Strategy, Economic Organization, and the Knowledge Economy
The Coordination of Firms and Resources

Strategy, Economic Organization, and the Knowledge Economy

The Coordination of Firms and Resources

NICOLAI J. FOSS

OXFORD
UNIVERSITY PRESS

OXFORD
UNIVERSITY PRESS

Great Clarendon Street, Oxford ox2 6DP

Oxford University Press is a department of the University of Oxford.
It furthers the University's objective of excellence in research, scholarship,
and education by publishing worldwide in

Oxford New York

Auckland Cape Town Dar es Salaam Hong Kong Karachi
Kuala Lumpur Madrid Melbourne Mexico City Nairobi
New Delhi Shanghai Taipei Toronto

With offices in

Argentina Austria Brazil Chile Czech Republic France Greece
Guatemala Hungary Italy Japan Poland Portugal Singapore
South Korea Switzerland Thailand Turkey Ukraine Vietnam

Oxford is a registered trade mark of Oxford University Press
in the UK and in certain other countries

Published in the United States
by Oxford University Press Inc., New York

© Nicolai J. Foss 2005

The moral rights of the author have been asserted
Database right Oxford University Press (maker)

First published 2005
First published in paperback 2006

British Library Cataloguing in Publication Data
Data available

Library of Congress Cataloging in Publication Data
Foss, Nicolai J., 1964.
Strategy, economic organization, and the knowledge economy : the coordination of firms and resources /
Nicolai J. Foss.
p. cm.
Includes bibliographical references (p.   ) and index.
1. Industrial organization (Economic theory) 2. Strategic planning. 3. Knowledge management. I. Title.
HD326.P67 2005
338.6.6–dc22
2004027324

Typeset by SPI Publisher Services, Pondicherry, India
Printed in Great Britain
on acid-free paper by
Biddles Ltd., King's Lynn, Norfolk

ISBN 0–19–924064–7   978–0–19–924064–7
ISBN 0–19–920532–9 (Pbk.)   978–0–19–920532–5 (Pbk.)

1 3 5 7 9 10 8 6 4 2

For Kirsten and Elisabeth

Preface and Acknowledgments

We are regularly told by politicians, high-ranking bureaucrats, CEOs, the business press, and many business administration academics that the emergence of the 'knowledge economy' both prompts and necessitates dramatic changes not only at the macro level of technology, science, and education policies, but also at the micro level represented by firms.

Thus, firms, it is argued, are increasingly becoming players in a 'hyper-competitive' game (D'Aveni and Gunther 1994), and engaging in extensive knowledge sourcing from all sorts of knowledge producers—whether they be suppliers, customers and clients, universities, or employees controlling critical knowledge—to support the 'knowledge-based' strategies that are appropriate for the 'new competition' (Best 1990). Strong implications for the organization of firms in terms of firm boundaries, organizational structure, and the employment relation are argued to follow. For example, firms are said to be increasingly 'knowledge intensive' (Starbuck 1992) and therefore increasingly dependent on expert talent in the form of 'knowledge workers' (Newell et al. 2003); to be shrinking their boundaries, yet still have an increasing number of technologies in-house (Brusoni, Prencipe, and Pavitt 2001); to be flattening their structures and delegating decision rights to employees to an increasing degree in order to foster local responsiveness and entrepreneurship (Cowen and Parker 1997); and to be increasingly reliant on softer forms of organizational control, such as 'clan' organization (Ouchi 1980; Adler 2001). Often the boundary conditions of such claims are not transparent. It is not clear to which firms in which industries the claims are supposed to apply. Mechanisms are black-boxed in the sense that it is not clear how propositions about the knowledge economy are connected to propositions about economic organization or firm strategy. There is little systematic empirical evidence that speaks directly to the issue of how the knowledge economy impacts on organization and strategy.

Moreover, the reach of existing theorizing in economics and business administration with respect to grappling with these issues is unclear. There is a diversity of perspectives, but relatively little shared theoretical ground. To use an evolutionary metaphor, there is rather substantial variation, but weak selection mechanisms. This volume is a modest attempt to grapple with some of the foundational issues that pertain to theorizing on organization and strategy in the knowledge economy. It is (one of) the result(s) of more than ten years of research into the theory of economic organization, and in particular into how this body of theory connects to knowledge issues in strategy. It is therefore also the result of more than ten years of interaction with other researchers. While

I myself internalize all the costs in the form of blame for obscurities, misinterpretation, errors, lack of coherence, etc., I do not want to appropriate all of the benefits. Thus, portions of the book have been presented at seminars at Zürich University, the Norwegian School of Economics and Business Administration (NHH), Bergen, Copenhagen Business School, Freiburg University, Caén University, Erasmus University, Rotterdam, Pisa University, Paris University I (the Sorbonne), Paris University X (Nanterre), and the Max Planck Institute for Research in Economic Systems, Jena, and I am grateful for comments and discussion from the seminar audiences.

Numerous people have provided comments on portions of this manuscript in various incarnations. In particular, Eric Brousseau, Bruno Frey, Robert Gibbons, Anna Grandori, Geoff Hodgson, Margit Osterloh, George B. Richardson, Svein Ulset, and Ulrich Witt have commented directly on portions of the text. Anna Grandori, Peter G. Klein, and Thorbjørn Knudsen have provided particularly helpful comments and discussion on a number of occasions. I am also grateful to a number of colleagues for stimulating discussions, notably Keld Laursen, Torben Pedersen, and Henrik Lando, and I thank Nicolai Pedersen for very efficient research assistance. I am extremely grateful to David Musson at OUP for his very considerable patience. My greatest thanks go to my wife, Kirsten, not only because she has been willing to internalize the hefty negative externalities of a husband struggling with a book, but also because her sharp mind has, I hope, helped me to avoid the worst blunders.

Many of the ideas set out in this book have appeared in previously published work. Most chapters are based on one or two already published articles. The relevant articles have, however, been rewritten, and much new material has been added, so most chapters are to a large extent original pieces of work.

Chapter 1 ('Strategy and Economic Organization in the Knowledge Economy') has been written for this volume.

Chapter 2 ('The "Strategic Theory of the Firm"') uses excerpts from 'Research in the Strategic Theory of the Firm: "Integrationism" and "Isolationism"', *Journal of Management Studies*, 36 (Nov. 1999): 725–55, and 'Competence and Governance Perspectives: How Much Do They Differ? And How Does It Matter?' (with Kirsten Foss), in Nicolai J. Foss and Volker Mahnke (eds.), *Competence, Governance, and Entrepreneurship* (Oxford: Oxford University Press, 2000). I am grateful to Blackwell for permission to use excerpts from the former paper.

Chapter 3 ('The Resource-based View: Aligning Strategy and Competitive Equilibrium') uses excerpts from 'The Resource-based Tangle: In Search of Sustainable Foundations' (with Thorbjørn Knudsen), *Managerial and Decision Economics*, 24 (2003): 291–307. I am grateful to Wiley for permission to reproduce excerpts from this paper.

Chapter 4 ('Knowledge-based Views of the Firm') uses excerpts from 'Bounded Rationality and Tacit Knowledge in the Organizational Capabilities Approach: an Evaluation and a Stocktaking', *Industrial and Corporate Change*, 12 (2003): 185–201.

Chapter 5 ('Strategy, Resources, and Transaction Costs') has been written for this volume.

Chapter 6 ('Economic Organization in the Knowledge Economy') uses excerpts from 'Coase vs Hayek: Economic Organization in the Knowledge Economy', *International Journal of the Economics of Busines*, 9 (2002): 9–36. I am grateful to Abingdon for permission to use substantial parts of this paper.

Chapter 7 ('Internal Organization in the Knowledge Economy: The Rise and Fall of the Oticon Spaghetti Organization') draws on 'Selective Intervention and Internal Hybrids: Interpreting and Learning from the Rise and Decline of the Oticon Spaghetti Organization', *Organization Science*, 14 (2003): 331–49, and is reprinted by permission of the copyright holder, the Institute for Operations Research and the Management Sciences, 901 Elkridge Landing Road, Suite 400, Linthicum, MD 21090 USA.

Chapter 8 ('Performance and Organization in the Knowledge Economy: Innovation and New Human Resource Management Practices') uses large parts of Keld Laursen and Nicolai J. Foss. 'New HRM Practices, Complementarities, and the Impact on Innovation Performance', *Cambridge Journal of Economics*, 27 (2003): 243–63.

Chapter 9 ('Cognitive Leadership and Coordination in the Knowledge Economy') uses excerpts from 'Leadership, Beliefs and Coordination', *Industrial and Corporate Change*, 10 (2001): 357–88.

Contents

Figures

Tables

Abbreviations

AT&T	American Telephone and Telegraph Company
CA	Competitive advantage
CEO	Chief Executive Officer
EPR	Economics of property rights
HRM(P)	Human-resource management (practices)
IBM	International Business Machines
ICT	Information and communication technologies
KBV	Knowledge-based view
OE	Organizational economics
OECD	Organization for Economic Cooperation and Development
OS	Organization studies
R&D	Research and development
RBV	Resource-based view
SCA	Sustained competitive advantage
SCP	Structure-conduct-performance
SWOT	Strengths, weaknesses, opportunities, and threats
TCE	Transaction-cost economics
TQM	Total quality management

1

Strategy and Economic Organization in the Knowledge Economy

Introduction: The Knowledge Economy as Context

Ours is a knowledge economy. This claim has become increasingly prevalent, not only among politicians, journalists, bureaucrats in organizations such as the OECD, and fashionable philosophers, but also, though somewhat reluctantly, among academic economists, and, much less reluctantly, management academics. The terminology may differ; for example, the OECD has flirted with the 'learning economy' (OECD 1996), a notion introduced by Lundvall and Johnson (1994; see also Tomlinson 1999). Of course, the 'new economy' was all the rage until a couple of years ago, although this concept is only partly congruent with that of the knowledge economy, and now appears to have fallen into disgrace, no doubt as a result of the dot.com bust.[1] Sociologists increasingly use the notion of the 'network society' to cover similar tendencies (Castells 1996). And, of course, there is the 'new information economy' (e.g. Halal and Taylor 1998).

Such notions are perhaps all examples of those concepts that, because they are ill-defined at the core and fuzzy at the edges yet clearly seem to capture real phenomena, attract a great deal of scholarly effort from diverse fields and disciplines, from the stratospheric speculations of a Jean-Francois Lyotard or Jacques Derrida to painstaking econometrics exercises on the productivity impact of information and communication technologies. This book is much concerned with the impact of the knowledge economy on the knowledge production of management studies, broadly conceived.

More specifically, it is concerned with important parts of the theorizing that has emerged within the strategy and organization fields to accommodate the emergence of the knowledge economy, or, more precisely, accommodate those tendencies that we may think of as characterizing the knowledge economy.[2] Among these—real, alleged, and imagined—tendencies is the increasing importance of human-capital inputs, the generally increasing importance of immaterial assets and scientific knowledge in production, the increasing importance of immaterial products, the need to control in-house an increasing number of technologies (even if product portfolios are shrinking) (Brusoni, Prencipe, and

Pavitt 2001), and in general to tap an increasing number of knowledge nodes, not just internally but also through an increasing number of alliances and network relations with other firms as well as public research institutions (Doz et al. 2004). These tendencies—that in turn co-evolve with a host of other tendencies that may be placed under the knowledge-economy heading, such as increasing competitive pressure and an increasing extent of the market stemming from increased deregulation and internationalization (Rajan and Zingales 2001), increasing technological modularity (Langlois 2002), improved methods of measurement and cost allocation (Zenger and Hesterly 1997), and the increasing importance of ICT (Brynjolfsson, Hitt, and Yang 2002; Paganetto 2004)— profoundly impact on economic organization and competitive advantages.

Reflecting this, management academics have firmly stressed the role of organizational factors in the process of building knowledge-based strategies that will bring sustained competitive advantage (Nonaka and Takeuchi 1995; Grant 1996; Myers 1996; Brown and Eisenhardt 1998; Day and Wendler 1998). For example, firms are said to adopt 'network organization' (Miles and Snow 1992) and engage in 'corporate disaggregation' (Zenger and Hesterly 1997), so as to become the 'information age organizations' (Mendelson and Pillai 1999) that can build the 'dynamic capabilities' that are required for competing in the knowledge economy.

It is hard to overestimate the impact that the tendencies that are typically associated with the notion of the knowledge economy and its diverse aliases have had on business administration.[3] In fact, business-administration scholars themselves have been among the most eager proponents of such notions (e.g. Halal and Taylor 1998; Drucker 1999). The impact manifests itself in a number of ways. Most visibly, perhaps, it has led to a whole new field in business administration, appropriately titled knowledge management, which has emerged partly to reflect the changed competitive and organizational realities (Grant 2002). However, it has also led to strong changes of focus in more established disciplines in business administration, such as strategy (e.g. Grant 1996; Brown and Eisenhardt 1998), organization (e.g. Brown and Duguid 2002), and international business and management (e.g. Doz, Santos, and Williamson 2001).[4] The impact has also been felt in such areas as accounting, industrial marketing, and business law. The favorite concepts of the knowledge movement—that is, notions of 'competence', 'capabilities', 'dynamic capilities', 'core competence', etc.—are becoming generally adopted outside their original strategy and organization context. Indeed, it is fair to say that a knowledge movement has been sweeping across business administration since the beginning of the 1990s, almost attaining the character of a Kuhnian paradigmatic shift. While the knowledge theme may occasionally have been oversold by its advocates, there is little doubt that the change in business administration is profound and and that many of the intellectual changes induced by the knowledge movement will be irreversible.

However, these kinds of major intellectual changes are usually quite messy. The Keynesian revolution is a somewhat comparable example. Keynes (1936) swept through the economics profession and led to a massive wave of conversions, an entirely new vocabulary and a new field (macro-economics). The reasons for this conversion still occupy economic methodologists and doctrinal historians, but there is probably little doubt that external circumstances (the Depression) played a major role. However that may be, the economics profession adopted virtually overnight an approach that was characterized by unclear constructs (e.g. 'aggregate demand'), unclear or non-existent micro-foundations (e.g. consumption seemed to be treated in an ad-hoc manner), unclear causal relations (e.g. How exactly did investments influence aggregate production?), and unclear policy implications (e.g. What was the role of monetary policy?). Sorting all this out occupied the creative energies of macro-economists for more than three decades. Some of the issues may still not have found a fully satisfactory solution (e.g. the micro-foundations issue).

There is no reason to think that the intellectual puzzles introduced by the emergence of the knowledge economy will take any shorter time to resolve. In fact, the puzzles are not unlike each other, as the knowledge movement in business administration also suffers from unclear constructs (e.g. What exactly is a 'capability'?), unclear micro-foundations (What is assumed about the motivation and information of agents?), unclear causal relations (e.g. How exactly do capabilities relate to competitive advantage and economic organization?), and unclear 'policy' recommendations (e.g. Are flat organizational structures necessarily more conducive to the development of dynamic capabilities than more traditional hierarchical ones?). Moreover, the external phenomenon that has partly prompted the emergence of the new approach is not identified with as much precision as one could wish. Economic historians still debate the root causes of the Great Depression. Relatedly, knowledge of the knowledge economy appears to be rather unsystematic and anecdotal. The following section discusses this in some detail.

What Do We Know about the Knowledge Economy?

Continuity and Discontinuity

One of the striking features of much talk of the knowledge economy is what may be called the 'discontinuity thesis'; to wit, that the knowledge economy represents a qualitative leap in a number of dimensions relative to earlier economies. For example, in a recent paper (2003) one of the key scholars behind the development of the notion of 'national systems of innovation' and a former high-ranking OECD bureaucrat, Bengt-Åke Lundvall, argues that what he calls the 'learning economy' is indeed such a historical discontinuity, because it represents a significant change in 'techno-economic paradigm'.[5]

One well-known problem with this kind of historical-stages thinking is that what may look like revolutionary change is actually an accumulation of incremental change; that is, the ancient problem of the 'conversion of degree into kind'. Indeed, as Lundvall rightly points out, the perception of change is partly determined by discipline, (economic) historians and economists being sceptical of talk of 'new', 'knowledge', 'learning', etc. economies (e.g. Nakamura 2000: 15), and management scholars and sociologists typically embracing such talk much more eagerly.[6] Of course, at a sufficiently high level of abstraction (or lack of precision), there is very little change that is qualitatively new. Those who have been present at conferences where the notion of 'new organizational forms' has formed the subject of debate will know this. If such forms are characterized by extensive delegation and high-powered performance incentives, are conglomerates that are organized with divisions as profits centers 'new organizational forms'—even though this form is decades old? Of course, exactly the same can be said of the notion of the knowledge economy. Isn't it the case that all economies, past and present, have been 'knowledge economies'? For example, didn't the aboriginal economy in Australia prior to the advent of the Europeans rely on much knowledge that was extremely specialized and sophisticated relative to the problems faced by this social group? And so on.

Such debates are usually not productive, and they will be eschewed here by not taking a stand on whether the tendencies that we may associate with the knowledge economy are new ones or rather intensifications of existing ones. Rather, if, as is the case in this volume, the purpose is to examine how the advent of the knowledge economy has prompted the emergence of a set of theories that place knowledge centrally as an explanatory concept, and to examine the resulting explanations, it is simply not necessary to take a stand in the continuity/discontinuity debate. For example, one can ask about the micro-foundations of the knowledge-based view of the firm, how the growing importance of human capital impacts on organizational control, or how the increasing diversity of technological inputs in a large number of products impacts on firm boundaries quite independently of this debate.

The Knowledge Economy as Vision

In an academic context the significance of recent talk of the knowledge economy and its many partial and complete aliases may lie in the overall vision they supply for work of a much more detailed nature. When sifting through databases and identifying scientific papers on the basis of whether they make use of these concepts, it becomes apparent that relevant papers usually do not present much evidence for a 'knowledge economy' (or new techno-economic paradigm) per se, but rather adopt the notion in a taken-for-granted manner to frame an argument at a lower level of analysis. For example, Carmuffo (2002) uses the concept to frame an argument concerning the 'new employment relation'; Ewing (2002) applies it to an argument about the importance of 'employment brand-ing'; Garicano and Rossi-Hansberg (2003) use it to frame an argument about how information technology influences wages and organization; Adler (2001) uses it as the context for an argument concerning how trust influences economic organization; and so on. Indeed, this volume, too, uses the notion of the knowledge economy to frame a number of specific arguments that relate to firm strategy and organization. However, because I am more specifically con-cerned (particularly in Part II) with how the knowledge economy influences firm strategies and organization, it will not do simply to take the notion for granted. Therefore, below I briefly survey some of those tendencies that we may place under the heading of the knowledge economy.

More comprehensive attempts to define the notion of the knowledge econ-omy usually take place at the level of policy and policy advice, and academic papers and books often simply adopt such definitions. However, it is also the case that policy-level definitions of the knowledge economy—such as OECD defin-itions of the knowledge economy as 'an economy based on knowledge' and 'an economy that is established directly on the basis of the production, distribution, and utilization of knowledge and information' (OECD 1996)—serve as devices to frame lower-level policy recommendations, for example on regional policy or educational policies. Therefore, definitions remain ambiguous and broad. For example, the World Bank defines the knowledge economy 'in terms of four major pillars that support any knowledge economy':

An economic and institutional regime that provides incentives for efficiently creating, acquiring, disseminating, and using knowledge to promote growth and increase welfare [. . .] An effective innovation system, including a system of research centers, universities, think tanks, consultants, firms and other organizations that can tap into a growing stock of global knowledge, assimilate it and adapt it to local needs, and create new knowledge; [. . .] A dynamic information and communication infrastructure that facilitates the effective dissemination and processing of information. An educated and well-trained population that can create, acquire, disseminate and use knowledge.[7]

There are several problems with such conceptualizations. First, the 'knowledge economy' is simply taken as an overall framing argument—or, in the case of policy-making bodies, a desirable state for ongoing policy initiatives—about which it is implicitly assumed that agreement exists. Second, the definitions may be severely mis-specified or incomplete. Third, we are not given information about any possible causal relations between the 'major pillars', which indeed seem to refer to outcomes as much as to drivers.

More generally, getting to grips analytically with the knowledge economy would seem to require an identification of relevant endogenous and exogenous variables, but such an identification is seldom forthcoming, mainly because of the tendency in both academic and policy-oriented work to treat the knowledge economy as an overall framing vision. Modeling the knowledge economy is, to put it mildly, an undertaking of very considerable complexity, because the number of relevant variables would seem to be overwhelming and causality would seem to be so complicated that any model can only capture select mechanisms.[8] Therefore, it is perhaps not surprising that model-oriented social scientists have typically refrained from taking on the knowledge economy in its forbidding complexity. However, although the knowledge economy may well best be treated under rubrics such as 'co-evolution' or 'cumulative causation' (concepts that often cover for ignorance), the existing academic contributions do suggest that certain tendencies may, in a shorter-run perspective, best be understood as drivers, while other tendencies are best understood as outcomes. Below I discuss the knowledge economy briefly in such terms.

Information and Communication Technologies

Virtually all discussions of the knowledge economy invoke recent information and communication technologies (ICT) as a main driver and primary characteristic of the knowledge economy. In addition to the apparently mandatory mention of Moore's Law, discussions often point to the extremely high annual growth rates in western countries of real investments in ICT, the explosion of e-commerce, the surge in the number of Internet hosts, the household adoption of computers, etc. However, it is often overlooked that much of this may well have been driven by substantial government funding of key 'new-economy' technologies (the Arpanet being the most familiar example). Moreover, the increase in ICT investments may at least partly have been driven by structural changes in the organization of R&D towards more open standards and a more important role for smaller firms connected in networks, as well as changes in financing towards a greater role for venture capital (and therefore a higher propensity to engage in perhaps more risky investments in ICT) (Klein 2001). In other words, it is somewhat unclear what is driving what in this case.

Still, much work proceeds on the assumption that ICT is a fundamental driver and that what is fundamentally new about the knowledge economy relative to earlier historical stages is the digital revolution. The importance of ICT to discussions of the knowledge economy is, of course, that many see it as the technology that the knowledge economy revolves around in the sense that ICT make information cheaper to process, store, and transmit; that is, as the heartbeat that animates the knowledge economy. For example, arguments are put forward that ICT drive productivity increases, facilitate the formation of networks between and inside firms, flatten hierarchies, reduce overall firm size, facilitate (external and internal) scale economies, ease the modularization of production, and so on.

Carefully gathered evidence lags somewhat behind such claims, however, although there is now evidence that ICT, when coupled with certain organizational practices, have had significant consequences for (US) productivity (Bresnahan, Brynjolfsson, and Hitt, 2002; Brynjolfsson, Hitt, and Yang 2002) and have impacted negatively on firm size (Brynjolfsson et al. 1994; Garicano and Rossi-Hansberg 2003; Paganetto 2004) and vertical integration (Culnan, Armstrong, and Hitt 1998).[9]

While there is evidence of ICT's transformative implications, this does not rule out that other drivers are also important, and perhaps as important. However, the conspicuous nature of the digital revolution may have drawn attention away from such other drivers. For example, rather little attention has been devoted to the 'quality revolution', notably in the form of total-quality management, of the last twenty years. There are reasons to believe that this has had implications for economic organization, such as the tendency for organizational units to decrease in size and to offer more high-powered incentives inside firm hierarchies (Zenger and Hesterly 1997). The reason is that methods such as TQM make it possible to measure the output performance of small units, easing benchmarking of such units against each other and the rewarding of performance based on precise measures. Also, advances in accounting, such as activity-based costing, allow for better measures of the true profitability of organizational units, easing benchmarking and perhaps leading to spin-offs of lacking units. There is an identification problem here, because a number of the organizational outcomes that are often claimed to be driven by changes in ICT may equally well be driven by changes in how quality is measured and costs are allocated.[10]

The Increasing Importance of Human Capital

Given the context of 'knowledge economy', it may seem more reasonable to look at those tendencies that are 'knowledge' rather than 'information' related. Many writers have stressed the distinction between information and knowledge (Nonaka and Takeuchi 1995; Spender 1996; Boisot 1998; Teece 2001). Knowledge is seen as a partly tacit and context-dependent capacity to select, interpret, and aggregate information, which in turn is explicit and less contextual. As Teece (2001: 130) puts it: 'A Bloomberg or Reuters newsfeed is information. The opinions of the leading analysts and commentators, putting the news into context and enabling it to be used to create value, are more akin to knowledge.' The information/knowledge distinction is one of the key dogmas in the knowledge movement in business administration, and is usually defended on epistemological grounds. From an economic perspective, however, what matters are the costs of absorbing, transferring, storing, and processing information/ knowledge (Demsetz 1991; Jensen and Meckling 1992; Casson 1997). Below, the convention is adopted of referring to information that is costly to absorb, etc. as 'knowledge' and information that is inexpensive to absorb, etc. as 'information'.

Given this distinction, the knowledge economy is indeed remarkable for the growing importance of not only information, but also of knowledge. A manifestation of this is the strongly growing importance of human capital. Acquiring human capital is largely a matter of reducing the costs of selecting, interpreting, and aggregating information and knowledge. A number of studies and indicators suggest that the importance of human capital has increased massively. Thus, in terms of general statistics the proportion of 'knowledge workers', such as managers, professionals, and technical workers, increased from 10 per cent of the US workforce in 1900 to 17 per cent in 1950 to 33 per cent in 1999. 'Creative workers', such as engineers and architects, artists and entertainers, increased from 1 per cent in 1900 to 2 per cent in 1950 to 5.7 per cent in 1999. Large-scale econometric studies provide the same message. Jorgenson and Fraumeni (1995) show that in the US economy human capital overwhelms physical capital in terms of contributing to value added, and that its weight has been continuously increasing. Machin and van Reenen (1998) present evidence that the relative demand for skilled labor increased in the 1990s in the seven OECD countries they investigated. Berman, Bound, and Griliches (1994) find a similar tendency in the US economy, as do sector- and industry-specific studies. For example, Demsetz (1996) shows that the share of high-skilled employees in US banking has strongly increased (around 8 percentage points from 1983 to 1995)—the most pronounced increase in any US industry.

In business administration the increasing importance of human capital has been reflected in notions of 'knowledge workers' (Zuboff 1988) and 'knowledge-intensive firms' (Starbuck 1992); that is, 'organizations staffed by a high proportion of highly qualified staff who trade in knowledge itself' (Blackler 1995: 1022). According to current influential thinking, such firms may be differentiated from 'traditional' firms in terms of organizational control in that they rely less on direction through the exercise of authority, eschewing high-powered performance incentives, and embracing 'culture' and 'clan' modes of organizational control (Adler 2001; Child and McGrath 2001). This kind of thinking can increasingly be found outside management studies. Thus, corporate finance scholar and organizational economist Luigi Zingales (2000: 1641) argues that:

in 1994 a firm like Saatchi and Saatchi, with few physical assets and a lot of human capital, could have been considered an exception. Not any more. The wave of initial public offerings of purely human capital firms, such as consultant firms, and even technology firms whose main assets are the key employees, is changing the very nature of the firm.

'Software'

In a discussion of the issues under consideration here Paul Romer (1998) argued against the idea of the knowledge economy as representing a novel historical stage. As he points out, the transition from a mechanized economy to one based on 'software' in a broad sense (not just the software underlying computer-assisted manufacturing and computer-aided design) is characteristic of economic development over the last hundred years or so. The notion of 'software' is deliberately chosen for two reasons. First, because it implies the notion of program, and Romer maintains that arguably the most important (in terms of contribution to economic growth) 'programs' (he calls them 'recipes') are firm routines and specific ways of organizing economic activities, such as business-format franchising, Wal-Mart's retailing system. Knowledge protected by intellectual property rights presumably also falls within the software category. Thus, scientific knowledge is also an instance of software, although it may need adaptation to become truly 'software-like'; that is, practically applicable and replicable.

Second, it is characteristic not only of computer software but also of software in this broad sense that it may have high initial costs of production, but will typically have much lower costs of replication. These characteristics yield the increasing returns that have often been heralded as the fundamental economic driver of the knowledge economy. They have pervasive implications for firm strategies, introducing dynamic complementarities (accessing, processing, etc. knowledge improves the ability to access, process, etc. future knowledge), making standard-setting an important competitive weapon, etc. (Shapiro and Varian 1999; Leibold, Probst, and Gibbert 2002).

Distributed Knowledge and Innovation

While information is becoming continuously cheaper to process, store, and transmit (Garicano and Rossi-Hansberg 2003), an increasingly influential argument asserts that the knowledge needed to create value is becoming increasingly dispersed, either in direct geographical terms (e.g. Doz, Santos, and Williamson 2001) or in terms of technological disciplines (Granstrand, Patel, and Pavitt 1997; Matusik and Hill 1998; Coombs and Metcalfe 2000; Brusoni, Prencipe and Pavitt 2001). The division of labor is becoming increasingly complex, particularly in the generation of science and technology (e.g. Coombs and Metcalfe 2000: 209). Firms need to build and maintain an increasing number of 'knowledge nodes' with lead users, universities, technical-service institutes, user communities (e.g. Hippel 1988; Granstrand, Patel, and Pavitt 1997; Hodgson 1998; Coombs and Metcalfe 2000; Smith 2000; Wang and Tunzelman 2000; Brusoni, Prencipe, and Pavitt 2001; Jeppesen 2002). Because firms increasingly need to rely on a growing number of knowledge specialists, be they employees or outside knowledge agents, they also need to have the absorptive capacity to be able *potentially* to source an increasing number of technologies. In fact, it is arguable that many knowledge nodes, particularly to universities, are established in order to create this absorptive capacity (Pavitt 1991). The tendency for many firms to have an increasing number of technological disciplines in-house, even if product portfolios are shrinking, may also be a reflection of the need to increase absorptive capacity in the face of an increasingly complex division of labor in science and technology (Brusoni, Prencipe, and Pavitt 2001).

The notion of 'distributed knowledge', coined in computer science just over a decade ago (Halpern and Moses 1990), has fast become a household concept in various branches of business administration as a handy way of framing these tendencies. Loosely, 'distributed knowledge' is knowledge that is not possessed by any single mind, but 'belongs to' a group of interacting agents, somehow emerges from the aggregation of the (possibly tacit) knowledge elements of the individual agents, and can be mobilized for productive purposes. While a division of labor will almost always imply that knowledge is distributed (Hayek 1945),[11] recent contributions actually assert that in some sense knowledge has become *more* distributed.

This tendency is seen as having strong transformative implications for economic organization; notably, the employment relation, internal-organization structure, and the boundaries of the firm. For example, the increasing reliance on 'knowledge workers', specialists, expert talent, etc. that is seen to accompany the increasingly distributed nature of productive knowledge challenges traditional authority relations (because knowledge workers have much more bargaining power; Rajan and Zingales 2001) and makes extensive delegation of decision rights necessary in firms' internal organizations (so as to co-locate rights with knowledge; Mendelsson and Pillai 1999). With respect to 'external organization' (to use Marshall's phrase (1920)), firms increasingly engage in relational forms of contracting that can simultaneously keep opportunism at bay and create the rich interfaces that are necessary for sharing and integration of complementary knowledge (Helper, McDuffie, and Sabel 2000; Heimann and Nickerson 2002). Thus, a picture is emerging of a new kind of firms that 'tend to be non-vertically integrated, human-capital-intensive organisations that operate in a highly competitive environment' (Zingales 2000: 1643), yet are still strongly networked to other firms and to knowledge institutions. Some of these characteristics are discussed very briefly below.

Changing Internal Organization

Virtually all of those who have written on the subject agree that tasks and activities in the knowledge economy need to be coordinated in a manner that is very different from the management of traditional manufacturing activities (as portrayed in (e.g.) Chandler 1962). Variations on the following account (Cowen and Parker 1997: 28) are very common:

[M]arket changes are moving manufacturing farther and farther away from steady-state, low variety, long-batch production runs, relevant to Taylorist methods, to high variety and small runs [...] Organizations are adopting new forms of decentralization to cope with the instability, uncertainty, and pace of change of the market-place [...] In clusters of network working, employees of undifferentiated rank may operate temporarily on a certain task or tasks in teams. The clusters are largely autonomous and engage in decentralized decision-making and planning [...] They are conducive to individual initiative ('intrapreneurship') and faster decision-taking. They facilitate organizational flexibility.

The notion of 'new organizational forms' is often used to capture these phenomena. The notion began to gain currency about a decade ago (e.g. Daft and Lewin 1993). It was propagated as shorthand for what was seen as a surge of firms experimenting with their governance of transactions; that is, adopting new ways of structuring their boundaries and their internal organization. This surge was related to but followed in the wake of the corporate refocusing wave; much of it consisted in a strong increase in the adoption of organizational practices such as total-quality management, business process re-engineering, and outsourcing (Bowman and Singh 1993), and it was probably to some extent inspired by organizational practices characteristic of recent Japanese economic organization (Aoki and Dore 1994). The concept was quickly adopted by those management thinkers who embraced concepts such as the 'knowledge economy' (e.g. Halal and Taylor 1998), and who argued that the advent of the Internet would have revolutionary implications for the organization of transactions (Tapscott 1999). New organizational forms were seen as a characteristic way of 'organizing in the knowledge age' (Miles et al. 1997). The 'virtual organization', 'shamrock firm', 'the boundary-less organization', and 'intelligent organization' quickly became household words in the discourse of management studies.

However, while many scholars have agreed that there is a marked tendency towards increased decentralization and that this may be caused by attempts to foster 'individual initiative ('intrapreneurship') and faster decision-taking', there is a fair degree of divergence in the accounts of what exactly is involved in the 'new organizational forms'.

Thus, some argue that 'traditional' coordination mechanisms such as price, authority, routines, standardization, etc. will diminish in relative importance, because knowledge-intensive production requires the increased use of mechanisms such as trust, communication, community, democratic procedures, etc. that can better cope with the particular metering problems and exchange hazards that are characteristic of knowledge transactions, and thus stimulate the emergence of knowledge management (in a broad sense) capabilities (Zucker 1991; Ghoshal, Moran, and Almeida-Costa 1995; Kogut and Zander 1996; Adler 2001; Grandori 2001). The new organizational forms are characterized as relying upon cross-functional processes, extensive delayering, and empowerment (Child and McGrath 2001: 137). The aim is to create highly specialized and motivated units by means of extensive delegation of discretion. Cross-functional processes substitute for hierarchy in the coordination of tasks.

Scholars promoting this view will tend to see the boundaries of firms blurring and employment relations undergoing dramatic change as a result of knowledge networks increasingly cutting across the boundaries of the firm and participative governance being increasingly adopted. Moreover, they will tend to question the traditional allocation of economic activities to discrete governance structures (notably markets and hierarchies), pointing out instead that governance mechanisms increasingly seem to be combined in such a way that much of the 'discreteness' of governance structures is disappearing and that this reflects the increasing volume of knowledge transactions (see particularly Grandori 1997, 2001).

Others take a more hard-nosed and less rosy view of the ongoing changes in economic organization. An important part of the tendencies constituting the knowledge economy is an intensification of competition as industry boundaries are eroded, and as internationalization and liberalization increase. In response to such competitive pressures, as Paul Adler (2001: 220) points out, 'firms are fine-tuning their management structures and planning processes, demanding greater accountability at every level, and enforcing more discipline in the planning and execution of operations'. As Zenger and Hesterly (1997) note, improved methods of cost allocation, more widespread use of ICT, and better measures of input and output performance have decreased the costs of monitoring employees and organizational units, in turn promoting a tendency to smaller organizational units that face more high-powered incentives (i.e. 'corporate disintegration').

These diverging accounts may well reflect the fact that the knowledge economy is pushing the employment relation, and the internal organization it is embedded in, in different directions. There is impressive evidence of the increasing application of 'high-performance work practices' (e.g. Ichniowski et al. 1996; Capelli and Neumark 2001; Goddard and Delaney 2001), by which reference is made to employee involvement in teams, quality circles, total-quality-management initiatives, and other more cooperative and participative ways of mobilizing employees' services. On the other hand, there is also considerable evidence that firms increasingly provide high-powered incentives, not only to their CEOs, but also to middle management and workers on the shop floor (Lawler, Mohrman, and Ledford 1998). And there is some evidence (Laursen 2002; Chs. 7 and 8 in this book) that high-performance work practices designed to foster innovation and/or knowledge management capabilities matter most (perhaps only *really* matter) if they are applied as parts of a *complementary* system together with high-powered performance incentives. In other words, ongoing changes in internal organization, including the employment relation, may reflect attempts simultaneously to reap different kinds of benefits. This introduces complicated trade-offs and will probably be very challenging to management. The story in Chapter 7 below of the rise and fall of the famous 'spaghetti organization' in the Danish hearing-aid producer Oticon illustrates a number of these challenges.

Changing Firm Boundaries

The same kind of seemingly diverging tendencies found in the case of the employment relation may also be operative with respect to the boundaries of the firm. According to Langlois (2003: 373), '[v]ertical disintegration and specialization is perhaps the most significant organizational development of the 1990s'. Everybody is familiar with the anecdotal evidence, such as AT&T spinning off its equipment division (now Lucent Technologies), IBM selling off its data-networking division (Global Networks), and other instances of 'reshaping of the supply chain', but there is also rather compelling quantitative evidence for this phenomenon (e.g. Feenstra 1998 and the reference therein), as well as some excellent historical studies (e.g. Langlois and Robertson 1995; Jacobides 2002).

Economists, economic geographers, and management scholars ponder the causes of the phenomenon. For example, to the international economists the 'rising integration of world markets has brought with it a disintegration of the production process. . . . This represents a breakdown in the vertically integrated mode of production—the so-called "Fordist" production, exemplified by the automobile industry—on which American manufacturing was built' (Feenstra 1998: 31). Organizational economists argue that the increasing relative importance of human capital causes the break-up of the vertically integrated firm (Rajan and Zingales 2001), because the growing importance of human capital weakens the control conferred by the ownership of non-human capital. To the extent that innovations in ICT lower external costs of coordination more than they lower internal costs of coordination, this is a force pulling in the direction of vertical disintegration (Culnan, Armstrong, and Hitt 1998; Langlois 2003). Corporate-finance scholars may stress the increased emphasis on shareholder value as an independent force that prompts specialization and vertical disintegration. Many business-administration scholars and sociologists argue that the hierarchy 'encounters enormous difficulty in the performance of innovation tasks requiring the generation of new knowledge' (Adler 2001: 216), so that in an innovation-rich economy hierarchies will be selected against. The question is what all these tendencies (that may possibly be highly complementary) select *for*.

As in the case of the employment relation, predictions here range from the rosy to the hard-nosed, to some extent depending on disciplinary orientation. Thus, economists may stress the overall Smithian theme of how an increasing demand causes vertical disintegration into market relations. Sociologists and business-administration scholars, on the other hand, may counter that this view neglects the fact that markets are inefficient governance structures for the knowledge-intensive transactions, the increasing importance of which is one of the defining characteristics of the knowledge economy. Instead, networked and trust-based forms of inter-firm relations emerge to handle such transactions (Powell 1990: 304; Liebeskind et al. 1995: 7). These trust-based forms do not fall in-between markets and hierarchies, as hybrids do in the Williamsonian scheme (Williamson 1996); rather, they cut across discrete governance structures and blur the boundaries of the firm: 'The ethos of common destiny that underpins trust blurs the allocation of accountability and decision rights at the heart of both hierarchy and market forms' (Adler 2001: 223; also Helper, MacDuffie, and Sabel 2000).

Others assert that the 'central tendency' is not the emergence of trust-based ('community'-based) forms of organization but that 'the buffering functions of management are devolving to the mechanisms of modularity and the market—informational decomposition, flexibility and risk spreading' (Langlois 2003: 376). This does not necessarily imply that the boundaries of firms 'blur'; rather, firms specialize and disintegrate. Also, while a modular system often internalizes knowledge-intensive transactions in modules, it is entirely consistent with innovative efforts (Langlois and Robertson 1995). Thus, the information and knowledge richness associated with innovative efforts does not necessarily imply trust, rich information and knowledge transfer between firms, etc.

Again, the truth of the matter may well be that rather diverging forces are pushing the boundaries of firms. In some industries at specific periods of time the 'mechanisms of modularity', including standards and stable interfaces, may indeed push vertically integrated structures towards market-governance structures. In other industries products may possess so much 'integrality' that trust and continuous knowledge and information transfer between firms become necessary.

Implications

The preceding pages have set the stage for much of what will follow. The emergence of those tendencies that, taken together, constitute the knowledge economy has been reflected in intellectual innovations, or sometimes rediscoveries of earlier thinking, in the social sciences. In economics, the new growth theory has dressed up earlier ideas of Thorstein Veblen, Allyn Young, and Joseph Schumpeter in formal garb (Romer 1986, 1990; Foss 1998b), models of network externalities and network competition have become an important part of the antitrust toolbox for a knowledge-based economy (Shapiro and Varian 1999), and the measurement of human capital for purposes of national income accounting has become a major issue (Laroche, Mérette, and Ruggeri 1999). Prompted by the emergence of the knowledge economy, many sociologists have engaged in speculative flights of fancy (e.g. Castells 1996) or have delighted in the new potential for revitalizing such concepts as 'marginalization' as the knowledge economy increases the need for the workforce to adapt.

Organization and Strategy

Business administration is certainly no exception, as several new literatures and approaches have emerged since the end of the 1980s to address the changed business realities implied by the above tendencies.[12] There is a general debate in the history of ideas about the extent to which the emergence of new ideas can be explained by societal developments (Blaug 1985), but in the case of a field so near to practice as business administration (or 'management studies') it is hardly controversial that developments in practice play a major influencing role in intellectual development. This is particularly the case in the strategy and organization fields, the two fields to which this book primarily relates.

Seen in this light, the appearance in business administration over the last decades of a host of new approaches that all somehow place knowledge center stage is non-spurious. In fact, quite often knowledge-economy phenomena are invoked to motivate theory development. Thus, in the *strategy field* it has been argued that various manifestations of the knowledge economy (e.g. technological convergence) wreak havoc with traditional industry boundaries and that firms must begin strategic analysis from their existing resource portfolio rather than from industry analysis. The resource-based view of the firm (Barney 1991; Peteraf 1993) has been taken as the theoretical underpinning of this stance. Of course, this view also provides much of the intellectual discipline for ideas that firms should pursue corporate specialization. A parallel development at the end of the 1980s was the emergence of 'competence' or 'capabilities' perspectives and then, slightly later, the 'knowledge-based view of the firm'. 'The essence of the firm in the new economy', says David Teece (2000: 29), 'is its ability to create, transfer, assemble, integrate, protect, and exploit knowledge assets'. The increasing interest in real options (e.g. Sanchez 1993) reflects an interest in explaining competitive advantages in volatile environments (Coff 2003). The interest in modular production and organization (e.g. Langlois 2002, 2003) reflects an increasingly distributed innovation environment.

As discussed above, in the *organization field* the knowledge economy has given rise to substantial debate about the emergence of trust-based forms of organization, the blurring of firm boundaries, new organizational forms, etc. Moreover, debate has arisen about which analytical perspectives are the most appropriate ones for dealing with organization in the knowledge economy. In particular, many writers have been quite explicit that the advent of the knowledge economy increasingly questions the relevance of Coasian organizational economics (e.g. Boisot 1998; Helper, MacDuffie, and Sabel 2000). Organizational economists themselves have been forced to question some of their traditional assumptions (Zingales 2000). For example, Cowen and Parker argue that, contrary to the traditional views of governance structures as discrete structural alternatives (Coase 1937; Williamson 1985, 1996a),

firms and markets are not exactly the same, but rather they differ in empirical terms. They refer to different means of organizing economic activity, albeit means that do not differ substantially in kind. [...] This [...] view does not seek to find a clear-cut distinction between firms and markets. Rather the difference between the firm and the market as a resource allocator involves what might more usefully be viewed as subtle differences relating to contracting. (Cowen and Parker 1997: 15)

And two leading organizational economists, Bengt Holmström and John Roberts (1998: 90) observe that

Information and knowledge are at the heart of organizational design, because they result in contractual and incentive problems that challenge both markets and firms [...] In light of this, it is surprising that leading economic theories [...] have paid almost no attention to the role of organizational knowledge.

The Need for Foundational Inquiry

As quotations such as the one immediately above indicate, the ongoing discussion has the potential to become a truly interdisciplinary dialog on foundational issues. Indeed, such a dialog appears to be not only strongly needed, but also natural, given the long history of interaction between economics and management (Coff 2003). It is strongly needed, because the diversity of perspectives is too large and there is too little shared theoretical ground (cf. Pfeffer 1993). A consequence is that the selection mechanisms that eliminate the weak ideas do not work with sufficient force.[13] This implies not only that there will be substantial variation in what is being asserted, which may be welcomed, but, more seriously, that the scientific status of many of the claims that are made will be and remain rather uncertain.

This uncertainty may be most conspicuous in the empirical dimension. Thus, there is rather little empirical knowledge of how and to what extent knowledge assets generally drive competitive performance, although work exists on how product-development capabilities and patents influence performance. Empirical knowledge about organizational control in knowledge-intensive firms is rather scant, with very different accounts being given, as argued earlier. The fact that relatively little rigorous empirical work exists on such issues is to a large extent caused by difficulties of conceptualizing and operationalizing such notions as the 'knowledge economy' and 'knowledge-intensive firms' (cf. Starbuck 1992), and therefore pinpointing *what* exactly is driving the alleged changes in the strategies and organization of *which* firms. However, it is also a matter of lack of understanding of *how* ongoing societal change toward the knowledge economy is affecting organization and influencing the contents and sources of strategies that firms engage in.[14]

Since basic conceptual and theoretical work is often a requirement for empirical work, the upshot is that clarification of foundations is necessary. What is needed is fundamental conceptual and theoretical thought on the tendencies that are placed under the heading of knowledge economy and how it impacts on economic organization and the content and sources of firm strategies. This is certainly not to say that theoretical speculation has not taken place. As shown earlier, the emergence of the knowledge economy has witnessed a proliferation of theorizing on the nature of firm strategy and organization in such an economy. However, much of this work originated very recently, largely within the last decade, and even much of the academic work is like buildings put up by a few key contractors on a tight completion deadline and on the basis of somewhat different inputs. The pilings, foundations, and actual structures themselves may not fit perfectly, and the theoretical structures may show some crevices, making repair efforts necessary, perhaps even amounting to additional piling of the foundations, or, in some cases, a demolition attempt (for the latter, see Thompson 2004).

About this Book

The present volume is offered as a modest contribution to these foundational issues. It is very much in the nature of a set of critical essays (Part I being more critical than Part II) that are, I hope, bound together by some shared concerns.

One overall theme is the one flagged in this introductory chapter; namely, that there is reason to think that many of the societal tendencies encompassed by the portmanteau concept of the 'knowledge economy' are very real ones that are likely dramatically to impact on firm strategy and organization, that we know rather little about the relevant mechanisms, but that strategic and organizational theorizing need to get to grips with this. These issues are explicitly framed and addressed in Chapter 6 ('Economic Organization in the Knowledge Economy'), which sets the stage for Part II of the book. Implications of the knowledge economy for organizational-design issues are addressed in Chapter 7 ('Internal Organization in the Knowledge Economy: The Rise and Fall of the Oticon Spaghetti Organization'), while Chapter 8 addresses the innovation-performance effects of those 'high-performance work practices' that are often associated with the knowledge economy ('Performance and Organization in the Knowledge Economy: Innovation and New Human Resource Management Practices'). Finally, Chapter 9 ('Cognitive Leadership and Coordination in the Knowledge

Economy') addresses the coordination problems introduced by the knowledge economy and how cognitive leadership may cope with these.

A more specific overall theme, present in all of the chapters in Part I and in some in Part II, concerns resolving the existing tension between 'competence' and 'governance' approaches to organization and strategy (Williamson 1999; Foss and Mahnke 2000). The debate in the strategic-management field on 'The Strategic Theory of the Firm' is the subject of Chapter 2. Sub-themes in this debate here include the importance of transaction cost. A second sub-theme is the need for proper micro-foundations and the general usefulness of a rational-choice perspective for illuminating a number of 'knowledge issues'. This theme is addressed in Chapter 4 ('Knowledge-based Views of the Firm'). A third theme is the role of the competitive-equilibrium model with respect to furthering thinking in strategy. In Chapter 3 ('The Resource-based View: Aligning Strategy and Competitive Equilibrium'), the argument is developed that the currently highly influential resource-based view of strategy is at the core founded on a patched-up version of the competitive-equilibrium model, and that this may be hindering the progress of the view. The three themes are clearly related, for transaction-cost economics supplies highly useful and alternative micro-foundations for much thinking in strategy and organization, as is argued in Chapter 5 ('Strategy, Resources, and Transaction Costs').

Other themes are, first, the importance of doctrinal history. While doctrinal history is generally held in rather low esteem, and has almost entirely disappeared from the modern economics or management curricula, some knowledge of a field's past is often quite useful for understanding contemporary currents (particularly in the management field, where most important ideas are recycled on a twenty-five-year basis). The argument in Chapter 3 that strategy's dominant 'resource-based view' has been founded on the competitive-equilibrium model has already been mentioned. Another example is that a number of the weak spots in the knowledge-based view, notably the above-mentioned absence of proper micro-foundations for that view, can be traced back to what is arguably *the* seminal contribution to this line of thought, namely Nelson and Winter (1982). A final, overall theme, and perhaps the most important one, is the need to embrace 'integrationist' thinking and eschew 'isolationism', to use concepts from Chapter 2; that is, to engage in disciplined and focused work that transcends compartmentalization. Getting to grips with strategy and organization in the knowledge economy requires such an approach.

Notes

1. Specifically, the notion of the 'new economy' was a strange amalgam of ideas, notably the 'end of the business-cycle hypotheses', an emphasis on the increasing role of information technology and new business practices (e-commerce, increased reliance

on intangible assets, and markets with network effects), and a claim that productivity growth had jumped discretely, presumably because of information technology and new business practices.

2. Not treated here is 'knowledge management'. See Foss and Mahnke (2003) for a discussion of knowledge management that is broadly in the spirit of this volume.

3. In economics the impact is manifest in the 'new growth theory' (Romer 1986, 1990, 1998) and in the resurgence of the evolutionary-economics research program since the mid 1980s (Nelson and Winter 1982; Dosi 1988).

4. Tallman has recently drawn attention to a 'transition of the dominant conceptual model of the multinational firm from the market failure approach of internalization theory and transaction cost economics theory to the market imperfections approach of capabilities or knowledge-based theories of the firm' (2003: 495) that took place during the 1990s. *Mutatis mutandis*, something similar may be said of the strategy and organization fields.

5. Originally launched by Brazilan political economist Carlota Perez (1983), a techno-economic paradigm is a 'set of interrelated technical and organizational innovations [that] gradually comes together as a best-practice model...capable of guiding the diffusion of each specific technological revolution. As it spreads, this new paradigm gradually takes root in collective consciousness, replacing the old ideas and becoming the new "common sense" of engineers, managers and investors for the most efficient and "modern" productive practice across the board' (<http://www.carlotaperez.org/papers/2-technologicalrevolutionsparadigm.html>).

6. But for a highly skeptical view from a business-administration position see Thompson (2004).

7. Taken from <http://www.worldbank.org/wbi/knowledgefordevelopment/k4d community/whatis_ke_k4dcomm.html>.

8. Still, modeling exercises such as Milgrom and Roberts (1990*b*), while not directed at modeling the 'knowledge economy' per se, may still capture many relevant mechanisms and variables.

9. For a transaction-cost interpretation of these tendencies see Picot, Ripperberger, and Wolff (1996).

10. Adding to the complexity, ITC and such practices as TQM and activity-based costing may be complementary with respect to their impact on economic organization.

11. Save, perhaps, for some primitive societies.

12. Here, too, much of the relevant work is rather strongly indebted to older economists, perhaps particularly the Austrians (Morck and Yeung 2001: 61). For example, ideas on creative imagination (Shackle 1972), competition as rivalry (Hayek 1948; Mises 1949), tacit knowledge (Hayek 1948), and entrepreneurship (Mises 1949; Kirzner 1973) have become increasingly prevalent in firm-strategy research (e.g. D'Aveni and Gunther 1994; Hamel and Prahalad 1994; Hunt 2000). The recent 'resource-based view' in strategy research (see Ch. 4) has even been characterized as an 'Austrian theory of strategy' (Jacobson 1992). (However, see Lewin and Phelan (2000) for a discussion of the presumed Austrian character of the resource-based view.) Many contributions to the related 'capabilities view' (Langlois 1992; Foss 1997) or the 'knowledge-based view' (Nonaka and Takeuchi 1995; Grant 1996) bear

a strong Austrian imprint. For an attempt to read the Austrians, mainly Hayek and Mises, as anticipating key currents in economics and business administration see Foss (1994).

13. A possible example is the notion of 'hyper-competition', originally proposed by D'Aveni and Gunther in 1994, and invoked in countless studies in business administration since then. However, in the single existing rigorous empirical test of the notion (McNamara et al. 2003), published almost ten years after its launch, the notion does not do well empirically.

14. To give an example, it is often argued that one consequence of the knowledge economy is that the knowledge bases to which firms must secure access increasingly take a 'distributed' form (Rooney et al. 2003: 10), and that this is a key driver of ongoing changes in economic organization (e.g. Coombs and Metcalf 2000). However, the notion of distributed knowledge is seldom defined with much precision (if at all). And it is not made clear how distributed knowledge impacts on economic organization. This issue is discussed further in Ch. 6.

Part I

Strategy: Critical Perspectives

2

The 'Strategic Theory of the Firm'

Introduction

Strategy research has been increasingly, and heavily, influenced by economic theories of the firm; notably, modern organizational economics (henceforth, 'OE')[1] and a host of currents that may be placed under the umbrella term of the 'knowledge-based view of the firm' (henceforth, 'KBV').[2] The main message of this chapter is that there has been a tendency in strategy research, narrowly to draw on only one of these two approaches—what is here called 'isolationism'—and to neglect the fact that it may be productive to join key insights of the two approaches—what is here called 'integrationism'.

Perhaps the first detailed arguments that (the then relatively recent) OE may be helpful in a strategy context were made by Caves (1980) and Rumelt (1984). Caves argued that in general corporate-strategy issues should be framed as constrained-optimization problems, and that recent work in the OE would be helpful in adding detail to such exercises. Rumelt claimed that 'it appears obvious that the study of business strategy must rest on the bedrock foundations of the economist's model of the firm' (ibid. 557). More specifically, he argued that by building on the work of Coase (1937) and Williamson (1975) the strategy field could arrive at a 'strategic theory of the firm'. Echoing Rumelt (1984), Williamson (1991, 1998) has more recently argued that the transaction-cost brand of OE aspires to become such a 'strategic theory of the firm'.

However, critical voices have pointed to the inability in the modern OE adequately to incorporate bounded rationality, limited cognition, and other phenomena of crucial interest to strategy scholars (Zajac 1992; Langlois and Foss 1999). In fact, during the last decade accumulating frustation in the strategy field with the modern OE has resulted in the gradual crystallization of a knowledge-based view of competitive advantage and economic organization (for a recent summary see Kaplan et al. 2001). This view is seen by many of its proponents as a rival to OE (e.g. Kogut and Zander 1992; Madhok 1996) and has (partly for this reason) been surrounded by a good deal of enthusiasm in the strategy field. Thus, there is controversy concerning what type of theory of the firm should be 'the bedrock foundation' for the study of strategy.[3]

In fact, much has happened with respect to the issue of the strategic theory of the firm since Caves (1980) and Rumelt (1984), and it is increasingly pertinent to perform a stocktaking and evaluation of the existing contenders and the options open to researchers in the field. However, this discussion does not have a retrospective and expository purpose per se.[4] Rather, it is an attempt to take a more forward-looking position and identify, criticize, and compare the research options that exist in the field of the strategic theory of the firm. Thus, this chapter aims to help researchers to make informed theory choices.

To be more specific, I identify two broad and archetypal research strategies that, as already indicated, I call 'isolationism' and 'integrationism'. The first research strategy—which I shall argue is often seriously incomplete—implies that the strategic theory of the firm should be founded either on the KBV or on OE. Thus, it consists of two mutually exclusive sub-strategies. While seldom found in pure forms, many contributions come close to taking the isolationist position (e.g. Kogut and Zander 1992; Grant 1996; Madhok 1996). In all cases it is certainly productive to discuss it, because it is a benchmark. The second research strategy, 'integrationism', implies that research on the strategic theory of the firm should be based on ideas from both OE and the KBV. Having criticized the isolationist research strategy, I state and defend the integrationist position. In particular, I argue that when there are interaction effects (trade-offs or complementarities) between governance and knowledge considerations, there is a strong argument in favour of integrationism, while isolationism is likely to produce too biased a view. Finally, I suggest some integrationist paths along which research in the strategic theory of the firm may proceed. Many of the themes described and developed in this chapter will also emerge in later chapters in different guises.

The Strategic Theory of the Firm: Meaning and Relevance

Following Rumelt (1984) and a number of other writers (e.g. Grant 1996), I take a 'strategic theory of the firm' to mean a theory that addresses the following four issues:

1. *The existence of the firm*—that is: Why do firms exist as distinct mechanisms for resource allocation in a market economy?
2. *The boundaries of the firm*—that is: What explains why certain transactions are governed in-house while others are governed through market relations?
3. *Internal organization*—that is: Why do we find different types of (formal and informal) organizational structure and accompanying phenomena, such as internal labor markets, job ladders, profit centers, etc.?

4. *Competitive advantage*—that is: Which factors account for superior rent-earning capability? Ultimately, this issue concerns why firms are heterogeneous.

To fully qualify as a strategic theory of the firm a candidate theory must be comprehensive in the sense that it addresses all four issues. This requirement simply has to do with the fact that a strategic theory of the firm brings together issues from the theory of economic organization (issues 1, 2, and 3) with issues from strategy (issue 4); if a theory fails to do this, it cannot be a strategic theory of the firm.

In this chapter I shall use the comprehensiveness criterion to evaluate the KBV and OE.[5] Intuitively one might expect the latter to be strong on issues 1, 2, and 3, and to be weak on issue 4, whereas the opposite might be expected to hold in the case of the knowledge-based view. The fact that this expectation is confirmed, as we shall see, no doubt has something to do with the historical development of the two approaches. Thus, whereas OE historically began with issues 1–3 (existence, boundaries, and internal organization of the firm) and then moved on to be applied to issue 4 (competitive advantage), the KBV began with the analysis of issue 4 and has during the last decade (or even less) moved on to consider the other issues.

The fact that these intellectual developments have taken place, and have taken place in a practice-related field such as strategic management, may in itself be taken as an indication of both the theoretical and empirical relevance of the project of constructing a strategic theory of the firm. At any rate, it is hard to disagree with the proposition that issues 1–3 in the above deal with themes that are crucial to strategy research (by definition issue 4 is crucial). Consider Rumelt, Schendel, and Teece's discussion of firm strategy (1994*b*: 9):

Because of competition, firms have choices to make if they are to survive. Those that are *strategic* include: the selection of goals; the choice of products and services to offer; the design and configuration of policies determining how the firm positions itself to compete in product markets (e.g. competitive strategy); the choice of an appropriate level of scope and diversity; and the design of organization structure, administrative systems, and policies used to define and coordinate work [...] It is the integration (or reinforcing pattern) among these choices that makes a set a strategy.

On this understanding, the issues of where to draw the boundaries of the firm and how to design internal organization are among a firm's important strategic choices. More specifically, the issue of the boundaries of the firm, for example, relates to a number of strategic issues, such as the firm's sourcing of resources (e.g. internal or external procurement of technology), supplier relations, the terms on which resources are acquired (e.g. the firm may internalize activities if it can carry them out more cost-efficiently), appropriation of rents (e.g. internalization may be an appropriation strategy), etc. To put it briefly, virtually all issues of corporate strategy, and many of business strategy, involve the boundaries of the firm. Therefore, theory that illuminates the issue of the boundaries of the firm is also likely to be helpful for understanding strategic choices. Quite similar arguments may be put forward in connection with the issue of internal organization.

However, this is certainly not to say that all strategic choices can be neatly linked to the issues of existence, boundaries, and internal organization of the firm and interpreted using organizational economics insights. For example, choices relating to the selection of goals, the choice of products and services to offer, as well as the issue of how to establish 'the integration (or reinforcing pattern) among these choices that makes a set a strategy' are hard to link directly to these issues. Thus, positioning and organizational coordination are not easy to comprehend through the lens provided by OE. It is ironic given Coase's status as *the* precursor of the modern economics of organization that these are issues that he saw as crucial in a retrospective comment (Coase 1988) on his seminal 1937 paper. Coase argued that economists have tended to neglect the main activity of a firm, namely organizational coordination. He himself had neglected this issue in the 1937 paper:

I did not investigate the factors that would make the costs of organizing lower for some firms than for others. This was quite satisfactory if the main purpose was, as mine was, to explain why there are firms. But if one is to explain the institutional structure of production in the system as a whole it is necessary to uncover the reasons why the cost of organizing particular activities differs among firms (ibid. 47)

Thus, the mature Coase suggested that the questions traditionally considered in the economic theory of the firm be extended to also include the issues of differential organizing capability, and, at least by implication, competitive advantage (see Madhok 2002 for a more extensive discussion). It is to those contributions to the economics of organizations that have taken their cue from Coase's early work (Coase 1937) that I now turn. The aim is to discuss the extent to which OE is a satisfactory strategic theory of the firm.

Isolationist Strategy No. 1: Organization Economics as a Foundation for the Strategic Theory of the Firm

Organizational Economics

Williamson (1994: 401) argues that what is needed in the strategy field is a 'core theory'; that the 'microanalytic, comparative institutional, economizing orientation of transaction cost economics deals with many of the key issues' of the field; and that what is needed to make transaction-cost economics 'even more germane' is more effort, extensions, and refinements. In other words, given sufficient time and research efforts, transaction-cost economics is likely to develop into a full-blown strategic theory of the firm. On all relevant indicators OE has in fact had a steadily increasing impact on the strategy field, and indeed on management studies in general. There is an increasing number of readers and textbooks, aimed at an audience consisting of management students and practising managers, and based on and presenting the main texts or the main principles of OE.[6] The journals present a similar picture. Inspection of randomly selected copies of the major journals from recent years reveals that OE is indeed a strong voice in the conversation. Nevertheless, it will be argued here that although OE has yielded valuable insights and asked interesting questions (cf. ibid. 381–2), it does not constitute a satisfactory strategic theory of the firm.

As already indicated, it is conventional to trace the origin of OE back to Coase's landmark 1937 essay on 'The Nature of the Firm'. In this paper Coase argued that the reason for the existence of firms ultimately had to be traced to some market failure, so that there would be a 'cost to using the price mechanism' (ibid. 390). At an overall level, all modern theories of the firm begin from roughly the same premise that Coase began with: It is necessary to introduce some spanners into the works of the perfectly competitive model (e.g. Debreu 1959), whether these be imperfect foresight, small-numbers bargaining, haggling costs, private information, cost of processing information or inspecting quality, increasing returns, etc., in order to tell a convincing story about economic organization. With perfect and costless contracting it is hard to find room for anything resembling firms (even one-person firms), since consumers could contract directly with factor owners and would not need the services of the intermediaries known as firms.

Ironically, these insights began to surface at exactly the time that Coase (1972: 63) lamented that his 1937 essay had been 'much cited and little used'; namely, in the work of Williamson (1971) and Alchian and Demsetz (1972). These two contributions helped found different approaches within the modern economics of organization. Thus, Williamson's work pointed the way not only to his own (as well as various associates') work on transaction cost economics but also to the more formal recent work of, notably, Oliver Hart and associates (Grossman and Hart 1986; Hart and Moore 1990; Hart 1995). Alchian and Demsetz's work, in turn, pointed the way to later work on the principal–agent relation (e.g. Holmström 1979, 1982; Holmström and Milgrom 1991, 1994).

These two traditions typically differ with respect to *which* spanners in the works of the perfectly competitive model they focus on, where the relevant spanners have to do with contracting (Holmström and Tirole 1989; Maskin and Tirole 1999; Tirole 1999). In the perfectly competitive model it is assumed that (1) agents can foresee all future contingencies and can costlessly write contracts that cover all contingencies (so that there are no incomplete contracts), and (2) there is symmetry of information concerning 'states of nature' (so that there are no principal–agent incentive problems of either the moral hazard or adverse-selection variety). It is these two basic assumptions that are challenged in incomplete contract theories and principal–agent theories respectively. I briefly discuss these two theories in terms of how well they meet the requirements of a strategic theory of a firm.

Incomplete Contract Theories

Incomplete contract theories are founded on the assumption that it is for some reason costly to draft complete complex contracts, and that there is therefore a need for *ex post* governance—a key theme in the work of probably the most influential follower of Coase, Oliver Williamson (1985, 1996a). In spite of the richness of Williamson's narrative, it is fair to say that there is one central character in his story: asset specificity. Assets are highly specific when there is a substantial difference between their value in present (best) use and next best use. This opens the door to opportunism. Once the contract is signed and the assets deployed, one of the parties may threaten to pull out of the arrangement— thereby reducing the value of the specific assets—unless a greater share of the surplus of joint production finds its way into the threatener's pockets. Fear of such a 'hold-up' *ex post* will affect investment choices *ex ante*. In the absence of appropriate contractual safeguards, the transacting parties may choose less specific—and therefore less specialized and less productive—technology. Often the parties to a contract do incorporate such safeguards or other mechanisms (such as reputation effects) to keep opportunism at bay. But for transactions characterized by very high levels of asset specificity not even this may be sufficient; pooling capital in a single enterprise may be the chosen solution, a solution that partly removes the incentives for opportunism, and may also imply (other) benefits in terms of *ex post* governance; notably, a superior ability to effect adaptive, sequential decision-making in the face of unforeseen contingencies (Williamson 1996a). Thus, Williamson's basic story addresses central points in a strategic theory of the firm, such as existence, boundaries, and internal organization. What is not, however, treated in his story—at least in any systematic way—is the issue of competitive advantage, since there is little in the transaction-cost story that allows us to say much about sustained inter-firm differences.

The work of Oliver Hart and various associates (Grossman and Hart 1986; Hart and Moore 1990; Hart 1995)—usually called 'the property-rights approach'—is often seen as a formal version of Williamson's work, although there are subtle but important differences (Kreps 1996). This work distinguishes two types of rights under contract: specific rights and residual rights. The latter are generic rights to make production decisions in circumstances not spelled out in the contract. The choice between market contracting and internal organization reduces to a question of the efficient allocation of the residual rights of control when contracts are incomplete and assets highly specific. If, again, assets are specific it may be efficient to place the residual rights of control in the hands of only one of the parties by giving that party ownership of both sets of assets. In general, the owner ought to be the party whose possession of the residual rights maximizes incentives to invest, which typically means the party whose contribution to the joint surplus of cooperation is greater. Hart and his colleagues hold that the possession of the residual rights of control necessitates ownership of the firm's capital assets and that the boundaries of the firm can be defined in this way.[7]

Although it is often seen as a formalization of (and improvement on) Williamson's work, the property-rights approach actually leaves out much of the richness in his work (see Kreps 1996), and is even less suitable than the transaction-cost approach as a strategic theory of the firm. In contrast to Williamson's work, there is very little in the property-rights theory about *ex post* governance and about issues of internal organization. Some of this may relate to the different behavioral assumptions that underlie the two theories. Incomplete-contract theorists explicitly deny the need in the theory of the firm for a notion of bounded rationality (cf. Hart 1990). To Williamson contractual incompleteness is clearly derived from bounded rationality, whereas to the property-rights theorists it is a matter of an assumed non-contractability of the use of the assets in a relation. In the latter case a welfare improvement may be brought about by reallocating residual rights of control; however, changes in organization structure and other information channels are not likely to have welfare consequences. To Williamson, on the other hand, organization structure and information channels strongly influence the boundedness of rationality. By economizing on bounded rationality, organization structure (which may be influenced by integration) may have welfare consequences for the agents involved with the firm. Moreover, to Williamson the incompleteness of contracting shifts some of the burden of efficient economic organization on to *ex post* governance, including management—something that is notable by its absence in the work of the property-rights theorists.[8] Thus, it may be argued that the inclusion of bounded rationality in Williamson's work allows him to stay closer to the traditional concerns of the strategy field than the property-rights theory. Moreover, in principle, bounded rationality opens the door for a theory of firm heterogeneity (cf. Nelson and Winter 1982); this, however, is a theme that Williamson has not pursued.

Complete Contract Theories

Complete contract theories break with the assumption that information concerning states of nature is symmetric. Thus, they allow agents to write elaborate contracts characterized by *ex ante* incentive alignment, but only under the constraints imposed by the presence of asymmetric information and (divergent) risk preferences. The agency problem (in its moral hazard manifestation) basically stems from a conflict between insurance and incentives. Sharing profit between a risk-neutral principal and a risk-averse agent—the standard assumptions about risk preferences in the literature—has the risk-neutral principal bearing all of the risk. This leads to the so-called 'first-best outcome'. However, this is only so if incentive issues are set aside (or the agent has no choice of action). In the standard bilateral setting the principal in fact cannot propose a first-best contract to the agent because the agent's action cannot be observed by the principal. The asymmetric information in question may be a matter of either hidden action or hidden knowledge (i.e. the principal does not know some characteristics of the agent that are relevant to the relation). The (moral hazard) problem then is that the agent selects an action which has random consequences, and those consequences can be ascertained by the principal, but the action and the state of nature (that both 'produced' the consequences) cannot. In this case risk-sharing and incentive considerations will interact. The contract specifies a reward schedule so that the agent is paid by the principal as a function of the verifiable consequences. In general, such a contract will only be second-best. The first-best (output maximizing) contract would be to let the agent compensate the principal with a fixed lump-sum payment and be awarded the residual; however, risk aversion on behalf of the agent will rule out this solution.

Principal–agent theory has produced many insights that are helpful for understanding contractual arrangements in general and the internal organization of firms in particular.[9] However, strictly speaking, these theories are not theories of the firm per se. Principal–agent theory is probably best understood as an extension of the neoclassical theory of the firm that inquires into the incentive conflicts that may hinder the firm from reaching its production-possibility frontier. However, the reward schedules that may modify the effects of asymmetric information are independent of any particular organizational structure. In principle, a reward schedule for a legally independent supplier firm may be completely identical to an employee reward schedule. Thus, principal–agent theory doesn't allow us to discriminate between inter-firm and intra-firm transactions. Thus, it does not address the issues of the existence and boundaries of the firm, nor, we may add, that of competitive advantage. Principal–agent theory cannot aspire to the title of a strategic theory of the firm.

Why Organizational Economics is Not a Strategic Theory of the Firm

So far, it has been argued that organizational economics fails to meet the criteria for qualifying as a strategic theory of the firm that were presented above (p. 24) (although some theories failed more than others). In this section I want to examine more closely the deeper reasons why economics-of-organization theories are not strategic theories of the firm.

Whatever their differences may be, one heuristic is characteristic of the various contributions that constitute OE: an overriding emphasis on conceptualizing virtually *all* problems of economic organization as problems of reducing incentive conflicts through *ex ante* contractual alignment and through *ex post* governance mechanisms. The role—the potentially very important role—of cognitive frames, routines, and capabilities as coordinating devices is neglected in this literature (Langlois and Foss 1999). Thus, the set of possible coordination problems, as well as the set of mechanisms for alleviating coordination problems, is very narrowly defined (Grandori 2001).

A specific example of this heuristic can be found in a recent paper by Rotemberg and Saloner (1994). They address one of the key ideas of the corporate-strategy and knowledge-based literature; namely, that firms may be best off choosing narrow strategies. Specifically, Rotemberg and Saloner use the incomplete-contract framework to argue that a firm may choose a narrow strategy (and thus ignore profitable opportunities) because strategic breadth leads to implementation problems *ex post* that distort *ex ante* incentives. They do note (p. 1131) that 'increasing returns to specialization' (because of learning advantages) from concentrating on well-defined knowledge-based may be an independent reason for narrow strategies, but they do not investigate that possibility—because this would mean breaking with the heuristic of reducing all problems of economic organization to problems of aligning incentives.

In a later paper (1995) the same authors discuss 'overt inter-functional conflict', which they exemplify by conflicts between production and marketing-and-sales functions. Conflicts sometimes arise between these functions, because 'production' prefers long, uninterrupted runs, while 'sales and marketing' prefers to be able to offer customers diversity. In the story Rotemberg and Saloner tell, these preferences are motivated by employees' wanting the firm to make particularly extensive use of their accumulated human capital, so that their bargaining position can be improved and they can increase their salary. Again, the authors do mention that an alternative explanation may have to do with different world-views among people in production and sales and marketing, but choose not to inquire into this.

A third, more general, example concerns the argument in the property-rights literature that strongly complementary assets should for reasons of efficient governance be under common ownership (Hart and Moore 1990; Hart 1995). In terms of the logic of the model, this conclusion is, of course, impeccable. But the model basically overlooks the argument, pointed out more than thirty years ago by George Richardson (1972), that although assets may be strongly complementary, they may still be dissimilar—in which case there is the possibility that governance by *separate* organizations is superior.

These examples are not isolated ones. Rather, they are representative of the explanatory stance characterizing OE. In this logic, factors such as differential cognition, values, routines, capabilities, etc. that may often be crucial to the traditional organization or strategy scholar when addressing, for example, core competencies, inter-functional conflict, or the organization of dissimilar capabilities do not enter the argument at all. The only explanatory mechanisms considered relate to the alignment of incentives. The problem is not that the explanatory logic pursued by OE is faulty, given its assumptions. It is not. Rather, the issue is empirical; it concerns whether the explanatory mechanisms identified in OE are plausible explanations of the phenomena under study. In fact, it is quite likely that the mechanisms underneath, for example, the narrow firm strategies that Rotemberg and Saloner (1994) talk about have little or nothing to do with the alignment of incentives, and have everything to do with limited knowledge, understanding, and perception.[10]

However, one may argue that whether narrow strategies ultimately turn on incentives or on capabilities is essentially an unsettled empirical question, and that therefore reformulating traditional organization and management issues in terms of OE is a respectable scientific activity. This may be granted. On the other hand, one may also validly argue that to translate the basic assumptions of organizational economics into an exclusive and near universal research strategy arguably closes off a range of plausible alternative explanations of what firms are and do, and of the activities of managing and strategizing.

Indeed, the claim here is that its full commitment to the narrow incentive-alignment research strategy is one reason why OE cannot, at least at the present, aspire to the role of a comprehensive strategic theory of the firm. First, it means that a very biased view is produced of a number of phenomena. For example, OE is characterized by relative inattention to issues of management, strategizing, and leadership (Coase 1988; Miller 1992)—all of which become reduced to merely a matter of providing the right incentives.[11] Moreover, it neglects those determinants of economic organization that are not related to incentive conflicts, such as information processing and organizational 'codes', 'languages', etc. (Radner 1996; Wernerfelt 1997). Second, but relatedly, the narrow research strategy of the modern economics of organization means that a number of issues that are crucial to the strategy field are not considered at all. These omissions include issues relating to positioning (but see Nickerson 1997); path-dependency (but see Williamson 1998)—which may lead the theorist to think of organizations as much more flexible than they in reality are (Winter 1991; Rumelt 1995)—and organizational learning (cf. Williamson 1998), as well as other dynamic phenomena and issues, such as innovation (Williamson 1985).

While a satisfactory strategic theory of the firm certainly does not have to take all this into account, it is clear, on the other hand, that issues such as path-dependency, organizational learning, differential capabilities, and the like have been very much present in the discourse of the strategy field within at least the last decade, and that the inability of the economics of organization to come to grips with them may be seen as a problem. Most seriously, their neglect in OE means that it becomes very difficult to account, within this body of thought, for systematic and sustained differences among firms.[12] In fact, this is the decisive objection against viewing OE as a strategic theory of the firm, for without a theory addressing the sources and persistence of heterogeneity among firms it is hard to tell a convincing story of (sustained) competitive advantage (Barney 1991).

One important reason why it is so hard to treat heterogeneity within OE is that this body of thought does not challenge the basic theory of production in economics; that is, 'the production function view' (Nelson and Winter 1982). In other words, it is implicitly accepted that the production function and its attendant assumptions tells us what we need to know about production. However, in basic economics technological knowledge is seldom portrayed as asymmetric, let alone tacit; on the contrary, it is assumed to be explicit, freely transmissible, and easily encapsulated in blueprints.[13] Thus, it is next to impossible to rationalize heterogeneity and competitive advantages in terms of different underlying capabilities, and, moreover, the governance choice cannot hinge on differential capabilities. The relative suppression of production in the modern economics of organization may simply be a pragmatic methodological postulate (Williamson 1985: 88), and differential production costs may eventually be more fully treated in OE (e.g. Lewis and Sappington 1991; Williamson 1998). But it is still a good approximation to say that in OE it is not recognized that (1) knowledge may be imperfect in the realm of production, and (2) firms may play the role not only of mitigating incentive conflicts but also of linking existing imperfect knowledge and of making knowledge less imperfect through learning.[14] I now turn to a body of theory that tries to make provision for these points.

Isolationist Strategy No. 2: The Knowledge-based View as a Foundation for the Strategic Theory of the Firm

Penrose and the Knowledge-based View

The conceptualization of the firm that underlies the KBV is often attributed to Penrose (1959). 'The firm', Penrose says, 'is . . . a collection of productive resources the disposal of which between different uses and over time is determined by administrative decision' (ibid. 24). She points out that allocation by means of 'administrative decision' is fundamentally different from allocation by means of the price mechanism (ibid. 20), thus establishing a link to Coase.[15] But whereas Coase (1937) was eager to emphasize that he was simply extending existing economic analysis, Penrose makes an explicit break with mainstream economics. Hers is a constructivist and disequilibrium theory of the firm.[16] In Penrose's story, the management team holds *images* of the external environment and of the firm's internal resources (this is the constructivist part of her analysis). She further argues that these images are produced through internal learning processes. Moreover, they determine the constantly changing 'productive opportunity set' of the firm (this is the disequilibrium part of her story); that is, the productive possibilities that the firm's ' "entrepreneurs" see and can take advantage of' (Penrose 1959: 31).

Thus, Penrose explicitly begins from a theory of (limited) cognition. In contrast, modern contributions to the knowledge-based view typically begin merely from the empirical generalization that firm-specific knowledge is 'sticky', distributed,[17] and tacit, without arguing this on the basis of a theory of individual cognition and knowledge.[18] This is not an unimportant point, for the problem of missing micro-foundations is a severe one in the knowledge-based view. However, both starting points imply that organizations are necessarily limited in what they know how to do well. These characteristics of productive knowledge are often summed up by means of the concept of 'capabilities', and basic ideas on capabilities form the backdrop to an analysis of firm heterogeneity, competitive advantage, and differential rents. Differential capabilities imply differences in terms of the efficiency with which resources are deployed, which yield rents that, in turn, may be long-lived because the inherent characteristics of capabilities make them hard to imitate (Lippman and Rumelt 1982; Wernerfelt 1984; Barney 1991; Peteraf 1993). I shall not spend more time here rehearsing these familiar arguments. What is important in the present context, however, is the increasingly influential idea that the characteristics of capabilities that make them interesting for the study of competitive advantage are actually *also* crucial for the study of the main issues in economic organization (Conner 1991; Langlois 1992; Kogut and Zander 1992; Foss 1993; Langlois and Robertson 1995; Conner and Prahalad 1996; Grant 1996; Kogut and Zander 1996; Madhok 1996). Thus, in prospect, we are being told, is a strategic theory of the firm derived from knowledge-based considerations rather than from incentives, opportunism, and transaction costs.

The Knowledge-based View as a Theory of Economic Organization

As a theory of economic organization the KBV may be reconstructed along the following lines. In a (Penrosian) world of bounded rationality and tacit, sticky, and distributed knowledge—that is, of differential capabilities—production and transaction costs are arguably cast in a different light relative to the modern economics of organization. First, in such a world firms will not confront the same production costs for the same type of productive activity, primarily because they are unlikely to control the same stocks of tacit knowledge (Nelson and Winter 1982). Second, and as a consequence of the first point, the costs of transacting may go beyond those that arise in the course of safeguarding against opportunism or reducing moral hazard problems through monitoring or incentive contracts. In particular, economic activity may be influenced by costs related to the process of gathering, coordinating, and communicating knowledge (Demsetz 1991; Langlois 1992; Foss 1993; Langlois and Robertson 1995; Casson 1997).

In such a setting the costs of making contacts with potential partners, of educating potential licensees and franchisees, of teaching suppliers what it is one needs from them, etc. may influence where the boundaries of firms will be placed. Likewise, the internal structure of firms may not just reflect incentive alignment but may also reflect the costs of transmitting knowledge (Radner 1996). This suggests, albeit loosely, that the KBV may be interpreted as an emerging *alternative* theory of economic organization, for the sort of costs of transacting that are highlighted in the KBV are not comprehensively treated in the modern economics of organization. As Jean Tirole (1988: 49), a key contributor to the modern economics of organization, admits, '[n]eoclassical theory pays only lip service to the issue of communication'.

The idea that a knowledge-based view may have implications for economic organization is not quite new. In what is still one of the best contributions to the literature, G. B. Richardson (1972) suggested that we begin not from the Coasean idea of transaction costs but from the idea that production can be broken down into various *activities*, not unlike the treatment of Porter (1985). Some activities are *similar*, in that they draw on the same general capabilities, and activities can also be *complementary*, in that they are connected in the chain of production, and similarity and complementarity may obtain to varying degrees. The main point in Richardson (1972) is that economic organization is strongly influenced by these dimensions of activities. For example, closely complementary and similar activities are best undertaken under unified governance, whereas closely complementary but dissimilar activities are normally best undertaken under some sort of hybrid arrangement (to use Williamson's terminology (1996)). Thus, Richardson's basic point clearly is that capabilities may be determinants of the boundaries of the firm, a point that was later elaborated by Kogut and Zander (1992) and Langlois (1992). They argued that differential capabilities would typically give rise to different production costs, and that such cost differentials may crucially influence the make or buy decision. Thus, firms may internalize activities because they can carry out these activities in a more production- not transaction-cost-efficient way than other firms are capable of (see also Madhok 1996).

In economics the next major knowledge-based critique (after Richardson 1972) of OE is probably Demsetz (1991), who argues that firms may exist for reasons of economizing on expenditures on communicating and coordinating knowledge. Thus, the employment contract, and hierarchy more generally, may exist because it is efficient to have the less knowledgeable being directed by the more knowledgeable.[19] Within the strategy field, a number of knowledge-based contributions have echoed Demsetz's points about the firm existing for reasons of superior ability to coordinate knowledge (Conner 1991; Conner and Prahalad 1996; Grant 1996). For example, Conner and Prahalad (1996) argue that the existence of firms can be explained in terms of the superior flexibility relative to market contracting that the authority relation may confer and in terms of economizing with the communication of knowledge, thus combining Coase's ideas (1937) about authority with Demsetz's ideas (1991) about conserving on expenditures on communicating knowledge. Whereas market contracting may require prolonged haggling and sharing of knowledge, firms may save on haggling costs and costs of communicating knowledge, and may exist for this reason.

A possible conclusion on this section is that the KBV is in fact reaching for a *distinct* perspective on economic organization, since it appears that explanatory mechanisms that are different from those of OE are emphasized. Specifically, the perspective begins from many of the ideas that were developed in order to understand competitive advantage, such as heterogeneous, firm-specific, path-dependent, and hard-to-imitate production and organization knowledge, and tries to build a theory of economic organization on this basis, specifically a theory that addresses the existence and boundaries of firms.

Weaknesses of the Knowledge-based View

There is, it is fair to say, an optimistic tone to the new knowledge-based approach to economic organization. The reason is easy to detect: it is an approach to economic organization that avoids (what its proponents may regard as) the worst excesses of the modern economics of organization,[20] and it deals directly with strategy issues, staying in close contact with both behavioral perspectives and more content-oriented strategy perspectives (cf. Zajac 1992). Thus, part of the optimism may have to do with a conviction that in prospect is a distinct theory of the firm that will largely be developed *within* the strategy field rather than merely being imported from economics. However, there are reasons to curb enthusiasm somewhat. In fact, the purpose of this section is to identify a number of weaknesses that beset the KBV. Whereas the view is at its strongest when it comes to the analysis of firm heterogeneity and competitive advantage, its approach to economic organization appears at present considerably more shaky, particularly considering that many of the weak points have been dealt with rather convincingly by the modern economics of organization. For example, I shall argue that the KBV has difficulties accounting for the existence of the firm. In addition to these difficulties of explaining economic organization, there are also difficulties of a more methodological nature, such as the view's lack of clear micro-foundations and its inability to put forward clear predictions.

*Economic Organization: The Existence of the Firm, Asset Ownership,
and the Boundaries of the Firm*

Perhaps the strongest arguments that the KBV can successfully address the issue of the existence of the firm have been put forward by Conner (1991), Kogut and Zander (1992), and Conner and Prahalad (1996), Grant (1996). The arguments fall in two different categories. First, there is an argument that firms exist because they can create certain assets—such as learning capabilities or a 'shared context'—that markets purportedly cannot create.[21] Second, a different (but perhaps complementary) argument is that firms exist because of their superior flexibility relative to market contracting; for example, they may be more flexible when it comes to deploying assets because they can rely on the authority mechanism rather than on the haggling that characterizes market contracts. However, the problem with both views is they that do not sufficiently characterize *firms*. Markets can cultivate learning capabilities and shared context (as in industrial districts), and markets can certainly be flexible, too; indeed, superior flexibility has often been invoked as very much part of their rationale (e.g. Hayek 1945). Likewise, the literature on user–producer interaction (e.g. Hippel 1988) makes essentially the same claims for cooperative relations between legally independent firms.

To illustrate further what is wrong with these views, consider the much cited Kogut and Zander (1992) paper. They are representatives of the view that firms exist because they can create certain assets that markets cannot create. As they argue,

organizations are social communities in which individual and social expertise is transformed into economically useful products and services by the application of a set of higher-order organizing principles. Firms exist because they provide a social community of voluntaristic action structured by organizing principles that are not reducible to individuals (ibid. 384)

—a view, they claim, that 'differs radically from that of the firm as a bundle of contracts that serves to allocate efficiently property rights' (ibid.). Firms' advantages over markets derive from their being able to supply 'organizing principles that are not reducible to individuals', and in which the members of the organization are embedded.[22] Markets (inherently?) cannot supply these principles. Thus, according to Kogut and Zander, the efficient development of capabilities and the full creation of the values of assets/resources can only take place within firm organization, because firms offer embeddedness (shared codes, knowledge, expectations, etc.) advantages that markets cannot offer. Presumably, this is what some writers have called 'the organizational advantage' (Ghoshal and Moran 1996; Nahapiet and Ghoshal 1999).

The basic problem with this reasoning is that embeddedness of the sort that these authors talk about does not require firm organization. Thus, in a moral utopia, characterized by the absence of opportunistic proclivities, the gains from embeddedness could be realized in *the market*. Agents could simply meet under the same factory roof, own their own pieces of physical capital equipment or rent them to each other, and develop value-enhancing 'organizing principles' (to use Kogut and Zander's term) among themselves, or in other ways integrate their specialized knowledge (as a team) (Putterman 1995; Foss 1996a). Firms would not be necessary. Even in an opportunism-prone world there may be much embeddedness 'outside' firms, as it were; for example, in single industries, in firm networks, industrial districts, etc., depending on the presence of various control and enforcement mechanisms.

The OE critique of the embeddedness argument is that in the absence of opportunism (or incentive conflicts more generally), the first-best (efficient) outcome can always be realized in the market and firms are strictly unnecessary. But there is another knowledge-based argument that cannot be killed by this critique. This is put forward by Conner (1991) and Conner and Prahalad (1996). They argue that firms derive their *raison d'être* from their superior flexibility relative to markets, particularly with respect to creating and redeploying knowledge, an advantage that is very closely connected to the incompleteness of the employment contract and the existence of authority. Admittedly, Conner and Prahalad (ibid.) go some way towards an improved understanding of the bargaining- and communication-cost advantages of the employment contract, and Wernerfelt (1997) presents an interesting formalization of a related idea. The problem here is whether the employment contract sufficiently characterizes the firm. According to a number of theorists, now including Coase (1988) himself, it does not.

As argued by Williamson (1985, 1996a), Grossman and Hart (1986), and many others, the key to defining the firm lies in asset-ownership rather than in the employment relationship. In fact, the latter is derived from the former. In this tradition the firm is defined as the collection of assets that the firm's owners/ managers control. One reason why asset ownership matters is that it allows us to understand bargaining power and hence the derived concept of authority: the owner/manager, who controls assets, can threaten the employee with depriving him of the assets with which he is currently working (here is the link to the employment contract). We may disagree with the idea that the pattern of asset ownership is indeed the essence of the firm,[23] but it is hard to disagree with the proposition that the pattern of asset ownership is a crucial aspect of the firm, and that any comprehensive theory of the firm must address this issues. Knowledge-based theories of the firm do not in their present version address it.[24]

In spite of this, many contributions to the knowledge-based view (e.g. Kogut and Zander 1992; Madhok 1996) present it as an alternative and *general* perspective on economic organization.[25] One interpretation of what it means for the KBV to be a general theory is that observed economic organization—always and everywhere—must be predominatly explained using knowledge-based ideas, and that economics-of-organization ideas enter the explanation in a secondary way (if at all).

The starting point of the KBV, we have seen, is differential capabilities and derived knowledge problems. But what if capabilities are not that 'dissimilar' (in Richardson's terminology (1972)), as, for example, they may not be in an industry characterized by a mature underlying technology. In such an industry, one may conjecture that incentive-conflict considerations will dominate differential capabilities, in which case an OE perspective is appropriate. If it is conceded that the knowledge-based view is complementary (rather than rivalrous) to the modern economics of organization, reasoning that allows the analyst to be more precise about when capabilities matter and when they don't is still needed. It may be argued that the 'balance' between capabilities and incentive/governance considerations hinges on the degree of overlap in the technological knowledge underlying firms' activities, but this does not go significantly beyond the formulation of Richardson (ibid.). Of course, it is possible to provide some rationalizations of differential capabilities; for example, by pointing to path-dependency, tacitness, and team-based knowledge (Winter 1991; Foss 1993; Langlois and Robertson 1995; Argyres 1996). But to some extent this begs the question, for we are still not much wiser about how capabilities are influenced by these factors and how this translates into knowledge dimensions such as 'similarity' (Richardson 1972). Knowledge of these links seems, however, to be required to make the KBV predictive. The virtual absence of theorizing here indicates a broader problem; namely, the lack of clear micro-foundations and modeling heuristics.

Methodological Problems: Lack of Predictive Power and Modeling Heuristics

The KBV is certainly not without empirical content; however, as it now stands the KBV is more of an explanatory than a predictive approach. That is to say, it allows the analyst to tell an *ex post* story about the causes of the success of a given firm, or why the boundaries of that firm are placed where they are, but it is considerably weaker with respect to predicting future success or future patterns of economic organization (Argyres 1996). This may be contrasted with the substantial base of empirical support that OE has now accumulated (on which see Klein and Shelanski 1995). What makes this comparison pertinent is not only that the KBV and OE may be seen as theoretical rivals. It is also that they both make heavy use of concepts—capabilities and transaction costs respectively—whose empirical counterparts are not immediately apparent.

However, in fairness it should be noted that it has taken OE two decades to accumulate its present base of empirical support, and one may argue that there is nothing in the KBV that makes it inherently non-predictive. Any theory contains terms and concepts that are not testable and, indeed, are not meant to be tested at all. And it is often held that what should be tested are the implications of the theory, not its assumptions (Machlup 1955). However, capabilities hardly partake of the role of assumptions; rather, they are crucial explanatory variables, so the issue of operationalization is hard to avoid. In particular, operationalization must proceed so that it is possible to distinguish between competing hypotheses.

This is a problem with the one quantitative empirical study that comes out unambiguously in favor of the KBV as it applies to economic organization, namely Kogut and Zander (1993). This paper is essentially an application to the multinational corporation, with an accompanying test, of the reasoning in their 1992 paper. In their story, the *raison d'être* of the multinational corporation lies in its superior ability to transfer tacit knowledge across borders, rather than in any market failures. They present quantitative evidence for the proposition that the harder to codify and teach a given technology is, the more likely is it that the technology will be transferred by means of wholly owned operations. Thus, the boundaries of the multinational firm are shown to depend on knowledge considerations. However, Kogut and Zander do not control for a possible competing transaction-cost explanation; namely, that tacit technologies may also tend to be more proprietary and therefore at greater risk of expropriation by contractual partners. Thus, an alternative micro-explanation can rationalize the finding that such technologies are not transferred over the market but through wholly owned subsidiaries. It is worth exploring the issue of micro-foundations, and relatedly, modeling heuristics, further.

Because it is largely derived from mainstream economics, OE is characterized by rather unambiguous micro-foundations and modeling heuristics. Basically, one may say that there is agreement that the aim is to explain economic organization (patterns of property rights, incentives, and monitoring) as an equilibrium outcome of interaction among self-interested agents in a setting characterized by asymmetric information (principal–agent theory) and/or incomplete contracting (incomplete contracts, transaction-cost economics). This heuristic guides almost all work done within OE. In contrast, there is no agreement on the micro-foundations of the KBV, and, what is worse, very little interest in providing such micro-foundations.[26]

A further, but related, problem is that how knowledge considerations relate to more economic considerations is seldom made clear. This is because the micro-logic of the arguments is very seldom spelled out. (More on this in Chapter 4.) To what extent can knowledge-based arguments about economic organization be interpreted in terms of information costs? What exactly is the relation between, for example, tacitness and complexity, on the one hand, and information and communication costs on the other? Moreover, how do we build up from assumptions about individual behavior and cognition to firm-level outcomes?

Is the knowledge-based view consistent with equilibrium or does it adopt other principles for making sense of the outcomes of interactions? In other words, clear modeling heuristics are lacking. Arguably, this problem besets the whole knowledge-based literature, and it is easy to agree with Williamson (1996a: 357–8) when he observes that ' "[c]ore competences", which is an elusive but important concept in the recent corporate knowledge-based literature [. . .] should be conceptualized more rigorously'.

The Knowledge-based View as a Strategic Theory of the Firm?

As the preceding sections indicate, there are reasons seriously to doubt whether the KBV can pretend to be a strategic theory of the firm in the sense in which that term is being used here. There are deep substantive as well as methodological problems. Thus, there are problems with the explanatory logic of the view, particularly as it applies to issues of economic organization; moreover, the view is non-formal and non-predictive. While these latter characteristics do not constitute grounds for rejection (or perhaps even critique) per se, they do imply that the KBV in important ways runs counter to both the strong formalistic tendency of OE and the positivistic tendency of the strategy field. One may seriously question for how long a theory can survive in environments in which formalization and the production of testable hypotheses appear to be important selection criteria.

The KBV has to a large extent been developed within the strategy field, and one may argue that it is characterized by the weaknesses (ambiguous terminology, little cumulative theory development, etc.) that have been claimed to characterize this field. This may in itself explain its continued existence, since it may not be such a weak theory after all—if seen in the context of its environment. Thus, while economists may wish to give short shrift to the perspective, the tolerance of management scholars may be considerably greater. In a more friendly interpretation, however, the KBV has emerged and continues to develop because it is up to something that is (1) interesting and (2) not treated in the modern economics of organization. Before this can be seen, it is necessary to undertake a more systematic analysis of the relations between the two bodies of theory in terms of their explanatory apparatuses. This is done in the following section.

A Theory-of-science Perspective

As already stated, the relation between the KBV and OE is often seen as one of rivalry. For example, Kogut and Zander (1992: 384) argued that their view 'differs radically from that of the firm as a bundle of contracts that serves to allocate efficiently property rights'. One would perhaps expect such inter-theory conflicts to be settled through empirical tests. One problem here is that empirical work that aims at testing the predictions of the KBV (Kogut and Zander 1993) does not control for a possible competing OE explanation, and vice versa (Klein and Shelanski 1995).[27] Indeed, empirical work in this area is fraught with severe difficulties in defining and operationalizing key concepts.

Possible Theory Relations

In order to be able to discuss the relation between the KBV and OE in a more precise manner, I rely on Krajewski (1977). He suggested a useful framework for classifying and discussing relations between different theories. The taxonomy in Table 2.1 reflects this framework. Krajewski's framework and taxonomy are here used as a heuristic tool. The aim is not unambiguously to place KBV and OE in one of the categories of Table 2.1. Rather, the taxonomy provides useful insights with respect to the dimensions in which theories may differ.

The taxonomy maps possible relations between two theories, T_1 and T_2, in terms of their domain of application (D) (i.e. their explanandum) and their theoretical language (V) (i.e. their explanans). The domain of application refers to what the theory is designed to explain. For example, OE is designed to explain the existence, boundaries, and internal organization of firms (cf. Coase 1937; Alchian and Demsetz 1972; Williamson 1985, 1996a; Hart 1995). Initially, the KBV was developed to address competitive advantage (Wernerfelt 1984; Barney 1986), but it has, as we have seen, increasingly expanded its explananda phenomena to also include those traditionally considered in OE (see Table 2.2).

Table 2.1 reveals that the KBV and OE have overlapping domains of application (D1 ∩ D2 ≠ ∅). They are therefore commensurable, which is a precondition for comparing them. Given commensurability, there are then several possible relations between the KBV and OE, of which the extreme possibilities are equivalence and contradiction. The possible relations between the theories all intimately involve the question of the relation between the respective theoretical languages. The concept of theoretical language refers to the explanatory framework of the theory, including terminology, explanatory variables, behavioral assumptions, and type of explanation. For example, while OE relies on an explanatory framework largely derived from mainstream economics, the KBV relies instead on a framework drawn from strategy, organizational, and behavioral research and emphasizes bounded rationality, routines, capabilities, and the like, rather than incentives, asymmetric information, property rights, and contracts. A key question then is what is the relation between these theoretical languages. For example, can equivalence be established through translation of KBV language into OE language or vice versa? If this cannot be done, this still leaves us with numerous other possibilities. For example, the theories may be contradictory, as asserted by some proponents of the KBV (e.g. Kogut and Zander 1992; Madhok 1996). In terms of Table 2.1, this means that while the domain of

TABLE 2.1. A taxonomy of theory relations

Type	Domain	Theoretical language	Relation
Commensurability	$D1 \cap D_2 \neq \varnothing$	—	—
Equivalence	$D_1 = D_2$	$V_1 \leftrightarrow V_2$	$T_1 = L_1(T_2)$
			$T_2 = L_2(T_1)$
Reduction:			
Homogeneous	$D_1 \subset D_2$	$V_1 \subset V_2$	$T_1 \wedge A \Rightarrow T_2$
Heterogeneous	$D_1 \subset D_2$	$V_1 \rightarrow V_2$	$T_1 \wedge A \wedge S \Rightarrow T_2$
Contradiction	$D_1 = D_2$	$V_1 \neq V_2$	$T_1 \Rightarrow \neg T_2$
			$T_2 \Rightarrow \neg T_1$
Correspondence:			
Homogeneous	$D_1 \subset D_2$	$V_1 = V_2$	$T_2 \Rightarrow aT_1$ in D_1
			$T_2 \Rightarrow \neg aT_1$ in $D_2 - D_1$
Heterogeneous	$D_1 \subset D_2$	$V_1 \rightarrow V_2$	As above

Note. The notation is standard notation; however, some of the expressions used deserve explanation: '$\leftrightarrow$' means that there is a one-to-one correspondence (so that double translation between two theories is possible); 'L' is a translation operator (metaphorically speaking, a sort of 'dictionary'); '$\rightarrow$' is used to indicate a one-sided correspondence (so that double translation is not possible); '$\Rightarrow$' refers to implications of a theory (e.g. '$T_1 \Rightarrow \neg T_2$' means that the negation of T_2 follows from T_1); 'A' refers to supplementary hypotheses; 'S' are bridging principles (e.g. principles of aggregation); finally, 'a' means 'approximates'.

Source. Reproduced from Krajewski (1977: 67) with modifications.

application (D) of the theories is the same, the theories work with different untranslatable languages (V), and their implications with respect to the domain of application contradict each other (i.e. $T_1 \Rightarrow \neg T_2$ and $T_2 \Rightarrow \neg T_1$). This would seem to make integrationism untenable, and isolationism the only possible approach. However, such a conclusion may be too hasty.

In order to find out what is the true relation between the KBV and OE, one can begin by examining to what extent it is possible to arrive at the same insights by trying to translate the theoretical language of the KBV into OE language (or vice versa). This allows for an identification of not just 'semantic' differences, but genuine theoretical differences.

We may begin by asking whether a *reduction* is possible? Two general types of reduction may be distinguished. First, a homogeneous reduction is obtained if it is possible to show that the KBV is a special-case theory of organizational economics (or vice versa), in the sense that one can obtain OE by adding hypotheses (A) to the KBV, and that the theoretical language of the KBV is a subset of OE. Second, in the case of a heterogeneous reduction we also need bridging principles (S), which generally refer to how one moves from one level of analysis to another one. For example, there may be principles that explain how the notion of 'routine' is obtained from aggregating individual actions.

TABLE 2.2. The knowledge-based approach and organizational economics: explananda and key contributions

Explanandum phenomenon	Knowledge-based contributions	Organizational-economics contributions
Why do firms exist?	Conner (1991), Conner and Prahalad (1996), Grant (1996), Kogut and Zander (1996)	Alchian and Demsetz (1972), Coase (1937)
What factors determine firms' boundaries relative to the market?	Kogut and Zander (1992, 1993), Madhok (1996), Penrose (1959), Richardson (1972), Winter (1991)	Hart (1995), Hart and Moore (1990), Williamson (1985, 1996a)
What determines firms' internal organization?	Dosi and Marengo (1994), Ghoshal, Moran and Almeida-Costa (1995), Ghoshal and Moran (1996)	Barzel (1997), Holmstrom (1982), Holmstrom and Milgrom (1991), Putterman (1995)
What determines competitive advantage?	Barney (1986, 1991), Peteraf (1993), Wernerfelt (1984)	Kreps (1990a), Williamson (1994)

Note: Some of the contributions address more than one of the explananda phenomena. However, they have been classified according to their main thrust.

Finally, there is the possibility of *correspondence*. In a homogeneous relation of correspondence the two theories apply identical explanatory apparatuses, and T_1 is an adequate approximation to T_2 within D_1, while the more general theory T_2 corrects T_1 in $D_2 - D_1$ by taking into account new variables, assumptions, etc. A final possibility is the heterogeneous relation of correspondence, which differs from the homogeneous relation by taking into account differences in theoretical languages.

The basic KBV position seems to be that because OE does not conceptualize economic organization in knowledge-based terms it cannot come to grips with either the analysis of competitive advantage or the knowledge-based determinants of economic organization (e.g. Madhok 1996). However, many of the explanatory concepts and insights of the KBV can be given an OE interpretation, or at least be further illuminated by this approach, as exemplified below.[28]

Translating the Knowledge-based View: Some Examples

Perhaps the key explanatory insight of the KBV is resource heterogeneity, particularly heterogeneity of knowledge resources. Ultimately, it is heterogeneity that explains performance differences between firms and why, for example, different firms organize different activities (i.e. the boundaries of the firm)

(Madhok 2002). Can OE handle heterogeneity and economic organization in a way that does justice to KBV insights?

Resource heterogeneity.   Resource (input) heterogeneity is in fact a key theme in organizational economics (e.g. Alchian and Demsetz 1972; Barzel 1982; Williamson 1996*a*). Not only do different resources have many and different uses, but even assets of the same type are heterogeneous. In fact, if resources were homogeneous, there wouldn't be room for the contracting problems that are central in organizational economics, save, perhaps, for very trivial agency problems. This insight is explicit in the Alchian and Demsetz (1972) theory of the firm. They argue that resource heterogeneity is a necessary condition for the existence of the team problem for which firm organization provides an efficiency-enhancing solution. They go on to argue that sometimes 'gains from specialization and cooperative production may better be obtained within an organization like the firm' (p. 75), because continuity of association among resource owners and specialized monitoring services reduce the costs of ascertaining quality differences across heterogeneous resources. Both depend on the specific allocation of property rights inside firms. First, continuity among resource owners is a matter of the duration of contracts. Second, the manager is in a unique position to acquire superior information about the diverse services that can be extracted from heterogeneous resources of variable quality, because he has the right to monitor employees. Based on this information he is also able to specify property rights—that is, specify the rights and obligations of employees—in ways that will yield the highest returns. Given this, efficiency differences between firms are 'a result not of having *better* resources but in [*sic*] *knowing more accurately* the relative productive performances of those resources' (ibid. 94; emphasis in the original). Thus, an important source of competitive advantage lies in such 'organization capital' (Prescott and Visscher 1980). It is hard to see how such reasoning as this could in any essential way be at variance with KBV reasoning; on the contrary, it may be seen as contributing parts of a much-needed micro-foundation for the KBV (more on this in Chapters 4 and 5).

The boundaries of the firm.   A common argument in the KBV literature (e.g. Kogut and Zander 1992; Langlois and Foss 1999) is that what ultimately sets the KBV apart from OE is that the former is much more explicit about productive knowledge that cannot be specified in blueprints (i.e. tacit, skill-like knowledge). Such knowledge, it is argued, holds the key to understanding the boundaries of the firm. However, it is not made clear why the coordination mechanisms characterizing firms are more efficient than markets in making use of tacit, skill-like knowledge. In order to understand this, we can employ property rights arguments. Thus, we may associate tacit, skill-like knowledge with imperfectly specified rights to valuable attributes of assets, notably the human capital of employees. Given the high costs of writing explicit contracts over such knowledge, the firm may have advantages relative to market contracting, because its property-rights system allows it to make less costly use of the services that tacit human capital may yield. This is because the continuous association between the employee and the firm allows the manager to extract information about the true skills of employees, as argued above. Finally, the firm is particularly efficient in enforcing the implicit elements of contracts (Williamson 1996*a*), such as the norms and conventions that emerge from the continued interaction among employees.

Which Theoretical Relations Obtain?

The two brief examples above amount to a suggestion that key KBV insights in fact may be reformulated in terms of, or at least furthered by means of, OE insights. This raises the question of how we can use the taxonomy in Table 2.1 to cast light over the relation between OE and the KBV.

To begin with, note that OE and the KBV attempt to address the same domain of application (the same explananda; see Table 2.2). However, I have suggested that the KBV does not provide convincing *independent* explanations of the existence and internal organization of firms, because KBV arguments here can be recast as OE arguments. If generalized, this suggests that the true domain of application of the KBV is a subset of the domain of application of OE. It is more complicated to sort out the relations between the KBV and OE with respect to how they explain the boundaries of the firm and competitive advantage. Note that the KBV explanation of these relies on concepts—such as routines and capabilities—that are not part of the OE language (explanans). This then raises the question of the relation between the languages used in OE and the KBV.

Essentially, it has been suggested that the language of the KBV (V_1) may to some extent be translated into the language of OE (V_2). This is because concepts such as routines, capabilities, and heterogeneity can to some extent be given an OE interpretation. Therefore, the KBV explanation of the boundaries of the firm and competitive advantage may be translated into OE insights, but only after first translating insights about routines and capabilities into OE insights. Thus, OE may provide a sort of micro-foundation for these more aggregate concepts. Note that in order to build up from OE insights to KBV insights one needs bridging principles (S) that help us to move from one level of analysis to another level. For example, routines may be seen as emergent properties of interaction between agents constrained by transaction costs and the property-rights system of the firm. On the other hand, it does not seem possible to translate the other way around; that is, translate OE language into KBV language. This is because there are no bridging principles that will allow one to go from routines and capabilities to property rights, asymmetric information, transaction costs, etc. As a first approximation, this means that there is a 'one-sided correspondence' between the two languages ($V_1 \rightarrow V_2$).

The reasoning so far points to either a heterogeneous reduction or a heterogeneous correspondence (see Table 2.1) as the 'true' relation between KBV and OE. In the case of the heterogeneous reduction, the theories have the same implications ($T_1 \wedge A \wedge S \Rightarrow T_2$), provided one of them is supplemented with additional hypotheses (A) and bridging principles (S). In the case of the heterogeneous correspondence, one of the theories approximates the other one in the latter's domain of application ($T_2 \Rightarrow a\ T_1$ in D_1), while adding some new implications that cannot be reached by the latter theory ($T_2 \Rightarrow \neg a\ T_1$ in $D_2 - D_1$). In the view espoused here, the true relation between OE and the KBV comes closest to that of the heterogeneous correspondence, because OE has implications with respect to competitive advantage, and the existence, boundaries, and internal organization of the firm that cannot be reached by the KBV. However, it may be argued that we have only been able to reach these conclusions by implicitly sidestepping issues such as bounded rationality, learning, and (differential) cognition—in short, ideas that relate to the endogenous creation of heterogeneity. Can these ideas be reduced to OE insights? And are they important to the KBV?

Knowledge-based Challenges to Organizational Economics?

There are, in fact, important concepts and insights in the KBV that cannot be reduced to OE insights, and may in fact challenge OE. Some of these are briefly discussed here.

Bounded rationality and learning.   According to KBV writers (e.g. Ghoshal, Moran, and Almeida-Costa 1995; Conner and Prahalad 1996; Grant 1996; Spender 1996), one strength of the KBV relative to OE is its (somewhat) more explicit treatment of bounded rationality and learning.[29] The treatment of bounded rationality in OE (Williamson 1985, 1996a) is arguably narrow, since it at best figures as a constraint on a decision problem.[30] Changing bounds of rationality through, for example, satisficing search activities is not inquired into. And learning only appears in OE as changes in human-asset specificity ('the fundamental transformation'; ibid.), while the learning process itself is largely neglected. However, OE is not inherently cut off from treating learning and bounded rationality (see Foss 2001).

For example, learning by doing requires the exercise of use rights over assets. One may even suggest that the more well specified and easily monitored use rights are, the less can asset users experiment, and the more constrained will their learning be (Foss and Foss 2002). Experimentation is important as a way of finding solutions to coordination problems (e.g. finding the optimal sequence of activities). Managers holding residual use rights over assets are able to conduct controlled experiments without continuously having to renegotiate contracts, and it is by exercising residual rights that managers change the conditions under which skills, conventions, norms, and other types of socially shared knowledge emerge. This suggests one way in which OE may better come to grips with the knowledge processes that are central in the KBV. But obviously much more needs to be done here.

Cognition.   OE follows virtually all of economics in assuming cognitive homogeneity (that is, agents hold the same, correct, model of the world) and cognitive constancy (that is, agents' model of the world does not change (see further Foss 2004)). In contrast to the narrow view of learning in OE, learning in firms is also a social process of cognitive development in which cognitive categories (e.g. business conceptions) arise and are adopted and possibly changed (Penrose 1959; Bandura 1977; Dosi and Marengo 1994; Witt 1999; Lindenberg 2003). This goes significantly beyond both the information processing view and conventional views on bounded rationality (Foss 2003*a*). If indeed such an emphasis on cognition is key in the KBV (consult Kogut and Zander 1996; Spender 1996; Witt 1999; Teece 2001: ch. 4; Lindenberg (2003) for different variations on the cognitive theme), then it should be acknowledged that here is a genuine challenge to OE.

It is possible that a cognitive view may have important implications for the understanding of the main explananda of OE and the KBV; namely, competitive advantage, and the existence, boundaries, and internal organization of the firm (see further Witt 1999). One we may think of the distribution of competitive advantages in an industry as stemming from both the resources that firms control and the cognition of managers—for example, with respect to how resources should be deployed (cf. Penrose 1959) and how elements in the external environment should be categorized (Teece 2001: ch. 4). Moreover, it may be conjectured that a cognitive perspective has implications also for the remaining explananda. For example, internal organization may be understood in terms of conflicts and disagreements stemming from different cognitive categories, and a major organizational-design problem may actually be to create shared cognitive categories, and in general to manage. It should be noted that such a cognitive perspective may both further OE (Williamson 1998) and itself be furthered by OE insights. Thus, on the one hand, the property rights system of the firm may, by defining the social relations and positions of individuals (Jones 1983), crucially influence the processes of interaction that may lead to shared cognitive categories. On the other hand, problems stemming from the delegation of rights may arise from differential cognition inside the firm, as well as from transaction costs (Miller 1992). In practice, it may be difficult to separate organizational problems stemming from differential cognition from those stemming from opportunism (a problem that the courts are all too familiar with).

Opportunism. It has been argued that a main difference between the KBV and OE lies in the KBV not being dependent upon the assumption of opportunism (Conner and Prahalad 1996; Madhok 1996). It is true that much of the modern economics of organization builds on this assumption, and that it is often held within this approach that it is not possible to explain much of observed economic organization without this concept (Foss 1996*a/b*; Williamson 1996*a*). It is also true that the assumption has served theorists well, and that many new insights have been produced building on this assumption. Nevertheless, KBV critics are right in asserting that aspects of economic organization that do not turn on incentive conflicts have been overly neglected. For example, Hart (1995) argues that in the absence of incentive conflicts the optimal outcome can always be realized. But this claim requires the theorist to abstract from misallocation caused by misunderstandings, communication costs, different cognition, etc. Opportunism is not the sole cause of management problems (e.g. Loasby 1991; Hendry 2002).

However, it should be noted that many contributors to OE are actually uncomfortable with the notion of opportunism, because it is not precisely defined compared to the ordinary assumption of self-interest (e.g. Hart 1985; Barzel 1989). And Williamson (1985, 1996*a*), who is the inventor of the concept of opportunism, tends to use it in connection with the hold-up situation only. Moreover, not all contributors to OE have made the assumption of opportunism. Instead, they have focused attention on opportunism-independent costs, such as measurement costs (Barzel 1989), costs of communicating (Segal 1996; Wernerfelt 1997), search costs (Casson 1994), and costs of storing, retrieving, and processing information (Marschak and Radner 1972; Bolton and Dewatripont 1994). As these OE theorists point out, it is possible to say a good deal about economic organization without relying on the assumption of opportunism. For example, Casson (1994) argues that decision rights within firms will be distributed according to who has important ('decisive') tacit knowledge and the costs of communicating this knowledge. Segal (1996) argues that understanding the managerial task requires that we take account of communication costs. If all computations and observations can be communicated without any cost, it will never pay to concentrate managerial effort (i.e. appoint a manager). Finally, Wernerfelt (1997) argues that the choice between markets, hierarchies, and intermediate forms also reflects economizing on costs of communication.

These are promising avenues of research that help correct a strong bias in OE. Moreover, in various ways they link up with the KBV. For example, an emphasis on communication costs fits naturally with the KBV. This is because it is largely specific and tacit knowledge that gives rise to communication costs which, in turn, produce coordination problems (Langlois and Robertson 1995). This, we believe, is one way to interpret the KBV theory of the boundaries of the firm (e.g. Richardson 1972; Kogut and Zander 1992): Because of firm-specific and tacit knowledge in firms, it may be more costly to communicate across the boundaries of the firm than inside the firm. Efficient boundary choice may therefore reflect communication costs (Monteverde 1995).[31]

Integrationism in the Strategic Theory of the Firm

Taking Stock

The argument so far can be summarized as follows. In searching for a strategic theory of the firm, we are confronting two different and imperfect contenders. To put it briefly, while OE is of considerable relevance to the strategy field, and while it is characterized by relative explanatory elegance and simplicity, it is also likely to misrepresent many strategy issues because of the heuristic that these issues must always and everywhere be framed as turning on problems of aligning incentives. On the other hand, while the KBV may in some respect be truer to the traditional interests and concerns of the strategy field, it is at present much too unclear in various dimensions to serve as a strategic theory of the firm.[32]

The extreme complexity of the issues involved partly explains why no existing theories of the firm are satisfactory strategic theories of the firm. For example, the very framing of the issue of, for example, the existence of firms is, as we have seen, complex.[33] And if a strategic theory of the firm must also explain competitive advantage (cf. Grant 1996), ideally it should address all strategic choices and how they interact in functional and/or dysfunctional ways. Thus, we are talking about complex sets of variables, and even about interaction among these sets. This is very much—and perhaps much too much—to ask of a single theory. What we need, given this complexity, are focused views that work from key aspects.

Arguments may thus be advanced in favor of the proposition that isolationist research strategies economize on the scarce mental resources of strategy and OE scholars. And nobody is in the position to claim that either the KBV or OE may not eventually develop into full-blown strategic theories of the firm; we simply do not know. The argument here has rather been that as they stand presently both theories are handicapped in some, widely different yet important, respects. Given this, there is a third possibility; namely, to pursue an integrationist research strategy that aims at combining key ideas of the KBV and OE.[34] Below I discuss, first, which arguments may be advanced in favor of integrationism, and, second, what an integrationist research strategy might look like.

Why Do We Need Integrationism?

A number of writers have already suggested that a fuller integration of knowledge-based and OE perspectives is something to be striven for (e.g. Mahoney

1992; Seth and Thomas 1994), although they have not fundamentally explained *why* such a fuller integration is desirable. However, if the starting point is that we are interested in assumptions and explanatory insights that take us better into 'the deep structure of economic organization' (Williamson 1996*b*: 49), it seems that it is possible to advance both methodological and substantive arguments in favor of an integrationist research strategy.

At the methodological level one could argue that a problem with isolationist strategies is that they suffer from an implicit and narrow essentialism; that is, they are founded on the basic idea that 'the essence of the firm' lies either in knowledge considerations or in incentive-alignment considerations. Such essentialism is pointless. First, there are no criteria for determining what is really the immutable essence of the firm. We can safely say that firms are indeed both contractual and knowledge-bearing entities, but they possess a good deal of other characteristics as well (some of which we may not even know). Second, the appropriate conceptualization of the firm depends on the purpose at hand. For some purposes a knowledge-based conceptualization may be the most appropriate one; for other purposes it may be an OE conceptualization; and for other purposes again (discussed later), it may be a combined view that is appropriate.

A somewhat different methodological argument is that a benefit of a cooperative effort between economists of organization and knowledge-based scholars is that knowledge-based arguments may be placed on the same footing as the one that characterizes OE. Assuredly, the benefits of formalization may often be exaggerated, and organizational economists may argue that it is hard (if not ultimately impossible) to formalize the phenomena that occupy the minds of knowledge-based theorists. Of course, strategic-management scholars should not let their conceptualizations of phenomena be wholly dictated by what formal tools are available (as is arguably the tendency among mainstream economists). Moreover, formalization often leads to a loss of content, so that subtle points are lost (Kreps 1996). But some formalization exercises may lend a much needed discipline to the KBV. What sort of game forms does the perspective work with? What is assumed about the timing of the relevant games? About the distribution of information? About information-processing capacities? And so on. Such questions are useful to ask, not because the Holy Grail of the strategic theory of the firm is to be found in fancy formal models, but simply for the sake of clarification and precision, not least with respect to understanding what are really the micro-foundations of the KBV and whether existing (verbal) knowledge-based ideas on, for example, the existence of the firm really hold water. This attempt is likely to require the efforts of organizational economists and to draw on their insights and heuristics.[35]

With respect to substantive arguments that may be advanced in favor of an integrationist program, these primarily turn on considerations of understanding real phenomena that are hard to comprehend through the lens provided by either the knowledge-based view or the economics of organization, or that may be significantly more illuminated by a combined view. Notably, there may be interaction effects (trade-offs or complementarities) between governance and knowledge considerations, so that adopting only one view is likely to lead to a biased understanding.

One such phenomenon may very well be what Coase (1988: 47) called 'the institutional structure of production'; that is, the issue of why specific firms undertake specific productive tasks. Understanding this, Coase argued, requires a theory of differential organizing capabilities *as well as* the established insights of the modern economics of organization. In fact, the very concept of organizing capability may be a phenomenon whose full understanding requires a cooperative effort between knowledge-based scholars and organizational economists. While organizing capability may be a matter of shared context, cognition, and of routines (see Nahapiet and Ghoshal 1999), it is also a matter of the allocation of incentives and property rights in an organization (Putterman 1995; Foss and Foss 2000a); fully understanding the phenomenon requires bringing both perspectives to bear on it.

It is possible to invoke many other empirical phenomena whose understanding may be furthered by a combined view. The dynamics of diversification may be one such view, because knowledge-based considerations help us understand the production of excess resources (Penrose 1959) and organizational-economics insights help us understand the organization of those resources (Teece 1982; Dosi, Winter, and Teece 1992). Another example may be understanding outsourcing in a dynamic context (Jacobides and Winter 2003), and in particular the perils that may accompany excessive outsourcing, such as the loss of learning capability (Bettis, Bradley, and Hamel 1992). Clearly, the strategic dangers of excessive outsourcing are hard to comprehend through a pure organizational-economics lens, in much the same way that the incentive benefits of outsourcing (i.e. getting access to the 'high-powered incentives' of the market) are hard to comprehend through a pure knowledge-based lens. Similar arguments may be invoked in connection with understanding phenomena such as the organization of the innovative process, incentives for R&D, the role of the corporate headquarters, and the shifting of the locus of learning from markets to firms and vice versa (Langlois and Robertson 1995). All of these arguably involve both knowledge and governance considerations, and their understanding may be furthered by a combined view. However, rather than continue to drop examples and merely note that these involve both governance and knowledge considerations, is it possible to generalize further and more precisely?

The key point seems to be that the phenomenon in question not merely involves both knowledge and governance considerations, but that these interact in essential ways. Important instances of 'interaction' are trade-offs (in the usual sense) and complementarity, in the sense of activities or asset stocks feeding on each other (Milgrom and Roberts 1990*b*, 1995). Both may be defined in an inter-temporal context. For example, there are likely (inter-temporal) interaction effects between the provision of incentives and the production of knowledge, although those effects are not simple (Holmström and Milgrom 1991; Ghoshal and Moran 1996). Thus, the conjecture may be formed that it is particularly profitable to adopt a combined KBV/OE view when dealing with phenomena where there are strong interaction effects between knowledge and governance, and in particular where this interaction is characterized by complementarities and has an inter-temporal dimension. Without interaction effects a combined view is unnecessary. Since a strategic theory of the firm is particularly likely to involve interaction between knowledge and governance considerations, a combined view would appear to be particularly natural here.[36]

What Might Integrationism Look Like? Some Entry Points

When pondering what integrationism might look like in theorizing and in application, we are not completely left in the dark, for some broadly integrationist work does exist (e.g. Teece 1982; Reve 1990; Dosi, Winter, and Teece 1992; Langlois and Robertson 1995). Reflection and generalization from these papers indicate that one attractive form that modeling efforts may take has to do with constraints on contracting. More specifically, knowledge-based considerations constrain the contracting space by influencing, for example, what principals know about agents and what assets and activities can be contracted for. Along these lines, the following entry points for modeling may be suggested.

Agency problems and capabilities.   Arguably, cognitive factors are important aspects of capabilities (Dosi and Marengo 1994). Firms will often be characterized by a distinct 'way of doing things'—that is, shared problem-solving heuristics—which is shared among input owners and which arises through continuity of association among agents in the firm. This shared-knowledge aspect of capabilities may significantly reduce agency problems, by making asymmetric-information problems less severe. In turn, rents are produced that may be sustainable to the extent that the relevant knowledge is hard to imitate. The other side of the coin—that less shared knowledge may worsen agency problems—is captured in the next point.

Capabilities and the scope of the firm.   Casual empiricism confirms that almost no firm has integrated the entire value chain, the common explanation being that the firm confronts increasing diseconomies of scope as it integrates activities that demand capabilities that are increasingly dissimilar to the firm's own capabilities (Coase 1937; Richardson 1972). However, a contracting-cum-capabilities view suggests the following story. As the firm moves increasingly away from its core business, it confronts increasingly severe adverse-selection and moral-hazard problems, as management becomes increasingly unable efficiently to monitor employees or evaluate their human capital. Agency costs rise correspondingly, producing the net-profitability disadvantage associated with further integration.

Agency problems and learning capabilities.   Although the presence of capabilities may reduce the severity of agency-type contracting problems, the accumulation of new capabilities is often fostered by a diversity of preferences, beliefs, and knowledge. In turn, this diversity may produce agency problems, so that there is (at least in the short run) a trade-off between learning (dynamic efficiency) and incentive alignment (static efficiency).

Capabilities, clustered transactions, and asset specificity.   Winter (1991: 178–9) argues that knowledge-based considerations suggest 'that the concept of human asset specificity is central to understanding the functioning of the firm as a repository of knowledge. For understanding to progress, however, the idea of "specificity" must be refined and linked to the broader context in which quasi-rents to various sorts of productive knowledge are determined' (see also Klein 1988). Knowledge-based theorists often have a detailed understanding of this 'broader context' (e.g. Nahapiet and Ghoshal 1999), and their knowledge is likely to further the understanding of clustered transactions involving human capital to a significant extent.

Heterogeneity of transactions.   To many KBV writers the import of capabilities clearly lies in their *limitations*; because of what are essentially cognitive limitations, firms must specialize (e.g. Richardson 1972). To put it differently, the heterogeneity of activities and transactions matters to economic organization. Because of its likely impact on economic organization, heterogeneity needs to be treated as a dimension of transactions. For example, a loose, possible conjecture is that there may be trade-offs between heterogeneity and asset specificity.[37] However, at present we know precious little about how to operationalize 'the degree of heterogeneity' of activities and transactions, and about how this connects to economic organization. One possible reason why heterogeneity of transactions matters turns on communication costs. Heterogeneous transactions may be heterogeneous precisely because (or, in the sense that) communicating about them is costly.

Admittedly, all these points in a sense take the OE perspective as given and merely ask how ideas on capabilities can be used to formulate specific constraints on various optimization problems. This is somewhat akin to the program for orienting transaction-cost economics more towards the concerns of the strategy field that has been sketched by Williamson (1999). Thus, he suggests that instead of asking in a standard way which generic mode of economic organization (markets, hybrids, firms) best organizes a particular transaction, the interesting question to ask in a strategy context is how a particular firm, with particular strengths and weaknesses, organizes a particular transaction. However, one may also look at the matter from a different angle, taking the KBV as given, and asking how OE insights complement knowledge-based ideas. For example, to what extent may understanding of 'the organizational advantage' (Nahapiet and Ghoshal 1999) be furthered by OE insights in the provision of incentives, reputations, hostage taking, etc.? There is reason to believe, however, that the former rather than the latter integrationist strategy may be the most productive, at least in the shorter run. The reason is that OE provides a more precise and coherent framework into which it is easier to introduce knowledge-based insights rather than the other way around.

Conclusion

This chapter has had two overall and closely related aims. First, I hope to have demonstrated that in searching for a strategic theory of the firm we confront rather imperfect alternatives that, moreover, are imperfect in different ways. Admittedly, both alternatives, OE and the KBV, may be on their way to becoming strategic theories of the firm in the sense of the term employed here. Thus, both have things to say about the four issues that enter into the construction of such a theory; that is, the existence, organization, boundaries, and competitive advantage of the firm. It has also been pointed out, however, that these four issues are quite complicated and that substantial theoretical imperfection is therefore a predictable state of affairs.

Given this situation, two overall possible research strategies immediately come to mind: to develop further OE *or* the KBV in isolation; or to pursue a strategy of combining the good ideas of both approaches in focused ways. The fact that OE is weak on the analysis of competitive advantage and firm heterogeneity and strong on issues of economic organization, and the opposite holds true for the KBV, in itself weakly suggests a possibility for integrative efforts. The existence of focused work with an integrative ambition (e.g. Teece 1982; Langlois and Robertson 1995; Argyres 1996; Silverman 1999; Coff 2002; Nickerson and Zenger 2002) gives somewhat stronger indications that such work may be fruitful.

This chapter has set the stage for much of the discussion that will follow. Thus, all of the subsequent chapters are taken up with the central issue in the discussion of the strategic theory of the firm: How can the knowledge considerations of strategic management be aligned with the issues highlighted in the economics of organization. Thus, the next two chapters (3 and 4) subject resource-based and knowledge-based theories to more critical scrutiny. In the spirit of the integrationism defended in this chapter, Chapter 5 develops a number of ways in which ideas on transaction costs and property rights may be integrated with the resource-based view of strategy. And all of the chapters in the second part of this volume in different ways explore links between knowledge and economic organization.

Notes

1. In strategy research, organizational economics is usually associated with transaction-cost economics (Williamson 1996a), principal–agent theory (Jensen and Meckling 1976), and the nexus-of-contracts approach (Alchian and Demsetz 1972; Cheung 1983). In this chapter and the rest of this volume I take modern organizational economics to also include contributions to contract economics, such as Holmström (1979, 1982), Grossman and Hart (1986), Hart and Moore (1990), Holmström and Milgrom (1991, 1994), Hart (1995), Maskin and Tirole (1999), and Tirole (1999), to mention some representative and seminal contributions.

2. In this case, too, a broad set of theories is involved, including 'the evolutionary theory of the firm' (Nelson and Winter 1982; Marengo 1995; Foss 1997b), 'the competence perspective' (e.g. Foss 1993), 'the knowledge-based view' (Loasby 1991; Langlois and Robertson 1995), 'the dynamic-capabilities perspective' (Teece, Pisano, and Shuen 1997), 'the resource-based approach' (Wernerfelt 1984), and 'the knowledge-based theory of the firm' (Grant 1996; Spender 1996). Note that in later chapters I explicitly distinguish between resource-based and knowledge-based theories (discussed in Chs. 3 and 4 respectively).

3. Issues of the *Strategic Management Journal* (special winter issue 1996, vol. 17), *Advances in Strategic Management*, (1992, vol. 8), and *Organization Science* (1996, no. 5, vol. 7) have been devoted to this.

4. In this respect Mahoney (1992) and Seth and Thomas (1994) cover more material than this chapter, although they do not go much into recent contract theory. However, they argue in favor of pluralism, but do not show in which ways the various theories may be combined or why this produces intellectual added value.

5. Obviously, a discussion of how good alternative theories are at addressing these issues requires that the relevant theories possess the same understanding of key terms, notably 'the firm'. Of course, it is also required that they are commensurable in the sense of Thomas Kuhn (1970)—which Mahoney (1992) convincingly argues that they in fact are. However, we may imagine a knowledge-based theorist and an organizational economist being in disagreement about whether a certain entity is really 'a firm' (Grandori and Kogut 2002). I will disregard this difficulty (primarily because so far the participants in the debate have not been troubled by it) and think of economic organization as 'firm-like' when decision rights are relatively concentrated (cf. Coase 1937; Jensen and Meckling 1992; Demsetz 1995; Hart 1995) (although this is not entirely unproblematic; cf. Aghion and Tirole 1997).

6. For example, Barney and Ouchi (1986) and Rubin (1990).

7. It is perhaps worth mentioning that although the literature has tended to focus on physical assets, non-physical assets, such as client lists, patents, and the like, may play the same role in the story. However, human-capital assets cannot do this, because human-capital assets are not alienable.

8. Actually, the more formal a contribution to the literature is, the less emphasis there is on *ex post* governance and the more on *ex ante* incentive alignment.

9. However, sometimes the theory has been helpful in a rather paradoxical way; namely, in pointing to phenomena that are clearly anomalous to economic reasoning and which therefore represent a challenge. An example is provided in Holmström and Milgrom (1991, 1994). They wonder why the payment schemes that are actually established by firms are often so different (usually much simpler) from what theory would predict. For example, why are incentives in firms often 'low-powered' (to use Williamson's terms (1985)), and why do firms rely so much on fixed wages, even when good output measures are seemingly available? The answer essentially turns on agents working on multidimensional tasks or agents working on multiple tasks. In this situation incentive pay not only influences efforts and allocates risk; it also directs the effort of agents among tasks. Some possibly essential tasks (or dimensions of a task) may be very costly to measure for the principal; as a result, the principal risks the agent allocating all his effort to tasks (dimensions of a task) that are easier to measure. If principals want agents to allocate effort to all tasks (dimensions of a task), they may be better off offering a fixed wage; that is, low-powered incentives.

10. Interestingly, Milgrom and Roberts (1988: 450), two of the leaders in the modern economics of organization, made the following observation and prediction ten years ago: 'The incentive based transaction costs theory has been made to carry too much of the weight of explanation in the theory of organizations. We expect competing and complementary theories to emerge—theories that are founded on economizing on bounded rationality and that pay more attention to changing technology and to evolutionary considerations.'

11. Williamson (1998: 11) argues that although he does not 'claim that the firm-as-a-governance structure makes *adequate* provision for management, it certainly makes *significant* provision for management'.

12. While bounded rationality may be related to, for example, causal ambiguity and other barriers to imitation (as in Williamson 1998), this is in no way systematically done in the literature.

13. However, note that the basic idea of the production (or transformation) function certainly does not rule out tacit knowledge, and that the critique may be more justified as a critique of production functions in macro-economics and growth theory than in micro-economics. See Nelson and Winter (1982: ch. 3) for a discussion of these issues.

14. It is true that Williamson has modified his basic 'efficiency hypothesis' so that it now reads: '*align transactions, which differ in their attributes, with governance structures, which differ in their costs and competencies in a discriminating (mainly, transaction cost economizing) way*' (Williamson 1991: 79; emphasis in the original). However, the word 'competencies' as used by Williamson does not mean the same thing as it means to

knowledge-based theorists. Rather, it means that there are things that some governance structures can do that others can't because of their transaction cost properties.

15. Although her book was apparently written in ignorance of Coase (1937).

16. How well this aligns with the so-called 'resource-based view of the firm' of which Penrose is often seen as an important precursor will be discussed in Chapter 3.

17. That is, the relevant knowledge can only be mobilized in the context of carrying out a multi-person productive task, and is not possessed by any single agent. More on 'distributed knowledge' in Chapter 6.

18. This is illustrative of a wider problem of missing micro-foundations in this approach, to be discussed further in Chapter 4.

19. One can speculate about the extent to which this is consistent with another key knowledge-based idea; namely, that firms will avoid integrating 'dissimilar' stocks of knowledge (Richardson 1972).

20. For example, it is 'opportunism-independent' (Conner and Prahalad 1996; Ghoshal and Moran 1996; Madhok 1996). Indeed, opportunism appears to be the major point of contention in the debate (see Williamson's response (1996b) to Ghoshal and Moran 1996). However, it is not entirely clear how important opportunism, in Williamson's sense, really is to the modern economics of organization. What is important is incentive conflicts, but incentive conflicts are something much broader than opportunism.

21. The most radical version of this argument can be found in Lazonick (1991).

22. It is not entirely transparent what these organizing principles may be, but from the discussion they would seem to include 'shared coding schemes', 'values', 'a shared language', as well as 'mechanisms by which to codify technologies into a language accessible to a wider circle of individuals' (Kogut and Zander 1992: 9).

23. Holmström and Milgrom (1994) argue that the great theoretical challenge in the theory of the firm is not so much to understand *separately* (1) the employment contract versus independent contracting, (2) issues that relate to ownership of assets, and (3) monitoring and compensation issues. Taken separately, these issues are relatively well understood. Rather, it is to understand how these choices are intertwined, and why they are intertwined in the ways characteristic of real-world firms.

24. This is not to say that we cannot tell a story about ownership that begins with capabilities. For example, we can tie knowledge and ownership together via the classic arguments that knowledge is a good that is particularly prone to market failures (Nelson 1959; Arrow 1962). Along such lines, Foss (1993) and Casson (1997) argue that those who discover new knowledge have an incentive to use it themselves because of the transaction costs of knowledge transfer, and that there is a general tendency for resource ownership to move to the knowledge source (rather than the other way around), because knowledge is harder to trade than most other resources. In general, ownership of resources is acquired by those who have a complementary, non-tradable resource, which may often be a knowledge-related resource, such as, perhaps, a firm capability. See Brynjolfsson (1994) for an incomplete-contracts perspective on related issues, and Jensen and Meckling (1992) for the nexus-of-contracts perspective on these matters.

25. However, some KBV writers (e.g. Conner and Prahalad 1996) think of it as complementary to the modern economics of organization.

26. This is argued in greater detail in Chapter 4.

27. However, at least three studies empirically confront the relevant theoretical contenders; namely, Poppo and Zenger (1998), Knott and McKelvey (1999), and Schilling and Steensma (2002).

28. Chapter 5 of this book shows how the resource-based view, which shares some key ideas with the KBV, may be illuminated by ideas on transaction costs and property rights.

29. However, in Chapter 4 it will be argued that the KBV does not actually give much attention to bounded rationality as an individual-level construct.

30. See Foss (2003a) for how, in organizational economics, bounded rationality has been much cited but little used. In formal contract theory bounded rationality is either entirely absent (Holmström 1979) or simply a rhetorical device designed to make contractual incompleteness plausible (Grossman and Hart 1986).

31. This is something of a rational reconstruction; KBV writers are not entirely forthcoming about these causal mechanisms, as is argued in greater detail in Chapter 4. Monteverde (1995) may represent the KBV contribution that is most detailed in its treatment of 'technical dialog' as a potential motive for vertical integration.

32. As already suggested, one possible route that proponents of the knowledge-based approach may take is relentlessly to pursue and elaborate the idea that economic organization to a large extent turns on those costs of transacting that are independent of considerations of incentive conflicts. Existing work here (such as Demsetz 1991; Monteverde 1995; Conner and Prahalad 1996; Grant 1996) has concentrated on the costs of acquiring, communicating, and coordinating knowledge, the underlying idea being that within the firm it is possible to generate more and, in some sense, richer coordinative activity than can be obtained in markets, and that firms may indeed exist because of this coordination gain. In order to develop this more rigorously, it may be productive to link up with efforts in team theory (e.g. Bolton and Dewatripont 1994; Radner 1996).

33. Thus, do we simply refer to explaining the presence of employment contracts in a market economy? To a specific pattern of property rights to assets? To the presence of low-powered incentives in institutions called 'firms'? Or, to the presence of employment contracts *and* property rights to assets *and* low-powered incentives in a complementary way, so that what we really address are alternative three-tuples (cf. Holmström and Milgrom 1994)?

34. To repeat, like isolationism, integrationism is, of course, an archetype. Some existing integrationist work may be rather close to the modern economics of organization (e.g. Putterman 1995; Nickerson and Zenger 2002; Nickerson and Silverman 2004), while other integrationist work may lie closer to the knowledge-based view (e.g. Langlois and Robertson 1995; Monteverde 1995; Teece 2003).

35. Whether they will actually take an interest is a different matter. Mahoney (1992: 104) rightly notes that intellectual pluralism is valued (or, at least, allowed) to a greater extent in the strategy field than in economics, and suggests that the integra-

tion of knowledge-based views and the economics of organization is more likely to take place within the strategy field than within economics.

36. A final argument that may be invoked in favor of integrationism is that incentive conflicts are, whether we like it or not, facts of the real world. To the extent that the knowledge-based approach insists on abstracting from them (e.g. Kogut and Zander 1992), it simply does away with important determinants of economic organization, in the same way that organizational economics may be criticized for doing away with differential capabilities as determinants of economic organization.

37. Thus, one may speculate that a firm may avoid integrating transactions characterized by high asset specificity, because they are too heterogeneous and the management costs would be prohibitive.

3

The Resource-based View: Aligning Strategy and Competitive Equilibrium

Introduction

The key issue in strategic management is usually seen as the creation and sustainability of firm-level competitive advantage. Increasingly, sustained competitive advantage is interpreted as earning (efficiency) rents in equilibrium. Although this framing of the field's central concern is now conventional, it is also relatively recent. In fact, it was not until the advent of the resource-based view of the firm (henceforth the 'RBV') that the issue became thus framed. Until then, the strategic-management field entertained a much less focused approach with a less clear hierarchy of research issues (see (e.g.) Hofer and Schendel 1978). Partly as a result of its relatively clear conceptualization of strategy's central concern and the development of clear and simple schemes designed to handle this concern (Barney 1991; Peteraf 1993), and partly because of a strong marketing effort, the RBV has become the dominant contemporary approach to the analysis of sustained competitive advantage, and therefore the dominant strategic-management approach. Hardly an issue is published of the *Strategic Management Journal*, the field's leading periodical, without at least one paper that applies the RBV. The view is clearly dominant in the Academy of Management's Business Policy and Strategy Division.

An aspect of the RBV so successfully capturing the space of strategic-management discourse is that it has attracted rather little critical examination (but see Lewin and Phelan 1999; Priem and Butler 2001*a*/*b*; Bromiley and Fleming 2002; Foss and Knudsen 2003). The purpose of this chapter is to look critically at the RBV.[1] Specifically, the discussion will concern the role that economic equilibrium, particularly in the form of 'competitive equilibrium' (i.e. equilibrium under perfectly competitive conditions), plays in the RBV.

The competitive-equilibrium model has long been recognized as a useful benchmark in strategy; thus, according to Knott (1998: 3), '[t]he field of strategy is concerned with the conditions under which the microeconomic equilibrium of homogeneous firms with zero profits can be overcome.' However, it is one thing to use a model as an extreme benchmark which, for example, shows the extreme conditions that must be present for competitive advantage to be non-existent. It is another thing to *build* theorizing on that extreme benchmark,[2] as has clearly been the ambition in the RBV (Lippman and Rumelt 1982; Peteraf 1993). While the former use of an extreme benchmark does not put constraints on theorizing, the latter does. The underlying theme in this chapter is that this difference may not have been recognized in the RBV. The basic or 'pure' RBV model (Barney 1991; Peteraf 1993) is founded on a patched-up competitive-equilibrium model, in which a few select information asymmetries represent the spanners in the works that are just sufficient for producing rents in equilibrium (see the section 'Main Tenets of the Resource-based View' below). The origin of this can be found in the works of Chicago-UCLA industrial-organization economists, notably Harold Demsetz (1973) (see 'On the Pedigree of the Resource-based View' below). Observing this goes beyond doctrinal history. The questions that can meaningfully be raised, framed, and answered in strategic management are constrained by underlying theories and models. It is the contention here that because of the theoretical path-dependence in the development of the RBV the view is still explanatorily constrained by the limitations of the competitive-equilibrium model (see 'Competitive Equilibrium and Explanation in the Re-source-based View' below. For a discussion with a similar thrust, see Lippman and Rumelt 2003*b*).

Main Tenets of the Resource-based View

The main structure of the RBV as it pertains to the analysis of sustained competitive advantage was built with a handful of contributions that appeared from the mid 1980s to around the end of that decade (notably Wernerfelt 1984; Rumelt 1984, 1987; Barney 1986, 1991; Dierickx and Cool 1989). Barney (1991) is probably the first full development of the RBV; that is, the first paper that draws together all of those elements that today would be considered indispensable in the RBV—one of the most heavily cited papers in business administration in general. Peteraf (1993) provides another canonical summary of the main tenets of the RBV. The gestation period of the approach would therefore seem to have been a very short one if compared, for example, to the almost forty years of transaction cost economics (or almost seventy years, if we go back to Coase 1937; Williamson 1999).

Rather than providing a comprehensive review of the evolution of the RBV, the main focus here will be on the 'pure' RBV, as represented by two authoritative papers that elegantly but rather differently pull together in simple frameworks the diverse theoretical components that enter into the RBV analysis of SCA. These two papers are Jay B. Barney's 'Firm Resources and Sustained Competitive Advantage' (1991) and Margaret A. Peteraf's 'The Cornerstones of Competitive Advantage' (1993).[3]

Barney's 1991 Analysis

The RBV is usually distinguished from other approaches to strategy by its taking the individual resource as the unit of analysis when it comes to understanding the sources of SCA. Moreover, the RBV is also often characterized as a distinctive approach by its beginning from the factor-market side rather than from the product-market side (Barney 1986), again somewhat in contrast to other approaches to strategy. Thus, attention is focused on various characteristics of resources, including the price at which their services are acquired, in order to clarify whether these resources may be sources of SCA. However, Barney begins by formulating the analysis of SCA in terms of the strategies that firms implement in product markets:

A firm is said to have a *competitive advantage* when it is implementing a value creating strategy not simultaneously being implemented by any current or potential competitors. A firm is said to have a *sustained competitive advantage* when it is implementing a value creating strategy not simultaneously being implemented by any current or potential competitors *and* when these other firms are unable to duplicate the benefits of this strategy. (Barney 1991: 102; emphasis in the original.)

Thus, sustained *uniqueness* of product-market strategies appears to be a necessary condition for SCA to obtain.[4] Now, it is not immediately clear what is meant by a (unique) 'value creating strategy not simultaneously being implemented by any current or potential competitors' (i.e. CA), the 'benefits' of which cannot be 'duplicated' by other firms (i.e. SCA). For example, if a number of firms in an industry implement cost strategies based on learning curves that are identical save for the learning curve of the cost leader, which lies just a fraction below the learning curves of the other firms, can the cost leader be said to have a competitive advantage? Aren't they really implementing the same strategy, albeit with slightly different success? Perhaps all that is meant is that a firm has an SCA if it is more efficient at some value-creating activity than any current or potential competitor in a way that cannot be imitated by said competitors. However, in that case the unit of analysis should have been activities rather than strategies.

Barney does not explicitly address these issues; however, he arguably provides an implicit answer by turning his attention to the resources underlying strategies. By examining the implications for SCA if resources are mobile and homogeneous, Barney is led to the conclusion that 'in order to understand sources of sustained competitive advantage, it is *necessary* to build a theoretical model that begins with the assumption that firm resources are heterogeneous and immobile' (Barney 1991: 105; emphasis added). However, there is then a jump in the argument from the two 'primitives' of heterogeneity and immobility to four *other* conditions of SCA. In order to have the 'potential' for SCA, Barney explains, a resource 'must have four attributes: (a) it must be valuable [. . .] (b) it must be rare among a firm's current and potential competition, (c) it must be imperfectly imitable, and (d) there cannot be strategically equivalent substitutes for this resource that are valuable but neither rare or imperfectly imitable (ibid. 105–6).

Referring to the SWOT framework, Barney defines resources as being *valuable* when they help in seizing an opportunity in the firm's environment or when they help in neutralizing some threat in that environment, or at least in shielding the firm against the threat. By resources being *rare* Barney seems to have a simple counting sense (as distinct from an economic sense) in mind.[5] Firms that control valuable and rare resources possess a competitive advantage and will be able to obtain a CA. If furthermore the relevant resources are *non-imitable* and *non-substitutable*, a SCA may be obtained. The non-imitability (or more correctly: 'costly-to-imitate') condition directs attention to whether (or, at what cost) competitor firms can acquire or accumulate resources with attributes and levels of attributes similar to some desired resource (Barzel 1997) which produces a competitive advantage. The non-substitutability (or, 'costly-to-substitute') condition directs attention to whether (or, at what cost) competitor firms can access (different) resources that will allow them to implement the same strategies as some successful firm. It is also these two criteria that allow Barney to define SCA in terms of situations in which all attempts by competitor firms at imitating or substituting a successful firm have ceased. Thus, SCA is a property of an equilibrium. Barney's framework is summarized in Figure 3.1a.[6]

Before leaving Barney's (1991) contribution, we note that he defines the dependent variable in the RBV as unique product-market strategies. This is different from Barney (1986), which is framed with above-normal profits as

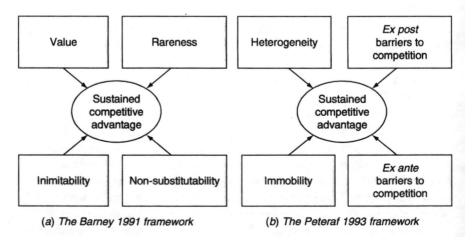

(a) *The Barney 1991 framework*   (b) *The Peteraf 1993 framework*

Figure 3.1*a/b*. Sustained competitive advantage in Barney (1991) and Peteraf (1993).

the dependent variable. In Barney (1991) the key to SCA is inter-firm differences in efficiencies; however, such efficiencies may have nothing to do with differences in profit, as we argue later. Barney (ibid.) singles out two necessary 'primitives' that must obtain for SCA to exist, namely heterogeneity and immobility. However, the relation between these two 'primitives' and the four other conditions of SCA (i.e. resources being rare, valuable, costly to imitate, and costly to substitute) is not made clear. The implication of Barney's discussion is that the four latter are collectively sufficient for SCA, and if they (all) obtain, heterogeneity and immobility also obtain. However, the four conditions are not all necessary, whereas immobility and heterogeneity are. In other words, possessing resources that are rare, valuable, costly to imitate, and costly to substitute is not the only way to gain and sustain competitive advantages, as long as the relevant ways conform to the criteria of resources being immobile and heterogeneous. This, however, is not clarified in Barney's paper.

Peteraf's 1993 Analysis

Peteraf's analysis of the conditions for SCA, which is summarized in Figure 3.1*b*, is quite different from Barney (1991) in terms of its explicit reliance on economics, unit of analysis, and substantive content. Thus, Peteraf more clearly draws on price theory (specifically the economics of rent), takes individual resources as the relevant level of analysis (not strategies), and reaches different conclusions with respect to the conditions of SCA. According to Peteraf, resources yield an SCA to the firm that controls them when they meet four conditions:

four conditions underlie competitive advantage, all of which must be met. These include superior resources (heterogeneity within an industry), *ex post* limits to competition, imperfect resource mobility and *ex ante* limits to competition.

While heterogeneity is not precisely defined in Peteraf (1993), indications of its meaning are given by arguing that resource bundles differ across firms in terms of efficiencies and that these different efficiencies give rise to different levels of value creation. These efficiency differences may translate into differences in rents, or, if you like, differential profits. In turn, rents are the relevant dependent variable in Peteraf (ibid.). Thus, her definition of SCA differs from Barney (1991) in the requirement that firms must earn relatively more on a sustained basis than other firms in order to possess an SCA. While heterogeneity is the condition under which a firm may generate a rent/differential profit, the remaining three conditions are sufficient to realize these rents and make them sustainable. Thus, '*ex ante* barriers' means that factor markets do not appropriate all of the rent; 'imperfect mobility' means that not all of the rent differential is eliminated through factor-market competition; and '*ex post* barriers' that the rent differential is not eliminated through product-market competition.[7]

What is Competitive Advantage?

A comparison of Barney (1991) and Peteraf (1993) leaves us unsure about whether the RBV is a theory of sustained competitive advantage in the sense of unique product-market strategies where the uniqueness can be sustained in equilibrium (Barney), or in the sense of differential rents/profits in equilibrium (Peteraf), or perhaps both? Apart from the obvious reason that it is unfortunate that disagreement exists with respect to something so basic as the definition of sustained competitive advantage, this is important to clarify because the two understandings have no necessary relation. Thus, sustained competitive advantage in the sense of sustaining a unique strategy in equilibrium (Barney) does not necessarily imply the earning of rents in that equilibrium (Peteraf), and vice versa. For example, a firm may persistently implement a unique strategy based on resources acquired in fully competitive and informationally efficient factor markets, in which case the firm may in principle have a sustained competitive advantage in the sense of Barney, but only realize 'normal' profits (and thus not have a sustained competitive advantage in the sense of Peteraf). This is because in informationally efficient and competitive factor markets the firm would have to pay the full value of the resources necessary for creating the relevant sustained competitive advantage.[8] Peteraf's understanding of sustained competitive advantage as referring to differential profits in excess of opportunity costs avoids this problem, and in general addresses the issue of appropriability of profit streams more thoroughly.

The Recent Evolution of the RBV

Peteraf's identification of the four 'cornerstones' of sustained competitive advantage provides a starting point for putting the strengths and weaknesses of the RBV into perspective, as well as for describing the recent evolution of the RBV.

Heterogeneity.   It has often been argued that the work of Penrose (1959) is the single most important precursor of the RBV. However, that may be (and it will be discussed critically later in this chapter), it can at least be argued that Penrose's contribution represents the first sustained attempt to argue for the importance to strategic analysis of resource heterogeneity, and that the RBV is thoroughly Penrosian in this sense. Given this, the causes of firm heterogeneity have actually been surprisingly under-researched in the RBV—surprising, that is, given that the approach is supposed to start out from this condition, and that part of the marketing effort of RBV scholars has been to argue that the RBV in contrast to industrial-organization economics places firm heterogeneity center stage. It is perhaps telling that a recent special issue of the *Strategic Management Journal*

(Oct. 2003) on the RBV was (sub)titled 'Towards a Theory of Competitive Heterogeneity'!

Ex post *barriers to competition.*   Lippman and Rumelt (1982), Rumelt (1984), and Wernerfelt (1984) added the cornerstone of '*ex post* barriers' (although their respective terminologies differed from this). This gave rise to a spate of work, of which Dierickx and Cool's short, but extremely influential, discussion (1989) still stands out, and which was taken up (1) with examining the generic mechanisms that may sustain competitive advantage (e.g. Dierickx and Cool 1989; Reed and DeFilippi 1990; Williams 1992) and (2) with classifying resources on the basis of their potential contribution to sustainability (e.g. Grant 1991). Notable empirical work has also grown out of this focus, such as Miller and Shamsie's discussion (1996) of the sources and sustainability of competitive advantage in the Hollywood film studios in terms of 'property-' and 'knowledge-based' resources, or Knott, Bryce, and Posen's empirical work (2002) on the characteristics of asset-accumulation processes.

Ex ante *barriers to competition.*   Barney (1986) established the cornerstone of '*ex ante* barriers' to competition with his strategic factor-market argument; that is, the argument that informational asymmetries are needed to produce that divergence between resource price and discounted net present value that is a condition of competitive advantage. Some of the most innovative recent work in the RBV has been the refinements and extensions of this argument; notably, in the works of Richard Makadok (e.g. Makadok and Barney 2001; Makadok 2003). Thus, Makadok and Barney (2001) develop the Barney (1986) factor-market argument into a story of information acquisition in which the ultimate determinant of competitive advantage is the firm's skill at researching the future value of resources.

Immobility.   Perhaps the least examined cornerstone has, until rather recently, been that of 'immobility'. The notion that those input owners whose services are regularly acquired by the firm (notably employees) have bargaining powers and that the distribution of these powers determines how surplus is split surfaced rather late in the RBV (although Wernerfelt (1989) was quite explicit about it).[9] Russell Coff's work (1997, 1999) in particular has drawn attention to this. Lippman and Rumelt (2003*b*) show how game-theoretical bargaining theory may inform an RBV perspective on how rents are split between resource owners.

Thus, it is apparent that some of the cornerstones have attracted more attention than others, and that the theoretical evolution of the RBV during the last twenty years is a matter of (1) gradually expanding the understanding of the determinants of sustained competitive advantage in the sense of incorporating more determinants and (2) refining the analysis of each individual determinant (i.e. each 'cornerstone'). The RBV has not yet completed this evolution. Thus, disproportionate attention has been paid to, notably, the '*ex post* barriers to competition' condition, usually in the form of trying to clarify which resource attributes make resources costly to imitate. It is only quite recently that the other three cornerstones have begun to receive similar attention. Seen in the light of the underlying theme of this chapter—that the RBV is founded on the competitive-equilibrium model—this is far from surprising. The divergence from competitive equilibrium is smaller when strategy is modeled in terms of making some *given* advantage costly to copy than if one seeks to endogenize heterogeneity, model factor-market competition with asymmetric information, or model bargaining processes, all of which has been notoriously hard to align with competitive equilibrium. It is time to pursue the theme of the connection between the RBV and competitive equilibrium in greater detail.

On the Pedigree of the Resource-based View

When the origins of the RBV are pondered, one name unavoidably comes up; namely, that of Edith Tilton Penrose. In their magisterial study of the research process that produced Penrose (1959), as well as the impact of this book and the challenges it still raises for strategic-management research, Kor and Mahoney (2000) document how numerous Penrosian themes can be found in modern resource-based writings. However, their interpretation of the RBV is considerably broader than the one adopted in this chapter, encompassing also, for example, the knowledge-based view of the firm. If a more narrow interpretation of the RBV is adopted, as in this chapter, Penrose's status as the matriarch of the RBV becomes more questionable, and it makes sense to look elsewhere for precursors of it.[10]

Edith Penrose on the Theory of the Growth of the Firm

The basic idea in Penrose's 1959 book, *The Theory of the Growth of the Firm*, is well known and will be only briefly summarized. Firms are collections of productive resources that are organized in an administrative framework that partly determines the amount and type of services that the resources yield. As they proceed with their productive operations, firms—in Penrose particularly management teams—acquire increased knowledge of the services that may be obtained from resources. The (related) results of such learning processes are, first, the expansion of the firm's 'productive opportunity set' (the opportunities that the firm's management team can see and can take advantage of) and, second, the release of managerial excess resources that can be put to use in other, mostly related, business areas. Since the opportunity costs of excess resources are zero, there will be a strong internal incentive for such diversification. Because the firm's expansion to a large extent builds on its 'inherited' resources, and because there 'is a close relation between the various kinds of resources with which the firm works and the development of the ideas, experience and knowledge of its managers and entrepreneurs' (ibid. 85), this expansion will tend to take place in areas of competence that are close to the firm's existing areas of competence.

The basic skeleton of some of Penrose's ideas may be cast in the language of equilibrium and (dynamic) optimization characteristic of mainstream economics, and this has been tried repeatedly (see Kor and Mahoney 2000 for details). For example, one may argue that at any given point in time there is a set of product-market applications (business areas) that maximizes the rents on the firm's existing resources and corresponds to an organizational equilibrium (à la Montgomery and Wernerfelt 1988), and a part of the optimization problem is the information costs that the firm's management team confronts (Casson 1997). However, in Penrose's own view her theory constituted a powerful critique of certain aspects of the neoclassical theory of the firm (if not necessarily of neoclassical economics in general; cf. Rugman and Verbeke 2004). In the neoclassical theory of the firm there is 'no notion of an *internal* process of *development* leading to cumulative movements in any one direction' (Penrose 1959: 1), a notion that in her view is absolutely crucial for understanding firm development. Rather, growth is simply a matter of adjusting to the equilibrium size of the firm. However, if services are produced endogenously (and continuously) through various intra-firm learning processes involving increased knowledge of resources, 'new combinations of resources' (ibid. 85), and an expanding productive-opportunity set, there is no equilibrium size.

There is clearly what we today would recognize as a Schumpeterian (change 'from within') and Veblenian (cumulative causation) flavor to such arguments (Foss 1998a). Penrose's basic vision of the competitive process in general, and of the firm in particular, is disequilibrium-oriented and subjectivist,[11] and it stresses entrepreneurship, flexibility, change, and uncertainty. 'In the long run', Penrose explains,

the profitability, survival and growth of a firm does not depend so much on the efficiency with which it is able to organize the production of even a widely diversified range of products as it does on the ability of the firm to establish one or more wide and relatively impregnable 'bases' from which it can adapt and extend its operations in an uncertain, changing and competitive world (ibid. 137)

Thus, seemingly paradoxically, flexibility is just as much a message of the analysis as specialization is. The paradox vanishes when it is realized that specialization is specialization in terms of the underlying resource base (rather than products) and that such specialization may be fully consistent with reacting to new business opportunities. In fact, as Penrose makes clear, there may be a considerable option value associated with a specialized resource base:

A firm is basically a collection of resources. Consequently, if we can assume that businessmen believe there is more to know about the resources they are working with than they do know at any given time, and that more knowledge would be likely to improve the efficiency and profitability of their firm, then unknown and unused productive services immediately become of considerable importance, not only because the belief that they exist acts as an incentive to acquire new knowledge, but also because they shape the scope and direction of the search for knowledge (ibid. 77).

Thus, firm development is an evolutionary and cumulative process of 'resource learning' (Mahoney 1995), in which increased knowledge of the firm's resources both helps create options for further expansion and increases absorptive capacity (Cohen and Levinthal 1990). Therefore, a major focus of *The Theory of the Growth of the Firm* lies in the *application* of resources.

To sum up, while the RBV is Penrosian in its emphasis on firm-level heterogeneity, most of Penrose's basic themes—flexibility in an uncertain world, organizational learning as an evolutionary discovery process, path-dependency, the vision of the management team, entrepreneurship, firm differences being traceable to the efficiency with which resources are applied rather than to resources themselves, etc.—seem to lie outside the orbit of the RBV, at least as it has been defined in this chapter. And it is indeed the contention here that the most important source of inspiration for the RBV is not the work of Penrose, but rather Chicago-UCLA price theory, notably as represented by the work of Harold Demsetz.[12]

Harold Demsetz on Industrial Economics

Harold Demsetz has worked within a number of economic sub-disciplines, such as the theory of property rights, the theory of the firm, and industrial organization. It is primarily Demsetz's contribution to industrial-organization economics that is relevant here. Much of Demsetz's work (see, in particular, Demsetz 1974) in this area has been concerned with critically discussing doctrines developed by economists associated with the so-called 'structure-conduct-performance' school in industrial organization (Bain 1959; Scherer and Ross 1990); that is, the main source of inspiration for Michael Porter's work (1980, 1981). In particular, Demsetz has subjected their thinking on entry barriers and on the link between industry structure and performance to critical scrutiny. Thus, Demsetz was probably the first economist to develop an understanding of barriers to entry as essentially informational in nature (e.g. advertising), and to argue that this understanding should influence antitrust policies. This focus on information asymmetries and costs as the real entry barriers is clearly related to the overall resource-based idea that the primary barriers that hinder the equalization of rents across firms are informational in nature (e.g. Lippman and Rumelt 1982).

However, there are other, even more direct, similarities. In fact, in Demsetz's 1973 article 'Industry Structure, Market Rivalry, and Public Policy' we encounter very clear anticipations of what would eventually become the RBV. At the beginning of this paper Demsetz notes that the presence of information costs, uncertainty, and less-than-fully-mobile factors may imply that 'a differential advantage in expanding output develops in some firms' (Demsetz 1973: 1). And the returns (rents) that such differential advantages may yield

need not be eliminated soon by competition. It may well be that superior competitive performance is unique to the firm, viewed as a team, and unobtainable to others except by purchasing the firm... The firm may have established a reputation or goodwill that is difficult to separate from the firm itself [...] Or it may be that the members of the employee team derive their higher productivity from the knowledge they possess about each other in the environment of the particular firm in which they work, a source of productivity that may be difficult to transfer piecemeal (p. 2)

Note the emphasis placed on heterogeneity, on different resource bundles as the sources of heterogeneity and therefore differential efficiencies that in turn are the basis for differential competitive advantages. In the same article, Demsetz also clearly anticipates the RBV conditions of *ex post* barriers to competition and *ex ante* barriers to competition that were considered above:

One such enterprise happens to 'click' for some time while others do not. It may be very difficult for these firms to understand the reasons for this difference in performance or to know [to] which inputs to attribute the performance of the successful firm. It is not easy to ascertain just why GM and IBM perform better than their competitors. The complexity of these organizations defies easy analysis, so that the inputs responsible for success may be undervalued by the market for some time. [...] inputs are acquired at historic cost, but the use made of these inputs, including the managerial inputs, yields only uncertain outcomes. Because the outcomes are surrounded by uncertainty and are specific to a particular firm at a particular point in its history, the acquisition cost of inputs may fail to reflect their value to the firm at some subsequent time. By the time their value to the firm is recognized, they are beyond acquisition by other firms at the same historic costs, and, in the interim, shareholders of the successful or lucky firm will have enjoyed higher profit rates (ibid.).

Sufficient evidence has now been presented to allow us to infer that Demsetz should indeed be reckoned as among the important precursors of the RBV, particularly with respect to the analysis of the conditions of sustained competitive advantage, the first key research theme within the RBV. In *this* respect he is more important than Penrose, for she does not really inquire into these conditions in her 1959 book. An important issue is whether these ideas were first developed by Demsetz and then independently discovered by later resource-based strategy theorists. Or, is there a more direct route through which Demsetz's ideas may have spread?

The UCLA Environment

Jay Barney, who is one of the prime movers behind the emergence of the resource-based approach in the 1980s, as argued that the rational-reconstruction approach to the history of the RBV—according to which the development of the RBV can be dated back to Selznick and Penrose and shown to progress rather smoothly from there—is simply a 'myth' (Barney 1995). Instead, Barney argued that the RBV largely owes its origin to the interaction—mainly at UCLA—between such economists and strategy scholars as William Ouchi, Michael Porter, Richard Rumelt, Oliver Williamson, and Barney himself. Only subsequently came the recognition that much of the early work of Selznick, Penrose, Chandler, and Andrews anticipated modern resource-based thought.

From the interaction at UCLA emerged two seminal contributions that came to play a founding role for the emerging RBV in the 1980s. The first was Lippmann and Rumelt (1982), which models equilibria with firms that earn different returns (rents) because of differential productive efficiencies, and imitation barriers that hinder the equalization of such rents. The other seminal paper is Barney (1986), which develops the first RBV account of *ex ante* barriers to competition. Both papers extend and (in the case of Lippman and Rumelt) formalize reasoning that was present much earlier in Demsetz's work.

Some evidence has been provided that, at least in its purer and explicitly economics-oriented incarnations (such as Lippman and Rumelt 1982; Barney 1991; Peteraf 1993), the RBV owes much to the Chicago approach to industrial organization (Brozen 1971; Demsetz 1973, 1974, 1982, 1989; Peltzman 1977). To resource-based writers, and notably the highly influential Richard Rumelt and Jay Barney, the Chicago approach represented an appealing way to reconcile the emphasis on the idiosyncratic and firm-specific that is characteristic of the strategic-management field with economic-equilibrium theory. In particular, Barney's analysis of the conditions of sustained competitive advantage is rather Chicago-ite in its emphasis on resources being costly to copy, etc. (compare Brozen 1971; Demsetz 1973, 1974, 1982, 1989; Peltzman 1977). His argument that all performance differences are explainable in terms of differential efficiencies of the resources underlying strategies, and that, therefore, superior returns are fully compatible with social welfare, is straight out of the Chicago book (e.g. Demsetz 1974). Barney's earlier emphasis (1986) on factor-market, rather than product-market, imperfections as a condition of competitive advantage is, as already suggested, also vintage Chicago (e.g. Demsetz 1973).

Looking back at the twenty years of evolution of the RBV, it is easy to jump to the conclusion that the application of economic equilibrium theory (of the specific Chicago-UCLA variety) in many ways furthered the field by reconciling strategic management and industrial organization economics in a way entirely different from Michael Porter's (1980). It expanded the vocabulary and the toolbox of the strategy field significantly by introducing efficiency rents, factor-market imperfections, costly-to-imitate resources, and other Chicago insights. However, this came at a price. Something unwanted sneaked in through the back-door.

Competitive Equilibrium and Explanation in the Resource-based View

Competitive Equilibrium in the RBV

What sneaked into the RBV was the competitive equilibrium (or 'perfect competition') model with its many constraining assumptions (Hayek 1948; Machovec 1995; Makowski and Ostroy 2001; Foss 2003*b*). Although borrowing from the Chicago approach in many ways furthered strategic management, it is also arguable that the set of phenomena relevant to strategic management that can be framed by relying on this approach is rather limited. Fundamentally, this stems from the basic Chicago research methodology, which is to cast virtually all social phenomena in terms of competitive equilibrium—what Chicago School insider Melvin Reder (1982) characterized as the 'tight-prior-equilibrium' assumption.

The competitive equilibrium that is used in RBV core contributions (such as Lippman and Rumelt 1982; Barney 1991; Peteraf 1993) may not be entirely of the perfect-competition textbook variety. For example, some superior technology may be costly to imitate (Demsetz 1973; Lippman and Rumelt 1982) or there may be some asymmetric information in factor markets (Demsetz 1973; Barney 1986). Still, the basic model is one of instantaneous market clearing in markets populated by traders with no bargaining power, and firms that—within a given industry—are essentially identical. We can see the legacy of the competitive equilibrium model in a number of the shortcomings or weaknesses of the RBV. I elaborate below.

Excluding Market Power?

Since firms have no bargaining power in product markets—because of the assumption of price-taking—competitive advantage cannot be a matter of 'market power' in the sense of raising price above cost through restricting supply (as in (e.g.) Porter 1980). Thus, there can be no profits from market power, only scarcity rents. This runs counter to the empirical evidence, which strongly suggests that firms' returns are composed of both rents and profits (Montgomery and Wernerfelt 1988; Demsetz 1989; Sanderson and Winter 2002). This could be defended by invoking a division of labour in which the RBV addresses the efficiency rent parts of sustained competitive advantage, leaving the profit parts to industrial organization approaches (Barney 2001). Moreover, the argument may also be put forward that it is sensible to begin analysis by assuming the harshest possible competitive environment, that is competitive conditions.[13] Such a procedure would allow the environment to be black-boxed, because it eliminates the need to bother with complicated oligopolistic interdependence and with forms of competition other than pure Bertrand competition.

However, such arguments are not entirely unproblematic. For example, note that under Bertrand competition returns come to a firm through low costs (as in Peteraf 1993). However, profits come to an *industry* through cost *heterogeneity*. This implies that there is a collective incentive to install an industrial structure that maximizes cost heterogeneity—even if this does not minimize costs. Thus, it is not only the form of competition that matters for performance, but also the organization of industry. For example, Farrell et al. (1998) examine the vertical organization of complementary activities by analytically separating whether firms compete in terms of selling an end product (a 'system') or whether firms compete in terms of selling individual components (that together make up the system). Contrary to intuition, even under Bertrand competition these two ways of organizing industry are not perfect substitutes (in terms of overall efficiency and firm performances), provided that firm resources (proxied by production costs) differ. This means that the organization of industry (here in terms of systems or component organization) is a choice variable for firms, and that firms may have an incentive to organize industry in such a way that cost heterogeneity is maximized (which may not minimize costs). Thus, differential resources clearly matter (in fact, the whole analysis of Farrell et al. 1998 requires taking such a starting point), but they matter for reasons that are somewhat different from those normally identified in the RBV.

This line of reasoning suggests that while it may make sense to *begin* from harsh competitive conditions, it is unsatisfactory to let analysis *stop* here. And if it does not, that is if non-competitive conditions are admitted, it becomes problematic to uphold the division of labor between the RBV and industrial-organization-inspired approaches (Porter 1980; Ghemawat 1997), because non-competitive conditions invite the consideration of, for example, entry deterrence as a means of sustaining competitive advantage. Moreover, once non-competitive conditions are admitted and market power is allowed, some pet RBV themes seem to break down. Consider the notion that sustained competitive advantage is a matter of unique, value-creating strategies. This idea may run into problems when strategies are *complementary*. An important distinction in recent industrial-organization economics concerns whether firm strategies are substitutes or complements (Bulow et al. 1985; Tirole 1988). If firm A's return from implementing a strategy is increasing in firm B's return from implementation of its strategy and vice versa, then the strategies of the two firms are complementary. A special case of this obtains when A and B implement the same strategy. This can be the case in oligopoly industries in which firms will benefit from implementing and enforcing the same pricing strategies.[14] Product-market strategies are not unique, yet firms may earn profits in excess of opportunity costs. In fact, in the latter case homogeneous resources may be a distinct *advantage*, since such homogeneity may ease the enforcement of oligopolistic collusion (Tirole 1988). The notion of heterogeneity as a necessary condition of sustained competitive advantage also runs into problems if market power is allowed for. As a simple example, consider an industry where incumbents control homogeneous resources and implement the same strategies based on these resources, but where competition is Cournot and high entry barriers exist for whatever reason. Firms will earn returns above the competitive level, although the resources they control, and the strategies they implement, are identical.[15]

Neglect of the Interaction Between Value Creation and Value Appropriation

It is a basic insight of economics that although determining the size of the pie is something different from dividing the pie, how the pie is divided may influence the size of the pie. Economists often conceptualize this insight—which, as we shall see later (Ch. 5), only holds true if (some) transaction costs are positive—in terms of interaction between allocation (creating value) and distribution (dividing value). It is crucially important for understanding the economic implications of reward systems and the allocation of property rights. Much of the modern economic theory of the firm revolves around it, the 'hold-up problem' (Hart 1995; Williamson 1996a) being an important manifestation of the expected sharing of surplus impacting on the creation of that surplus (through the effect on investment incentives). And yet it is an insight that is conspicuously and surprisingly absent from the RBV (an exception being Kim and Mahoney 2002). One reason is that bargaining is abstracted from, so that dissipation of value from bargaining activities (i.e. the 'pie' being reduced as a result of haggling) cannot be treated. By the same token, creating value by means of reducing such activities (as in Williamson 1996a) cannot be treated either. This is a manifestation of the neglect of transaction costs in the RBV.

Transaction Costs Are Absent

Because transaction costs are not explicitly considered in the RBV, the reduction of transaction costs—for example, through choosing governance structures that are more efficiently aligned to the relevant transactional dimensions than those that were previously in place (Williamson 1996a)—cannot be a source of value creation in such a world. In other words, the sources of competitive advantage cannot lie in economizing on transaction costs. It is also not clear how the strategic opportunities implied by transaction costs being positive (Foss 2003b) may be handled, if the competitive model is the starting point. As Makowski and Ostroy (2001: 529) note, '[w]ith the standard model as the point of departure, the simplicity of price-taking behavior leaves the perfect competitor unprepared for the entirely new strategic considerations he confronts when transaction costs are positive'.

No Theory of the Firm

The view of the firm in the competitive equilibrium model is what Williamson (1996a) calls the 'production function view', which is an important part of the neoclassical theory of production, as stated in basic economics textbooks. While this view has been contrasted with the RBV (e.g. Conner 1991), it is not clear what exactly is the difference between saying that the firm is a production function and saying that the firm is a bundle of resources. True, 'resources are heterogeneous' in the RBV whereas 'inputs are (usually) homogeneous' in the production-function view. But the latter assumption is simply made for calculational convenience. The production function describes the relation between inputs, that is resources, and output, and such a production function may of course be constructed for any firm (Wernerfelt 2003). It is not logically committed to an assumption of resource homogeneity. In fact, some of the critical assumptions of the production function carry over to the RBV.

From a TCE point of view there are two problems with the production-function view. First, it contains no predictions with respect to the optimum scope of the firm (Teece 1982; Williamson 1996a).[16] Second, it assumes what should be explained; namely, that input factors (resources) are optimally used inside a firm. Because its view of productive activities is not essentially different from that of the production-function view, the RBV similarly contains no implications for the optimum scope of the firm and similarly works from the assumption that resources are optimally used inside the firm. Differences in competitive advantages are therefore not a matter of how well resources are organized or managed, but of the inherent efficiencies of the resources that firms control. This means that there is little or no attention to the managerial task or to organizational matters in the RBV. The 'resource-based view of the *firm*' may therefore be a bit of a misnomer, because the RBV says very little about firm organization and because it is not clear how the view fundamentally differs from basic economic-production theory.

Disequilibrium is Not Considered

Since by the basic Chicago methodology all phenomena that relate to strategic management must be expressed in terms of equilibrium, those aspects of strategic management that are best understood as disequilibrium phenomena are hidden from view. Notably, it is hard to make room for entrepreneurship in an 'equilibrium-always' approach, because the essence of entrepreneurship is to either restore or upset equilibrium (Kirzner 1973; Machovec 1995; Lewin and Phelan 2000). Of course, it is possible to use equilibrium models to examine the *effects* of entrepreneurship (e.g. in terms of earning rents in equilibrium), but the models themselves do not allow for the phenomenon itself, except in the very stylized form of draws from probability distributions over technologies with differing costs (as in Lippman and Rumelt 1982). Related to this, dynamics becomes a matter of performing comparative-static exercises; that is, comparing equilibria where the variables differ because of changes in underlying data.[17] While disequilibrium characterizes the transition from one equilibrium to another, it is not treated in the model. In an alternative interpretation, disequilibria may indeed be induced by entrepreneurs, but a new equilibrium is very quickly restored, because transaction costs are zero: 'When equilibrium is disturbed in a positive transaction cost world, price adjustment is not expected to be instantaneous.' Of course, this is in contrast to a zero-transaction-cost world, where 'when equilibrium is disturbed a new equilibrium is instantaneously attained because, given zero transaction costs, the cost of adjustment is zero' (Barzel 1997: 101). Thus, the reason why the RBV is an equilibrium approach is not just a matter of not explicitly addressing entrepreneurship and innovation (Teece 2003), it is also a matter of abstracting from transaction costs.

Summing Up

The implication of the above is that with respect to the key strategic-management issues of understanding value creation and appropriation, a competitive equilibrium starting point has quite a number of constraining consequences. Thus, value creation by means of product innovation or differentiation (Machovec 1995), advertising, improving contractual arrangements and internal organization (Akerlof 1970; Williamson 1994, 1996a), and other ways of reducing inefficiencies becomes difficult to represent. This is caused by the suppression of entrepreneurship, disequilibrium, and transaction costs in the competitive-equilibrium model. In fact, quite a number of the shortcomings discussed above derive from the zero-transaction-cost property of the competitive model.

Conclusions

During the last decade and a half the RBV has emerged as perhaps the dominant approach to strategy-content theory. Indeed, as Kor and Mahoney (2000: 119) note, a number of recent textbooks 'situate the resource-based view as the crown jewel of strategic management'. There can indeed be little doubt that the RBV has not only been influential but also very useful. However, as noted at the start of this chapter, the RBV was built in a hurry by a few key contributors, and although the view is now approaching its twentieth birthday, this is a short life in a social-science context. It is therefore not surprising that some aspects of the RBV are less clear and less developed than one might wish them to be. Boundary conditions may not always be identified (Priem and Butler 2001*a*; Foss and Knudsen 2003). And there is a certain path-dependency in the RBV, caused by the initial reliance of some of the key RBV writers on the competitive-equilibrium model. Concentrating on the representative and elegant formulations put forward by Barney (1991) and Peteraf (1993), this chapter has argued that, at least in these pure forms, the RBV is underpinned by a patched-up version of the competitive equilibrium model (Chicago-UCLA style), and that this has introduced an explanatory straitjacket that the RBV seems only now to be breaking out of (Lippman and Rumelt 2003*a*/*b*).

Many strategic management writers have noted that the RBV may be limited in dimensions such as endogenizing resources and allowing for disequilibrium (e.g. Teece 1993; Teece, Pisano, and Shuen 1997). These writers have generally embraced knowledge-based (or 'dynamic capabilities') approaches. Others have argued that the RBV can best overcome its limitations by making contact with organizational theory, including organizational economics (e.g. Mahoney 1992; Kor and Mahoney 2000; Foss 2003*b*). The following two chapters relate to these two strategies, as the next chapter discusses the knowledge-based view of the firm and Chapter 5 discusses how notions of transaction costs and property rights may further the RBV.

Notes

1. Note that the focus in this chapter is on what may be called the 'pure' RBV, here exemplified by Barney (1991) and Peteraf (1993), and not on the various related approaches such as dynamic capabilities, competence, or knowledge-based approaches. These are dealt with in Chapter 4.
2. Cf. the discussion in Mises (1949) of the 'evenly rotating economy' (*aka* competitive equilibrium) and the discussion in Coase (1988) of the explanatory role of zero-transaction-cost settings. See also Coddington (1983), Furubotn and Richter (1997), and Foss and Foss (2000*a*) for further methodological reflection on these issues.
3. Foss and Knudsen (2003) raise a number of critiques of these two papers that are not reproduced here.
4. Barney is not the only one to argue this. Thus, according to Aharoni (1993: 31), '[c]ompetitive advantage can be achieved if the firm is able to be *different*. Success is based on using a unique strategy. The ability to protect the uniqueness against imitators ensures continued success.' The emphasis on uniqueness goes back to the founding fathers of the strategy field, such as Selznick (1957) and Andrews (1971).
5. Thus, if a million firms control a certain resource it is not likely to be rare (even if a billion firms badly need the relevant resource). From an economic point of view, resources cannot be valuable if they are not rare; thus, a rare resource is a valuable resource (Lewin and Phelan 1999).

6. It should be mentioned that Barney (1997) later added the efficient organization of resources as an independent necessary condition for SCA.

7. Unfortunately, Peteraf is not entirely forthcoming about whether her conditions constitute the minimum set of *jointly* necessary conditions for SCA, or whether they are *individually* necessary conditions, or whether they are merely collectively *sufficient* for SCA. However, she does say that all conditions must be met (Peteraf 1993: 185), that the four conditions are 'related' (p. 185), that heterogeneity is 'necessary for sustainable advantage but not sufficient', and that we require '*ex post* limits to competition as well'. Because the conditions are related, Peteraf spends some time explaining how the meeting of one condition may mean that another one is also met. She does not, however, say that the four conditions constitute the bare-minimum necessary (and sufficient) conditions for SCA, and qualifies her discussion by saying that the four conditions are 'distinct', yet 'related'.

8. Or to take the inverse case. A firm may adopt the same strategy as a large number of competitors, but may still exploit informational advantages or bargaining advantages in factor markets or be favoured by luck, so that, while it does not have a sustained competitive advantage in the sense of Barney, it does earn higher profits than the competition and thus realizes a sustained competitive advantage in the sense of Peteraf (1993).

9. Perhaps this is because immobility is hard to distinguish from factor-market competition, and may be placed under '*ex ante* barriers to competition'. Surprisingly, while bargaining power has been important in connection with 'immobility', it has played no role in connection with the '*ex ante* barriers to competition' cornerstone (leading to the incorrect conclusion that with perfect factor markets the supply side will always appropriate all rent).

10. The first paper to explicitly make and develop this point seems to be Foss (1999*b*), on which the following section draws. Rugman and Verbeke (2002) is the most extensive argument that in key dimensions Penrose cannot rightly be considered a precursor of the RBV. This view is amplified in Rugman and Verbeke (2004).

11. Penrose's subjectivism is particularly apparent in her adoption of Kenneth Boulding's concept of 'the image': 'the environment is treated . . . as an "image" in the entrepreneur's mind of the possibilities and restrictions with which he is confronted, for it is, after all, such an "image" which in fact determines a man's behaviour' (1959: 5). In other words, the environment is basically 'enacted'—to use Weick's terminology.

12. Conner (1991) also mentions Chicago-UCLA industrial-organization theory as an input into the development of the RBV, but not as a particularly important one.

13. In fact, it may be argued that as a matter of general modeling practice it is wise to begin by assuming the harshest possible kind of competition, since all sorts of behaviors and performances may be rationalized by assuming less harsh competition.

14. Another example concerns network industries (i.e. industries characterized by network externalities), in which case incumbents, or a subset of the incumbents, may benefit from adopting identical strategies. The application of the RBV to such industries is an important unexamined issue.

15. This further suggests that the boundary conditions of RBV analysis may not be entirely clear. See Foss and Knudsen (2003) for such a critique.

16. Relatedly, it is hard to see what is distinctly resource-based about Conner and Prahalad's 'resource-based theory of the firm' (1996).

17. Foss (1996*b*) speculates that the suppression of disequilibrium issues is what explains the branching of the 'resource-based view', broadly conceived, into, first, the RBV proper, and, second, various 'competence-based', 'capabilities', 'dynamic-capabilities', etc. approaches which all try to highlight dynamics in various ways (e.g. Hamel and Prahalad 1994). Priem and Butler (2001*a*) recently also noted the lack of dynamics in the RBV.

4

Knowledge-based Views of the Firm

Introduction

As discussed in Chapter 2, knowledge-based views (henceforth 'KBV') of the firm have become very influential in a host of disciplines and sub-disciplines in business administration, notably in the strategy, organization, and inter-national-business fields (Kogut and Zander 1993; Grant 1996; Spender 1998). It has also made some headway into economics (Hodgson 1998) and economic geography (Maskell et al. 1998). A conclusion in that chapter was that knowledge-based views of the firm are trying to capture some important, perhaps essential, aspects of economic organization that have been imperfectly theorized in other theories, or have not been addressed at all (Holmström and Roberts 1998; Williamson 1999). A case was made for 'integrationism'. However, an important prerequisite for successful integrationism may well be a disciplined dialog between proponents of governance (organizational economics) perspectives and propon-ents of knowledge-based views based on shared insights and terminology. How-ever, so far there has not been much dialog between these, communication being limited to proponents of knowledge-based views criticizing governance perspec-tives. It is also questionable to what extent there exists a body of shared insights and terminology, a 'pfefferdigm' (Pfeffer 1993). Partly because of this, not much concrete integrative work has actually emerged (e.g. Argyres 1996; Silverman 1999; Coff 2002; Heimann and Nickerson 2002).

One reason for the relative lack of dialog is that different disciplinary and institutional backgrounds (economics and universities vs. business administration and business schools) are involved. Another one is that the sources of the KBV are many more and more diverse than the sources of organizational-economics approaches. Whereas organizational economics is mainly a continuation of main-stream economics, its theoretical core essentially consisting of game-theoretical information economics (Williamson's brand of transaction cost economics being an exception), the KBV is an amalgam of ideas from evolutionary economics (Nelson and Winter 1982), Austrian economics (Hayek 1964), organizational-learning theory (March 1991), the behavioral theory of the firm (Cyert and March 1963), the resource-based view of strategy (Barney 1991), Penrose's work (1959), and epistemology (Spender 1996).

Not surprisingly, it is a task of considerable complexity to identify what is the (knowledge-related) unit of analysis of the KBV, how this unit is dimensionalized, which causal mechanisms it posits with respect to the unit of analysis, and the outcomes at the level of organization and competitive advantage that the perspective wishes to address. A fundamental reason why communication and integrative efforts are bound to be severely handicapped for some time to come is that the KBV suffers from some fundamental explanatory problems. At the most fundamental level, its micro-foundations are at best unclear, and perhaps non-existent. A consequence of this is that the fundamental explanatory notions in the KBV—notions such as 'capabilities', 'competencies', 'dynamic capabilities', and even 'routines' (depending on which subset of the KBV one focuses on)—are notions in search of micro-foundation. As they appear in the literature, these notions are aggregate concepts that may be located in firms, among firms, and even in industrial districts (Foss and Eriksen 1995). However, we are rather in the dark about how they relate to individual actions and learning. Because the fundamental mechanisms, the micro-foundations, are unclear, a number of explanatory difficulties emerge in knowledge-based views.

Rather than examining the entire body of KBV contributions, this chapter focuses in on one important early contribution to this stream of research; namely, Richard Nelson and Sidney Winter's celebrated 1982 book, *An Evolutionary Theory of Economic Change*. A fundamental argument in the previous chapter on the RBV was that an understanding of the nature and causes of some of the explanatory weaknesses that beset the RBV could be gained by examining the pedigree of the RBV. This chapter similarly pursues a theme of intellectual path-dependence. Specifically, the claim here is that some of the conceptual and explanatory difficulties that the modern KBV confronts are at least partly traceable to Nelson and Winter (1982). This is particularly the case with respect to the problem of missing micro-foundations.

Particular attention is devoted to Nelson and Winter's much-cited treatment in chapters 3–5 of their book of bounded rationality and tacit knowledge in the context of firm organization and behavior—a treatment that Nobel Prize winner Reinhardt Selten (1990: 649) characterized as having 'brought new impulses to the modeling of boundedly rational behavior in economics'. This examination is primarily undertaken because the Nelson and Winter approach to conceptualizing the firm and understanding its organization and behavior has been extremely influential for writers within the KBV.

The KBV is quite often seen as an approach to the theory of the firm that puts much more of an emphasis on bounded rationality than is the case in, notably, transaction cost economics (e.g. Fransman 1994; Conner and Prahalad 1996; Marengo et al. 2000). It is also seen as one that goes beyond information processing and stresses the tacit and socially embedded aspects of knowledge (Fransman 1994). Both of these characteristics hark directly back to Nelson and

Winter. Below I engage critically with this influential view. Specifically, the following points are developed. First, the theory of the firm put forward in Nelson and Winter (1982) is considerably less about bounded rationality than it is about socially held tacit knowledge. Bounded rationality and tacit knowledge do not logically imply each other. It may, in fact, be argued that Simonian bounded rationality and Polanyi's notion of tacit knowledge are ultimately founded on very different, and perhaps incompatible, epistemologies (see Nightingale 2003). Attempts to combine the two are likely to be unsuccessful, one driving out the other. This is largely the case in Nelson and Winter (1982), in which tacit knowledge looms much larger than bounded rationality. The tipping of the balance in favor of tacit knowledge has become even more pronounced in subsequent work within the organizational capabilities approach. Second, the emphasis on socially held knowledge in the form of 'routines' and the downplaying of bounded rationality in Nelson and Winter (ibid.) mean that there is very little attention given to the level of the individual agent. Indeed, the Nelson and Winter theory (as well as many subsequent contributions to the KBV) may be criticized for not being consistent with methodological individualism, at least in the sense that it works with aggregate entities (i.e. routines and capabilities) that are not explicitly reduced to individual behavior. Third, I argue that the absence of a clear behavioral foundation for the organizational-capabilities approach is the root cause of the difficulties, discussed in Chapter 2, that the KBV has with respect to illuminating the key organizational economics issues of the internal organization and boundaries of the firm.

Nelson and Winter (1982): A Foundation of the Knowledge-based View

The Place of An Evolutionary Theory of Economic Change in the Evolution of the KBV

Nelson and Winter (1982) has arguably appealed more to business administration and management scholars than to economists. One paper after another, in such fields as strategy, organizational learning, international business, and organizational behavior, has generously cited the book, particularly the three chapters (3–5) that deal with issues pertaining to individual and organizational behavior and capabilities. These three chapters may well be the single most important reason why strategy scholars are increasingly converging on organizational capabilities as a key construct in strategy research (e.g. Cockburn and Henderson 1994; Teece, Pisano, and Shuen 1997; Eisenhardt and Martin 2000) (Felin and Foss 2004). In fact, rereading the chapters makes one realize that perhaps not so much essential has happened in two succeeding decades of work on capabilities, competence, evolutionary, etc. theories of the firm that goes beyond Nelson and Winter's treatment. It is arguable that later knowledge-based ideas on competence traps, the central importance of tacit and socially complex 'resources' for explaining competitive advantage, knowledge replication, and dynamic capabilities can be found in at least an embryonic, and often a quite explicit, form in Nelson and Winter (1982).

Quite appropriately, contributors to the organizational capabilities approach have therefore often treated Nelson and Winter (1982) not only as a source of inspiration, but also as a foundation. At first sight this may appear somewhat surprising, given that building a distinct theory of the firm was never the intention of Nelson and Winter (1982). However, what may appeal to knowledge-based theorists of the firm is the attempt in that book to treat in a unified fashion bounded rationality and tacit knowledge, and at the same time place these in a social context—all of which converges in a single, intuitively plausible concept, namely that of 'routine'. These ideas, as well as the use of them to help explain revealed competitive advantages, innovation, and limited aspects of economic organization, cannot really be found in any other of the precursors of the capabilities approach. While Cyert and March (1963) have much to say about bounded rationality and standard operating procedures, and touch on competitive advantage, they have next to nothing to say about socially held tacit knowledge. And while Penrose does treat the latter theme, she says nothing about bounded rationality and competitive advantage. The single unifying theme in the diverse streams of research that make up the KBV, that is 'capabilities' (Richardson 1972; Chandler 1992; Langlois 1992), 'dynamic capabilities' (Teece and Pisano 1994), 'competence approaches' (Sanchez 2001), and, of course, the 'evolutionary theory of the firm' (e.g. Dosi 2000; Marengo et al. 2000), is indeed an emphasis on the central explanatory importance of experiential, localized, socially constructed, and embedded knowledge and learning in understanding firm organization and behavior. Of all the many precursors of the KBV, only Nelson and Winter (1982) explicitly feature this theme.[1]

Skills, Routines, and Organizational Behavior

The KBV literature is often interpreted as an attempt to make more room for bounded rationality in the theory of the firm than is standard in the economics of organization (e.g. Fransman 1994; Conner and Prahalad 1996). However, it is seldom made clear in exactly what sense the KBV may be characterized as starting from bounded rationality. Because bounded rationality is, unfortunately, a concept that comes with a legacy of diverse and even conflicting meanings, it does matter where exactly one starts from, and it is rather uninformative to say that the organizational capabilities approach builds on bounded rationality, unless one specifies what kind of bounded rationality. Thus, are we talking about Newell and Simon's work on heuristic search, or Selten's aspiration-adaptation theory, or Lipman's or Rubinstein's axiomatic foundations for bounded rationality, or regularities established in experimental-psychological research, or any other of the great number of different—indeed, very different—variations on Simon's Grand Theme?

However, such information is virtually never forthcoming. Indeed, it is easy to become skeptical about the real role played by bounded rationality in the KBV for the basic reason that out of the many sources that the approach builds on, notably the works of Philip Selznick, Alfred Chandler, Edith Penrose, G. B. Richardson, and Nelson and Winter (1982) (see Foss 1997 for a sample), only Nelson and Winter explicitly address and try to incorporate bounded rationality. All this raises suspicions that talk of bounded rationality in connection with the KBV may in actuality be more rhetorical (in the pre-McCloskeyan, derogatory sense) than substantive. Understanding the extent to which the KBV builds on a foundation consisting of bounded rationality requires that we take a look at Nelson and Winter, because, as argued, this contribution has been hugely influential in the development of the KBV conceptualization of firms.

Quite early in Nelson and Winter (1982), namely when discussing 'the need for an evolutionary theory', the authors observe that their 'basic critique of orthodoxy is connected with the bounded rationality problem' (p. 36), and that, therefore, they 'accept and absorb into our analysis many of the ideas of the behavioral theorists' (pp. 35–6), notably Cyert, March, and Simon. In particular, they are attracted to the behavioralist notion that short- and medium-run firm behavior is determined by relatively simple decision rules (Cyert and March 1963). They also make use of behavioralist models of satisficing search (Simon 1955). In a later contribution they note that '[t]he view of firm behavior built into evolutionary economic theory fits well with the theory of firms contained in modern organization theory, especially the part that shares our own debt to the "Carnegie School" (March and Simon 1958; Cyert and March 1992)' (Nelson and Winter 2002: 42). However, in the 1982 book Nelson and Winter go significantly beyond behavioralism by examining populations of firms with differing decision rules, by addressing the interplay between changing external environments and changing decision rules (see also Pierce, Boerner, and Teece 2002), and, the most interesting theoretical innovation in the context of this paper, by trying to bring bounded rationality together with tacit knowledge. It is the last aspect of Nelson and Winter's 'updating exercise' that I shall argue is not entirely successful.

Nelson and Winter's main problem with 'orthodox' theory, and particularly the neoclassical theory of the firm, does not appear to be that this theory rules out diversity in terms of productive or organizational capabilities between firms in an industry per se. Indeed, that theory does allow for variety in these dimensions. For example, to the extent that differences in how well ('competently') a firm is run reflects owners' on-the-job consumption, and these owners are able and willing to bear the consequences of this consumption (Demsetz 1997), the neoclassical theory of the firm allows for differential competencies to exist in equilibrium. Moreover, differential initial endowments of some costly-to-copy resources may simply be postulated (à la Lippman and Rumelt 1982), so that firms with differential efficiencies may exist in equilibrium. However, the main point of Nelson and Winter's critique is that in mainstream economics heterogeneity is at best exogeneously determined (as in the cases of differing preferences for on-the-job consumption or different initial endowments). To paraphrase their argument, in the setting of the (basic) neoclassical theory of the firm, it has to be this way, because the production set is assumed not only to be given (or at best changing through given technological-progress functions or similar constructs) but also to be fully transparent (Langlois and Foss 1999). The implication, as Demsetz (1991) notes, is that if information costs are thus assumed to be zero, what one firm can do at the level of production another firm can do equally well.

Unlike Demsetz, Nelson and Winter do not cast their argument in terms of the information (and other) costs of copying rival firms' resource endowments. Instead, they devote a whole chapter (ch. 4) to an analysis of skills. By a 'skill' they mean 'a capability for a smooth sequence of coordinated behavior that is ordinarily effective relative to its objectives, given the context in which it normally occurs' (1982: 73). The attractions of the notion of skill are apparent. First, it provides a way of introducing dynamics at the level of production, since skills need to be nurtured and tend to grow with practice. Second, it provides an analogy to the behavioralist notion that behavior is strongly guided by relatively rigid decision rules, and thus serves to underscore Nelson and Winter's critique of maximization in the sense of forward-looking, informed deliberate choice. They put much emphasis on this, noting that 'the sort of choice that takes place in the process of exercising a skill is choice without deliberation' (p. 82), although they are careful to note that the behavioral 'programs' embodied in skills may be initiated through deliberate, but presumably boundedly rational, choice.

However, this and the notion that routines may be changed through metaroutines (i.e. search routines) is the only substantive connection that the notion of bounded rationality makes to skills and the organization-level counterpart to individual skills, namely routines. Neither concept is directly derived from bounded-rationality considerations. Third, starting from skills and developing the organization-level analogy to skills allow Nelson and Winter to bring considerations of tacit knowledge into the picture and to develop a strong critique of the 'blueprint' view of neoclassical production function theory. Fourth, it helps them to establish a link between individual action and organizational behavior. That link is initiated in a rather straightforward way by the observation that 'directly relevant to our development here is the value of individual behavior as a *metaphor* for organizational behavior' (ibid. 72; emphasis in the original).

In turn, 'organizational behavior' is addressed in terms of 'routines' that serve as organization-level metaphorical equivalents to individual skills. Like skills, routines represent stable sequences of actions (i.e. they coordinate actions) that are triggered by certain stimuli in certain contexts and which, in a sense, serve as memories for the organizations that embody them. However, because routines are social phenomena, they go beyond the skill metaphor and raise issues of motivation and coordination. However, Nelson and Winter sidestep the motivation issue, arguing that routines represent 'organizational truces'—an idea going back to Cyert and March (1963).

Thus, quite a lot—and perhaps too much—is packed into the notion of routine, including a variety of behaviors (e.g. heuristics and strategies), organizational processes and arrangements, cognitive issues (e.g. 'organizational memories'), and incentives ('truces'). Nelson and Winter defend this by noting that, in actuality, 'skills, organization, and "technology" are intimately intertwined in a functioning routine, and it is difficult to say where one aspect ends and another begins' (1982: 104). Although it is true that the boundaries are blurred, it is not clear why one is not allowed, for purposes of analytical clarity, to look at one aspect at a time. It is one thing to claim that ontologically things are a mess. It is another thing to openly admit the mess into analysis. This is perhaps only a minor problem for Nelson and Winter. Because their level of analysis lies higher than the firm, they can afford to keep the firm level messy. However, their all-inclusive notion of routine may have contributed to the thick terminological soup that characterizes the organizational-capabilities approach, as well as the difficulties of giving precise content to the notion of routines (cf. Cohen et al. 1996), and derived and related notions, such as capabilities, competencies, etc. Below, another possible source of conceptual and explanatory problems in the organizational capabilities approach is considered; namely, the absence of a clear foundation, rooted in individual, boundedly rational choice behavior, for the notion of routines.

Micro-foundations, Bounded Rationality, and Tacit Knowledge

At first glance bounded rationality appears to be quite crucial to Nelson and Winter's argument (Fransman 1994). Thus, firm members can only learn routines through practising them; routines are simply repeated until they become too dysfunctional; learning is myopic, search is satisficing; etc. All of these very strong assumptions about individual and organizational behavior would seem to make room for a rationality that is very bounded indeed. Apparently, this is Williamson's impression when he argues that Nelson and Winter work with a version of bounded rationality, 'organic rationality', that assumes less intentionality, foresight, and calculativeness than his own notion of bounded rationality (Williamson 1985: 47).[2] However, (re)reading chapters 3–5 in Nelson and Winter suggests that what ultimately interests them is not really bounded rationality per se, in the sense of a commitment to building specific models of boundedly rational individual behavior that, in turn, may be fed into models of organization-level behavior and outcomes. What interests them is rather tacit knowledge and its embodiment in their firm-level analogy to individual skills, namely routines, and how these notions assist the understanding of sluggish organizational change and adaptation. These claims are substantiated below.

The Limited Role of Bounded Rationality in Nelson and Winter

Bounded rationality has a bad reputation for being used as a sort of catch-all category that can 'explain' all observed deviations from maximizing rationality (Conlisk 1996; Casson and Wadeson 1997). The Simon dictum that man is 'intendedly rationality, but only limitedly so' is an example. In itself it is vacuous and therefore explains or predicts virtually nothing. Explanation and prediction that begin from a foundation of bounded rationality require that bounded rationality be focused through specific models of behavior (such as Simon 1955). This is where the link to the skill metaphor of organizational behavior becomes important, for it is the use of the notion of skill and particularly its transfer to the organizational level that step in and fill the explanatory and predictive vacuum left by invoking bounded rationality in general terms. In other words, it is skills and, particularly, routines that allow Nelson and Winter (1982) to work out an explanatory and predictive theory of firm behavior. However, the further assumptions that are added to the basic invocation of bounded rationality are not drawn from the existing evidence, notably from psychology, on boundedly rational behavior per se, although Nelson and Winter (2002: 31) in a later paper argue that '[i]n contrast to the usual quest for microfoundations in economics, seeking consistency with rationality assumptions, our quest is for consistency with the available evidence on learning and behavior at both the individual and organizational levels'.

In fact, it turns out that what they mean by the 'available evidence' may be somewhat idiosyncratic. They go on to argue, in the 2002 paper, that '[w]ith respect to individual learning, the plausibility of our behavioral foundations for evolutionary economics has received support from an unexpected quarter. Studies linking cognitive abilities and brain physiology have established the existence of anatomically distinct memory processes supporting the skilled behaviors of individuals' (ibid. 33). Not only is such memory 'highly durable', it also 'functions in some ways that are alien to theories of calculative rationality' (p. 34). While this cognitive science support for the notion of skilled behavior seems compelling, the evidence they present in support of the critical move from individual skilled behavior to the organizational, routine level is less so. The only cited evidence is an experimental study of card-playing teams (Cohen and Bacdayan 1994) that demonstrated that team-level skills (i.e. 'routines') acquired under one specification of the game played made the adaptation to a new specification of the game sluggish. While this has much to do with skilled and inertial behavior and problems of adaptability at the level of teams, it is not clear what exactly all this has to do with bounded rationality (or indeed with firm behavior). Thus, Nelson and Winter's recent stocktaking (2002) reinforces the tendency in Nelson and Winter (1982) to lump together an almost empty characterization of bounded rationality with a much richer description of skilled behavior. Bounded rationality is, in effect, suppressed as a result of this exercise. This raises the question of why bounded rationality is treated as a background assumption while individual and organizational-level skilled behavior takes precedence.

Why Tacit Knowledge is More Important than Bounded Rationality in Nelson and Winter

Nelson and Winter (1982) explicitly compare skilled behavior to the execution of a computer program. The outcomes of computer programs are predictable, given knowledge of what is fed into them and knowledge of the program itself. When triggered in a certain context, skilled behavior is also predictable, and knowledge of an individual's skill set, the relevant context, and the relevant stimulus may also allow for reasonably accurate prediction of his behavior. By implication, organizational routines, the organization-level counterpart to individual skills, may also be understood as programs that make aggregate (i.e. organization-level) behavior predictable and inert. And it is inert organizational behavior that Nelson and Winter (ibid.) are after, because this is a necessary part of their evolutionary mode of explanation. Thus, tacit knowledge, as embodied in skills and routines, can do the job. Can bounded rationality do the job; that is, can it explain inert organizational behavior?

In Nelson and Winter bounded rationality is mainly treated to the extent that it provides an underpinning for the behavioralist notion of decision rules, particularly in connection with search. Such decision rules may be understood as manifestations of bounded rationality at the individual level (cf. Simon 1955) and, less obviously, at the organizational level (Cyert and March 1963). One may expect rule-bound behavior also to provide a strong explanation of inert organizational behavior. However, there are two reasons why bounded rationality and the decision rules it gives rise to may not be a strong foundation for a theory of organizational inertia. First, decision rules that are explicit (i.e. Cyert and March's 1963 'standard operating procedures') may arguably be changed at lower cost than complex routines that embody huge amounts of tacit knowledge. In this sense, routines that are rationalized in terms of skills and tacit knowledge offer a stronger explanation of organizational sluggishness than standard operating procedures. Tacitness beats bounded rationality with respect to the explanation of inertia, as it were. Second, it is far from clear that individual bounded rationality produces inert behavior at the aggregate level. To be sure, such stories can be told (e.g. Heath, Knez, and Camerer 1993; Egidi 2001), but they require that bounded rationality and the interaction between boundedly rational agents be specified in certain ways. To take an almost trivial example, if similar agents all suffer from status quo biases, their aggregate behavior may indeed manifest inertia. In contrast, it is not clear that inert aggregate behavior will in general follow from individual-level rule-following; for example, in the form of some satisificing model.

Thus, bounded rationality alone cannot do what Nelson and Winter wish their behavioral assumptions to do for them; hence the invocation of skills, and the use of the skill metaphor to address aggregate behavior. In the end, bounded rationality is more a sort of background argument that serves to make plausible the notion of organizational routine (including search routines), and therefore the sluggish organizational adaptation that is so crucial to Nelson and Winter's evolutionary story. Thus, the whole construct works from an initial argument about bounded rationality, goes from there to behavioralist decision rules, jumps via analogy to ideas on tacit knowledge as embodied in skilled behavior, and then transfers skills to the level of routines and organizational capabilities. Bounded rationality re-enters the story when changes in routines and capabilities have to be explained; namely, in the form of dynamic search routines.

This is a complicated exercise that has some unfortunate consequences. In addition to the various problems identified in the Cohen et al. symposium (1996) on the meaning of routines, there are at least two further problematic consequences of this exercise. First, tacit knowledge and bounded rationality tend to become indiscriminately lumped together, because it is not transparent where the one ends and the other begins. Of course, tacit knowledge and bounded rationality are different things and do not necessarily imply each other. Thus, there can be tacit rules for maximization, as Machlup (1946) argued. Or, agents can cope with bounded rationality by means of fully explicit operating proced-ures. While one can certainly construct an argument that boundedly rational agents make use of experientially produced—and 'skilled'—decision rules that are likely to embody a good deal of tacit knowledge (Langlois 1999), there is simply no necessary connection between bounded rationality and tacit know-ledge. Second, and perhaps more seriously, bounded rationality at the level of the individual becomes suppressed. This makes it hard to understand the link between bounded rationality, on the one hand, and routines and other organ-izational phenomena, on the other. In other words, what exactly is the nature of the mechanism that aggregates from individual behavior to routines and organ-izational behavior? This mechanism is never really identified in Nelson and Winter (1982). It also means that there is a certain interpretative ambiguity surrounding the notion of routines to the extent that it is related to bounded rationality. Is organization-level routinization produced by interaction effects among the members of a team or is it ultimately founded in aspects of individual cognition (Egidi 2000: 2). These issues are not resolved in Nelson and Winter (1982). In fairness, it should be noted that this is perhaps not surprising, since not much work existed on this issue when Nelson and Winter wrote their book.

Wider Consequences: Explanatory Difficulties and Lack of Micro-foundations

Explanatory Difficulties

Nelson and Winter (1982) is indeed a high point in the development of the KBV, and their work has been foundational for much subsequent work within this approach. In Chapter 2 the KBV's aspiration to become a full-blown theory of economic organization, a point at which it goes beyond Nelson and Winter (ibid.), was discussed. The argument that will briefly be developed here is that certain characteristics of Nelson and Winter (ibid.) were carried over into the organizational capabilities approach, characteristics that may not be so problematic if the analytical purpose is one of explaining rigidity in firm behavior as part of a broader evolutionary story, but which are much less appropriate for the purpose of building a theory of economic organization. The relevant characteristic is a strong emphasis on aggregate entities, notably routines and organizational capabilities, an emphasis that comes at the expense of attention to individual behaviors, and derives from Nelson and Winter's attempt to establish a metaphorical solution to the aggregation problem of moving from the level of the agent to the level of the organization. Because they fully recognize the metaphorical character of this maneuver, they do not commit the mistake of conflating an ontological claim with a useful research heuristic. Later contributors to the knowledge-based view may not have been as careful here as Nelson and Winter are.

Problems seem unavoidably to emerge as soon as Nelson and Winter's ideas on organizational routines and capabilities are transferred from their original place in the analysis of a changing population of firms to an analysis of the behavior and, particularly, organization of individual firms. While these notions have indeed been of value for the understanding of, for example, the sources of competitive advantage (although much of this literature is also plagued by conceptual ambiguity), their application to economic organization is more problematic.

The boundaries of the firm. The problem is apparent in another founding contribution to the KBV that actually introduced the 'capabilities' construct, namely Richardson (1972). In Richardson the import of capabilities is their limitations. Because of what are effectively cognitive constraints, all organizations must specialize; and, since the chain of production in an advanced economy requires a diversity of very different capabilities, the costs of integrating across many links in that chain are necessarily high, and firms must rely on various kinds of market and hybrid arrangements to coordinate their activities even in the face of contractual hazards. In Richardson's terminology, production can be broken down into various stages or *activities*. Some activities are *similar*, in that they draw on the same general capabilities. Activities can also be *complementary* (in both a technical and an economic sense) in that they are connected in the chain of production and therefore need to be coordinated with one another. Juxtaposing different degrees of similarity against different degrees of complementarity produces a matrix that maps different types of economic organization. Notably, Richardson argues, closely complementary activities (which are in need of substantial coordination) that are, however, dissimilar are organized more efficiently in inter-firm relations than under unified governance or market governance.

Richardson's argument is intriguing and the first systematic attempt to explain economic organization in terms of the capabilities construct (as well as one of the few attempts in the literature to dimensionalize capabilities). However, it suffers from some of the same kind of problems that also characterize later developments in the KBV. Thus, capabilities are only loosely defined in Richardson (ibid.); namely, as firm-specific 'knowledge, experience and skill . . . [that] may depend upon command of some particular material technology, such as cellulose chemistry, electronics or civil engineering, or may derive from skills in marketing or knowledge of and reputation in a particular market' (p. 888). Also, what are 'similar' or 'dissimilar' and 'complementary' and 'closely complementary' capabilities is mainly explained in terms of examples, and Richardson, like virtually all writers in the KBV, is not very forthcoming in defining these dimensions of his unit of analysis.[3]

In these respects, there are no differences between Richardson (ibid.) and Kogut and Zander (1992), in spite of the twenty years that separate these two heavily cited papers. Thus, like Richardson, Kogut and Zander (ibid.) argue directly from organizational capabilities to the boundaries of the firm; that is, from an aggregate construct to an aggregate phenomenon. And, like Richardson, they do not offer an elaborate micro-argument to support this. The supporting argument is that 'firms know more than their contracts can tell'. However, there is no attempt to address this is in terms of comparative contracting, and, ultimately, individual behavior. What exactly is it that cannot be written in contracts? Even if writing costs in fact are prohibitive, why cannot relational contracting, involving highly incomplete contracts, between independent parties handle the transfer of knowledge? Why is it only vertical integration that economizes with what are presumably writing and communication costs? No compelling answers are given to such questions. This is the case for most of this literature as it is applied to economic organization. A partial exception is the work of Langlois (1992). Langlois attempts to supply the missing mechanism from organizational capabilities to the boundaries of the firm by means of the concept of 'dynamic transaction costs', which are essentially communication costs that arise because of 'dissimilar' (Richardson 1972) capabilities in a vertical structure of firms. Presumably, efficient economic organization minimizes such costs (as well as other more 'traditional' transaction costs—allowance being made for possible trade-offs between these).

Internal organization.   However, this idea may imply another difficulty, one that is also present in Nelson and Winter (1982) and in virtually all of the KBV. This difficulty is that knowledge inside firms is very often assumed to be homogeneous (or, less strongly, not very costly to communicate), while knowledge between firms ('differential capabilities') is taken to be (very) heterogeneous (and therefore costly to communicate) (notably Kogut and Zander 1992).[4] Thus, Winter (1986: 175) assumes that 'the search for information from external sources does not proceed with the same ease as for internal sources'. Knott (2003: 691) argues that the firm's 'knowledge stock' is a 'public good inside the firm that can be redeployed on other projects. What makes the knowledge stock a public good are the facts that it is *non-rival*—once the firm has acquired the knowledge it can be used by multiple departments at zero cost—and *nonexcludable*—the department which developed the knowledge can't (or would have no reason to) keep other departments from using it.' It is easy to see why such assumptions are made in the KBV. It makes it plausible that communication costs could carry implications for the boundaries of the firm, as in the Kogut and Zander (1992) argument that the boundaries of firms are strongly influenced by firms knowing 'more than their contracts can tell'.

However, although there may be some intuitive appeal in the assumption, it is hard to accept as true in general. There are many examples of firms where the bandwidth of the communication channels between some business unit of the firm and an external firm (e.g. buyer or seller) is much higher than the bandwidth between the unit and, say, corporate headquarters. Moreover, the implicit assumption that knowledge in hierarchies can be taken, at least as a first approximation, to be communicable at zero cost makes it hard to understand hierarchical organization, since with zero cost communication the managerial task has no economic rationale (Demsetz 1991; Casson 1994).

Methodological Individualism

It seems fairly obvious that the essentially ad hoc assumptions that knowledge inside firms can be communicated at low cost while knowledge between firms can only be communicated at high cost slip into the analysis when the units of analysis are routines or organizational capabilities. It is then easy to postulate that 'firms know more than their contracts can tell' and that all organizational aspects are 'intertwined in a functioning routine'. If instead the analysis had started in an explicit individualist methodological mode, that is from individual choice behavior, the argument that communication costs within, for example, certain business units may be lower than the communication costs between people in the unit and people in a supplier firm might have been derived as an outcome of a properly specified model instead of being postulated. The problem is that there is no theory of individual choice behavior in KBV, so that KBV writers have to treat economic organization in a collectivist methodological way; namely, in terms of postulating crude causal relations between capabilities and economic organization, little attention being paid to the microanalytic issues involved. Not surprisingly, these stories are vulnerable to critiques from more microanalytic perspectives (Foss 1996; Williamson 2000).

Ironically, therefore, it turns out that much of the KBV is vulnerable to the *same* critique that Winter (1991) forcefully (and justifiably) launched against the neoclassical theory of the firm. Specifically, and borrowing directly from Winter, it is in potential 'conflict with methodological individualism' (p. 181) (because of the emphasis on routines and organizational capabilities), 'provides no basis for explaining economic organization' (p. 183) (because transaction costs and comparative contracting are not considered), lacks 'realism' (because of its 'unrealistic' treatment of decision-making as entirely guided by routines), and provides a 'simplistic treatment of its focal concern' (e.g. because it is simply assumed that it is easier to gather, combine, source, etc. knowledge inside firms than between firms). The main underlying problem, it has been argued here, is that too little attention is devoted to individual decision-making, and that much of the KBV de facto subscribes to methodological collectivism (Felin and Foss 2004).[5] To see this, consider the following diagram, which is an adaptation of the familiar 'bathtub diagram' from Coleman (1990).

The KBV relies heavily on mode (4) explanation; that is, aggregate-level explanation where aggregate 'social facts' *directly* cause aggregate social outcomes.

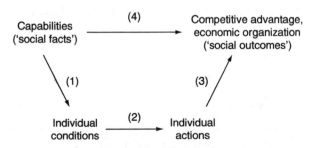

Figure 4.1. Explanation in the organizational-capabilities approach.
Source: Adapted from Coleman (1990).

For example, 'capabilities' are argued to cause the boundaries of the firm as well as overall firm performance. This is methodological collectivism, whereas methodological individualism would dictate substituting for mode-(4) explanation, an explanation that involved at least mode (3) and possibly also modes (1) and (2). The fundamental problems with such methodological collectivism are that it (1) ascribes independent causal powers to collective entities; (2) suppresses more 'micro'-explanatory mechanisms that are located at the level of individual action; and therefore also (3) neglects the complicated processes of interaction between individuals (Hayek 1952; Ullman-Margalitt 1977). Not surprisingly, there is a strong tendency in methodological collectivism to treat individuals as homogeneous.

We can see all these characteristics in the KBV. The problems at least partly go back to Nelson and Winter and their sidestepping of individual behavior in favor of aggregate notions (i.e. routines and capabilities). Although Nelson and Winter were aware of the limitations and problems of sidestepping individual behavior in favor of collective entities as the explanatory 'primitives', and Winter certainly seems committed to methodological individualism (Winter 1991), later KBV writers seem more at variance with individualistic explanation, and some explicitly abandon it (Spender 1996).[6] In fact, Howard Aldrich argues for a potential shift completely away from individuals, conjecturing that 'if we truly focused on routines, competencies, practices and so on, we would *not* follow people anymore in our research' (Murmann, Aldrich, Levinthal, and Winter 2003: 25–7; emphasis in the original). Recent work has also argued for the existence and importance of aggregates or collections of routines and nth level capabilities (Nelson 1994; Eisenhardt and Martin 2000; Zollo and Winter 2002; Helfat and Peteraf 2003; Winter 2003; Zott 2003). This seems somewhat problematic, given that clarity on the basic constructs has not yet been achieved (Felin and Foss 2004).

Conclusion

In conclusion it is appropriate to set the argument in this chapter in a somewhat broader context. In an excellent recent paper (2003) Paul Nightingale's argument parallels the one developed here. He argues that Nelson and Winter (1982) seek to 'bring together two very different ways of thinking about knowledge'; namely, the more appreciative 'tacit knowledge tradition that derives, in part, from Polanyi's phenomenology' and the more formal 'objectivist information processing, problem-solving approach that derives, in part, from Simon' (2003: 1). This is visible in their attempt to conceptualize firms both in terms of information processing and in terms of tacit and socially embedded knowledge. Nightingale argues that a number of tensions in the science-and-technology policy literature are traceable to this problematic attempt in Nelson and Winter to fuse two epistemologies, the tensions between which have fuelled other recent debates, notably in artificial-intelligence research.

Much of the argument in this chapter may be cast in similar terms. The attempt in Nelson and Winter to combine ideas on routines and skilled behavior derived from Polanyi with ideas on bounded rationality and satisficing search derived from Simon has not been entirely satisfactory, and may be an important source of some of the explanatory difficulties that confront the modern KBV. An indication that Nelson and Winter's reconciliation exercise was not entirely successful is that tacit knowledge and bounded rationality simply are not equal partners in the 1982 book; the three central chapters on firm-behavior and organization are to a much larger extent about tacit knowledge than about bounded rationality. Thus, contrary to a commonly held view, the role of bounded rationality in the knowledge-based view is very much a background one. Its precise relation, if any, to the notion of the central concepts of routine and capability is unclear. Its role seems more rhetorical than substantive. At any rate, boundedly rational behavior at the level of the individual agent is not modeled either in Nelson and Winter's seminal 1982 book or in the many contributions to the KBV that are so heavily indebted to this contribution.

Finally, lest this chapter be taken as a general attack on the KBV, it is important to stress that its real message is a methodogical one. In the spirit of what was called 'integrationism' in Chapter 2, the position here is that the KBV embraces interesting issues, but that KBV theorists should devote more analytical energies to getting the micro-foundations right. It will not do in the long run to continue working with concepts whose micro-foundations are unclear. This is not just a matter of conforming to the conventional methodological individualist approach of most economics and business administration. It is also, and more substantively, a matter of the explanatory and predictive capabilities of the KBV being less impressive than they could be as a result of the lack of micro-foundations for concepts such as routines, capabilities, etc. Also in the spirit of integrationism, the central argument in the following chapter is that various ideas that belong to the broad theoretical body of 'new institutional economics' (including organizational economics) have the potential to further the KBV as well as the RBV.

Notes

1. Penrose (1959) does treat localized, tacit knowledge, but only at the level of the management team.
2. For discussions of the role of bounded rationality in organizational economics see Foss (2003a).

3. It is not surprising that the balance between theoretical and empirical work in the capabilities perspective seems weighted towards the theoretical side, and that most empirical work is qualitative.

4. While this is the most common assumption in the KBV, Nickerson and Zenger (2003) point out that some KBV make exactly the opposite assumption. For example, Conner and Prahalad (1996) invoke the Demsetz (1991) argument that the main advantage of authority (i.e. order giving) is that it allows use to be made of knowledge without communicating this knowledge.

5. For an excellent extended critique of the KBV along these lines see Felin and Hesterly (2004).

6. Although a few knowledge-based writers explicitly try to eschew the dangers of methodological collectivism (notably Grant 1996).

5

Strategy, Resources, and Transaction Costs

Introduction

Transaction cost economics (henceforth 'TCE') has for a long time been a favorite whipping boy of sociologists and heterodox economists of various colours (e.g. Hodgson 1998). TCE bashing continues to be a thriving industry in these fields, but new entrants are increasingly recruited from the ranks of management scholars, particularly from the strategic management field. As noted in Chapter 2, work in economics on transaction costs and their role in structuring economic organization attracted a great deal of sympathetic attention and influence at the beginning of the 1980s in the strategic-management field (e.g. Dundas and Richardson 1980; Rumelt 1984) following the seminal work of Williamson (1975). However, during the 1990s transaction cost economics became increasingly subject to critical discussion and even opposition, as knowledge-based approaches swept across business administration. In the strategy field, resource-based and knowledge-based theorists have been particularly vocal critics, and have explicitly used the critique of TCE as a starting point for developing their own approaches to the firm (Kogut and Zander 1992; Conner and Prahalad 1996; Ghoshal and Moran 1996; Madhok 1996). At much the same time similar critiques were put forward in economics (e.g. Langlois 1992; Foss 1993; Hodgson 1998; Witt 1999), drawing on somewhat similar sources (notably Penrose 1959 and Richardson 1972).

While Chapter 2 was essentially an essay comparing the respective merits and drawbacks of existing theory of the firm-based approaches in strategy, this chapter is an attempt to go beyond existing positions. It does so in two ways. First, in the spirit of the 'integrationism' promoted in Chapter 2, it will be argued that TCE can further the resource-based view. More fundamentally, it will be argued that rather than supplying non-negligible, but still second-order, arguments about optimum sourcing and sales arrangements, internal organization, and the like (Seth and Thomas 1994), TCE arguments have the potential to add to the very core of strategic-management research; that is, value creation and appropriation. Second, the chapter does not build on Williamsonian foundations. As it is understood here, TCE is not limited to Williamson's work (Eggertson 1990; Barzel 1997; Furubotn and Richter 1997), and TCE is not committed with any logical necessity to the specific behavioral assumption of opportunism (Hart 1995) or the assumption of asset specificity (Barzel 1997).

Thus, the chapter will sketch an approach that is perhaps more dependent on the property rights branch of transaction cost economics (Barzel 1982, 1997) than on the Williamsonian branch. While entirely consistent with what follows, asset specificity and opportunism are not central characters. Instead, below we frame the fundamental questions of strategic management directly in a transaction cost context by asking questions such as: Is competitive advantage possible in a zero-transaction-cost world? How does the presence of transaction costs influence strategic opportunities? Does an explicit recognition of transaction costs direct attention to resource types that have been overlooked in previous strategic-management research? And so on. These questions go right to the heart of the matter of the central issues of strategic management in their concern with the creation and appropriation of value. What is added is a fundamental concern with the role that transaction costs play in such processes.

In addition to unfolding some of the relations between transaction costs and value creation and appropriation, the chapter links the discussion to the resource-based view (the 'RBV') (Barney 1991; Peteraf 1993) and the knowledge-based view (the 'KBV') (Kogut and Zander 1992; Grant 1996). It does so by drawing on the economics of property rights (the 'EPR') (e.g. Coase 1960; Alchian 1965; Demsetz 1967; Cheung 1969; Barzel 1997). Property rights over resource attributes consist of the rights to use, consume, obtain income from, and alienate these attributes. Property rights matter to strategy because a resource owner's ability to create, appropriate, and sustain value from resources partly depends on the property rights that she holds to those resources and how well protected these rights are. In turn, transaction costs—the costs of exchanging, protecting and capturing property rights—matter to strategy, because they influence the value that a resource owner can appropriate. This conceptualization unifies the theoretical constructs of property rights, transaction costs, and value creation and appropriation with the notion that resources are fundamental to strategic management.

The Strategic-management Debate on Transaction-cost Economics: Are the Right Questions Being Asked?

The debate—or, set of connected debates—in the strategic-management field on the role of TCE with respect to furthering insights in firm strategy that was surveyed in Chapter 2 has usually centered on Williamson's version of TCE (Williamson 1975, 1985, 1996a). This is arguably not surprising, because the link between transaction costs economics and firm strategy was first made explicit in Williamson's demonstration (1975) of the capacity of transaction cost reasoning to throw light on fundamental corporate strategy issues (i.e. the issue of efficient firm boundaries), as well as functional and organizational strategy issues (i.e. the issue of efficient internal organization). Also, Williamson and his students and co-authors have continued to be influential voices in the strategic-management field. The Chandler-Williamson M-form hypothesis quickly became a key insight in the strategic management field, particularly after being supported in a number of influential empirical studies (e.g. Armour and Teece 1978). The classic transaction cost papers on such issues as the multinational firm, vertical supply arrangements, joint ventures, franchising, sales force organization, etc.—most of which has been built on Williamsonian foundations—have become standard references in the strategic management field.

Given all this, it is not surprising that Rumelt, Schendel, and Teece (1994: 27) could introduce the proceedings from the 1990 Napa conference on 'Fundamental Issues in Strategy: A Research Agenda for the 1990s' with the observation that '[o]f all the new subfields of economics, the transaction cost branch of organizational economics has the greatest affinity with strategic management', and then go on to observe that within strategic management TCE 'is the ground where economic thinking, strategy and organizational theory meet' (Rumelt et al. 1994: 27). Their views echoed Rumelt's earlier argument (1984) that Williamsonian TCE should serve as the foundation for firm strategy research and, ultimately, managerial practice. Only TCE supplied an understanding of such foundational issues as the existence, boundaries, and, to a smaller extent, the internal organization of the firm, and a number of derived issues (e.g. the structuring of joint ventures, franchise contracting, diversification, etc.). However, the relevance of TCE seemed to be limited to corporate strategy issues; implicitly, it was acknowledged that TCE had very little to say about competitive strategy; that is, issues relating to positioning in an industry and defending such a position.

TCE was first openly challenged by attempts to frame the then relatively recent RBV as a theory of the firm (in particular, Conner 1991; Kogut and Zander 1992). These attempts were launched against a general background of critique of TCE, particularly Williamson's version of TCE. Critics of Williamsonian TCE attacked the theory on a broad front. Thus, it was argued that TCE (1) put too much emphasis on opportunism and too little on trust (Ghoshal and Moran 1996); (2) neglected 'transaction benefits' and focused solely on transaction costs (Zajac and Olsen 1993); (3) only considerd 'exchange' and excluded 'production' (Winter 1991); (4) could not explain firm heterogeneity (Conner 1991); and (5) was static (Langlois 1992). In contrast, it was argued that a new 'strategic theory of the firm' could be built from insights into such neglected phenomena as transaction benefits, firm heterogeneity, etc., the obvious implication being that Williamsonian TCE was not necessary for developing a strategic theory of the firm. As shown in Chapter 2, the debate has attracted numerous contributors and has sometimes provoked heated arguments and strong opinions. Important issues appear to be at stake. However, while the debate may have clarified positions, both substantive and meta-theoretical, it is questionable whether it has actually provided essential new insights.

One possible reason why the debates may not have been fruitful is that right from the start they implicitly assumed that the specific Williamsonian formulation of TCE contained the entire set of TCE assumptions and propositions relevant to strategic management. Thus, virtually all contributors to the debates on the role of TCE in strategic management research have tended to focus on theory-of-the-firm issues, and most have adopted different takes on the 'knowledge or opportunism in the theory of the firm' theme originally introduced by Conner (1991), Kogut and Zander (1992), Langlois (1992), and Foss (1993). This reflects the heuristic ideas that, first, the theory of the firm is very important to strategic management research, and, second, there is a choice to be made between knowledge and incentive issues in the explanation of economic organization.

Both ideas may be contested. Although I think that the first idea is ultimately sound (cf. also Chapter 2), while the second isn't, even the first idea and its various implications—notably, that strategic management research should explicitly begin from a theory of the firm—is open to some debate. Strategic management research has typically had a firm focus, and its fundamental concern has been to explain how firms can create and appropriate more value than the competition (e.g. Hofer and Schendel 1978; Porter 1980; Peteraf 1993). Economic theories of the firm fit neatly into this overall conceptualization. Their level of analysis is the firm (albeit units of analysis may differ) and they are fundamentally concerned with value creation and appropriation. To illustrate, in a recent paper Mahoney (2001; emphasis in the original) provides what he considers a fundamental reason why the Williamsonian transaction cost approach to the firm is important to strategic management:

asset specificity (sunk cost commitment) is a necessary condition for isolating mechanisms that sustain rents [...] Often the firm achieves sustainable competitive advantage (i.e., sustains rents) because it reduces opportunistic behavior and allows for firm-specific investment. *In the absence of opportunism the rent-generating firm need not exist.* In the absence of opportunism, contracting would be sufficient to support investments that are strategic commitments.

A number of things are noteworthy about such reasoning.[1] First, sustained competitive advantage, which is taken to be the central explanandum of strategy research, is unambiguously located at the firm level. However, it is strictly speaking not firms that appropriate value, but the numerous stakeholders that supply inputs to the legal fiction known as the firm. Second, this suggests that there is more to the TCE/strategic management nexus than asset specificity; for example, the role of TCE arguments would seem to be a general matter of exploring how well alternative contracting practices constrain the strategic behavior of the firm's stakeholders. Third, it is assumed that the TCE/strategic-management nexus is indirect in the sense that establishing it requires taking a route over the theory of the firm. Such a view is potentially constraining, because it seems to imply that a TCE approach to strategic management must necessarily involve Williamsonian notions of asset specificity and opportunism. However, this route is not the only possible one. While applications of the Williamsonian approach in strategic management continue to produce outstanding research (e.g. Oxley 1999; Silverman 1999; Nickerson and Zenger 2002; Nickerson and Silverman forthcoming), it is possible, and, it will be argued, worthwhile, to explore the strategic-management/TCE nexus along different routes.

The Argument: An Example

According to Coase (1992: 716), '[b]usinessmen in deciding on their ways of doing business and on what to produce have to take into account transaction costs [. . .] In fact, a large part of what we think of as economic activity is designed to accomplish what high transaction costs would otherwise prevent'. To illustrate Coase's idea, consider the strategy that a major player in the world's diamond industry, the DeBeers cartel, has adopted for organizing sales to its customers. The customer informs DeBeers of her wishes with respect to the number and quality of stones. DeBeers then offers the customer a packet of stones, a 'sight', that roughly corresponds to the customer's wishes, and that sight is offered on a 'take-it-or-leave-*us-permanently*' basis. The price is calculated on the basis of the gross characteristics of the stones, and no negotiation over the price is possible.

Does this strategy reflect the raw exercise of market power on the part of a player that controls 80 per cent of the world's market for raw diamonds? Economists (Barzel 1982; Kenney and Klein 1983) writing from the perspective of property-rights economics have argued that it does not. Rather, it is a practice that maximizes the created value in firm–customer relations by reducing the costs customers would otherwise have expended on sorting and negotiating, and exists for this reason (it would be superfluous in a zero-transaction-cost world). With this practice DeBeers sorts, but only in a coarse manner. The 'take-it-or-leave-us-permanently' practice and the posted price mean that costs of negotiation are effectively eliminated. Because only minimum resources (i.e. transaction costs) are spent on sorting and negotiating, DeBeers's practice maximizes the total created value that the parties to the transaction can split between them.[2]

Although strategic-management research has paid virtually no attention to such practices and how they can be explained, their theoretical explanation has important implications for strategic management, not least the RBV. First, transaction costs and value *creation* appear to be linked. Thus, sorting costs (an instance of transaction costs) reduce the value that is created through exchange.

However, certain practices (that would be irrelevant in the absence of transaction costs) may reduce transaction costs, increasing created value. In other words, they 'accomplish what high transaction costs would otherwise prevent'. Second, transaction costs and value *appropriation* appear to be linked. Suppose DeBeers posts prices that reflect the mean quality of the diamonds in a given sight. If DeBeers then allows customers to sort between the diamonds in a sight, customers will only pick high-quality stones. DeBeers's actual sales strategy raises customers' (transaction) costs of sorting to infinity, allowing DeBeers to maximize the share of created value that it can appropriate. Ideas on property rights in economics provide a convenient way of focusing these insights and at the same time relating them to the RBV and the KBV.

Relating Property Rights and Transaction Costs to Resources[3]

Although notions of property rights abound in the analysis of the strategic implications of intellectual-property issues (e.g. Liebeskind 1996; Teece 1987; Argyres and Liebeskind 1998), the EPR is a very unusual visitor to the pages of the strategic-management journals (Foss and Foss 2000a; Kim and Mahoney 2002; Foss 2003b). There are many reasons for this. First, while the property-rights approach was quite influential at the end of the 1960s and in the 1970s (Furubotn and Pejovich 1972), in the 1980s—the decade where strategic management was established as an academic field—micro-economists directed their interest to game-theoretical information economics. Ironically, however, ideas on property rights were reintroduced into the economics profession through the medium of game theory (Grossman and Hart 1986; Hart and Moore 1990), and the older, non-formal tradition in the EPR was given a new lease of life in the work of, particularly, Yoram Barzel (1994, 1997).[4] Second, much of the property-rights program was directed to understanding the allocational consequences of social institutions (e.g. Alchian 1965; Demsetz 1967); that is, the program primarily worked at a level of analysis that was substantially higher than those levels that strategic management is concerned with. Third, strategic management scholars tend to associate the EPR with intellectual property rights issues alone. However, the EPR goes far beyond issues of intellectual property. It is therefore appropriate to state the fundamentals of the EPR, especially as these relate to firm strategy issues, particularly the RBV.

Property Rights and Resources

The pioneering paper on the economics of property rights is conventionally and justifiably taken to be Coase (1960). In this paper Coase examines the economic implications of the allocation of legally delineated rights (liability rights) to a subset of the total uses of an asset; namely, those that have external effects on the value of other agents' abilities to exercise their use rights over assets. As part of his critique of the Pigovian tradition in welfare economics, Coase (ibid. 155) notes that a reason for the failure of this tradition fully to come to grips with the externality issue lies in its 'faulty concept of a factor of production', which—according to Coase—should be thought of not as a physical entity but as a right to perform certain actions. This right is a property right.

Following Coase, economists writing within the EPR stress that transactions involve the exchange of property rights rather than the exchange of goods per se. Hence, the unit of analysis is the individual property right. Clearly, this is a unit of analysis that is more microanalytic than those that are applied in the RBV and the KBV.[5] While the units of analysis of the EPR and the RBV thus differ, the EPR view is not at variance with the RBV position that for the analysis of sustained competitive advantage resources are what matters. Rather, the EPR refines the RBV understanding of resources and how resources create and appropriate value.

Different definitions of 'resources' are put forward in the RBV literature. For example, Wernerfelt (1984) thinks of resources as assets that are tied 'semi-permanently' to the firm, and Barney (1991) defines resources as anything that may be of potential value to a firm. Elaborate taxonomies of resources have been constructed, partly on the basis of the supposed contribution to sustained competitive advantage of different kinds of resources (physical, human, organ-izational, relational, financial, etc.). Because the standard definitions of resources are so broad (cf. Barney's definition, ibid.), confusion has occasionally surfaced in the literature with respect to the *levels* at which resources are located, and many writers have developed elaborate resource hierarchies (e.g. hierarchical structures that relate 'competencies', 'capabilities', and 'resources', such as in Sanchez 2001) to address what they see as a need to distinguish between mundane resources that can—through the application of 'higher-level' resources—be assembled into less mundane resources with the potential to bring sustained competitive advantage. Many contributions to the KBV take this perspective. One reason why such exercises may be warranted is that simply defining resources as 'anything that may be of value to a firm' risks obscuring the ways in which those resources that indeed create value to the firm (e.g. in the sense of helping it to obtain sustained competitive advantage) are built from other, more mundane, resources. High-lighting resource hieararchies may bring attention to mechanisms that are otherwise in danger of being black-boxed.

The EPR suggests a different way of refining the understanding of resources. From this perspective resources can be thought of as being composed of different functionalities and services (Penrose 1959); that is, different *attributes*. Property rights may be held to such attributes (Barzel 1997)—property rights over attributes consisting of the rights to consume, obtain income from, and alienate these attributes (Alchian 1965). A car is composed of numerous attributes, such as the ability to carry passengers and goods, the ability to drive fast or slow, etc. However, the set of property rights that a person may hold to the attributes is usually smaller than the set of attributes. For example, the use right to the attribute of delivering speed at 250 km per hour is constrained in most countries. Similarly, firm resources, such as a brand name, may also have attributes to which use rights are constrained. An owner of a brand name can decide in which contexts she wishes to deploy the brand name in the non-virtual world; that is, she holds property rights to the relevant uses (attributes) of the brand name and appropriates the value from the services it yields by allowing customers and suppliers to identify the firm that owns the brand name in various contexts (i.e. social, geographical). Her use rights may still be constrained, for she may not be allowed to use the brand name as a domain name on the Internet.

Resources, Property Rights, and Attributes

These examples suggest that it is useful to think of *resources* as *bundles of property rights to attributes*. The resource is an important aggregation of the unit of analysis (the individual property right), because often resources rather than individual property rights over attributes are traded or created. Trading bundles of property rights of which only some are specified is efficient because it is often too costly to specify and trade each individual attribute (Foss and Foss 2001). The implication is that how attributes are bundled to constitute a 'resource' is dependent on transaction costs. In other words, resources are *outcomes* of processes of economizing with such transaction costs. For example, the extent to which copying machines and servicing agreements are sold as a combined good (i.e. a 'tying arrangement') may depend on the costs to the seller or lessor of monitoring the impact of non-standard servicing on the machine (Elzinga and Mills 2001). Transaction costs often hinder resource owners from realizing their income rights to all of the attributes of a resource by selling individual attributes. For example, the transaction costs of trading production time mean that the practice of leasing such attributes to other firms is rather unusual.

The value that an owner of a resource potentially can create from a resource depends on the bundle of property rights (specified as well as unspecified) that he holds to the attributes of the resource.[6] For example, the value to the owner of the brand name mentioned earlier may be increased if she also has the right to use it (use rights) as a domain name on the Internet.

The value that an owner of a resource can appropriate from her resource depends on her right and ability to exclude non-owners from the attributes of the resource; for example, various uses of the resource. Thus, the value that a firm can appropriate from its brand name by selling it or by deploying it in-house depends on its legal rights to exclude non-owners (other firms) from using the name, as well as its ability to enforce this right. While the resource owner has the legal and moral right to exclude non-owners from using and obtaining value from his resources, he may still find it too costly to exclude non-owners from all possible uses of the resource. Relatedly, given the costs of protecting property rights over attributes, owners often choose to control the relevant property rights to varying degrees, and the value that a resource can appropriate will reflect this. For example, in a franchise chain the value of a brand name to the franchisor will be eroded (Dierickx and Cool 1989) when it is too costly to the franchisor to control franchisees' use of the brand name for selling products that are below the quality standards of the chain. The implication is that the value that a resource can appropriate depends on the costs of controlling the property rights to the attributes that make up the resource. These costs are transaction costs. Attempts to maximize resource value must take these costs into account.

The Capture and Protection of Property Rights

An important part of transaction costs are the costs of using legal and/or private means of protection. The existence of transaction costs means that most property rights are not fully protected and can be subject to capture attempts; that is, resource-consuming activities of appropriating value from other players *without compensating them*. Thus, capture is the source of negative externalities. Moral hazard, adverse selection, and hold-up are familiar examples of capture. While capture is different from exchange, it may take place in exchange relations. For example, two parties to a transaction agree on a price for a resource with certain attributes (e.g. a certain quality level); however, the supplier may deliver a resource of a lower quality. Such post-contractual opportunism on the part of the supplier amounts to capturing (some) valued resource attributes from the buyer.[7]

Given this definition of capture, 'protection' can be defined as the resource-consuming activities that players undertake in order to reduce others players' possibilities of capturing value. Since capture takes many forms, the notion of protection that is present in the EPR goes significantly beyond making and keeping resources costly to imitate or substitute (Teece 1986; Barney 1991). Protection includes such activities as using the legal system, establishing private orderings (Williamson 1996), deterring entry (Tirole 1988), establishing isolating mechanisms (Wernerfelt 1984; Rumelt 1987), writing contracts, and adopting sales strategies to avoid adverse sorting, as in the DeBeers example (Barzel 1982; Kenney and Klein 1983). The RBV and the KBV mainly consider a subset of these protection activities; namely, protecting against competitive imitation. However, there are many other relevant kinds of capture and corresponding protection activities, and there is no inherent reason why the RBV should not consider a much broader set.

To see why this is so, consider a hypothetical insurance company that is the first to market a particular kind of accident-insurance concept that is in heavy demand, and can be fully protected from imitation by legal means. Moreover, assume that factor markets can only bargain for a small part of the value created by the new concept, and that customers also have weak bargaining powers. Given all this, the insurance company would seem to implement 'a value creating strategy not simultaneously being implemented by any current or potential competitors and [. . .] these other firms are unable to duplicate the benefits of this strategy' (Barney 1991: 102); that is, to realize a sustained competitive advantage. However, this may not be the case. Because of transaction costs, the price of insurance contracts cannot perfectly reflect the true accident risks of each individual who takes out insurance. Given variation in risks, some customers, namely those with high accident risks, capture value in excess of what they pay for (i.e. 'adverse selection', Akerlof 1970). At the limit, all of the rents from the new strategies will be eroded through the value capture/adverse selection of customers. As this example suggests, resources are not fully protected from value erosion unless they are protected from *all* kinds of capture. And it suggests that protection of resource value goes beyond keeping resources inimitable. In the example, the proper way to protect value is to segment the customer base.

This suggests that the EPR contains implications for value creation and appropriation, and therefore sustained competitive advantage, that add to the RBV and the KBV. In order to spell this out more clearly, it is useful first to examine value creation and appropriation in a setting where transaction costs are zero; that is, the setting underlying the Coase theorem (Coase 1960, 1988), and then add transaction costs and trace the implications for value creation and appropriation. Thus, essentially the same strategy that Coase (1937, 1960) followed is followed here. Examine an extreme setting (i.e. the Coase theorem setting) to see what this tells us about the phenomenon that we are interested in understanding (i.e. the firm (Coase 1937), the law (Coase 1960)—and strategic management (this chapter))—and then demonstrate that this understanding is furthered by the introduction of transaction costs.

A Coasian Benchmark

Value Creation and Appropriation when Transaction Costs Are Zero

A compact way of stating the Coase theorem is that in the absence of transaction costs all the value that can conceivably be created from the exchange and use in production of the available resources in the economy will, in fact, be created. An underlying assumption is that in such a surplus-maximizing equilibrium players have full information.[8] Therefore, there are no costs of bargaining and of measuring the attributes of resources, and property rights to (all attributes of) all resources are defined and protected at zero cost. Because the costs of exchanging property rights are zero, all property rights to all attributes will be tradable.[9]

All rights will therefore move to their highest valued uses, so that in this benchmark situation the total value that resources can create, and which therefore will be imputed to them, will be at its maximum.

Another way of stating that the costs of exchanging property rights are zero is that prices for all relevant resource uses (attributes), namely those that are realized in the surplus-maximizing equilibrium, emerge immediately from costless bargaining processes. As an example, consider a car park that is located adjacent to a supermarket. Since information and bargaining costs are zero, the owner will bargain with users of the car park so that all attributes will be priced. Relevant attributes may be the time and date and how close one can park to the supermarket entrance. Different prices for different attributes will probably emerge. Because prices are perfect signals of scarcities, all attributes will be perfectly rationed; that is, no queues emerge and reallocating the use rights to the parking spaces cannot increase created value. The division of the created value between the owner of the car park and each of the customers depends only on bargaining powers. Moreover, for any resource the bundle of attributes will be well defined and will be the one that maximizes resource value.

This reasoning suggests a further remarkable implication of the zero-transaction-cost assumption; namely, that the value created by the use of resources is always independent of the value that each individual resource appropriates, because in such a world resources will always get at least their opportunity costs, and resource investments will always be covered (Hart 1995). One may think of parties to transactions (i.e. resource owners) as first agreeing to maximize the value that can be created from their resources, and afterwards splitting this value through bargaining that defines each party's share of the created value (Milgrom and Roberts 1992). In other words, value creation is independent of value appropriation when transaction costs are zero.

However, while the zero-transaction-cost notion informs us that total resource value will be maximum for the coalitions chosen by maximizing players, it does not directly speak to the issue of value appropriation. Game-theoretic reasoning shows that there is an upper limit to what a player can appropriate; namely, no more than his contribution to overall value creation (Hart 1989). Making this more determinate requires that more assumptions be added; for example, that agents can join and leave 'coalitions' as they please, that there are 'many' agents, etc. Taking this to the extreme brings us to the competitive equilibrium model, where agents receive their marginal product value. In other settings it is usually not possible to say exactly how cooperating agents will split the value they create, in the absence of rather detailed knowledge about the size of the transfer payments that will normally be required to sustain an efficient outcome, bargaining powers, the structure of interaction, etc.[10] It may be split in any possible way within the bounds given by opportunity costs and reservation prices. However, the Coase theorem implies that bargaining processes are instantaneous, consume no resources, and that there is no feedback effect from the splitting of value to the creation of value.

The Coase Theorem and Strategic Choice

As Coase (1960) notes, rents may be earned when the supply of input resources is not perfectly elastic, independently of whether transaction costs exist or not. Because property rights are perfectly protected, these rents are sustainable. Thus, the rudiments of the resource-based view of sustainable competitive advantage (Barney 1991; Peteraf 1993) are consistent with the zero-transaction-cost assumption; firms may implement strategies based on resources that are valuable, rare, and (infinitely) costly to imitate and substitute, even if transaction costs are zero. However, maximum value would be created instantaneously in each time period, all rent streams would be perfectly protected, bargaining over the division of these streams would take place instantaneously and costlessly, there would be no problems of implementing a strategy (since organizational costs would be zero), etc. In sum, value creation and appropriation would pose no problems whatsoever.

Arguably, a significant part of the content of strategic management seems to lie in all these processes not being instantaneous, costless, and unproblematic. Extreme settings, such as the one underlying the Coase theorem or its cousin the competitive-equilibrium model, leave little room for strategic choices. To see this, observe that the Coase theorem implies that all possible uses of assets are fully known, all returns from all uses of all assets are perfectly known, all legitimate and illegitimate uses of assets are perfectly specified, and all this is perfectly enforceable (Barzel 1997). If all rights are completely defined in this way, by definition no conflicts can arise over the use of scarce resources or the returns from assets, because individuals do not have any discretion in the use of resources. Somewhat paradoxically, because there are no impediments to efficiency, there is also no genuine discretion, including no room for strategic choice.

In order to find a role for strategic choice, 'imperfections' have to be thrown into this perfect world, as has been argued. This has, of course, been known ever since strategy became established as an academic field, as various kinds of 'market failures' (e.g. Dundas and Richardson 1980; Porter 1980, 1981) have been invoked to make sense of strategic opportunities. However, such failures have seldom been explicitly related to transaction. Market failures arise as transaction costs are introduced into the perfect world of the Coase theorem.[11] One consequence is that the choice of, for example, organizational arrangements now matters, because—in contrast to the perfect world underlying the Coase theorem—different arrangements have different consequences in terms of created value. For example, contractual arrangements with suppliers, internal organization, quality systems, sorting of customers, etc. may all be sources of value creation, notably because organizational arrangements influence value appropriation (Milgrom and Roberts 1990*a*, 1992; Williamson 1996*a*; Barzel 1997).[12] There are, however, many other ways in which transaction costs influence value creation and appropriation. Some of these are discussed below.

Putting Transaction Costs into the Resource-based View

Like other economic approaches to strategy, the RBV is concerned with value creation and value appropriation. What needs to be given fuller attention in the RBV is the way in which these two processes interact. When transaction costs are zero, there is no such interaction. Accordingly, the RBV should embrace transaction costs. A manifestation of the interaction of value creation and value appropriation in a world of positive transaction costs is *dissipation* of value; that is, costly capture and protection. Dissipation results from players seeking to maximize the value that they can appropriate by means of engaging in costly capture and protection activities (Barzel 1997). This reduces created value. The presence of capture introduces a second feedback loop from value appropriation to value creation that is absent in the zero-transaction-cost world. Notably, the threat of hold-up, and imitation in relations may induce inefficient investments and thus reduce potential value creation (Hart 1995; Williamson 1996*a*; Kim and Mahoney 2002). The feedback loop from value appropriation to value creation suggests two ways of creating value that are absent in a zero-transaction-cost world. First, in a positive-transaction-costs world an important source of value creation stems from the reduction of dissipation. Second, a resource owner can devise means of protecting (in a low-cost manner) against capture attempts by other players and can thereby realize value from transactions that otherwise would not take place. This is exemplified below.

Creating Value through Reducing Dissipation: An Example

In a positive-transaction-costs world it will never be possible to realize the full potential of all resources with respect to value creation, because with scarce resources (so that competition over resource uses arise, Alchian 1965), *some* dissipation is unavoidable. Dissipation of value results from players' attempts to maximize the value that they can appropriate by means of engaging in costly capture-and-protection activities (Barzel 1997). Increasing protection of property rights in order to reduce capture reduces one kind of dissipation but increases another. Similarly, reducing protection in order to save on protection costs increases capture. This trade-off means that there is an optimal amount of dissipation (i.e. that amount which maximizes created value). An implication is that value creation requires that resource owners consider not only their own costs of protection, but also the costs to other players of engaging in capture

(Skaperdas 1994). Below, I exemplify how reducing dissipation increases created value. I then link the example to the RBV.

Consider a uniquely located (hence, inimitable) car park that is placed adjacent to and owned by a supermarket. Customers value a combined good; namely, the combination of what the supermarket offers and parking spaces. This will be reflected in both the demand the supermarket faces and the prices it can charge. The supermarket will earn a profit from being located next to the car park. The source of the profit is the positive externality in consumption. Thus, use rights to the parking spaces are unprotected in the sense that non-owners can use these attributes without directly compensating the owner, but it will still be rational for the owner to make available the car-park resource to non-owners when he can appropriate the value it produces through its complementarity to the supermarket.

Assume now that the supermarket's pricing decisions can be represented in terms of the monopoly diagram familiar from economics textbooks (see Fig. 5.1). D_1 is the demand curve for its goods that the supermarket would face in the absence of the car park. Created value is represented by the area IJHC. However, if the supermarket constructs a car park but does not police its use, D_2 is the combined demand curve for the goods offered by the supermarket *and* the free services of the car park. The price is lower in the absence of the car park (P_1), because consumers value having access to a car park. Total created value increases by BFHC to IJFB. The supermarket can capture EFHG (= BFHC) by charging the higher price (P_2). However, when the car park of a limited size is offered for

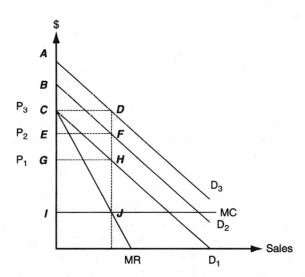

Figure 5.1. Pricing and value creation.

free, customers queue for the unpriced parking spaces. This results in dissipation of value in the form of waiting time. (In Fig. 5.1 it is assumed that not all value is dissipated in this way.) Dissipation can be reduced if the supermarket extends the car park or if it protects its property rights and charges patrons for parking. The demand curve will shift outwards, because customers no longer have to expend resources on queuing. Total created value increases by ADFB to IJDA. If the supermarket charges the equilibrium price that fully rations parking space (i.e. $P_3 - P_1$), and prices supermarket goods at P_1, it can capture the extra value CDFE that pricing the car park generates.[13] The cost of pricing the car park has to be subtracted from CDFE; in other words, as long as these costs are less than CDFE it will pay to price the parking services.

So far it has been assumed that the value of each parking space to customers is independent of location and time. However, it is much more realistic to assume that customers value a parking space adjacent to the entry of the super-market higher than other spaces and that they value parking at peak shopping hours higher than at other hours of the day. A single price will therefore not perfectly ration the use of high-valued parking spaces. If the supermarket can devise means of reducing the cost of pricing and enforcing property rights to these attributes, it will appropriate a greater part of the value that the resource can create. In the case of a car park this may require investments in developing sophisticated ticket systems and control systems. Incentives to invest in such transaction-costs-reducing technology stem from the ability to reduce dissipation and to capture a greater share of the value of attributes.

Pricing and Exchange as Sources of Value Creation

The above example runs counter to a recurrent theme in the RBV; namely, that strategically important resources are often *unpriced* (Dierickx and Cool 1989; Reed and DeFilippi 1990; Lippman and Rumelt 2003*a*: 1070, 2003*b*; Teece 2003). For example, it is often pointed out that strategically important resources are accumulated in-house, should also be deployed in-house, and are unpriced. However, the RBV is not entirely forthcoming about why resources are unpriced. Perhaps for this reason, it is not recognized that pricing may be a source of value creation.[14]

However EPR logic suggests two reasons why resource attributes are unpriced. First, attributes may be costly to define and measure in ways that are verifiable to the parties to a potential transaction. For example, defining and measuring the attributes of a firm-specific technological or organizational capability may be very costly. Second, it may be prohibitively costly to exclude non-owners from capturing property rights. For example, while firms may exclude non-owners (e.g. by means of secrecy and covenants not to compete) from firm know-how as long as the relevant know-how is deployed internally, firms cannot enforce their property rights through legal means if they seek to trade their know-how. When the costs of specifying the relevant attributes and protecting the property rights to those attributes exceed the benefits of trading the bundle of attributes the resource will not be priced.[15] This may lead to the conclusion that value creation is always sustained by *keeping* resources unpriced. However, the car-park example shows that pricing not only serves to divide the surplus created by the resource, but also serves to ration the use of the resource in such a way that dissipating competition over created value is avoided.

As a general matter, exchange is value-creating because it allows resources to move to better uses. Transaction costs represent one important reason why not all value-creating trade takes place. The transaction costs that inhibit trade are of various kinds and the measures that firms can take to reduce these transaction costs therefore differ. For example, costs caused by adverse selection and moral hazard may be reduced by the creation of brand name and reputations (Barzel 1982), and costs from opportunistic hold-up may be reduced by means of private orderings (Williamson 1996a). Trade increases as these costs are reduced. Perhaps because the reasons for such non-tradability (or 'non-transferability') are not clearly framed in the RBV, the opportunities for exchanging such resources have been neglected. To be sure, certain kinds of technological knowledge may be easily imitable, and this speaks in favour of in-house deployment. However, technological knowledge may also yield substantial returns if traded. This suggests that there is a trade-off between keeping resources in-house (which may contribute to making the resource costly to imitate: Reed and DeFilippi 1990), and trading it (which may contribute to value creation). However, firms may influence the trade-off in a manner favorable to themselves. For example, technology trading has emerged among firms in closely knit networks (Hippel 1988). The trading is supported by reciprocity norms and the ability to exclude free riders from the network. In-house deployment is substituted by within-network deployment.

In the EPR resources are perceived as bundles of property rights to attributes. In the zero-transaction-cost setting property rights to attributes can be traded separately; in actuality, transaction costs often inhibit such trade. However, value can be created if transaction costs can be reduced so that individual attributes can be employed in better alternative uses. For example, value can be created when use rights to production equipment or labor service that would otherwise be idle can be traded in rental arrangements. Trade can also create value when resources have attributes that are non-exclusive in use. Brand names used by several sales outlets at the same time are examples of this. Contractual innovations such as franchise contracts have allowed for substantial trade in such attributes. Lippman and Rumelt (2003b: 1082) note that the RBV predicts that firms will focus their energies on developing 'complex "homegrown" resources [...] Yet a glance at corporate reality reveals that much more effort is devoted to combinations, deals, mergers, acquisition, joint venture and the like'. They therefore suggest that more attention be devoted to such resource assembly. What is missing in their perspective, but supplied by the EPR, is the recognition that created value is constrained not only by knowledge about resource complementarities but also by the transaction costs that attend the exchange aspects of 'combinations, deals, mergers, acquisition, joint venture and the like'.

Sustained Competitive Advantage

The centerpiece of the RBV is the analysis of the conditions of sustained competitive advantage (cf. Ch. 3) (Barney 1991; Peteraf 1993). Below, the contribution of the EPR to this analysis is outlined, using Peteraf's identification (1993) of the 'cornerstones of competitive advantage' in terms of heterogeneity, barriers to *ex ante* and *ex post* competition, and immobility.

Heterogeneity. By stressing that resources are composed of property rights to attributes, the EPR contributes a further dimension to the RBV analysis of heterogeneity which stresses the inherent efficiencies of resources (Peteraf 1993) and resource complementarities (Dierickx and Cool 1989; Denrell, Fang, and Winter 2003). Property rights are typically bundled together in resources because of the costs of exchanging individual property rights, including the costs of protecting these rights. Thus, resources are *outcomes* of processes of economizing with such transaction costs, and vary in their efficiencies and potential for being combined in a complementary manner because they encompass different attributes. By implication, resource heterogeneity changes under the impact of innovations in sales practices, contracting practices, and other transaction-cost-reducing technologies.

Ex ante *competition.* The RBV stresses informational barriers to *ex ante* competition as a necessary condition of the existence of rents (Barney 1986). The EPR adds a different mechanism by which discrepancies between value and price may be established on strategic factor markets. In the EPR resource heterogeneity is caused by variation in the types and levels of valued attributes that resources embody. Such variation causes costly measurement (Barzel 1997). Costly measurement implies that (1) not all attributes are priced and (2) some actors may be able to capture value from unpriced attributes (Barzel 1982). Actors on strategic factor markets that have low costs of capture because of superior efficiencies in searching and/or in low opportunity costs of search will be able to purchase resources—that is, bundles of property rights over attributes, *including* the highly valued one—at prices below their value to the seller. This suggests that rent capture is connected to transaction costs, and that variation in the attributes of resources is a resource dimension that is important to understanding rent capture.

Ex post *competition.*   In the RBV *ex post* competition is mainly a matter of competitive imitation and of resource substitution. A condition of sustained competitive advantage is that there are barriers to imitation and substitution (Barney 1991). The EPR adds to this by pointing to *ex post* dissipation of value and to other kinds of capture than imitative competition and substitution. For example, moral hazard and adverse selection are instances of capture *and* cause *ex post* dissipation of value as victims of capture seek to protect themselves. The EPR also expands the avenue of research pursued in the RBV with respect to identifying characteristics of resources that may contribute to sustained competitive advantage. For example, causal ambiguity is often seen as a characteristic that supports sustainability (Lippman and Rumelt 1982). However, from an EPR perspective causal ambiguity may make it costly to write contracts and enforce performance norms. Causal ambiguity may therefore reduce value creation and appropriation. The general lesson from the EPR is that barriers to *ex post* capture as well as dissipation are a necessary condition for the sustainability of competitive advantage.

Immobility.   While the RBV suggest that from the firm's point of view resource immobility is preferable, transaction costs may imply that immobility leads to underinvestment. Granting resources outside options, such as giving patent rights to research scientists, may increase their bargaining power (make them more 'mobile') *and* improve their investment incentives (Hart 1995). This points to a trade-off in certain situations between immobility and value creation, and therefore refines the analysis of immobility as a condition of sustained competitive advantage.

Conclusion

The aim of this chapter has been to sketch in more precisely one specific route through which the integrationism that was endorsed in Chapter 2 could be developed. Specifically, the argument has been that the economics of property rights—a theoretical input into organizational economics—may complement and further the RBV (and therefore also the KBV where this overlaps with the RBV) by refining the notion of resource, adding insight into resource value, and suggesting new, transaction cost-based sources of value creation.

An implication of the discussion is that the contribution to competitive advantage of a resource depends not only on its use and its scarcity and the amount of capture in the form of competitive imitation and substitution (Barney 1991), but also on the costs of controlling capture in the form of, for example, moral hazard, adverse selection, and hold-up. Estimating the sustainability of competitive advantages must involve taking such costs into account. Another implication is that resources are not given, but are outcomes of processes of economizing with transaction costs. Therefore, what are physically the same resources may to different firms be economically different resources; for example because the relevant firms are not equally capable of protecting the relevant attributes. Finally, the discussion directs attention to those resources that may be advantages to firms by increasing created (and appropriated) value by means of reducing transaction costs; for example, specific ways of sorting goods (e.g. in the retailing industry and industries such as fruit and vegetables) or customers (e.g. credit classes in banking), contracting, the use of private orderings, etc. (Williamson 1996*a*; Barzel 1997). The conjecture here is that these resources are important sources of heterogeneity and competitive advantages in a number of industries. However, they have been largely neglected in the RBV. One may speculate that this is because these resources are only visible if a positive-transaction-cost world is assumed, and the RBV has not yet explicitly endorsed transaction-cost perspectives.

The RBV has proved to be an influential and useful analytical structure for the analysis of many strategic issues. However, it is also like a ten-to-fifteen-year old building built by a few key contractors on a tight completion deadline and on the basis of somewhat different inputs (Foss and Knudsen 2003). Some of the limitations are beginning to show up. First, as argued in Chapter 3, the RBV building was constructed on a foundation—the competitive-equilibrium model—that makes it hard to extend the building. Second, some essential materials—namely transaction costs—were not used to a sufficient degree. A number of deficiencies have resulted. Accordingly, the repair attempt should be a fundamental one, and will have to be directed at building a better foundation and adding the essential material of transaction costs. The first kind of repair attempt has been initiated by Lippman and Rumelt (2003*a/b*); the second one is that sketched out in this chapter. However, much more work is required to flesh out a satisfactory synthesis between resource-based and transaction cost ideas.

Among the important problems that must be addressed in such an undertaking are these. While notions of transaction costs and property rights may illuminate the notion of resource heterogeneity (and therefore firm heterogeneity), do they go far enough? Or do these arguments merely set the problem at a higher level, so that the question becomes: Why are firms different in recognizing and managing property rights and transaction costs? Admittedly, TCE, including the EPR, has devoted little effort to developing insights into issues such as tacitness of knowledge, social complexity, path-dependence, and the like and how these explain firm heterogeneity. Thus, the RBV and the KBV contain a number of ideas that are not present in TCE. Also, TCE directs primary attention to reducing inefficiencies associated with exchange as an important source of value creation. Evidently, there are numerous sources of value creation that do not fall within this perspective. For example, in many cases creating value through product and process innovations does not. Thus, TCE is not an all-encompassing strategic perspective. No perspective is. However, it directs attention to phenomena that, although important, have hitherto been comparatively neglected in strategic-management research.

Notes

1. I leave out the claim that asset specificity is a necessary condition for isolating mechanisms.
2. Similar practices can be observed in many industries, such as pre-packaging of fruit and vegetables in grocery stores or block booking in the movie industry; arguments about their existence similar to the explanation of the DeBeers sales practice can be advanced (Barzel 1982, 1997; Kenney and Klein 1983).
3. This section draws on Foss and Foss (2004).
4. Note that I here primarily rely on the Alchian-Barzel-Cheung-Coase-Demsetz brand of property-rights economics, rather than on the formal approach associated with Hart. For a comparison of the two property-rights approaches see Foss and Foss (2002).
5. Of course, it could be argued that the notion of resource is sufficiently flexible also to include the individual property right.
6. This adds a property-rights dimension to Penrose's distinction (1959) between resources and the services they yield. The services that a firm can derive from its resources (i.e. the fungibility of the resources) are not just constrained by path dependencies, the functionalities of the resources, and managerial imagination (Penrose 1959), but also by property rights.
7. Note that there is also a dimension of capture to competition, to the extent that competitive activities aim at capturing value without compensating the current holder. This is perhaps most conspicuous in the case of resource imitation, reverse engineering, and the like; however, competition in terms of investing in bargaining power, quality improvements, and technology may also be analyzed in terms of capture, because such activities reduce the value that a resource can appropriate without compensating the resource owner (Barzel 1994; Foss 2003a).
8. A strong version of the Coase theorem (as in Coase 1988 and Barzel 1997) is adopted here. Readers who recall the critique in Chapter 3 of founding strategy research on the competitive equilibrium model may wonder why the Coase theorem is any less constraining. However, there are some subtle, yet important, differences between the Coase theorem setting and the standard competitive-equilibrium model that are of relevance to their utility as benchmarks in strategy research. Thus, the Coase-theorem setting directs attention to individual agents bargaining with each other, rather than interacting anonymously through a price system as in the competitive-equilibrium model. And the Coase-theorem setting does not make any assumptions with respect to market structure (see also Makowski and Ostroy 2001).
9. For this reason, the very notion of a 'resource', strictly speaking, dissolves in this extreme world. Exchanges will only involve attributes.

10. Economists have come up with a number of more or less plausible concepts to resolve to bargaining problems. See Muthoo (1999) and Lippman and Rumelt (2003a) for an application to strategy.

11. Relating market failures to fundamental strategic issues takes the form of arguments such as 'asymmetric information is a necessary condition for internal capital markets to be superior to external capital markets'; 'the public goods nature of knowledge may make it more efficient to exploit excess knowledge through diversification rather than contracting'; 'because of asymmetric information, knowledge transfer may more efficiently take place inside firms than across firms'; etc. These are the arguments underlying the Alchian-Williamson argument in favor of internal capital markets (Williamson 1975), the economies of scope-cum-transaction-costs story of diversification (Teece 1982), and the theory of the multinational enterprise (Teece 1986) respectively; that is, theories that have been highly influential in the evolution of strategic management.

12. Williamson (1994) thinks that these choices are so fundamental that 'economizing is the best strategy'. Presumably this is because governance and contractual choices are ubiquitous, must be made by all firms, and can have an important impact on performance, whereas strategizing, which appeals to a market-power perspective, is only open to major players.

13. Here I have assumed that extending the car park is more costly than pricing parking services. In the example, although customers are never worse off, the monopolist supermarket captures all created value from the car park and from pricing parking spaces. In other words, customers have no bargaining power. Also, we have assumed that customers have similar queuing costs and valuations of parking spaces. Relaxing the assumptions does not compromise the overall conclusion.

14. Only Lippman and Rumelt (2003b: 1085) note that 'intuition suggests that a resource bundle will be more valuable if it can be accurately priced'.

15. Resources may also be unpriced because they are extremely firm-specific (Lippman and Rumelt 1982). Such resources are necessarily best used in-house, and the fact that there are no prices on such resources is not a sign of a potential for value creation. However, it may be doubted that such resources are common.

Part II

Organization: Critical Perspectives

6

Economic Organization in the Knowledge Economy

Introduction

During the last decade management academics have firmly stressed the role of organizational factors in the process of building knowledge-based strategies that will bring sustained competitive advantage (Nonaka and Takeuchi 1995; Grant 1996; Myers 1996; Brown and Eisenhardt 1998; Day and Wendler 1998).[1] Arguably, this emphasis is also reflected in managerial practice. Thus, firms are said to adopt 'network organization' (Miles and Snow 1992) and engage in 'corporate disaggregation' (Zenger and Hesterly 1997), so as to become 'information age organizations' (Mendelsson and Pillai 1999) that can build the 'dynamic capabilities' required for competing in the knowledge economy. These changes with respect to the organization of economic activities take place in tandem with changes in the composition of inputs toward knowledge inputs, an increase of the 'knowledge-content' in outputs, a stepping up of innovative activity, an increasing differentiation of demand, increasing globalization, and increasingly inexpensive networked computing—changes that are taken to indicate the emergence of the 'knowledge economy' (cf. Ch. 1 and Halal and Taylor 1998; Prusac 1998; Tapscott 1999; Munro 2000).

This chapter attempts to address economic organization in the context of the emerging knowledge economy. Thus, it asks what are the implications for our understanding of issues relating to the scope and organization of alternative governance structures of some of the key tendencies that we may take as characterizing the knowledge economy. As discussed in Chapter 1, these include such tendencies as that many industries become increasingly 'knowledge-intensive', an increasing share of the workforce is constituted by 'knowledge workers', commercially useful knowledge becomes increasingly distributed and needs to be accessed from several sources, many lying outside the boundaries of firms, etc.

Admittedly, significant analytical complexity is involved here. Moreover, any discussion of economic organization in the context of the emerging knowledge economy is unavoidably somewhat harmed by the lack of robust and clear definitions of, as well as a solid empirical knowledge base about, the 'knowledge economy'. However, understanding economic organization in the context of the emerging knowledge economy is an important challenge—for three reasons.

First, it arguably concerns important real tendencies and phenomena with respect to economic organization—which so far have only received sporadic attention from economists of organization.[2] Second, it goes right to the heart of the crucial and perennial issues in the theory of economic organization, challenging us to rethink issues such as: What are the limits to resource allocation by means of authority? What do we mean by authority? What defines the boundaries of firms? How do we distinguish an independent contractor from an employee? These 'classic' questions are pertinent ones, because it is an underlying theme in much recent work on economic organization in the knowledge economy that authority relations, the boundaries of firms, and the way in which mechanisms for coordinating economic activities are designed and combined will undergo significant change under the impact of knowledge that is complex, controlled by specialists, and distributed. Third, and closely related to the previous point, some writers on the knowledge economy (e.g. Boisot 1998; Helper, MacDuffie, and Sabel 2000) argue that existing approaches to the economics of organization, such as transaction cost economics, are not capable of providing an adequate explanation of economic organization in the knowledge economy. To illustrate:

firms are increasingly engaging in collaborations with their suppliers, even as they are reducing the extent to which they are vertically integrated with those suppliers. This fact seems incompatible with traditional theories of the firm which argue that integration is necessary to avoid the potentials for hold-ups created when non-contractible investments are made (Helper, MacDuffie, and Sabel 2000: 443)

The following arguments and positions are developed in this chapter. Admittedly, it is a justified complaint that post-Coasian organizational economics so far has not comprehensively addressed economic organization in the context of the knowledge economy. However, the insights developed in this body of thought are actually quite useful for framing the issues. Moreover, they help to temper—by making clear the limits of—more extreme claims about organization in the knowledge economy. Among such claims are that authority relations will strongly diminish in importance or at least change significantly in character (Zucker 1991); that ownership-based and legal definitions of the boundaries of firms will become increasingly irrelevant for understanding the organization of economic activities (Helper, MacDuffie, and Sabel 2000); and that constraints on the space of feasible combinations of coordination mechanisms will be very significantly relaxed (Miles et al. 1991). Below, such claims are all addressed and framed in the context of organizational economics, so as to examine their reach.

However, this does not mean that organizational economics can survive in a completely unchanged form confrontation with the knowledge economy. On the contrary, much work needs to be done with respect to understanding the importance of knowledge assets (cf. also Holmström and Roberts 1998), distributed knowledge (Foss 1999*a*), and environmental complexity (Athey et al. 1994) for organizational design.[3] Still, many of the basic insights and ideas survive and are very useful for the understanding of economic organization in a knowledge economy, including new organizational forms. Thus, the basic aim of this chapter is not theory building per se. It is rather to engage in a dialog with those management academics who have written on organization in the emerging knowledge economy, and in this context to examine the reach of organizational economics with respect to framing organizational issues characteristic of the knowledge economy.

Economic Organization in the Knowledge Economy: Framing Recent Debate

In this section some recent claims about how the advent of the knowledge economy will change economic organization are reviewed. In order to focus the discussion, six 'interpretive propositions' are identified. These are intended to summarize influential recent ideas on (1) the changing role of knowledge in production, (2) economic organization in the knowledge economy, and (3) how (1) and (2) are connected.

Some Recent Claims about Economic Organization in a Knowledge Economy

Many disciplines, fields, and sub-fields are involved in the ongoing discussion of efficient organization in the context of the emerging knowledge economy. Nevertheless, a number of distinct themes are discernible in much of the debate. Overall, a consensus seems to be emerging that tasks and activities in the knowledge economy need to be coordinated in a manner that is very different from the management of traditional manufacturing activities, with profound transforming implications for the authority relation and the internal organization and boundaries of firms. There are several reasons for this.

Because of the increasing importance in knowledge-intensive industries of combining knowledge inputs, sourcing knowledge for this purpose, and keeping sourcing options open, knowledge-based networks (Harryson 2000) increasingly become the relevant dimension for understanding the organization of economic activities. Such networks typically cut across the legal boundaries of the firm; for example, in the sense that inter-firm communication channels may have much greater bandwidth than intra-firm channels or that coordination requirements are more severe between firms than within firms.[4] Networks are particularly useful organizational arrangements for sourcing and transferring knowledge because of the costs of pricing knowledge (in a market) or transferring it (in a hierarchy) (Powell 1990: 304; Liebeskind et al. 1995: 7). The increased reliance on knowledge networks tends to erode authority-based definitions of the boundaries of the firm, because authority increasingly shifts to expert individuals who control crucial information resources and may not be employees of the firm. As Zucker (1991: 164) argues:

> While bureaucratic authority is by definition located within the firm's boundaries, expert authority depends on the information resources available to an individual, and not on the authority of office. Thus, authority may be located within the organization [...] but when an external authority market can provide information that leads to greater effectiveness, then authority tends to migrate into the market.

To the extent that important knowledge assets are increasingly controlled by employees ('knowledge workers') themselves, traditional authority relations are fading into insignificance. This is partly a result of increased bargaining power on the part of knowledge workers (stemming from the control over critical knowledge assets) (Coff 1999), and partly a result of the increasingly specialist nature of knowledge work (Hodgson 1998). The specialist nature of knowledge work implies that principals/employers become ignorant about (some of) the actions that are open to specialist agents/employees, thus making the exercise of authority through direction increasingly inefficient. The combined effect of the increased importance of knowledge assets that are controlled by knowledge workers themselves and the increasingly specialist nature of knowledge work is to wreck the traditional economist's criterion of what distinguishes market transactions from hierarchical transactions (Zingales 2000). Thus, direction by means of order giving (Coase 1937; Simon 1951; Williamson 1985; Demsetz 1991) and backed up by the ownership of alienable assets (Hart and Moore 1990) is increasingly irrelevant for understanding the organization of economic activities in a knowledge economy (Grandori 2000).

Not only does the emerging knowledge economy profoundly change the authority relation, and the boundaries of firms, it also influences the design of firms' internal organization; that is, their allocation of decision rights. As Miles et al. (1997: 7) argue:

> Each major era in business history has featured a particular form of organization. Early hierarchical, vertically integrated organizations have largely given way to network organizations that link the assets and know-how of numerous upstream and downstream industry partners. A number of leading companies today are experimenting with a new way of organizing—the cellular form. Cellular organizations are built on the principles of entrepreneurship, self-organization, and member ownership. In the future, cellular organizations will be used in situations requiring continuous learning and innovation.

By suggesting that radical internal hybrids, 'built on the principles of entrepreneurship, self-organization, and member ownership', are emerging as stable organizational modes, this quotation (and others like it) suggests that mechanisms for coordinating economic activities are more malleable, and that the set of stable discrete governance structures is larger than is conventionally assumed in much organization theory and in the economics of organization (e.g. Coase 1937; Williamson 1996*a*).[5] These new governance structures are increasingly often referred to as 'new organizational forms' (Daft and Lewin 1993; Zenger and Hesterly 1997). To the extent that new organizational forms represent new ways of combining mechanisms that have traditionally been seen as characteristic of governance structures that are polar opposites, they also exemplify the fading boundaries between markets and firms (Helper, MacDuffie, and Sabel 2000).

What is Going on Here? Six Interpretative Propositions

In order meaningfully to discuss economic organization in a knowledge economy there is a need for some conceptual clarification and some focusing of the issues. Most fundamentally, it is necessary to define the aspects of the knowledge economy that are most obviously relevant for an understanding of economic organization. Existing treatments emphasize such dimensions as increased knowledge content of outputs and the composition of inputs, hyper-competition and therefore the paramount importance of learning, decreasing corporate size, the importance of IT innovations, increasing differentiation of demand, increased general-environmental complexity, increasing importance of networks for the transfer and production of knowledge, etc. (e.g. D'Aveni 1994; Nonaka and Takeuchi 1995; Grant 1996; Miles et al. 1997; Boisot 1998; Matusik and Hill 1998; Leadbetter 1999; Coombs and Metcalfe 2000; Zingales 2000).

Needless to say, dealing with all of this as it impacts on economic organization is a task of forbidding complexity. A narrowing of the issues is required. In order to do so, I submit that *for the purposes of understanding economic organization*, recent claims about the impact of the knowledge economy on organization may usefully be narrowed down to two basic propositions about knowledge in production and four basic propositions about economic organization.[6] The first two assertions both turn on the increased importance of specialist knowledge:

Proposition 1: Because of the increased need for diverse, specialized knowledge in production, commercially relevant knowledge is becoming increasingly distributed in the Hayekian sense (e.g. Hayek 1945; Coombs and Metcalfe 2000).[7]

Proposition 2: Because of the increased importance of sourcing specialist knowledge, knowledge assets controlled by individual agents ('knowledge workers') are becoming increasingly important in production (e.g. Boisot 1998).

For convenience, settings in which Propositions 1 and 2 hold true are characterized as '*Hayekian*'. Further narrowing of the issues is produced by the three following (related) propositions about economic organization in a knowledge economy—all of which may be found in recent writings:

Proposition 3: In the emerging knowledge economy, authority relations will become increasingly inefficient and insignificant means of allocating resources (e.g. Semler, 1989; Hodgson 1998).

Proposition 4: The boundaries of firms blur because of the increasing importance of knowledge networks that transcend those boundaries. Thus, while legal and ownership-based definitions of the boundaries of the firm may formally be made, they will be increasingly irrelevant from an economic (and strategic) perspective (e.g. Zucker 1991; Helper, MacDuffie, and Sabel 2000).

Proposition 5: Coordination mechanisms will be combined in new, innovative ways, suggesting that these mechanisms are inherently combinable and not limited to being necessarily clustered in specific discrete governance structures (e.g. Grandori 1997; Helper, MacDuffie, and Sabel 2000).[8]

Although these propositions are rather open-ended, they are susceptable of theoretical treatment (and in principle of empirical test as well). Moreover, so is the final proposition:

Proposition 6: The effects described in Propositions 3–5 are driven by changes in the way in which knowledge enters into the productive process, as described in Propositions 1–2.

The strategy that I follow in the ensuing pages is that of critically discussing Proposition 3–6, taking Propositions 1 and 2 as *given* (i.e. accepted). In other words, I discuss the typically Coasian themes of authority, the boundaries of the firm, and the combinability of coordination mechanisms in the context of the typically Hayekian setting in which knowledge is distributed and subjectively held. The strategy is to discuss the role (if any) of authority in Hayekian settings, examine the connections between authority and ownership, and finally discuss how authority and ownership constrain the malleability and combinability of coordination mechanisms. Thus, as will become clear, the themes of authority, ownership, and the malleability of coordination mechanisms are connected. These themes are addressed seriatim below.

Authority in the Economics of Organization

The following is a discussion of the notion of authority as it appears in a few, crucial organizational-economics contributions. The reason for focusing on what economists of organization have said about authority is that these scholars offer clear and stark interpretations of authority and that this chapter is based on organizational economics. This is not to deny that much insight may be gained from the more encompassing classic discussions of Barnard (1938), Weber (1947), etc., and that economists of organization should pay more attention to these (cf. Aghion and Tirole 1997). However, at this stage a narrower and more focused approach is appropriate, particularly as the above propositions primarily relate to the relatively narrow notions of authority typically found in the works of organizational economists.

Coase and Simon

It is conventional to date the birth of organizational economics to Ronald Coase's 1937 paper 'The Nature of the Firm'. This is justified by Coase's stress on market failure caused by transaction costs as the starting point for any explanation of firms, and by his contractual approach, comparative institutionalism, and clear identification of the main explanatory requirements of a theory of the firm (i.e. explaining the existence, boundaries, and internal organization of firms).[9] Coase also founded the widespread practice of identifying the firm with the employment contract; indeed, he puts much emphasis on the flexibility afforded by incomplete employment contracts and the authority relation as the ultimate reason for the existence of firms.[10] Thus, as Langlois and Foss (1999) have argued, Coase's explanation for the emergence of the firm is ultimately a coordination one: The firm is an institution that lowers the costs of qualitative coordination in a world of uncertainty.[11] The employment contract is explained in related terms, as 'one whereby the factor, for a certain remuneration (which may be fixed or fluctuating) agrees to obey the directions of an entrepreneur *within certain limits*. The essence of the contract is that it should only state the limits to the powers of the entrepreneur. Within these limits, he can therefore direct the other factors of production' (ibid. 242).[12]

A later paper, by Herbert Simon (1951), provides a formalization of Coase's notion of the employment relationship and a clarification of the notion of authority. The latter is defined as obtaining when a 'boss' is permitted by a 'worker' to select actions $A^0 \subset A$, where A is the set of the worker's possible behaviors. More or less authority is then simply defined as making the set A^0 larger or smaller. The model is basically a multi-stages game in the context of an incomplete contract with *ex post* governance. In the first period the prospective worker decides whether to accept employment or not. Then nature intervenes, uncertainty is resolved, and the costs and benefits associated with the various possible tasks are revealed. To the extent that the boss cares about his reputation, he will not direct the worker to undertake tasks that lie outside the latter's 'zone of acceptance', and there may thus be an equilibrium in the three-stages game.[13]

To sum up, in the Coase/Simon view of authority the action space is well-defined and known both to the 'boss' and the 'worker', the boss observes those states of nature to which it is necessary to react (e.g. a realization of demand on the firm's product markets), he possesses the right to direct the worker, and the worker obeys the boss's instructions 'within limits'.

The Puzzling Notion of Authority

The Coase/Simon view of authority raises several questions. In the present context four such questions are particularly relevant:

1. What is ultimately the source of the employer's authority? In other words, why exactly is it that the employee accepts being directed? These are pertinent questions, given that slavery is prohibited (i.e. human assets are inalienable).

2. What happens to the Coase/Simon view if the employer does not possess full knowledge of the employee's action set (i.e. the actions that he can take when uncertainty is resolved), so that the employee can take actions about which the employer has no knowledge (in other words, the employer suffers from 'sheer ignorance' in the sense of Kirzner 1997)?

3. What happens to the Coase/Simon view of authority if the employee is better informed than the employer with respect to how certain tasks should (optimally) be carried out? In the Coase/Simon view there is an implicit assumption that the employer is at least as well informed, and presumably better, about the efficiency implications of alternative actions.[14]

4. What happens to the Coase/Simon view if employees control knowledge assets that they cannot, or will not, alienate (sell, transfer), and which may give them substantial bargaining power, so that they cannot automatically be depended on to obey instructions?

The last three questions relate to the issue of the limits of authority in Hayekian settings, while the first question asks about the sources of the employer's bargaining power over the employee.[15] Only the first question has been given extensive treatment in the economics of organization. In fact, it has been one of the classic points of contention in a long-standing debate in economics initiated by Alchian and Demsetz (1972). They argue that it is not meaningful to assume that an employer can force an employee to do what the employer wants in the absence of coercion.[16] An implication of this view is that the distinction between the authority-based and the price-based modes of allocation emphasized by Coase (1937) is superficial. One may perhaps talk about a nexus of contracts being more 'firm-like' when continuity of association among input owners increases and/or residual claimancy becomes more concentrated, but it is not in general useful to talk about 'firms' as distinctive entities. In reality, they argue, there is no economic difference between 'firing' one's grocer and firing one's secretary.[17]

Authority and Ownership

One response to the nexus-of-contracts view is that there are in fact fundamental economic differences between firms and markets, because the law makes an

explicit distinction between market transactions and employment transactions—
a distinction that makes the incentives faced by the parties to the relevant
transactions differ (Masten 1991), and provides an economic role for authority
(Vandenberghe and Siegers 2000). However, the work of Oliver Hart and others
(Grossman and Hart 1986; Hart and Moore 1990; Hart 1995, 1996)—called
the incomplete contracts literature—provides an approach to the understanding
of authority that is not dependent on legal considerations of this kind. In
one important respect this approach differs from all earlier treatments of authority. Whereas Weber, Coase, Barnard, Simon, etc. focus on direct authority over
(non-alienable) human assets, the incomplete-contracts literature, rather, explains authority over human assets as something that is *indirectly* acquired
through authority (ownership) over alienable assets. Since reference will be
made to this kind of reasoning later, it is worth examining it briefly.

Contributors to the incomplete-contracts literature distinguish two basic
types of decision rights ('property rights'): residual rights and specific rights.
The former are generic rights to make decisions in circumstances not spelled out
in the contract, and imply the ability to exclude other agents from deciding on
the use of certain assets. Residual control rights are conferred by legal ownership.[18] In contrast, specific rights are allocated through contract terms. If
contracts were complete, all rights would be specific, and there would be no
residual rights. Two kinds of assets are distinguished; namely, alienable (i.e. non-
human) and non-alienable (i.e. human) assets. Given this, the distinction between an independent contractor and an employee (i.e. between an inter-firm
and an intra-firm transaction) now turns on who owns the non-alienable assets
that an agent (whether independent or employee) utilizes in his work. An
independent contractor owns his tools etc., while an employee does not. The
importance of asset ownership derives from the fact that the willingness of an
agent to undertake a *non-contractible* investment (say, exertion of effort or
investment in human capital) which is specific to the asset depends on who
owns the asset.

As in Alchian and Demsetz (1972) the parties to a relation—whether customer and grocer, or employer and employee—are seen as being in a bargaining
situation, each having an outside option. Although the parties in the specific
models that are analyzed always reach an efficient agreement, the division of the
surplus from the relation will nevertheless depend on who owns the alienable
assets in the relation, since the pattern of ownership will influence the parties'
outside options. For example, if the employer owns all the alienable assets, the
employee can still quit if he dislikes the employer's orders (as in Alchian and
Demsetz 1972), but he cannot take the assets with him, and the employer can
ensure that if the employee leaves, somebody else can take over the job. Thus, as
Hart (1996: 379) explains, 'an employer's authority is represented not by the
ability to force an employee to do what s/he wants, but rather by the ability to

obtain a substantial share of the *ex post* surplus from the relationship through the control of non-human assets'. Efficiency considerations then suggest that authority (i.e. ownership of the alienable assets) should be allocated to the agent who makes the most important (non-contractible) relation-specific investment. Thus, in an elegant manner, Hart (and his colleagues) link together the issues of the boundaries of the firm (which are defined in terms of ownership of alienable assets) and authority.[19] However, this only provides an answer to the first of the four puzzles above. The remaining three are discussed in the next section.

The Knowledge Economy as a Challenge to Authority: Distributed Knowledge

So far, the debate in organizational economics has almost exclusively centered on the problem of providing explanations of what it is that makes the employer able to direct the employee and whether this differs fundamentally from market exchange. In contrast, the knowledge-related questions, made increasingly relevant by the emergence of the knowledge economy, have not been given much attention. The problem of what happens to the Coase/Simon notion of authority when agents are better informed than principals about how certain tasks should be carried out, the principal is ignorant about certain actions that the agent may take, or agents have considerable bargaining power because of their control over knowledge assets, is not necessarily one of 'asymmetric information', as this is understood in information economics. In a typical asymmetric-information problem an uninformed agent knows what he is uninformed about (e.g. the precise quality of a car). However, this excludes ignorance and how ignorance may be overcome through processes of discovery (Kirzner 1997; Foss 1999a). A possible interpretation of the claim that authority relations will be transformed, and perhaps vanish, in the emerging knowledge economy is that these relations will break down under the impact of principals becoming increasingly uninformed about the actions open to agents and *at the same time* becoming increasingly reliant on the knowledge controlled by agents. These are the characteristics of Hayekian settings.

Hayekian Origins of 'Distributed Knowledge'

Examining the relation between economic organization and distributed knowledge brings us into distinctly Austrian territory. Thus, it is no coincidence that so many of those who write on economic organization in the emerging knowledge economy approvingly cite Hayek's work (e.g. Ghoshal, Moran, and Almeida 1995; Nonaka and Takeuchi 1995; Grant 1996; Cowen and Parker 1997). The first systematic argument that distributed knowledge represents a challenge to central planning and direction was in fact developed by Hayek (1935, 1937, 1945) in the context of the inter-war debate on the economic efficiency of socialism (see Lavoie 1985). In these early works Hayek does not directly criticize the use of authority as a mechanism of coordination; rather, his critical target is the notion that benevolent planners can draft complete contingent plans for the allocation of resources at a societal level, based on all relevant knowledge being concentrated in the hands of a central planner. Still, it is easy to see that Hayek's argument represents a challenge to authority in the sense of Simon and Coase. Consider his famous characterization of the economic problem (1945: 77–8):

The economic problem of society is [. . .] not merely a problem of how to allocate 'given' resources—if 'given' is taken to mean given to a single mind which deliberately solves the problem set by these 'data'. It is rather a problem of how to secure the best use of resources known to any of the members of society, for ends whose relative importance only these individuals know. Or, to put it briefly, it is a problem of the utilization of knowledge which is not given to anyone in its totality.

As the dating of the Hayek paper suggests, the problem of making optimal use of distributed (or 'dispersed') knowledge is, of course, not a novel one, only brought about by the emergence of the knowledge economy; rather, *any* complex social system confronts it (Hayek 1964). As Hayek later observes, it is only in the 'most simple kind of organization [that] it is conceivable that all the details of all activities are governed by a single mind' (Hayek 1973: 49).

Along these lines, what proponents of the position that economic organization is undergoing a radical transformation as a result of the emergence of the knowledge economy implicitly assert is that problems posed by Hayekian distributed knowledge have become increasingly pressing for firms (cf. Cowen and Parker 1997). Thus, because of the increased importance of specialist workers, the increased knowledge-intensity of production, and the increasing need to combine knowledge from multiple, diverse sources (Coombs and Metcalfe 2000), coping with the issue raised by Hayekian distributed knowledge has moved from being a problem for socialist planners to also being a problem confronted by managers of firms in capitalist economies. However, before the nature of this argument can be assessed, a more accurate characterization of distributed knowledge is required.

Distributed Knowledge

During the last decade the notion of distributed knowledge has been used with increasing frequency as an apt description of the knowledge conditions in which modern firms, the argument goes, increasingly find themselves.[20] Thus, in the strategy field Tsoukas (1996) conceptualized the firm as a distributed knowledge system, and Granstrand, Patel, and Pavitt (1997) documented the increasing extent to which the knowledge bases controlled by major technology-intensive corporations are distributed. Lessard and Zaheer (1996) discussed the implications of distributed knowledge for decision-making, Hutchins (1995) and Gherardi (1999) discussed its implications for organizational learning, while Cohen and Regan (1996) applied the notion to technology management, Foss (1999*a*) discussed its implications for the modern economics of organization, and Larsen (2001) applied it to knowledge-intensive service firms.

Apparently, the notion rings a bell in a number of diverse contexts. But what does it mean to say that knowledge is distributed? Unfortunately, the above contributions are not entirely forthcoming with respect to precise definitions of this concept. The same critique may actually be directed against the Austrian literature. While suggestive, the famous passages from Hayek (1945) hardly qualify as definitions of the notion of distributed knowledge. Moreover, it is not clear whether Austrian dispersed knowledge is identical to distributed knowledge. Below, I attempt to go somewhat further in the direction of definition.

Distributed knowledge is a member of a set of concepts that relate to the different ways in which knowledge may 'belong' to a group of agents. Two other examples of this kind of concept are the game-theory notions of 'common knowledge' and 'shared knowledge'. An event is common knowledge among a group of players if each player knows it, each one knows that the other players know it, each player knows that other players know that the other players know it, and so on (Aumann 1976).[21] Shared knowledge differs from common knowledge by not requiring that each agent knows that the other agents know, etc. Thus, there is shared knowledge of a fact if each agent knows this fact, but does not know that the other agents know it.

If common knowledge lies at one end of the spectrum, distributed knowledge lies at the other end. Loosely, knowledge is distributed when a set of agents knows something no single agent (completely) knows. Thus, the notions that firms (Tsoukas 1996) or whole economies (Hayek 1945, 1973) are distributed knowledge systems mean that the set of agents comprising these entities collectively possesses knowledge that no single agent possesses. In this sense, distributed knowledge has the same characteristics as dispersed 'knowledge in society' as discussed by Hayek (1945). Note that this does not amount to asserting the existence of mysterious supra-individual 'collective minds'. Knowledge still ultimately resides in the heads of individuals; however, when this knowledge is combined and 'aggregated' in certain ways it means that, considered as a system, a set of agents possesses knowledge that they do not possess if separated. On the basis of epistemic logic (Hintikka 1962) distributed knowledge may be defined as follows:

Definition—Distributed Knowledge: *If $K_i p_i$ means that agent i knows proposition i, a set of n agents has distributed knowledge of a proposition q (i.e. Dq) when: $K_1 p_1 \wedge K_2 p_2 \wedge \ldots \wedge K_n p_n \Rightarrow Dq$, $q \neq p_i$, $\forall i$.*[22]

For example, Jack knows that p is the case and Jill knows that p implies y, but neither know that y is the case. However, if Jack and Jill's information states are 'added' there is a sense, which is more than metaphorical, in which they may know that y is the case (Gerbrandy 1998: 53). The information that y is the case is present in the system comprising Jack and Jill, but in a distributed form.

The above definition is open to some interpretation. At one extreme, Jack and Jill may both be completely ignorant about the knowledge controlled by the other party. Sometimes such an interpretation consists of the 'competitive-equilibrium' model in economics: Although knowledge of technologies and preferences is private, all this knowledge is utilized in the best possible way, so that the knowledge of how to bring about an allocation of resources with superior welfare properties is distributed in the economy. At the other extreme there is considerable, but not complete,[23] knowledge overlap (p_i may be close in some sense to p_j), but it is still the case that no single agent knows q. Between the extremes are different degrees of overlap between individual knowledge elements.

Changing Distributed Knowledge

Many writers argue that distributed-knowledge conditions have become increasingly important in modern competitive conditions, as firms to a greater extent need to access an expanding set of external knowledge sources (Arora and Gambardella 1994; Coombs and Metcalfe 2000; Smith 2000), and increasingly need to rely on specialist knowledge controlled and accumulated by specialist employees (Miles et al. 1997). There is nothing new per se in the notion that knowledge for productive purposes may be distributed; indeed, it is a necessary consequence of the division of labor and bounded rationality (Hayek 1945, 1973; March and Simon 1958; Arora and Gambardella 1994). Rather, what is being asserted by a number of authors seems to be that there are significant discontinuities in the evolution of distributed knowledge, so that the distributed character of knowledge has strongly increased during the last decades. Thus, Granstrand, Patel, and Pavitt (1997) document the significantly increasing extent to which firms organize in-house distributed technological knowledge, drawn from a growing number of underlying technological disciplines. Wang and Tunzelman (2000) emphasize that not only is the number of disciplines that firms draw on expanding, it is also the case that these disciplines themselves evolve in terms of their depth and specialization; firms' sourcing of technological knowledge reflects this.

These observations and the above definition help us better to understand what it means to argue that 'knowledge is becoming more distributed'. Thus, we may say that knowledge becomes more distributed when

1. n (i.e. the number of agents and propositions/knowledge elements) increases (cf. Granstrand, Patel, and Pavitt 1997); and/or

2. The overlap between individual knowledge elements is reduced. Knowledge overlap may be reduced for two principal reasons:
   (a) One (or more) knowledge element that was known by j ($\leq$ n) agents is now only known by h ($<$ j) agents. Thus, forgetfulness in this sense makes knowledge more distributed. Changing from a state with less division of labor to one with more may exemplify this, because each agent needs to control less different knowledge under more division of labor; and/or
   (b) Knowledge elements/propositions become more heterogeneous (cf. Wang and Tunzelman 2000). For example, whereas in an initial period a firm draws all its production-knowledge elements from the engineering discipline, in a later period it adds knowledge elements drawn from the discipline of organic chemistry.

Handling Distributed Knowledge

A well-known Hayekian point is that a market system (but not a socialist one) promotes a tendency towards allocating property rights to those who can make best use of them; a system with alienable property rights solves simultaneously both the assignment and the moral-hazard problem. However, firms solve these problems differently. Thus, within firms resources are directed (to a larger extent than in markets), and motivation of employees is engineered (to a larger extent than in markets). From a Hayekian perspective, firms would seem to be inherently disadvantaged relative to markets, for firms encounter a fundamental problem that markets do not; namely, 'the problem which any attempt to bring order into complex human activities meets: the organizer must wish the individuals who are to cooperate to make use of knowledge that he himself does not possess' (Hayek 1973: 49). In order to cope with the problem, designed orders, such as firms, must adopt some of the organizing principles of spontaneous orders; notably, the reliance on rules:

every organization must rely also on rules and not only on specific commands. The reason here is the same as that which makes it necessary for a spontaneous order to rely solely on rules: namely that by guiding the actions of individuals by rules rather than specific commands it is possible to make use of knowledge which nobody possesses as a whole (ibid. 48–9).

Such rules are 'rules for the performance of assigned tasks'. They are therefore 'necessarily subsidiary to commands' (ibid. 49).

Thus, Hayek does not *deny* that in practice the problem of making use of distributed knowledge can be solved by firms, and that authority, the central characteristic of firm organization, is consistent with distributed knowledge. However, observe also that Hayek does not *explain* how the problem is solved: If knowledge inside the firm is indeed distributed, how can management choose good 'rules for the performance of assigned tasks'? How are employees assigned to tasks and how are standards for performance chosen when these actions are partly dependent on knowledge that management does not itself hold?

An obvious way to handle the problem is to suppress distributed knowledge as far as possible by discouraging local initiative, indoctrinating employees harshly, and operating with rigid routines and operating procedures. The archetypal 'machine bureaucracy' fits this overall characterization. However, to the extent that competition is increasingly knowledge-based, this is a self-defeating strategy, because suppressing distributed knowledge in this way also implies that beneficial explorative and innovative efforts are suppressed. Therefore, an often more attractive way to handle the presence of distributed knowledge inside is to delegate decision rights (cf. Hayek 1945: 83–4; Galbraith 1974: 31–4; Jensen and Meckling 1992), balancing the resulting agency costs against the benefits from improved use of distributed knowledge. An interpretation of internal hybrids, such as team organization, 'molecular forms', and the like, is that these manifest attempts to delegate decision rights and structure reward schemes so that such optimal trade-offs are reached (Jensen and Wruck 1994; Zenger and Hesterly 1997; Foss and Foss 2002; Zenger 2002). However, this still does not resolve the issue of how management can rationally decide on delegation, install rules, etc. in the face of distributed knowledge. Such decisions, too, are acts of authority, and would therefore seem to be challenged by distributed knowledge. This is discussed further below.

Narrow and Broad Notions of Authority

Although there is mounting evidence that the employment relation is undergoing significant changes, we do not observe anything amounting to a complete breakdown of authority relations. One reason is the possibility of benefits of firm organization that offset the knowledge-related inefficiencies of authority. Another reason is the simple one that there is a large distance between the real phenomenon of authority and the usual way in which economists think of authority. In fact, both those who have criticized authority for being an increasingly inefficient coordination mechanism in the emerging knowledge economy and organizational economists may be criticized for working with a too narrow understanding of what authority is and can accomplish. For example, a representative of the first group, Grandori (1997: 35), argues that

whatever its basis, authority is a feasible governance mechanism only if information and competence relevant to solving economic action problems can be transferred to and handled by a single actor, a positive 'zone of acceptance' exists, the actions of other supervised actors are observable, and if the system is not as large as to incur an overwhelming communication channel overload and control losses

This critique seems to be directed at the Coase-Simon view of authority, and is, as such, a valid criticism. The Coase-Simon view is too narrow, because it implies that the boss performs a detailed direction of the worker's actions, based on a complete knowledge of the worker's action set, and because it implicitly asserts that the boss is always at least as, or more, knowledgeable about what actions should optimally be carried out. To the extent that authority is understood only in this narrow sense, it is not difficult to argue that indeed authority will become increasingly inefficient and therefore increasingly less prevalent as a coordination mechanism (i.e. Proposition 1).

However, as Simon (1991: 31) himself pointed out four decades after his initial paper on authority, '[a]uthority in organizations is not used exclusively, or even mainly, to command specific actions'. Instead, he explains, it is a command that takes the form of a result to be produced, a principle to be applied, or goal constraints, so that '[o]nly the end goal has been supplied by the command, and not the method of reaching it'. This notion of authority as commanding somebody to work towards a specified goal, for example backed up by some superior bargaining power, is entirely consistent with Assumptions 1 and 2. Although an employer may be ignorant of the efficient action, and perhaps of most of the employee's possible action, he can always tell him to 'Do *something* to fix it!'

This suggests the more general implication that *some* overlap of knowledge may be sufficient to make coordination by means of authority work in the presence of distributed knowledge. In particular, note that it is not in conflict with the notion of distributed knowledge (at least as defined earlier) that some agent possesses the knowledge that—in terms of the earlier example—if Jack and Jill's knowledge sets are somehow aggregated, this will result in their having, as a 'system', a knowledge that none of them possesses individually. This agent does not need to know that Jack knows that p is the case and Jill knows that p implies y. However, she does need to know that there is a set P of which p is a member and that these elements map to certain outcomes Y of which y is a member. Thus, though she may still be ignorant in an important sense about the knowledge controlled by Jack and Jill, she does not suffer from complete ignorance;[24] there is some, possibly rather modest, knowledge overlap. She may therefore be able to pass *judgment* on the overall abilities of Jack and Jill, and, in particular, on how actions based on Jack and Jill's knowledge may be coordinated. In other words, it is possible to have knowledge of interdependencies between actions based on different knowledge elements without possessing much knowledge of these elements themselves.

In his pioneer contribution Frank Knight (1921) made it clear that the effective exercise of authority does not require full knowledge of an employee's action set and precise knowledge of exactly which action should be picked in response to contingencies: 'What we call "control" consists mainly of selecting someone else to do the "controlling." Business judgment is chiefly judgment of men. We know things by knowledge of men who know them and control things in the same indirect way' (ibid. 291).[25] These principles also apply to hierarchical organization, which Knight conceptualizes as layers of agents exercising judgment of subordinates' judgment and other capabilities (particularly ibid. 291–7). Delegation, Knight argues, rests on judgment. Such judgment does not require that that the principal know the agent's entire action set.[26] Thus, when Hayek (1973) argues that authority in the sense of the delegation of decision rights, the imposition of rules on the organization, the checking of whether actions are in conformity with the rules, etc. is consistent with distributed knowledge conditions, this can be explained by invoking management judgment of subordinates.

This suggests that authority in the sense of direction and centralized decision-making—which does not necessarily require detailed knowledge about a subordinate's knowledge or available actions—may persist in Hayekian settings, including the emerging knowledge economy. Thus, authority may be based on judgment rather than perfect knowledge. Below, I discuss this further. To make it more concrete, situations involving distributed knowledge are approximated by 'hidden knowledge' (Minkler 1993) in principal–agent relations. That is, it will be assumed that the problem facing a principal is not just that she is uninformed about what state of nature has been revealed or of the realization of the agent's effort (i.e. hidden information), as in the standard agency paradigm. Rather, the agent's knowledge is superior to that of the principal with respect to certain production possibilities (i.e. hidden knowledge). The principal may be ignorant about some members of the set of possible actions open to the agent, or the agent may be better informed than the employer with respect to how certain tasks should (optimally) be carried out, or both. Given this, the issue is whether in these situations it is possible, under hidden knowledge, to make sense of this notion of authority on grounds of efficiency. It turns out that it is indeed possible to explain the presence of authority in such a setting. The key factors that will be considered in the following are (1) the urgency of decisions, (2) decisive knowledge, and (3) monitoring, incentives, and externalities. However, coping with distributed knowledge inevitably seems to lead in the direction of decentralization, as Hayek (1945: 83–4) forcefully argued:

If we can agree that the economic problem of society is mainly one of rapid adaptation to changes in the particular circumstances of time and place, it would seem to follow that the ultimate decisions must be left to the people who are familiar with these circumstances, who know directly of the relevant changes and of the resources immediately available to meet them. We cannot expect that this problem will be solved by first communicating all this knowledge to a central board which, after integrating all knowledge, issues its orders.

Coping with distributed knowledge would thus seem to require extensive delegation of rights. In fact, there is an argument that under Hayekian distributed knowledge de facto delegation of rights *already obtains*. Therefore, the formal right to decide need not confer effective control over decisions, as Aghion and Tirole (1997) point out, with a bow to Max Weber. Thus, real authority is already largely determined by the structure of information in the organization, including the distribution of Hayekian dispersed knowledge. Of course, agents who possess local knowledge may be subject to the exercise of authority by uninformed hierarchical superiors, but this is likely to harm incentives.[27] Thus, in Aghion and Tirole (1997) an increase in the agent's real authority is assumed to lead to control losses from the point of view of the principal but also to promote initiative; efficient organization produces value-maximizing trade-off. It is apparent that Hayekian distributed knowledge has important implications for understanding internal organization, such as the adoption of internal hybrids in the form of project- or team-based organization, 'molecular forms', 'cellular organizations', etc.[28]

However, while a Hayekian perspective is informative for understanding internal hybrids, it does not answer the question of why such hybrids are at all organized *inside* firms. Because they are organized inside firms, they are subject to the exercise of, at least formal, authority. Being overruled by formal hierarchical superiors may harm motivation. Thus, moving teams out of firms would seem to yield net benefits, since incentives would be strengthened.[29] In fact, spin-offs, carve-outs, and the like may be explained in these terms, so we should ask why not all internal hybrids are spun off.

A further issue is that the ownership-based notion of authority developed by Hart also seems to play only a limited role under Hayekian distributed knowledge. There are several reasons for this. First, in Hart's framework all residual decision-making power is concentrated in the hands of the owner/manager, whereas in actuality delegation often amounts to delegating at least some residual decision rights to hierarchical subordinates (e.g. division managers). Implicitly, the notion that, on the one hand, there are rights that may be clearly specified in a contract and allocated to another party, and that, on the other hand, there are rights that cannot be specified at all in a contract but can only be allocated to a single party through asset ownership means that the only room left for delegation is that agents receive well-specified rights to carry out well-specified actions. However, this implies that if agents can take actions about which principals have no knowledge, or are better informed about how certain actions should be carried out, the superior knowledge of agents cannot be utilized.

A second reason why Hartian ownership-based authority may be increasingly irrelevant under Hayekian distributed knowledge is that the assets that in Hart's scheme confer authority are primarily physical assets (Hart 1995). However, as many writers have emphasized, an important aspect of the knowledge economy is exactly that physical assets are of fast-waning importance (Myers 1996; Boisot 1998; Neef 1998). Of course, the implication is that ownership over such assets is an increasingly ineffective source of bargaining power and that, therefore, authority must wane as bargaining power increasingly becomes more symmetrically distributed over the owners of knowledge assets. The following section discusses this in greater detail.

Authority When Knowledge is Distributed

Authority in the Presence of Hidden Knowledge

This section further examines the role of authority, understood in the broad sense of direction, in a Hayekian setting of distributed knowledge. Distributed knowledge is here approximated by 'hidden knowledge' (Minkler 1993) in principal–agent relations. That is, it will be assumed that the problem facing a principal is not just that she is uninformed about what state of nature has been revealed or of the realization of the agent's effort (i.e. hidden information), as in the standard agency paradigm. Rather, the agent's knowledge is superior to that of the principal with respect to certain production possibilities (i.e. hidden knowledge). The principal may be ignorant about some members of the set of possible actions open to the agent, or the agent may be better informed than the employer with respect to how certain tasks should (optimally) be carried out, or both. The setting is one of incomplete contracts, so authority refers to the giving of direction in situations about which contracts are silent. Given this, the issue is whether it is possible, under hidden knowledge, to make sense of authority in the sense of direction on grounds of efficiency. It turns out that it is indeed possible to explain the presence of authority in such a setting. The key variables are (1) the urgency of decisions and, what is often the other side of the coin, the wish to avoid duplicative effort (Bolton and Farrell 1990), (2) decisive information (Casson 1994), (3) economies of scale in decision-making (Demsetz 1991; Hermalin 1998), and (4) the setting of incentives and the curbing of externalities (Holmström 1999). These are discussed below.

Urgency and Duplication Avoidance

While Hayek (1945) did much to identify the benefits of the price with respect to coping with the problems introduced by distributed knowledge and unexpected disturbances, he arguably neglected those situations where efficiency requires that adaptation be 'coordinated' rather than 'autonomous' (Williamson 1996a). Coordinated adaptation or action may be required when actions or activities are complementary (Milgrom and Roberts 1992; Foss 2001). Coordination problems are examples of this. In game theoretic parlance, these problems obtain when there is more than one equilibrium in pure strategies. Examples are Schelling's famous where-to-meet problems (Schelling 1960) or the choice of standards, such as which side of the road to drive on. Game theory demonstrates that even in extremely stylized and simple, but still decentralized, settings with players possessing perfect reasoning capabilities and common knowledge, they may still be unable to coordinate their independently taken actions or only coordinate these after costly trials and errors. Authority may be a least-cost response to such problems (cf. Ch.9).

In order to determine the costs and benefits of centralized and decentralized decision-making in a specific context, Bolton and Farrell (1990) study a coordination problem with private information in the setting of a natural-monopoly market. The coordination problem concerns who should enter the market when costs are sunk and are private information. Under decentralization, which is represented as a two-period incomplete-information game of timing (sink costs/enter or wait another period), each firm is uncertain about whether the other firm will enter. However, the incentive to enter depends on the height of a given firm's cost—low-cost firms being less worried that their rival will enter (and vice versa). If costs are sufficiently dispersed, the optimal outcome prevails; that is, the lowest-cost producer enters and preempts the rival(s). However, if costs are equal or are high for both, inefficiencies may obtain, since firms will then enter simultaneously (inefficient duplication) or will wait (inefficient delay).

Enter a central authority whose job is to nominate a firm for entry. In the spirit of Hayek, Bolton and Farrell assume that this central authority cannot possess knowledge about costs. In their model, s/he nominates the high-cost producer half of the times, which is clearly inefficient. However, this cost of centralization should be compared with the costs of decentralization (delay and duplication). Bolton and Farrell show that 'the less important the private information that the planner lacks and the more essential coordination is, the more attractive the central planning solution is' (1990: 805). Moreover, the decentralized solution performs poorly if urgency is important. Centralization is assumed not to involve delay and therefore is a good mechanism for dealing with emergencies, a conclusion they argue is consistent with the observed tendencies of firms to rely on centralized authority in cases of emergency.[30]

The inefficiencies under decentralization (duplication, delay) that Bolton and Farrell point to may arguably be particularly relevant for much 'knowledge-intensive' production. This is because much of this production is 'pooled' rather than 'sequential' or 'reciprocal', in the terminology of Thompson (1967); that is, involves relatively decentralized efforts aimed at a common end. Research-based organizations where much production takes place in decentralized project groups may be an example. A centralized authority may be necessary to give priority to certain projects rather than others, even though that authority is basically very ill informed about the projects.

Decisive Information

Even under distributed knowledge, where the centralized decision-maker by definition does not possess (at least some) local information, s/he may in many cases still hold the information that is *decisive*. Intuitively, information is decisive when actions taken on the basis of such knowledge impact strongly on the firm's pay-offs. According to Casson (1994), the extent to which a productive task involving the knowledge of several individuals has decisiveness features and the cost at which knowledge can be communicated help to explain the allocation of decision rights. For example, if supply conditions (changing technologies and/or input prices) are more volatile than demand conditions (changing sales and/or tastes), it may pay to investigate supply before investigating demand. In fact, if supply volatility is considerably higher, it may be evident what the firm should do in terms of its output and pricing decisions without checking demand conditions. In both cases, information about supply is decisive (and more so in the latter case). Note that decisiveness in the examples suggests that decision rights should be allocated towards the production side of the firm. The more general principle is that decision rights will tend to be concentrated in the hands of the individual who has access to the decisive information, and particularly so the more costly it is to communicate this information.

This means that there may be a role for authority under hidden knowledge; namely, when the latter is not decisive, it is costly to communicate the knowledge that is decisive, and the consequences of an incorrect decision are expected to be small relative to the costs of communicating the knowledge. In contrast, extensive information-sharing is only necessary if each party holds information which is highly likely to be decisive or if the costs of not making the correct decision if lacking some of the tacit information are high. In that case, knowledge transfer and delegation of decision rights are likely to characterize the organization.

Economies of Scale

Demsetz (1991) argues that economies of scale in managing are a neglected factor in the explanation of the existence of firms and the understanding of authority, but doesn't spell out the underlying reasoning. However, the relevant economies may relate both to managing the relations between agents inside the firm and managing relations to outside agents (customers, suppliers, government agencies) (Hermalin 1998). Not only may there be scale economies in such activities; there may also be substantial learning economies. Other agents may be happy to let a central agent incur the effort costs of negotiating, learning about potential suppliers, etc., and compensate him accordingly. At first glance, this only explains why a team may hire a 'consultant'; it does not explain why this consultant should have any authority (Foss 1996). However, as will be argued later, it may pay to give the consultant authority to the extent that he risks being held up by the other agents to whom he specializes his human capital. Giving the 'consultant' authority is tantamount to giving him ownership of the firm's alienable assets.

Setting Incentives and Curbing Externalities

As pointed out earlier, Hayekian distributed knowledge poses special problems for the use of monitoring mechanisms and incentive pay, as these are discussed in the mainstream agency literature (e.g. Holmström 1979) (Minkler 1993; Aghion and Tirole 1997; Foss 1999a; Foss and Foss 2000b). Minkler (1993: 23) argues that 'if the worker knows more than the entrepreneur, it is pointless for the entrepreneur to monitor the worker', which implies that to the extent that monitoring is a precondition for the exercise of direction, using the authority mechanism also seems to become 'pointless'. In the extreme case both the agent's type and actions may be fully observable by the principal but the latter may still not understand the full set of production possibilities open to the agent (all in contrast to the standard agency paradigm). Clearly, in that extreme case the problem is to design a contract that (1) allows the agent to use his superior knowledge *ex post*, and (2) gives him the incentive to do so efficiently. This will typically amount to allocating decision rights as well as rights to residual income streams to the agent, which indeed are key features of many new organizational forms.[31]

However, even under hidden knowledge there may still be a role for authority (as suggested in connection with the discussion of distributed knowledge earlier in this chapter). For example, Foss and Foss (2002b) construct a hidden-knowledge model in which the principal can, nonetheless, form conjectures of the pay-offs that result from the agent's activities (even though the principal cannot observe and fully understand these activities). The pay-offs are assumed to be related in a simple manner to the amount of discretion that is left to the agent. It can then be shown that the surplus from the relation may be maximized by choosing degrees of discretion that differ from those the agent would have preferred if he were completely on his own. The power to choose these levels of discretion (i.e. the exact delegation of decision rights) stems from the principal's ownership of the assets in the relation.

More broadly, the ability of a principal to form conjectures with respect to an agent's output even under hidden knowledge—what was earlier by Knight (1921) called 'judgment'—and enter into formal or informal contracts over this, implies that limited notions of monitoring and incentive pay may still have a role to play. For example, so-called 'forcing contracts', in which, for example, a bonus is paid only if a certain threshold of output is reached, may work under hidden knowledge. Subjective forms of performance assessment may be workable to the extent that the principal can form estimates of the level of output that can 'reasonably' be expected of the agent.[32] Even softer forms of incentive instruments—such as norms and the provision of intrinsic motivation—are arguably particularly important under hidden knowledge (see Jensen and Wruck 1994; Osterloh and Frey 2000).

In a somewhat speculative vein, it may be argued that the greater the departure from very simple settings where employees, undertaking routinized tasks, are very easily monitored, and the harder we make it to find out what the employee can deliver and actually delivers, the more likely it is that an employer will choose to rely on multiple-incentive instruments to influence employee behavior (Henderson 2000). Under these circumstances, a key managerial task is to 'balance' incentive instruments (Holmström 1999); that is, design and maintain coherence between the various ways in which an employee may be motivated so that negative spillover effects between these ways are minimized.[33] In a dynamic economy, maintaining coherence between such instruments may be a recurrent task. Economies of scale in this task may dictate that this activity is centralized. Moreover, centralization is required to the extent that externalities arise when the instruments are controlled by separate firms and transaction costs hinder the internalization of these externalities. Both arguments point towards the centralization of decision rights.

Summing Up

It has been argued that it is possible to give efficiency explanations of authority in the sense of direction and centralized decision-making in the context of Hayekian settings.[34] Thus, a response has been provided to Proposition 3 ('In the emerging knowledge economy, authority relations will become increasingly inefficient and insignificant means of allocating resources'). This is *not* to say that authority relations, and the allocation of decision rights in firms in general, will be unaffected by the increased reliance on specialist knowledge (i.e. by Propositions 1 and 2 becoming increasingly descriptively correct). The growing prevalence of internal hybrids that go beyond traditional hierarchies (Zenger and Hesterly 1997) may very well be caused by the increased importance of Hayekian distributed knowledge. Still, internal hybrids are organized inside the firm and are thus subject to the exercise of authority. Therefore, even if the hierarchy becomes flatter because of the existence of cellular organizations, authority persists.[35] A reason for this is that even in knowledge-based firms there may be a need for centralized coordination, as we have seen. When there is such a need, it is often efficient to centralize ownership to alienable assets, as the following section demonstrates. In turn, this suggests that centralized coordination is a feature of firms rather than markets. In other words, it will be argued that the presence of Hayekian settings does not invalidate the notion of the boundaries of the firm, even when these are conceptualized in legal and ownership-based terms.

Ownership and Firm Boundaries in Hayekian Settings

Ownership and Assets in the Knowledge Economy

The previous section did not say much about what backs up authority. However, we know from Hart (1995) and other economists of organization that ownership may play a key role in this respect; the purpose of this section is to go further into ownership issues—particularly the ownership of knowledge assets—and therefore the issue of the boundaries of the firm. One of the key characteristics of the knowledge economy is usually taken to be the increased importance in production of knowledge assets and the decreasing importance of physical assets (Boisot 1998). A further argument is that this transformation will also transform economic organization, because knowledge assets have different implications for the boundaries of firms than physical assets (e.g. Powell 1990; Zucker 1991; Kogut and Zander 1992; Boisot 1998).[36]

The category of 'knowledge assets' is a broad one—encompassing individually held tacit knowledge, firm-level capabilities ('organizational knowledge'), patents, client lists, etc.—and difficult to frame analytically.[37] Perhaps for this reason, there are different—albeit all somewhat underdeveloped—modeling strategies available. One such strategy is to stress problems of appropriability as a key determinant of the boundaries of the firm (Teece 1987; Liebeskind 1997). In this scheme the boundaries of the firm reflect attempts to maximize the rent streams from the firm's valuable knowledge assets (rather than the hold-up problem). A second one is to stress that many knowledge assets are collective or public goods (e.g. capabilities or reputational assets) and that this creates free-rider problems, bringing about a need to delimit access to such goods (Holmström and Roberts 1998). A third strategy is to argue that knowledge assets in the form of differential capabilities give rise to communication costs, and attempts to economize with such costs help determine the boundaries of the firm (Langlois 1992; Monteverde 1995). A fourth possibility is to rely on more standard transaction cost economics and incomplete contracts theory arguments about the need to protect specialized assets and investments specific to such assets from rent-capture attempts (Rabin 1993; Brynjolfsson et al. 1994; Putterman 1995). Since the latter strategy is the one that most obviously connects to the theme of authority that has been pursued in so much of this chapter, I briefly discuss this approach.

An Incomplete Contracts Approach to Knowledge Assets and the Boundaries of the Firm

Following Brynjolfsson et al. (1994), use will be made of the incomplete contracts modeling methodology of Hart and Moore (1990) to get an understanding of the implications of knowledge assets for the boundaries of the firm. This is a key issue, because asset ownership may provide the bargaining lever that backs up authority, and the concentration of decision rights that we call authority may have important efficiency implications, as already argued. Thus, this section connects the discussion of authority in a knowledge economy with the issue of the boundaries of the firm in such an economy. The emphasis is on supporting the claim made earlier that when there is a need for centralized coordination, efficiency considerations often suggest a need also to concentrate asset ownership (Hermalin 1999; Holmström 1999).

The primary required change in the basic Hart and Moore framework is a more explicit introduction of knowledge assets (which may be alienable or non-alienable). In fact, we can dispense entirely with physical assets, and discuss a purely knowledge-based firm.[38] It is assumed that agents enter into productive relations with other agents but that synergies between agents occur only through the assets that they control (and not through the actions they take). Furthermore, although assets may influence the value of actions, the reverse is not true (Brynjolfsson et al. 1994: 433). This means that we can write the cost of agent i's action as $c(x_i)$ and the marginal value of i's actions when he is in a productive relation with other agents simply as $v_i(A)$, where A is the set of all assets owned by agents (and their actions can be suppressed).[39]

For simplicity, assume that two agents interact and that one of these, the 'entrepreneur', owns a knowledge asset, K, that is 'inside his head' (e.g. an entrepreneurial idea) and the other agent, the 'scientist', owns the only other asset in the relation, P, which we may assume to be a 'patent'. Both assets are necessary to create value in the relation, and K and P are (strictly) complementary, so that the one is of zero value without the other. It is prohibitively costly to communicate the knowledge embodied in K from the entrepreneur to the scientist, so K is effectively non-alienable, although the services of K may of course be traded. Moreover, it is not possible to write a comprehensive contract governing the use of the assets in all contingencies. Given this, we may ask who should own the alienable asset P; which—in terms of the Hart and Moore (1990) analysis—is tantamount to asking who should own the firm.

In this setting, if the entrepreneur makes an effort investment, x_e, that is elaborates on his idea and creates extra value, the scientist can effect a hold-up on the entrepreneur, since the latter needs access to the patent to create value (and the contract is incomplete). Of course, the reverse also holds, so that if the scientist makes an effort investment, x_s, (e.g. makes a spin-off patent), the entrepreneur can hold up the scientist by threatening to withdraw from the relation. Under the standard assumption of Nash bargaining, the entrepreneur and the scientist each realizes half of the extra value created as a result of their efforts. Because of the externality problem, each underinvests; specifically, each party invests to the point where the marginal cost of effort investment equals half of the marginal value.[40] Suppose instead that the entrepreneur owns *both* the patent and the entrepreneurial idea. This will strengthen the entrepreneur's incentives (the scientist cannot hold him up any more) and it will leave the scientist's incentives unaffected.[41] Obviously, this ownership arrangement should be chosen.[42]

A conclusion at this stage is that it *is* possible to speak of the boundaries of the firm in terms of ownership (and therefore also in legal terms)—even in a situation where all assets are knowledge assets.[43] However, this does not yet demonstrate the point made earlier; namely, that concentration of coordination tasks produces a need for concentration of ownership. We can address this issue, however, by assuming that one of the agents has decisive information (in the sense of Casson 1994). While efficiency may require that this agent should have decision rights amounting to authority, should he also be an owner?

Consider a 'knowledge-based' group of scientists in which each scientist owns a patent, P_i. One of the scientists possesses decisive knowledge, C, and the other scientists communicate directly with him rather than with each other.[44] For example, this agent aggregates information from the messages of the other agents and issues directives. His knowledge is decisive in the sense that without it all actions of the other agents produce zero value. The coordinator may improve on this decisive knowledge. Each agent needs access to his own patent and to C in order to be productive. Given this assumption (which means that we need only consider relations between any agent and the coordinator), we have the by now familiar underinvestment problem for both the coordinator and the scientists.[45] If the coordinator is given ownership to all patents things change. While the incentives of the scientists are not affected,[46] the incentives of the coordinator to invest in augmenting his decisive coordination knowledge are strengthened. Thus, this ownership arrangement should be chosen.

Summing Up

Although the framework that has been applied in this section is extremely stylized and in many ways quite limited (Holmström 1999; Foss and Foss 2001), it does succeed in providing an answer to Proposition 4 in Section II that '[t]he boundaries of firms blur because of the increasing importance of knowledge networks that transcend those boundaries. Thus, while legal and ownership-based definitions of the boundaries of the firm may formally be made, they will be increasingly irrelevant from an economic (and strategic) perspective'. The analysis shows, first, that it makes perfect sense to address ownership issues in terms of knowledge assets, and, second, that ownership of such assets may be important in situations where agents need to be provided with incentives (and where contracts are incomplete). Therefore, ownership-based (and therefore also legal) definitions of the boundaries of the firm will continue to be crucially important. The discussion ties together the notions of authority and ownership in the context of knowledge-based production. As will be argued in the following section, this has implications for the malleability of coordination mechanisms; for example, the extent to which market mechanisms can be introduced in firms.

Coordination Mechanisms in Hayekian Settings

The Malleability and Combinability of Coordination Mechanisms

The dominant perspective in much of organization theory and organizational economics has been that there are stable, discrete governance structures that combine various coordination mechanisms in predictable ways. The specific combinations are typically seen as dependent upon the underlying technology, characteristics of the environment, such as exchange conditions, and the strategy of the firm (Thompson 1967; Williamson 1985, 1996a; Holmström and Milgrom 1994; Nickerson and Zenger 2002).

In contrast to this, it has been argued that there are *no* compelling reasons why specific coordination mechanisms should necessarily cluster in a few ideal-typical governance structures of the 'firm-hybrid-market' variety (see Grandori 1997, 2000). In particular, advances in networked computing, management-information systems, and methods of measuring performance have made possible a richer set of combinations of coordination mechanisms. 'Cellular' or 'molecular' forms are examples. The fact that these forms—which operate on very market-like principles—are still organized inside firms serves to illustrate the flexibility with which coordination mechanisms may be combined. This raises the issue of whether there are constraints on the ways in which coordination mechanisms may be combined.

There is a substantial literature on these points. For example, in economics much emphasis has been placed on the need to design organizational structures so that their constituent elements are complementary (Holmström and Milgrom 1994; Zenger and Hesterly 1997). Organization theory has long highlighted 'consistency' among constituent elements (Burns and Stalker 1961; Thompson 1967). The following section briefly discusses this. Later chapters (7 and 8) exemplify and undertake further analysis.

Incentive Limits to the Use of Market Mechanisms

The problem of combining market and hierarchy has been much discussed in economics. In an early contribution the Austrian economist Ludwig von Mises (1949: 709) argued that there are inherent contradictions involved in 'playing market'; that is, trying to simulate a market in the context of hierarchy. With reference to various socialist schemes of his day that tried to preserve some market relations while eliminating capital and financial markets, Mises argued that these schemes would be unworkable. The concentration of ultimate decision-making rights and responsibilities, and therefore ownership, in the hands of a central planning board would dilute the incentives of managers. Thus, while planning authorities could delegate rights to make production and investment decisions to managers, these rights were likely to be used inefficiently. First, since managers could not be sure that they would not be overruled by the planning authorities, they were not likely to take a long view, notably in their investment decisions. Moreover, since managers were not the ultimate owners, they were not the full residual claimants of their decisions and, hence, would not make efficient decisions. Therefore, Mises declared, the attempt to 'play market' under socialism would lead to inefficiencies. In modern parlance, Mises argued that the economic institutions of capitalism are strongly complementary, so that (unhampered) capitalism is a stable system, consisting of interlocking elements, where changes away from pure capitalism will result in serious allocational inefficiencies.

In a related vein, the attempt to simulate markets in a firm hierarchy may lead to inefficiencies. Later research has clarified that (1) handling the problem requires that the planning authorities can credibly commit to a non-interference policy, and (2) the problem goes beyond the comparative systems context. It is latent in all relations between 'rulers' and 'ruled' (North 1990; Miller 1992; Williamson 1996a). The problem arises from the fact that it is hard for the ruler to commit to a non-interference policy, because reneging on a promise to delegate will in many cases be extremely tempting and those to whom rights are delegated will anticipate this. Loss of motivation results. The problem is not unknown in organizational studies (e.g. Vancil and Buddrus 1979: 65). In particular, Williamson's concept (1985, 1993, 1996a) of the 'impossibility of selective intervention' is highly relevant, and will be discussed further in Chapter 7.

Suffice it here to note that it is, in fact, conceivable that the ruler may credibly commit to not intervene in such a way that his sub-goals are promoted. The logic may be stated in the following way (cf. Baker, Gibbons, and Murphy 1999). Assume that a subordinate initiates a project.[47] Assume further that the manager has information that is necessary to perform an assessment of the project, but that he decides up front to ratify any project that the subordinate proposes. Effectively, this amounts to full informal delegation of the rights to initiate and ratify projects—'informal', because the formal right to ratify is still in the hands of the manager and because that right cannot be allocated to the subordinate through a court-enforceable contract (cf. Williamson 1996*a*). Because the subordinate values being given freedom—she is partly a residual claimant on the outcomes of his activities—this will induce more effort in searching for new projects (Aghion and Tirole 1997). To the organization the expected benefits of these increased efforts may be larger than the expected costs from the bad projects that the manager has to ratify. However, a problem arises when the manager has information about the state of a project ('bad' or 'good'), because he may then be tempted to renege on a promise to delegate decision authority; that is, intervene in a 'selective' manner. If he overrules the subordinate, the latter will lose trust in him, holding back on effort. Clearly, in such a game a number of equilibria, each one characterized by different combinations of employee trust and managerial intervention, are feasible. What determines the particular equilibrium that will emerge is the discount rate of the manager, the specific trigger strategy followed by the subordinate (e.g. Will he lose trust in the manager for all future periods if he is overruled, or will he be more forbearing?), and how much the manager values his reputation for not reneging relative to the benefits of reneging on a bad project (Baker, Gibbons, and Murphy 1999).

The implication of this reasoning is that mixing very different coordination mechanisms may lead to efficiency losses, and may not be sustainable for this reason. The basic problem is that emulating market organization inside firms amounts to 'playing market'. Unlike independent agents in markets, corporate employees never possess ultimate decision rights. They are not full owners. This means that those who possess ultimate decision rights can always overrule employees. Thus, there are fundamental incentive limits to the extent to which market principles can be applied inside firms.

These insights imply that coordination mechanisms are not combinable in an arbitrary fashion. In other words, using the case of internal hybrids, an argument has been made that Proposition 5 (i.e. 'Coordination mechanisms will be combined in new, innovative ways, suggesting that these mechanisms are inherently combinable and not limited to being necessarily clustered in specific discrete governance structures') needs substantial qualification. There are inherent (incentive) limits to the extent to which such mechanisms can be combined. It is the tension between authority (backed up by ownership) and delegated rights that creates limits to the combinability of coordination mechanisms. To the extent that authority persists in the knowledge economy, so will these limits.

Conclusion

Addressing economic organization in the context of the emerging knowledge economy is a task of almost forbidding complexity. It is also inherently speculative, suggesting to some that the use of scenario techniques is appropriate (Hodgson 1998) or that a multidisciplinary approach is justified (Daft and Lewin 1993). However, this chapter has taken a narrower approach, by trying to distill some key assumptions and propositions that characterize much of this literature, and examine these in the light of organizational economics. This has the advantage of making explicit what may be the issues of contention and the terms of the debate, thus contributing a possible starting point for further empirical and theoretical work. Thus, it has been argued that the recent literature on economic organization in the knowledge economy may be summarized in a handy way by means of two basic assumptions about knowledge conditions, three propositions about economic organization, and one proposition that relates the former to the latter. Admittedly, this is a much too crude way to say much that is definite; however, it serves to identify what needs to be explained and to examine the reach of some popular arguments. Thus, using this framework, it was argued that what matters to economic organization is not so much the prevalence of knowledge assets per se as it is the growing importance of inalienable assets. Moreover, it was argued that it is possible to give efficiency explanations of authority under distributed-knowledge conditions. One import of this argument is that most economists work with a notion of authority (called above the 'Coase-Simon view') that is perhaps too far removed from the real phenomenon (cf. also Grandori 2001).

However, the discussion also implies a further challenge to the knowledge-based view (the KBV) of the firm in addition to those discussed in Chapter 4. The KBV argues that economic organization is explainable in knowledge terms rather than in terms of efficiently allocating property rights and incentives to maximize joint surplus. For example, the boundaries of the firm reflect partly differential capabilities (Richardson 1972; Kogut and Zander 1992). However, in their present manifestation these arguments may not be sufficiently worked out fully to convince. Thus, the above discussion has exemplified how difficult it is to relate certain knowledge conditions (i.e. distributed knowledge) to organizational outcomes (i.e. the use of authority). Problems introduced by distributed knowledge can be overcome by means of delegation and judgment. It may not matter (or matter much) for allocative outcomes if a manager does not know how exactly an agent produces an output, but can pass precise judgment on the levels and quality of that output. The right to choose the means to produce this output may be delegated to the agent, possibly backed up by some incentive mechanism that mitigates the attendant moral-hazard problem (Jensen and Meckling 1992).

If this is the case, it is hard to see how distributed knowledge constrains firms. It may well do so, but before this issue can be clarified, it is necessary to look into underlying issues such as: How exactly does increased ignorance on the part of employers/principals influence the quality of the decisions they make? Exactly what do we mean, in an economic context, by more or less ignorance? Which factors limit the efficacy of managerial judgment? Heterogeneity of the relevant knowledge inputs (e.g. delegating decision-making rights to employees with widely different disciplinary backgrounds)? If so, what does it mean that knowledge is more or less 'heterogeneous'? And so on.

Notes

1. However, the pedigree of this goes back a long time, including, for example, Burns and Stalker (1961).
2. By the 'economics of organization' reference is made to principal–agent theory, incomplete-contract theory, and transaction-cost economics. Thus, on this definition proponents of resource-based, knowledge-based, capabilities, or evolutionary theories of the firm are not economists of organization.
3. It is also true that organizational economics needs to develop a better understanding of external and (particularly) internal hybrids (Zenger 1997).
4. From such a position the legal boundaries of the firm will only coincide with the boundaries of knowledge-based networks if considerations of appropriability, imposing a strong need for protecting knowledge, completely dominate considerations of sourcing knowledge from networks. More probably, however, the boundaries between markets and firms are fading into insignificance as generalized, reciprocal knowledge exchange in communities of practice and other network forms, as well as hyper-competitive conditions, make knowledge-protection issues less relevant. What will matter for long-run competitive advantage will not be the extent to which, for example, technical capabilities can be protected from imitation, but the dynamic capability continuously to source, integrate, and recombine diverse knowledge inputs (D'Aveni and Gunther 1994; Grant 1996).
5. See Grandori (2000) for a sophisticated argument that because both organization theory and organizational economics have put too much emphasis on discrete, stable, 'consistent' governance structures, and too little on more microanalytic coordination mechanisms (e.g. price, norms, authority, teams, etc.), the number of ways in which such mechanisms may be combined has been strongly underestimated.
6. The assumptions and propositions are extremely crude, so there is clearly a straw-man issue here. Although it may be possible to find authors who present Propositions (3)–(6) in an extreme form, it may also be argued that one can always dig up unimportant extremists, smash their arguments, and obtain an easy victory. Two responses are pertinent here. First, the proponents of Propositions (3)–(6) who have been cited are not unimportant extremists, but established and respected academics. Second, even if the statements contained in Propositions (3)–(6) were the brainchildren of intellectual extremists, investigating them would still be a worthwhile task.

This is because such an activity helps establish the boundaries of the discussion. For example, although it may be argued that nobody truly believes that all authority relations will disappear completely in the knowledge economy, we still need to know why authority relations will persist and how they will change. Answering this question makes us better understand the limits and potentials of authority in Hayekian settings. For example, as I have argued, it furthers understanding of the extent to which coordination mechanisms that are characteristic of market allocation can be introduced in firms' internal organization.

7. 'Distributed knowledge' is knowledge that is not possessed by any single mind and which may be private and tacit, but which it may nevertheless be necessary somehow to mobilize for the carrying out of a productive task (Hayek 1945). Many writers have argued that such distributed knowledge is of increasing importance in an innovation-rich, knowledge-based economy (e.g. Ghoshal, Moran, and Almeida-Costa 1995; Hodgson 1998; Coombs and Metcalfe 2000). Grant (1996: 378) argues that Hayekian distributed knowledge is crucial to the understanding of organizational capabilities: 'Although higher-level capabilities involve the integration of lower-level capabilities, such integration can only be achieved through integrating individual knowledge. This is precisely why higher-level capabilities are so difficult to perform.'

8. By 'coordination mechanisms' reference is made to a wide set of mechanisms for allocating resources, such as authority, norms, teams, prices, contracts, voting, etc. For an innovative overview see Grandori (2001).

9. In other respects, however, Coase is not so obvious a precursor. For example, the emphasis in the modern economics of organization on incentive conflicts, including the hold-up problem (Williamson 1985; Hart 1995), as a main explanatory principle cannot be found in Coase's paper, as he himself has stressed (Coase 1988).

10. 'It may be desired to make a long-term contract for the supply of some article or service', Coase writes. 'Now, owing to the difficulty of forecasting, the longer the period of the contract is for the supply of the commodity or service, the less possible, and indeed, the less desirable it is for the person purchasing to specify what the other contracting party is expected to do. It may well be a matter of indifference to the person supplying the service or commodity which of several courses of action is taken, but not to the purchaser of that commodity or service. But the purchaser will not know which of these several courses he will want the supplier to take. Therefore, the service which is being provided is expressed in general terms, the exact details being left until a later date. [. . .] The details of what the supplier is expected to do is not stated in the contract but is decided later by the purchaser. When the direction of resources (within the limits of the contract) becomes dependent on the buyer in this way, that relationship which I term a "firm" may be obtained' (Coase 1937: 242–3).

11. Apparently, some organization scholars disagree with this. Thus, Grandori (1997: 37) notes that it has been 'well-documented' in organization studies that 'authority is not very effective in managing uncertainty'. It will later be argued that this depends to a large extent on the context; for example, if strong interdependencies ('complementarities') between activities are involved, authority may be extremely effective for 'managing uncertainty'.

12. See Hodgson (1998*b*) for an interesting critical discussion of Coase's notions of authority and the employment contract.

13. A problem with Simon's paper is that he does not really address the issues in the manner of comparative contracting. Thus, the worker only has the choice of accepting or not accepting to work for the boss; the parties are not seen as choosing between an employment relation and *alternative* contractual arrangements for regulating a relation. In an interesting contribution, Wernerfelt (1997) begins from Coasian and Simonian premises. By portraying governance mechanisms as game forms (spot contracting, price lists, hierarchy) chosen to regulate trade, Wernerfelt makes precise Coase's idea that the choice of a governance mechanism is partly determined by the flexibility afforded by that mechanism, and he extends Simon's analysis by explicitly comparing alternative mechanisms. Specifically, game forms determine how players adapt to changes in the environment and communicate about these changes. Wernerfelt's conjecture is that these different game forms will be systematically characterized by different levels of costs of making adaptations. For example, in the case of the hierarchy, the employer and the employee avoid the costs of negotiating either a very complex agreement or a series of short-term contracts. Instead, the parties negotiate a once-and-for-all wage contract. In this context, authority is simply an implicit contract which states that one of the parties should have the authority to tell the other what to do (as in Coase 1937). This game form requires less bargaining over prices than the market game form, and is selected to save too on communication (adaptation) costs. The agreement to play by the least costly adaptation mechanism is upheld by the parties' concern for reputation in a repeated game.

14. This is explicitly argued in Demsetz (1991) and Conner and Prahalad (1996).

15. However, as will become apparent later, the four questions are closely related.

16. Relatedly, Barnard (1938) argued that for authority to be effective it has to be accepted.

17. Note that this 'nexus-of-contracts' position is remarkably close to the position that in a knowledge-based economy the firm/market boundary is unclear and the notion of authority elusive at best, although its conceptual basis is rather different.

18. For a critique of these aspects of the incomplete-contracts literature see Foss and Foss (2001).

19. Although the property-rights approach of Hart and Moore succeeds in adding an important component to the understanding of authority, and provides a strong answer to the Alchian and Demsetz denial that authority is a useful concept, arguably it doesn't succeed in giving a full explanation of the employment contract, or the firm. For example, the bargaining power possessed by a principal who owns the complementary physical assets in a relation may be exercised over an employee *or* it may be exercised over a legally independent party who just happens to have given up ownership of alienable assets to strengthen incentives (i.e. vertical quasi-integration) (Foss and Foss 2001). In other words, there is no one-to-one correspondence between the firm and the Hart understanding of the exercise of authority. In fact, as Bengt Holmström (1999: 87) has recently argued, the incomplete-contracts literature 'is a theory about asset ownership by individuals rather than by firms'.

20. The term seems to originate with Halpern and Moses (1990).

21. Common knowledge is a core assumption in much contemporary game-theory-based micro-economics, such as agency theory (Salanié 1997). It is discussed in greater detail in Chapter 9.

22. p_i could be interpreted as a vector of propositions. Thus, it is not asserted here that each agent only knows one thing.

23. If knowledge overlap is complete, the agents will also know or be able to infer q (if they have perfect rationality/perfect reasoning assumptions and/or the knowledge elements, and how they connect is easy to comprehend).

24. On the other hand, it may not be entirely correct to say that she is 'asymmetrically informed'. In asymmetric information models, such as agency models, an agent knows precisely what she is ignorant about (e.g. the probability distribution associated with quality levels of a good). No such strong knowledge requirements are assumed here; only that the coordinator can pass judgment on the capacities of individual agents and on how their efforts may be aggregated into some coherent outcome.

25. Relatedly, Minkler (1993: 18) in parts of his modeling attempts assumes that the 'entrepreneur can form a conjecture about the worker's possible output without contemplating *how* that output can be produced'.

26. Note that the ownership-based notion of authority developed by Hart (1996) is somewhat problematized under distributed knowledge. In Hart's framework *all* residual decision-making power is concentrated in the hands of the owner/manager, whereas in actuality delegation often amounts to delegating at least some residual decision rights to hierarchical subordinates (e.g. division managers). Implicitly, the notion that, on the one hand, there are rights that may be clearly specified in a contract and allocated to another party, and, on the other, there are rights that cannot be specified at all in a contract but can only be allocated to a single party through asset ownership, means that the only room left for delegation is that agents receive well-specified rights to carry out well-specified actions. However, this implies that if agents can take actions about which principals have no knowledge, or are better informed about how certain actions should be carried out, the superior knowledge of agents cannot be utilized.

27. Here is a further limitation to the use of authority. As Frey (1997) argues, both the use of incentive instruments and authoritative direction may harm intrinsic motivation. Osterloh and Frey (2000) and Osterloh, Frost, and Frey (2002) explore some of the organizational implications of this.

28. The basic conclusion in such a perspective is that decision rights should be delegated in such a way that the benefits of delegation in terms of better utilizing local knowledge are balanced against the costs of delegation in terms of agency losses (Jensen and Meckling 1992; Jensen and Wruck 1994; Aghion and Tirole 1997; Foss and Foss 2002). An interpretation of much of the contemporary emphasis on internal hybrids, such as team organization, 'molecular forms', and other manifestations of organizational delegation and decentralization, is that these are prompted by a pressure to delegate decision rights and structure reward schemes in such a way that optimal trade-offs are reached (Zenger 2002; Zenger and Hesterly 1997).

29. In fact, some writers draw what appears to be the logical consequence of a Hayekian starting point, and flatly argue that only firms that explicitly emulate market organization to the largest possible extent can survive and prosper in the knowledge economy (Cowen and Parker 1997).

30. Although Bolton and Farrell don't note this, the example is vulnerable to the critique that the two firms may enter a court-enforceable contract that lets entry depend on the flipping of a coin. However, in many realistic situations, particularly when urgency is involved, contracts may not be court-enforceable, or the potential delay introduced by using the court system may be intolerable.

31. The problem and its solution are of course subtler than this suggests. The precise arrangements may also involve the payment of a lump sum from the agent to the principal (as in franchising relationships), and it will be shaped by the risk preferences of the parties and whether liquidity constraints are present or not.

32. See Prendergast (1999) for an argument that higher environmental uncertainty may lead to more performance pay (contrary to mainstream agency theory) because it complicates input monitoring.

33. For example, if motivation is mainly secured by pecuniary means, this may harm other instruments, such as trying to motivate by fostering a culture that emphasizes trust and sharing.

34. These reasons also seem broadly consistent with organization theory work on authority in the context of flat hierarchies (where Hayekian distributed knowledge is particularly prevalent). In a study of authority in newspaper publishing companies Brass (1984) identified the determinants of authority as 'criticality' (i.e. decisive knowledge), 'centrality' (i.e. centralized decision rights because of economies of scale in certain tasks), and 'the friendship network'.

35. For a discussion of the differences between authority and hierarchy see Ménard (1994).

36. In fact, two of the flag bearers of modern formal-contract economics, Bengt Holmström and John Roberts (1998: 90), recently observed that '[i]nformation and knowledge are at the heart of organizational design, because they result in contractual and incentive problems that challenge both markets and firms [. . .] In light of this, it is surprising that leading economic theories [. . .] have paid almost no attention to the role of organizational knowledge.'

37. For example, it is not clear whether it makes sense to speak of ownership of firm-level capabilities. For a discussion of this and related issues see Zingales (2000).

38. This is because the key issue is not whether assets are physical or immaterial, but whether they are alienable or non-alienable.

39. One may wonder what has happened to Hayekian distributed knowledge in this setting. Although it is a necessary assumption that the agents can observe each others' marginal product values, they don't need to observe each others' specific actions or know the underlying knowledge. Thus, Hayekian distributed knowledge is consistent with the assumptions being made here.

40. The first-order conditions are given by (1) $\frac{1}{2} v^e(K, P) + \frac{1}{2} v^e(K) = c'(x_e)$ and (2) $\frac{1}{2}v^s(K, P) + \frac{1}{2}v^s(P) = c'(x_s)$. Since it has been assumed that the value of the assets outside the relation is zero, the second term in (1) and (2) equals zero.

41. This may be seen from inspecting the first-order conditions when the entrepreneur owns both K and P: (3) $\frac{1}{2} v^e(K, P) + \frac{1}{2} v^e(K, P) = c'(x_e)$ and (4) $\frac{1}{2} v^s (K, P) = c'(x_s)$.

42. This shows somewhat more formally the argument made earlier that incentives are likely to be strengthened by spinning off employees who come up with idiosyncratic entrepreneurial ideas that are costly to communicate to the rest of the firm.

43. For applications of the basic model, for example with respect to what happens if knowledge (K) is made alienable, see Brynjolfsson et al. (1994).

44. Clearly, this is a strong assumption, but one that is made for analytical convenience. The main point is simply that there is a central agent whose centrality in the information network is crucial to the value-creating efforts of other agents.

45. For example, the first-order condition for any individual scientist is: (5) $\frac{1}{2} v^i(P, C) + \frac{1}{2} v^i(P) = c'(x_i)$, where the second term is zero.

46. The first-order condition for any individual scientist is now: (6) $\frac{1}{2} v^i(P, C) = c'(x_i)$, which is the same as (5).

47. This should be understood in a broad sense. A 'project' may refer to many different types of decisions or clusters of decisions.

7

Internal Organization in the Knowledge Economy: The Rise and Fall of the Oticon Spaghetti Organization

Introduction

In academic research, as well as in managerial practice, the search for the sources of competitive advantage has increasingly centered on organization-related factors (e.g. Barney 1986; Kogut and Zander 1992; Mosakowski 1998a; Nahapiet and Ghoshal 1999). Thus, many firms are said radically to have changed the way in which they structure their boundaries (e.g. Helper, MacDuffie, and Sabel 2000) as well as their internal organization (e.g. Miles et al. 1997). They have arguably done this in an attempt to foster the dynamic capabilities that are necessary for competing in the emerging knowledge economy. Fundamental advances in IT and measurement technologies have facilitated these changes (Zenger and Hesterly 1997), while equally fundamental developments in the organization and motives of capital markets as well as increasing internalization are said to have made them necessary (Halal and Taylor 1998).

From an organizational economics perspective these experiments with economic organization fall into the categories of either *external hybrids* (Williamson 1996a), that is market exchanges infused with elements of hierarchical control, or *internal hybrids* (Zenger 2002), that is hierarchical forms infused with elements of market control. The aims of the experimental efforts are to reduce coordination costs, improve incentives, and help to clarify the nature of the businesses the firm is in, thereby improving entrepreneurial capabilities and the ability to produce, share, and reproduce knowledge (Grant 1996; Miles et al. 1997; Day and Wendler 1998; Mosakowski 1998a). Although both internal and external hybrids are means to reach these aims, they would seem to be highly imperfect substitutes. For example, adopting an internal-hybrid form has the benefit of involving fewer lay-offs relative to adopting external hybrids. Also, spin-offs, carve-outs, and the like are often legally complex operations, whereas adopting an internal hybrid may simply be a matter of managerial fiat. Further, management may fear that leaving too many activities in the hands of other firms will hollow out the corporation (Teece et al. 1994), or make it difficult to protect valuable knowledge (Liebeskind 1996). Given this, one may wonder why firms should ever make governance choices in favor of external hybrids. However, a main point of this chapter is that internal hybrids are beset by distinct incentive costs that external hybrids (and markets) tend to avoid, and that this may explain why external hybrids are chosen over internal hybrids.

Research on new organizational forms is an emerging field (Daft and Lewin 1993; Zenger and Hesterly 1997), and rather little is known about the costs and benefits of these organizational forms. This chapter mixes empirical observation with theoretical reasoning, mostly drawn from organizational economics, in order to gain a better understanding of the organizational design problems of internal hybrids. The theoretical emphasis is on the (neglected) costs of internal hybrids, and in particular on motivational and commitment problems that derive from the delegation of decision rights. The root of such problems is that in firms, (delegated) decision rights are not owned; they are always loaned from the holder(s) of ultimate decision-making rights; namely, the top management and/or the shareholders. Given this, a fundamental problem for top management/owners is to commit to real delegation and refrain from *selective intervention* (Williamson 1996a) that harms motivation, and may reduce effort and investments in firm-specific human capital.

These ideas are developed and discussed empirically with reference to organizational changes that took place in the Danish electronics (primarily hearing-aid) producer Oticon A/S from 1991 onwards. Oticon became world-famous for its radical delegation experiment. The 'spaghetti organization', as it came to be called, was explicitly conceived by its designers as an attempt to infuse the Oticon organization with strong elements of market control (Kolind 1990; Lyregaard 1993), and was seen as a hard-to-replicate source of knowledge-based competitive advantage (e.g. Gould 1994). In fact, a recent cottage industry has treated the Oticon experience as an outstanding example of the sustained benefits that radical project-based organization may provide (e.g. Verona and Ravasi 1999; Lovas and Ghoshal 2000; Ravasi and Verona 2000). However, this literature fails to note that the spaghetti organization in its initial radical form does not exist any more—since about 1996 it has been superseded by more structured administrative systems. Below, these organizational changes will be discussed from an organizational-economics starting point. The approach followed with respect to understanding the nature of organizational changes in Oticon is a historical one that relies heavily on the large number of thick descriptions of Oticon that have been produced by a number of mainly Danish academics, journalists, and Oticon insiders throughout the 1990s (in particular, Lyregaard 1993; Poulsen 1993; Morsing 1995; Eskerod 1997, 1998; Jensen 1998; Morsing and Eiberg 1998). However, these sources have been supplemented with semi-structured interviews with the prime mover behind the spaghetti experiment, the then CEO Lars Kolind, as well as the current Oticon HRM officer (both June 2000).

The chapter begins by developing an organizational economics interpretation of the spaghetti organization ('The Spaghetti Organization: A Radical Internal

Hybrid'). The spaghetti organization appears to have been a particularly well-crafted internal hybrid. Still, it gave way to a more traditional matrix structure. It is not plausible to ascribe this organizational change to outside contingencies, or to dramatic changes in strategic intent. This suggests that the spaghetti organization may have been beset by organizational costs that came to dominate the benefit aspects, necessitating a change of administrative systems ('Spaghetti and Beyond'). The Oticon spaghetti experiment carries lessons for the design of internal hybrids. In particular, it directs attention to the incentive problems of delegating rights within a firm when top management keeps ultimate decision rights. Refutable propositions for the design of internal hybrids are derived ('Discussion: Implications for Internal Hybrids').[1]

It should be clear already at this stage that the following is an attempt to pursue *a specific interpretation* of the Oticon spaghetti organization. Organizational economics per se is hardly in an early stage of theory development any more, given that early work goes back almost seven decades (Coase 1937) and the last three decades have witnessed a flurry of work in this field. There is therefore little need to follow a logic of grounded theory per se (Glaser and Strauss 1967). Moreover, organizational economics is a particularly appropriate tool of interpretation in the present context, because only this body of theory *simultaneously* frames internal hybrids theoretically, casts the analysis in the relevant comparative-institutional terms (e.g. allows external and internal hybrids to be compared), and frames the kind of incentive problems that will be central in the analysis below. For example, information processing or motivation theory cannot accomplish all this.[2]

In sum, the contributions of this chapter are to (1) present a novel and in key respects more encompassing account and interpretation of a well-known organizational-change case, exemplifying the interpretative usefulness of organizational economics in the process; (2) analyze the (neglected) costs of internal hybrids in terms of the problem of selective intervention, thus contributing to understanding the efficient design of such hybrids; and (3) argue that the analysis under (2) is also helpful for understanding broader issues of economic organization, such as the governance choice between internal and external hybrids.

The Spaghetti Organization: A Radical Internal Hybrid

Recent work has used the Oticon spaghetti experiment for the purpose of developing notions of strategy making as 'guided evolution' (Lovas and Ghoshal 2000), and to discuss how the deliberate introduction of 'structural ambiguity' through the choice of loosely coupled administrative systems (Ravasi and Verona 2000) may help to build 'organizational capabilities for continuous innovation' (Verona and Ravasi 1999). This literature places all the emphasis on the benefit side (mostly innovation performance) of the spaghetti experiment and fails to note that (and explain why) the spaghetti organization has been largely abandoned. In contrast, this chapter accounts for the costs of this particular internal hybrid in terms of organizational economics, and uses this account to explain the change from the spaghetti organization.

Oticon: Background

Founded in 1904 and based mainly in Denmark, Oticon (now William Demant Holding A/S) is a world leader in the hearing-aid industry. In the early 1990s Oticon became a famous and admired instance of radical organizational change. CEO Lars Kolind and his new organizational design became favorites of the press, consultants, and academics alike. The new organization was cleverly marketed as the very embodiment of empowering project- and team-based organization. Moreover, it quickly demonstrated its innovative potential by revitalizing important, but 'forgotten', development projects that, when implemented in the production of new hearing aids, produced significant financial results, essentially saving the firm from a threatening bankruptcy, as well as turning out a number of new strong spin-off products. The background to the introduction of the spaghetti organization was the loss of competitive advantage that Oticon increasingly suffered during the 1980s as a result of increasingly strong competition (mainly from the USA), and a change in the technological paradigm (Dosi 1982) in the hearing-aids industry, which was gradually moving through the 1980s from 'behind-the-ear' to 'in-the-ear' hearing aids (Lotz 1998). Oticon's success in the 1970s was founded on miniaturization capabilities. While these had been critical for competitive advantage in the 'behind-the-ear' hearing-aid paradigm, new technological capabilities in electronics, which were not under in-house control by Oticon, were becoming crucially important in the emerging in-the-ear paradigm.

There is evidence (e.g. Poulsen 1993; Gould 1994; Morsing 1995) that at the end of the 1980s Oticon was locked into a competence trap that was reinforced by strong groupthink characterizing both the management team and the employees. A symptom of this was that the dominant opinion among managers and development personnel at Oticon was that the in-the-ear hearing aid would turn out to be a commercial fiasco. Moreover, in-the-ear hearing aids were not perceived to be Oticon turf, in terms of both technological and marketing capabilities (Poulsen 1993). The self-image of the company clearly was one of being a traditional industrial company with its strongest technological capabilities in miniaturization, and specializing in mass-producing behind-the-ear hearing aids, developing the underlying technology incrementally. Administrative systems were organized traditionally into functional departments, the managers of which together constituted the senior executive group. When problems began to accumulate, various attempts were made to change the situation, which, however, were either too insignificant or did not survive political jockeying inside Oticon. In 1988 Lars Kolind assumed the position of new CEO, concentrated all decision-making power in his own hands, and implemented drastic cost-cutting measures. However, he also quickly realized that something else had to be done to cope with the decisive changes that were under way with respect to products and processes in the industry. More radical measures were needed regarding the strategic orientation of the firm, the administrative systems that could back this up, and the technology that the firm sourced, leveraged, and developed.

Trying Spaghetti

The new, radical measures were first sketched in a six-page memo (Kolind 1990), which described a fundamental change of corporate vision and mission: The company should be defined broadly as a first-class service firm with products developed and fitted individually for customers, rather than narrowly as a manufacturing company producing standard behind-the-ear hearing aids. A new organizational form, namely the 'spaghetti organization' (so called in order to emphasize the point that it should be able to change rapidly, yet still possess coherence), would support this strategic reorientation. The new form should be explicitly 'knowledge-based'; that is, consisting of 'knowledge centres . . . connected by a multitude of links in a non-hierarchical structure' (Kolind 1994: 28–9). Making the organization 'anthropocentric', that is designing jobs so that these would 'fit the individual person's capabilities and needs' (ibid. 31), was argued to provide the motivational support for this knowledge network. Furthermore, basing the network on 'free-market forces' (Lyregaard 1993) would make it capable of actually combining and recombining skills in a flexible manner, whereby skills and other resources would move to those (new) uses where they were most highly valued. Clearly, the aim was to construct a spontaneously functioning internal network that would work with only minimal intervention on the part of Kolind and other managers; that is, 'essentially, a free market at work' (LaBarre 1996).

The new organizational form was primarily implemented at the Oticon headquarters (i.e. administration, research and development, and marketing). In order symbolically to underscore the fundamental transformation of Oticon, headquarters moved, at 8 a.m. on 8 August 1991, to a completely new location north of Copenhagen. In the new building all the desks were placed in huge, open office spaces, and employees did not have permanent desks, but would move depending on which projects they were working on. The number of formal titles was drastically reduced, resulting in a two-layered structure, with Kolind and ten managers representing the managerial team and the remaining part of the organization being organized into projects (Kolind 1994). Thus, the new organization represented a breakdown of the old functional department-based organization into an almost completely flat, project-based organization. Departments gave way to 'competence centers' (e.g. in mechanical engineering, audiology, etc.) that broke with the boundaries imposed by the old departments. The 'multi-job' concept represented a notable break with the traditional division of labor in organizations. It was based on two key features. First, there were no restrictions on the number of projects that employees could voluntarily join, and, second, employees were actively encouraged (and in the beginning actually required) to develop and include skills outside their existing skill portfolio. The underlying notion was that this would increase the likelihood that project teams would consist of the right mix of complementary skills and knowledge, because of the increase in the scope of the knowledge controlled by each team member. Moreover, the multi-job concept would ease knowledge transfer, because of the increase in the overlap of knowledge domains that it would produce, as employees familiarized themselves with other employees' specialized fields.

These changes were accompanied by an extensive delegation of the rights to make decisions on resource allocation. Notably, employees would in essence themselves decide on which projects they would join rather than being assigned to tasks and projects from above. Project managers were free to manage projects in their preferred ways. Wage negotiations were decentralized, project managers being given the right to negotiate salaries. Finally, although project teams were self-organizing and basically left to mind their own business once their projects were ratified, they were still to meet with a 'Products and Projects Committee' once every three months for ongoing project evaluation.

To meet the two, potentially conflicting, aims of making it possible for project teams rapidly and flexibly to combine the right skills, and achieving overall coherence between rather independently taken decisions, the new organization was founded on four fundamental ideas (Kolind 1994). First, as noted, the traditional, functional department structure was eliminated in favor of a project organization that went considerably beyond the traditional matrix structure. While this served to increase flexibility, other measures were directed towards achieving organizational coherence. Thus, second, new information-technology systems were designed and implemented to make it possible to coordinate plans and actions in this decentralized organization. Everybody was supposed to have full access to the same information. Third, the traditional concept of the office was abandoned, as already mentioned. Finally, Kolind worked hard to increase intrinsic motivation by developing a corporate value base that strongly stressed responsibility, personal development, and freedom. These fundamental organizing principles were backed up by other measures. For example, in order to increase motivation Kolind introduced an employee stock program, in which shop-floor employees were invited to invest up to 6,000 Dkr (roughly $US800) and managers could invest up to 50,000 Dkr (roughly $US7500). Although these investments may seem relatively small, in Kolind's view they were sufficiently large significantly to matter to the financial affairs of individual employees; therefore, they would have beneficial incentive effects. More than half of the employees made these investments.

The implementation of the spaghetti organization had quick and strong performance effects (Peters 1992; Poulsen 1993). Improved performance in terms of the use and production of knowledge was almost immediate, resulting in a string of remarkable innovations during the 1990s (Verona and Ravasi 1999; Ravasi and Verona 2000). Improved growth and financial performance followed somewhat later (see Table 7.1).

With respect to improvements in the use of knowledge, the spaghetti organization allowed significant shelved projects to be revitalized. For example, it was realized that Oticon had already embarked upon development projects for in-the-ear hearing aids as far back as 1979. These projects provided essential inputs into many of the product innovations that Oticon launched during the 1990s. Another effect of the spaghetti organization was that product-development time was reduced by 50 per cent. In 1993 half of Oticon's sales stemmed from products introduced in 1993, 1992, and 1991. A total of fifteen new products had been introduced since the implementation of the new organization, whereas none had been introduced in the last five years of the earlier organization.

A recurring theme in academic treatments of the Oticon spaghetti organization (Morsing 1995; Verona and Ravasi 1999; Ravasi and Verona 2000) is that an important cause of the observed increase in Oticon's innovativeness was the introduction of 'structural ambiguity'; that is, the deliberate engineering of freedom and ambiguity in the role system and in the authority structure by means of the introduction of a radical project organization. This condition facilitated the efficient and speedy integration and production of knowledge, resulting in the observed improvement in Oticon's innovativeness in the 1990s. This interpretation fails, however, to explain why the spaghetti organization was gradually abandoned from about 1996 in favor of a more traditional matrix organization. It also fails to account for the possible costs of the spaghetti organization. The following section presents a complementary interpretation, based mainly on organizational economics.

The Spaghetti Organization as an Internal Hybrid

A striking aspect of the spaghetti organization is the prevalence of the market metaphor in the commentaries on the new form by both insiders and outsiders (Peters 1992; Lyregaard 1993; LaBarre 1996). The spaghetti organization may indeed be interpreted as a radical internal hybrid, because the organization was strongly infused with elements characteristic of market exchange (see Table 7.2).

TABLE 7.1. Oticon financial and technological performance

	1988	1989	1990	1991	1992	1993	1994	1995	1996	1997	1998	1999
Net revenue (million Dkr)	423,8	449,6	455,4	476,5	538,8	661,3	750,3	940,2	1.087,3	1.413,4	1.613,1	1.884,3
Profit margin (%)	1,6	8	3,7	1,8	5,8	13,1	17,9	12,4	12,8	13,8	15,4	17,9
RoE (%)	-8,5	11,6	9,4	-1,5	7,2	37	37,9	25,9	24,3	30,6	35,7	53,8
Product innovation	–	–	–	Multi-Focus	Personic	Oticon 4 Kids	Noah	Micro-Focus	Digi-Focus	Spin-off innovations of Digi-focus	Spin-off innovations of Digi-Focus	Ergo Swift Digi-Focus II

Sources: Ravasi and Verona (2000); annual reports of Oticon A/S and William Demant Holding A/S.

TABLE 7.2. Market organization and the spaghetti simulation

Market organization	The spaghetti organization
Allocation by means of pricing	Transfer prices not used
Legal independence between parties (contract law)	Employment contracts (employment law)
Freedom of contract	Freedom of contract approximated by delegating rights to suggest and join projects
High-powered incentives	Variable pay; initially based on objective input and output measures
Dispersed residual claimancy	Employee stock schemes
Dispersed decision rights	Very widespread delegation of rights
Dispersed ultimate decision rights (dispersed formal authority)	Concentrated ultimate decision rights (concentrated formal authority)
Resource allocation decentralized, and strongly influenced by local entrepreneurship	Local entrepreneurship very strongly encouraged
	Project approval easily obtained
Strong autonomous adaptation properties	Secured through extensive delegation of decision rights

Although there was no attempt to price internal services in the spaghetti organization and Oticon employees did not become legally independent suppliers of labor services, in many other relevant dimensions Oticon was more like a market than a traditional hierarchical firm. Thus, employees (particularly project leaders) were given many and quite far-reaching decision-making rights. Development projects could be initiated by, in principle, any employee, just like entrepreneurs in a market setting, although these projects had to pass not the market test but the test of receiving approval from the Products and Projects Committee. Project groups were self-organizing in much the same way that, for example, partnerships are self-organizing. The setting of salaries was decentralized to project leaders, acting like independent entrepreneurs (Business Intelligence 1993). Incentives became more high-powered (i.e. efforts and rewards were more closely tied together), as performance pay was increasingly used and as the employee-stock-ownership program was introduced, thus mimicking the superior incentive properties of the market. Most hierarchical levels were eliminated and formal titles done away with, etc., mimicking the non-hierarchical nature of the market. In sum, market organization was indeed emulated in a number of dimensions.

As a general matter, the attraction of infusing hierarchical forms with elements of market control is that some of the basic advantages of the hierarchy, such as the superior ability to perform coordinated adaptation to disturbances (Williamson 1996a), build specialized social capital (Nahapiet and Ghoshal 1999), and share knowledge (Osterloh and Frey 2000), can be combined with the superior incentive properties of the market (Williamson 1996a) and its superior flexibility with respect to autonomous adaptation (Hayek 1945; Williamson 1996*a*). Along similar lines, Kolind explicitly saw the spaghetti organization as combining the superior abilities of a hierarchy to build knowledge-sharing environments and foster a cooperative spirit with the flexibility and creativity of a market-like project organization (Kolind 1994).

The Structure of Rights in the Spaghetti Organization

Organizational economics suggests that understanding the costs and benefits of any organizational form requires examining the structure of decision and income rights in the relevant form (Fama and Jensen 1983; Jensen and Meckling 1992; Hart 1995; Williamson 1996*a*; Barzel 1997; Baker et al. 1999, 2002; Holmström 1999). The benefits and the costs of the spaghetti organization can be comprehended through this lens. The remaining part of this section concentrates on the benefit side.

Centralized decision-making systems, particularly large ones, have well-known difficulties with respect to mobilizing and efficiently utilizing important 'sticky' knowledge (Hippel 1994), such as the precise characteristics of specific processes, employees, machines, or customer preferences (Jensen and Wruck 1994). They therefore often also have difficulties combining such knowledge into new products and processes. As Hayek (1945) explained, the main problem is that much of this knowledge is transitory, fleeting, and/or tacit, and therefore costly to articulate and transfer to a (corporate) center. Markets have advantages relative to pure hierarchies with respect to utilizing such knowledge, particularly when it is not required to utilize the relevant knowledge in conjunction with other knowledge sets (where a hierarchy may have comparative advantages).[3] Thus, markets economize on the costs of transferring knowledge by allocating decision rights to those who possess the relevant knowledge, rather than the other way around (Hayek 1945; Jensen and Meckling 1992). Rights will move towards the agents who place the highest valuation on those rights. Since these agents become residual claimants, effective use will be made of the rights they acquire. From this perspective, internal hybrids are fundamentally attempts to mimic, inside the hierarchy, the decentralization of decision and income rights that characterizes the market, in an attempt to improve the efficiency of processes of discovering, creating, and using knowledge.

The spaghetti organization may be understood through this lens; that is, as a hybrid organizational design that aimed at improving the co-location of knowledge and rights through extensive delegation, and backed this delegation of decision rights up by giving employees more income rights. By giving project teams extensive decision rights, requiring that ideas for projects be made public, and ensuring that project teams possessed the necessary complementary skills for a particular marketing, research, or development task, the spaghetti organization stimulated a co-location of decision rights with knowledge. High-powered incentives were provided in an attempt to make sure that efficient use was made of those rights. This improved the use of existing knowledge (cf. the revitalization of 'forgotten' projects) and eased the combination of knowledge in the production of new knowledge.

However, Oticon's use of 'free-market forces' (Lyregaard 1993) was fundamentally a simulation, because the allocation of decision rights in that organization (as in any firm) remained in important respects different from the allocation that characterizes market organization. In contrast to markets, firms cannot concentrate to the same extent income rights (i.e. residual claimancy) and decision rights in the same hands. An agency problem results from this separation. Many of the elements of the spaghetti organization may be seen as responses to this fundamental agency problem, most obviously the increased use of high-powered incentives. Consider also the rights to allocate resources to a particular project. These may be broken down into groups of decision-making rights; namely, rights to (1) initiate projects, (2) ratify projects, (3) implement projects, and (4) monitor and evaluate projects (cf. Fama and Jensen 1983). The efficiency of decision-making processes in project-based firms rests on the allocation and exercise of such rights. For reasons of efficiency, firms usually do not concentrate these rights in the same hands; rather, initiation and implementation rights may be controlled by one person (or team), while ratification and monitoring rights are controlled by other persons, usually hierarchical superiors.[5]

This allocation of decision rights was characteristic of the spaghetti organization. Whereas anybody could initiate a project, projects had to be evaluated by the Products and Projects Committee that was staffed by Kolind, the development manager, the marketing manager, and the support manager. The Committee either rejected or approved the project. The only formal criteria for getting a project accepted were that the relevant project relate to the business areas of Oticon and yield a positive return over a three-year period and with a discount rate of 30 per cent. Apparently, the Products and Projects Committee did not control the use of corporate resources by means of controlling the budgets of individual projects at the project-ratification stage. In particular, the use of human resources, the main input category, across projects was not monitored. The rights to implement a project following approval included the right to hire employees in open competition with other projects (Eskerod 1998). Operating projects would meet every third month with the Products and Projects Committee, or a representative thereof, for project evaluation (i.e. monitoring).

The fact that the Products and Projects Committee could veto a project *ex ante* suggests that it was the real holder of power in Oticon. Frequent intervention on the part of the Committee *ex post* project approval confirms this (ibid.). Thus, it became increasingly clear that the Committee could at any time halt, change, or even close projects. This kind of intervention took place frequently.

The Products and Projects Committee's exercise of its ultimate decision rights may be seen as simply reflecting the separation discussed above between decision management (i.e. initiation, implementation and daily project management) and decision control (i.e. project evaluation and monitoring).[5] However, this separation does not logically imply the kind of *ex post* intervention that the Committee engaged in. For example, one may imagine that the relevant rights might be allocated so precisely and with so much foresight that there are no incentives to intervene *ex post*, as in the case of a very detailed contract between two legally independent firms. However, the way in which the Products and Projects Committee exercised their ultimate decision rights is more akin to reneging on a contract, perhaps even to performing a 'hold-up' (Williamson 1996a). Thus, the Committee effectively reneged on implicit contracts with the projects as the efforts of projects became, in the eyes of the Committee, superfluous (e.g. because of new technological developments), moved in unforeseen directions, or were revealed to have been founded on ill-conceived ideas. In turn, this exercise of ultimate control rights caused unforeseen incentive problems, as will be discussed later.

Organizational Complementarities

An interesting aspect of the spaghetti organization is that an explicit logic of complementarity was present in the reasoning of its main designer. Observed Kolind: 'It was not strictly necessary to do all these things at the same time, but we opined that with a simultaneous implementation of the changes [in organizational elements]...they would reinforce each other' (in Mandag Morgen 1993: 17; my translation). Complementarities between elements of an organizational form exist when increasing the level of one element increases the marginal return from increasing the level of all the remaining elements (Milgrom and Roberts 1990b; Hemmer 1995; Zenger 2002). Loosely, when complementarity obtains, the dynamics of organizational elements imply that they move together. Changing one element in an isolated way is likely to set in motion (possibly unforeseen) processes of change in other elements, because the system will grope towards an equilibrium where all the elements have changed (Zenger 2002). The process of groping may be associated with serious inefficiencies. Therefore, organizational change initiatives should 'get the complementarities right'.

Apparently, the spaghetti organization did exactly this. Thus, the alteration in the rights structure of Oticon was such that decision rights changed in a way that was complementary to the change in income rights; specifically, widespread delegation of decision rights was accompanied by making incentives more high-powered through performance pay and employee ownership. In turn, the change in incentives was backed up by complementary changes in measurement systems. Thus, a performance evaluation system was implemented in which employee performance was measured in 3–8 different dimensions (depending on the type of employee) and pay was made dependent on these measures (Poulsen 1993).

Other initiatives may also be seen to be complementary to the increase in the delegation of rights in the spaghetti organization. For example, the open-office landscape and the strategically placed coffee bars and staircases were complementary to rights delegation in terms of utilizing and building knowledge, because they helped foster the knowledge exchange that gave rise to new ideas for project teams. With respect to the moral hazard problem introduced by delegating rights, the new, much more information-rich environment was also complementary to this delegation, because it helped to build reputational effects (cf. Eskerod 1997, 1998) and eased mutual monitoring among employees, keeping agency problems at bay. Kolind's strong emphasis (1990) on building culture in the new organization may be seen in a similar light. Influencing preferences through the building of shared values became an important activity in the spaghetti organization, because its strong delegation of rights introduced both problems of coordinating independently made decisions (Miller 1992) and agency problems—problems that are reduced as preferences become more homogeneous. The complementary nature of these organizational elements also explains the speed and toughness with which Kolind managed the transition from the old organization. This is because it is usually inefficient to change systems of complementary elements in an incremental manner; transition between such systems should normally be accomplished in a 'big-bang' manner (cf. Dewatripont and Roland 1995).

Spaghetti and Beyond

Retreating from Spaghetti

In his account of the spaghetti organization Gould (1994: 470) noted that 'Lars Kolind's vision was the right one for Oticon. In any case, one thing was certain: there could be no turning back'. However, from 1996 a considerable 'turning back' actually began: Oticon embarked upon a partial abandonment of the spaghetti organization and gradually adopted a more traditional matrix structure. In 1996 Oticon headquarters was divided into three 'business teams' that are essentially new administratives layers. In addition to the business teams, a 'Competence Center' has been set up. This unit is in charge of all projects and their financing and of an operational group that controls administration, IT, logistics, sales, and exports. It is one of the successors to the now abandoned Products and Project Committee. However, its style of managing projects is very different. In particular, care is taken to avoid the kind of intervention in already approved projects that characterized the Products and Projects Committee. The team leaders and the head of the

Competence Center comprise, together with the CEO, the 'Development Group', which may be seen as a second successor to the Products and Projects Committee of the original spaghetti organization. The Development Group, which is essentially the senior executive group, is in charge of overall strategy making. It is also the unit from which most of the initiative with respect to starting new projects comes. Many of the decision-making rights earlier held by project leaders have now been concentrated in the hands of the Competence Center, or the managers of the business teams. For example, project leaders' rights to negotiate salaries have been constrained. Project leaders are appointed by the Competence Center, so that the right to be a project leader is not something that one grabs, as under the spaghetti organization. Although the multi-job concept is still present, the extreme forms that characterized the spaghetti organization are not.

To sum up, recent changes of administrative systems at Oticon have amounted to a break with the radical bottom-up approach that characterized the original spaghetti structure. Thus, although Oticon is still characterized by considerable decentralization and delegation of rights, many of the crucial elements of the spaghetti organization have been abandoned.

Searching for Possible Causes of the Partial Failure of the Spaghetti Experiment

Although the spaghetti organization at first glance seems to have been a particularly well-crafted internal hybrid, closer inspection may reveal design mistakes that led to its abandonment. A number of candidates for design mistakes are discussed below. They may be grouped into problems of allocating competence, eliminating tournaments, sacrificing specialization advantages, coordination, knowledge sharing, and influence activities.[6]

Allocating competence.   Demsetz (1991) and Casson (1994) argue that firms are hierarchical because this is an efficient way of utilizing different, yet complementary, knowledge; direction may be less costly than instruction or joint decision-making. When this is the case, those with more decisive knowledge should direct those with less decisive knowledge. Thus, the hierarchy is an efficient method of allocating competence. The spaghetti organization eliminated most hierarchical levels. Thus, the extent to which hierarchy could be used as a sorting mechanism for allocating skills was much smaller in the spaghetti organization. For example, the delegation of project-initiation rights implied that competent and less competent employees had the same rights to initiate projects and get a hearing before the Products and Projects Committee. Knowledge-based inefficiencies may have resulted that could have been avoided in a traditional hierarchy.

However, this explanation implicitly asserts that managers are, on average, more knowledgeable with respect to what actions subordinate employees should optimally take than these employees are themselves. If this is not the case, bottom-up selection processes may sort better than hierarchical processes. In fact, the spaghetti organization was (at least in the official rhetoric) very much founded on the notion that bottom-up processes would select more efficiently than hierarchical processes. Hierarchical superiors may be more knowledgeable about which actions should optimally be taken by subordinates when there are strong complementarities between the actions of subordinates, hierarchical superiors possess superior information about these complementarities, and/or they possess private information about which states of the world have been realized (Foss and Foss 2002). To be sure, complementarities between subordinates' actions and knowledge sets obtained in the spaghetti organization. However, the purpose of the spontaneous, market-like, bottom-up processes was exactly to discover and utilize such complementarities—something that the earlier hierarchical organization had not been capable of. Thus, it seems unlikely that abolishing the hierarchy in Oticon led to serious inefficiencies related to the allocation of competence.

Eliminating tournaments.   From an incentive perspective, the extremely flat spaghetti organization implied that one particular incentive instrument was no longer available to the organization: Hierarchical job ladders could no longer function as incentive mechanisms in their own right, since the spaghetti organization essentially abolished what agency theorists call 'tournaments' between managers (Lazear 1995). Promotion was no longer a 'prize' that could be obtained through expending effort. However, while the spaghetti organization may have eliminated this particular incentive instrument, it introduced a number of new incentive instruments, such as performance pay. From the point of view of individual employees, these new instruments may have been stronger with respect to motivation than tournaments, because they were less open to political manipulation. Thus, the sacrifice of tournaments as an incentive instrument may not have been a major problem.

Sacrificing specialization advantages.   A key component of the spaghetti organization was the multi-job concept, which implied that each employee was (1) encouraged to develop skills outside her present skill portfolio, and (2) free to join projects as she saw fit. Much work on Oticon has treated the multi-job concept as a strong stimulus to knowledge exchange and integration (e.g. Verona and Ravasi 1999; Ravasi and Verona 2000), presumably quite rightly so. However, the concept may also have introduced distinct costs, most obviously the sacrifice of specialization advantages that it would seem to imply. However, there are indications that this was actually not the case. For example, an Oticon engineer might have been encouraged to develop English writing skills, which would place him in a better position to undertake technical translation relevant to his project, and do so in a more informed way than a professional translator would be capable of. Thus, this aspect of the multi-job concept may have led to beneficial exploitation of complementarities between different skills.

Problems of coordination.   However, there is strong evidence that the second part of the multi-job concept, the freedom to join projects, had significant costs.[7] Nobody kept track of the total time that employees spent on projects.[8] Moreover, project leaders were free to try to attract those who worked on competing projects, and in many cases they succeeded in doing so. This was a consequence of the explicit aim to emulate the market, but the effect was that it was hard to commit employees to projects and to ensure an efficient allocation of attention to projects (Gifford 1992). This led to severe coordination problems, because project leaders had no guarantee that they could actually carry a project to its end. Moreover, many employees joined more projects than their time resources could possibly allow for, creating problems of coordinating schedules and work hours. The Products and Projects Committee had no routines for dealing with these problems. Apparently, reputation mechanisms were not sufficient for coping with them either. It would seem perhaps that these problems could have been reduced by simply prohibiting employees from working on more than, say, two projects, that could not add up to more than 100 per cent of the employee's total work hours.[9] Establishing such controls in the original spaghetti organization would, however, have run counter to the official rhetoric of auton-omy, empowerment, and delegation. Alternatively, monitoring systems might have been refined to control dimensions of employee behavior that related to their attention and work allocation across the projects they participated in, so as to reduce coordination problems. However, the very elaborate monitoring sys-tem that was implemented alongside the spaghetti organization and involved the construction of objective measures on half a dozen aspects of employee behavior (Poulsen 1993) appears to have been quickly and tacitly shelved and substituted with a simpler system that relied much more on subjective performance assess-ment (Business Intelligence 1993). This suggests that the problem with mon-itoring systems under the original spaghetti organization was rather that they were already too complex and costly to administer in practice.

Problems of knowledge sharing.   The multi-job concept promoted knowledge sharing and, in turn, knowledge creation. However, there is evidence (Eskerod 1997, 1998) that knowledge sharing was not always spontaneous and uninhib-ited. In fact, in some cases knowledge tended to be held back within projects, because of the widespread, and correct, perception that projects were essentially in competition over corporate resources. Thus, by stressing so strongly a market-like competitive ethos and by making incentive systems more 'high-powered' (Williamson 1996*a*) than they had been under the old organization, the spaghetti organization to some extent worked against its stated purposes. The organization's measurement and reward systems apparently could not fully cope with these problems. It may be questioned how significant this problem was. The impressive innovation record of Oticon in the 1990s indicates that the firm's creation of knowledge may not have been significantly harmed by the competitive relations existing within the spaghetti organization. Still, the relevant question is whether the knowledge-sharing environment could have been better designed. Knowledge sharing is not necessarily best stimulated by a kind of project organization that simulates competitive markets. To the extent that knowledge sharing is a hard-to-measure performance variable, employees are likely to put less of an emphasis on it (Holmström and Milgrom 1991). Upon realizing this, resort to lower-powered incentives is likely (Holmström 1999). This corresponds to what has happened in Oticon. Although the performance-measurement systems in Oticon now include attempts to measure employees' contribution to knowledge sharing, it is also the case that the strong competitive ethos which characterized the spaghetti organization has been significantly dampened in the successor form.

Influence activities.   Influence activities are activities that subordinates engage in when they influence hierarchical superiors to make decisions that are in their own interests, rather than in the organization's (Milgrom 1988; Argyres and Mui 2000). Resources expended on influence activities are, from the point of view of the organization, waste. It is arguable that it is relatively more difficult under an organization such as the spaghetti organization to protect against influence activities. This is because everybody has, in principle, direct access to the management team. A comparative advantage of the traditional, hierarchical, and rule-governed organization is exactly that it may be better at protecting itself against influence activities, because access to those who hold ultimate decision rights is more difficult. In fact, the spaghetti organization, which actively stimulated competition between project groups for the approval of the only relevant 'hierarchical superior' left, namely the Products and Projects Committee, did produce such influence activities (Eskerod 1998). In contrast, under the hierarchical form existing prior to the spaghetti organization such activities had been much less prevalent, because of the aloof management style of the old management (Poulsen 1993). Personal relations to those who staffed the Committee became paramount for having a project ratified by the Committee. As Eskerod (1998: 80) observed:

Part of being a project group may be lobbying in the PPC trying to obtain a high priority status by influencing the PPC members. The reason for doing this is that a high priority project is regarded as a very attractive place for the employees, because the management sees this project as important.

It is, however, not clear from the existing empirical studies of the spaghetti organization that this was perceived as a serious problem in the organization, for example, whether it resulted in obviously unimportant projects being approved by the Committee. Rather, it was taken as an unavoidable, and relatively small, cost of the spaghetti organization.[10]

To sum up, the search for the causes of the partial abandonment of the spaghetti organization so far seems to lead only to inefficiencies stemming from the lack of well-functioning project management routines on the part of Products and Projects Committee being a serious problem. However, handling this problem did not necessarily require a major organizational change. Still, the many possible small liabilities of the spaghetti organization (problems of knowledge being held back in projects, influence activities, etc.) may together have added up to significant costs that could be reduced by adopting a more structured organizational form (Børsens Nyhedsmagasin 1999; interview with Henrik Holck, June 2000). Moreover, there is one fundamental problem left that was clearly present in the spaghetti organization, and which is a strong candidate for explaining the abandonment of that organizational form.

The Problem of Selective Intervention

Although infusing hierarchical forms with elements of market control seems attractive, crafting and implementing such internal hybrids is a highly complicated problem. One reason is a fundamental incentive problem that plagues all hierarchies, but is arguably particularly prevalent in the very flat kind of organization of which the Oticon spaghetti organization is an example. An early statement of the nature of this problem can be found in the comparative-systems literature in economics; that is, the literature taken up with the economic differences between capitalist and socialist systems. Thus, Mises (1949: 709) argued that there are fundamental problems involved in 'playing market' inside hierarchies.[11] Specifically, schemes for a socialist market economy would not work, because the concentration of ultimate decision-making rights and responsibilities (i.e. ownership) in the hands of a central planning board would dilute the incentives of managers. Thus, while planning authorities could delegate rights to make production and investment decisions to managers, these rights would be inefficiently used. First, because managers could always be overruled by the planning authorities, they were not likely to take a long view, notably in their investment decisions. Second, because managers were not the ultimate owners, they were not the full residual claimants of their decisions and, hence, would not make efficient decisions.

Later research has clarified that (1) handling the problem requires that the planning authorities can credibly commit to a non-interference policy, and (2) the problem goes beyond the comparative-systems context. It is latent in all relations between 'rulers' and 'ruled' (North 1990; Miller 1992; Williamson 1996a; Foss and Foss 2002). The problem arises from the fact that it is hard for the ruler to commit to a non-interference policy, because reneging on a promise to delegate will in many cases be extremely tempting and those to whom rights are delegated will anticipate this. Loss of motivation results. The problem is not unknown in organizational studies, (e.g. Vancil and Buddrus 1979: 65). In particular, Williamson's concept (1996a) of the 'impossibility of selective intervention' is highly relevant. He describes it as

a variant on the theme, 'Why aren't more degrees of freedom always better than less?' In the context of firm and market organization, the puzzle is, 'Why can't a large firm do everything that a collection of small firms can and more.' By merely replicating the market the firm can do no worse than the market. And if the firm can intervene selectively (namely, intervene always but only when expected net gains can be projected), then the firm will sometimes do better. Taken together, the firm will do at least as well as, and will sometimes do better than, the market (1996a: 150).

Williamson directly argues that (efficient) selective intervention of this kind is 'impossible'. Incentives are diluted, because the option to intervene 'can be exercised both for good cause (to support expected net gains) and for bad (to support the subgoals of the intervenor)' (ibid. 150–1). Promises only to intervene 'for good cause' can never be credible, Williamson argues, because they are not enforceable in a court of law. The wider implication of this reasoning is that since decision rights cannot be delegated in a court-enforceable manner inside firms (i.e. are not contractible), authority can only reside at the top. Authority cannot be delegated, even informally, since any attempt to do this will run into the problem of the impossibility of selective intervention. One would therefore expect to see little use of delegation. Given that delegation is clearly a viable and widespread organizational practice, this suggests that this implication is going too far.

   In fact, it is conceivable that the 'intervenor' may credibly commit to not intervene in such a way that the 'subgoals of the intervenor' are promoted. The logic may be stated in the following way (cf. Baker, Gibbons, and Murphy 1999). Assume that a subordinate initiates a project.[12] Assume further that the manager has information that is necessary to perform an assessment of the project, but that he decides up front to ratify *any* project that the subordinate proposes. Effectively, this amounts to full informal delegation of the rights to initiate and ratify projects—'informal', because the formal right to ratify is still in the hands of the manager and because that right cannot be allocated to the subordinate through a court-enforceable contract (cf. Williamson 1996a). Because the subordinate values being given freedom—she is partly a residual claimant on the outcomes of his activities—this will induce more effort in searching for new projects (Aghion and Tirole 1997; Foss and Foss 2002). To the organization the expected benefits of these increased efforts may be larger than the expected costs from the bad projects that the manager has to ratify. However, a problem arises when the manager has information about the state of a project ('bad' or 'good'), because he may then be tempted to renege on a promise to delegate decision authority, that is, intervene in a 'selective' manner. If he overrules the subordinate, the latter will lose trust in him, holding back on effort. Clearly, in such a game a number of equilibria, each one characterized by different combinations of employee trust and managerial intervention, are feasible. What determines the particular equilibrium that will emerge is the discount rate of the manager, the specific trigger strategy followed by the subordinate (e.g. Will he lose trust in the manager for all future periods if he is overruled, or will he be more forbearing?), and how much the manager values his reputation for not reneging relative to the benefits of reneging on a bad project (Baker, Gibbons, and Murphy 1999).

All of the above builds on standard-economics assumptions on motivation and cognition. Employees are motivated solely by being able to share in the outcomes of their activities, and managerial intervention decreases motivation because it means that the expected gain from putting effort into a project diminishes. Including richer motivational and cognitive concerns aggravates the problem of selective intervention. As argued in an extensive literature in psychology (summarized in Frey 1997), people are also likely to be intrinsically motivated. Such motivation may be sustained by psychological contracts that involve loyalties and emotional ties (Brockner et al. 1992; Robinson and Morrison 1995; Osterloh and Frey 2000: 541). Managerial intervention, particularly when it is perceived to be essentially arbitrary, may break such contracts and harms intrinsic motivation (Robinson and Rousseau 1994). Other aspects of psychological research (summarized in Bazerman 1994) suggest other ways in which the problem of selective intervention may be aggravated in practice. Thus, robust findings in experimental psychology show the presence of a systematic overconfidence bias in judgment; that is, people tend to trust their own judgments more than is 'objectively' warranted. Managers are not exceptions to this bias; perhaps quite the contrary. The presence of the overconfidence bias in the judgments that underlie managerial decision-making is likely to aggravate the problem of selective intervention, because it produces additional meddling in subordinates' decisions.

Selective Intervention in Oticon

It is arguable that the main reason why the spaghetti organization was changed into a more hierarchical organization has to do with the kind of incentive and motivational problems described above. The official Oticon rhetoric, stressing bottom-up processes in a flexible, market-like, and essentially self-organizing system, with substantial autonomy and a management team (i.e. the Products and Projects Committee) that acted as little more than a facilitator (Kolind 1990; Lyregaard 1993), became increasingly at odds with the frequent selective intervention that was undertaken by the Products and Projects Committee.[13] The need for selective intervention was rationalized by an external observer in the following terms:

PPC [the Products and Projects Committee] does not make general written plans, which are accessible to the rest of the organization . . . if this were done, plans would have to be adjusted or remade in an ever-continuing process, because the old plans had become outdated (Eskerod 1998: 80)

This entirely ad hoc approach was taken by the Products and Projects Committee to be an unavoidable feature of a flexible, project-oriented organization (ibid.: 89). However, it was also a direct signal to employees that the 'contract' between any project and the Products and Projects Committee was very incomplete (Williamson 1996a), and that the Committee might at any time exercise its ultimate control rights for the purpose of intervening in projects. This produced diluted incentives and badly harmed motivation (as documented at length by Eskerod 1997, 1998). Accumulating frustration finally resulted in a major meeting in 1995, which marks the beginning of the retreat from the spaghetti organization. At the meeting employees vociferously expressed their concerns about the contrast between, on the one hand, the Oticon value base, including the strong rhetoric of delegation, and, on the other hand, the way in which the company was actually managed. Frustration that projects were interrupted in seemingly arbitrary ways and that the organization was far better at generating projects than at completing them was explicitly voiced.

The preceding discussion suggests that a fundamental problem in the spaghetti organization was that Kolind and the Products and Projects Committee never committed to a policy of not intervening selectively; neither, apparently, did they intend to do so, or even see any rationale in it. Kolind's view appears to have been that in important respects and in many situations he and the Products and Projects Committee would possess accurate knowledge about the true commercial and technical possibilities of a given project, and that efficient utilization of corporate resources dictated intervening in, and sometimes closing down, projects. However, that view clashed at a basic level with the rhetoric of widespread delegation of decision rights, leading to the demise of the spaghetti organization, and the adoption of the current more structured matrix organization.

In principle, Kolind and the Products and Projects Committee could have committed to a policy of non-interference from the beginning, rather than acting on the belief that organizational flexibility required that they selectively intervene in projects. Conceivably, this might have made this radical internal hybrid viable. However, even if Kolind and the Products and Projects Committee had announced initially that they would refrain from selective intervention, there are reasons why this commitment might not have been sustainable in the longer run. Thus, it was increasingly realized that the elaborate system of measures that was initially installed was inadequate. It did not capture important dimensions of behavior (e.g. employees' contribution to knowledge sharing) and it may have caused some projects to hold back knowledge. Rather than trying to refine the system further, it was abandoned.[14] However, the implication was that management could no longer take place solely through incentives (following initial ratification of projects). The employee-stock-ownership program was arguably not sufficiently high-powered to truly motivate, and did not confer sufficient decision rights to halt the practice of selective intervention in employees' territory. The implication was that Kolind and the Products and Projects Committee had to engage in much more monitoring of the projects. Being able to do this without compromising team autonomy and harming motivation was unlikely.

The New Organization

A notable feature of the current Oticon organization lies in its much more consistent approach towards projects. Organizational expectations are that priorities do not change in the rapid and erratic manner that characterized the original spaghetti organization, and that employees can be much more sure that the projects they are working on will be seen through to the end. In the new organization projects are rarely stopped or abandoned, and there is an explicitly stated policy of sticking to ratified projects. Two reasons are given for this. First, projects are more carefully examined with respect to technical feasibility and commercial implications. An aspect of this is that the Competence Center now puts forward project ideas much more actively, and contacts potential project leaders, rather than relying on the bottom-up approach that characterized the original spaghetti organization. Thus, hierarchical selection has to some extent substituted for selection performed by bottom-up processes. Second, the wish to avoid harming motivation (i.e. diluting incentives) by overruling existing projects is firmly stressed. The management team has openly announced this policy, and has made it credible by (1) consistently sticking to it and (2) researching project ideas carefully *ex ante* so that employees' perception of the probability that intervention will occur is low. Some reasons why a more traditional hierarchy may be better at making such commitment credible are discussed in the following section.

Discussion: Implications for Internal Hybrids

Proponents of internal hybrids argue that their advantage lies in the ability to integrate the virtues of more conventional organizational forms (Miles et al.

1997). Specifically, internal hybrids combine the ability to achieve efficiencies through specialization that characterizes the functional form with the relative independence that can be granted in a divisional form and the ability to transfer resources and capabilities across division and business-unit boundaries that characterize the matrix organization (e.g. Miles and Snow 1992). Strikingly similar arguments were invoked by the designers of the Oticon spaghetti organization (Kolind 1990, 1994; Lyregaard 1993). This suggests that broader lessons with respect to the efficient design of internal hybrids may emerge from the Oticon experience.

Getting Complementarities Right

A basic proposition in much organization theory is that for reasons of efficiency organizational forms are aligned with environmental conditions, strategies, and exchange conditions in a systematic and discriminating manner (Thompson 1967; Meyer, Tsui, and Hinings 1993; Williamson 1996a; Nickerson and Zenger 2002). Thus, Zenger (2002: 80) argues that many attempts to infuse hierarchies with elements of market control break with this basic proposition and often 'violate patterns of complementarity that support traditional hierarchy as an organizational form'. For example, managers implement new structures without new performance measures and new pay systems, or they implement new pay systems without developing new performance measures. This results in unstable, possibly inefficient, hybrid forms. In contrast, viable internal hybrids are characterized by organizational elements clustering in certain characteristic, complementary combinations, just as in the case of markets and hierarchies (Williamson 1996a).

Did the spaghetti organization get the complementarities between organizational elements right? On first inspection, it did, as has been argued. However, closer inspection reveals a somewhat different picture. Thus, it may be argued that Oticon did not get the organizational complementarities exactly right, because the kind of radical internal hybrid that was adopted requires that projects be managed almost exclusively through the provision of incentives and ownership (Miles et al. 1997; Zenger 2002). The performance measurement systems in the spaghetti organization were not adequate to support precise performance evaluation. Some relevant performance dimensions (e.g. contribution to knowledge sharing) were not measured at all. Also, the incentive effects of the employee-stock-ownership program appear to have been limited. Thus, remuneration schemes may not have rested on sufficiently precise and encompassing measures and were not sufficiently high-powered to complement the widespread delegation of decision rights in the organization. This fostered a need for selective intervention on the part of Kolind and the Products and Projects Committee that went beyond what would have been necessary with better measures of employee performance, and which had the unintended effect that motivation was seriously harmed. This reasoning suggests the following proposition:

> **Proposition 1:** Internal hybrids that violate patterns of complementarity characteristic of this organizational form will be subject to more problems of selective intervention than hybrid forms that get the complementarities right.

A corollary to this proposition is that advances in measurement methods will result in less selective intervention, because the measurement of performance is improved so that the moral hazard stemming from the delegation of rights is reduced.

Problems of Intervention and Organizational Form

The motivational and incentive problems that may emerge from selective managerial intervention are not independent of organizational structure; notably, the number of hierarchical layers in the organization, and therefore the distribution of information and authority in a firm. Arguably, organizations that adopt internal hybrids that amount to drastically reducing the number of hierarchical layers, such as Oticon's spaghetti experiment, are more prone to the problem than more traditional hierarchical firms. There are (at least) three reasons for this.

First, decision rights are more solidly established in a traditional hierarchy, being associated with well-defined, distinct positions, than in a flat, project-based organization, where decision rights are more fleeting. Organizational expectations that certain positions come with certain decision rights are very well established, and potentially costly for a top manager to break with through selective intervention. The same kind of organizational expectations are not likely to be established in a flat, project-based organization. Second, a top manager who selectively intervenes in a hierarchical organization risks overruling the *whole* managerial hierarchy (all those below him), whereas this may be a smaller concern in a flat organization, where the CEO may only harm motivation in a specific project team if he overrules that team. Third, information processing perspectives (Thompson 1967; Galbraith 1974) suggest that the hierarchy is not just a structure of authority, but also one of information. The informational distance between projects and top manager may be enlarged by having a multi-layered hierarchy. This implies that the top manager knows that he is in key dimensions ignorant about the project (Aghion and Tirole 1997). In this case, his incentives selectively to intervene will be small. The preceding arguments suggest the following proposition:

> **Proposition 2:** An internal hybrid form that is organized within a firm with few hierarchical layers will be associated with larger efficiency losses caused by

problems of selective intervention than an internal-hybrid form that is organized within a firm with more hierarchical layers.

Problems of Intervention and the External Environment

A key reasons why the Products and Projects Committee considered that frequent selective intervention was necessary had to do with the impossibility of making detailed plans for future business development in an industry where unforeseen contingencies (e.g. new technologies) often occurred. This suggests a third proposition:

Proposition 3: There will be more selective intervention in internal hybrid forms that operate in turbulent industries than in internal hybrid forms that operate in tranquil industries.

This proposition may be taken to be the other side of the coin of the transaction-cost argument that *external* hybrids are unstable in 'dynamic' industries (Williamson 1996*a*) because in such industries unexpected contingencies that may give rise to hold-ups are more likely. Along similar lines, the argument underlying Proposition 3 is that in dynamic industries the implicit contract between teams/projects and management in *internal* hybrids is likely to be relatively more incomplete than in more tranquil industries. Therefore, management is likely to engage in more selective intervention in an attempt to influence how projects react to unexpected contingencies.

Internal and External Hybrids and Internal and External Markets

The problem of selective intervention casts a novel light over governance choices between internal and external hybrids and internal and external markets. These organizational forms may be seen as rather close substitutes. For example, they may be adopted in order better to exploit local knowledge (Cowen and Parker 1997), or to strengthen incentives because they make agents residual claimants to a higher degree than is the case in traditional hierarchies. However whereas internal hybrids/internal markets may suffer from problems stemming from selective intervention, external hybrids/external markets do not suffer from these. Of course, external hybrids and markets may suffer from inefficiencies caused by hold-up problems when specific assets are deployed. However, creating competition between suppliers, investing in hostages, having some tapered integration, etc. may strongly reduce problems related to hold-up. The legal system also constrains the hold-up possibility, however imperfectly. In contrast, a solution to the problem of avoiding harmful selective intervention cannot rely on market forces or court-enforceable contracts. The implication is that, on average, external markets and external hybrids are likely to have incentive properties that are superior to those of internal markets and internal hybrids, so that there will be (transaction and production) cost penalties associated with the use of the latter. This results in the following proposition:

Proposition 4: Firms that choose external hybrids (markets) over internal hybrids (markets) will have a cost performance that is superior to those that choose internal hybrids (markets) over external hybrids (markets).

This reasoning may be seen as a variation of a familiar theme of transaction cost economics (Williamson 1996a); namely, that vertical integration be considered the option of last resort.

Managing Commitment to Not Selectively Intervene

While theory suggests that the problem of committing to not selectively intervene is a tough one, we do seem to observe a substantial amount of delegation in real-world firms. This indicates that it is possible credibly to commit to non-intervention. There are two fundamental methods that managers may use for this purpose. Both essentially tie the hands of a would-be intervenor.

The first one is to commit oneself to being (rationally) ignorant. Thus, a manager may choose not to be informed about a number of critical dimensions in projects. In very hierarchical organizations this may be easy to accomplish because of the large informational distance between top management and projects. A second approach proceeds by managers making it harmful to themselves selectively to intervene. Open announcement of a non-intervention policy, ensuring such a policy is recorded in company documents, working to install it in corporate culture, etc. all go some way to meet this aim, since they make the possible clash between the communicated values and interventionist managerial practice extremely sharp, and make very obvious the breaking of the explicitly stated psychological contract (Brockner et al. 1992).

The Spaghetti Organization as a Modulation between Stable Organizational Forms

Although organizational forms that break with a logic of complementarity may incur penalties in terms of static efficiency (i.e. economizing with transaction costs and costs of production), they may still conceivably yield benefits in terms of dynamic efficiency (i.e. innovativeness). Calls for 'chaotic' organization (Peters 1992) often implicitly make such arguments. Organization design needs to consider both types of efficiencies (Ghemawat and Ricart i Costa 1993). An implication is that in an inter-temporal perspective, choosing 'consistent' configurations of organizational elements may not necessarily maximize the value of the firm. An ingenious argument of this kind has been developed by Nickerson and Zenger (2002). They suggest that considerations of efficiency may require modulating between discrete organizational forms—such as the old hierarchical Oticon organization and the post-spaghetti matrix structure—even in response to a *stable* set of environmental conditions. This is because the steady-state functionality delivered by a discrete organizational form may itself be discrete, and the desired functionality may lie in-between those delivered by the discrete organizational forms. Efficiency gains may then be obtained by modulating between the forms.

If indeed the Oticon spaghetti organization did incur inefficiencies with respect to the organization of its administrative systems, it is hard to dispute that it was also quite an innovative organization (cf. Table 7.1). These benefits may have overwhelmed the organizational costs. Although the spaghetti organization was not stable in the presence of the problem of selective intervention, it would still have made sense to choose this form, even if the designers had known it to be inherently unstable. In fact, much of the early discussion of the spaghetti organization made reference to the need to try something entirely new and admittedly chaotic, for the purpose of drastically shaking up the original, bureaucratic organization (Kolind 1990; Peters 1992; Poulsen 1993). This is consistent with Nickerson and Zenger's theory. The spaghetti organization may indeed be an example of modulating between the stable organizational form of the traditional, pre-spaghetti hierarchy and the stable matrix organization *post* spaghetti. What lends credence to this interpretation is that although the hearing-aid industry was technologically quite dynamic in the relevant period (Lotz 1998), it is not possible to identify environmental changes that might have caused the organizational change away from the spaghetti organization.

Firms and Markets

This discussion casts light over the classic question of the fundamental differences between firms and markets, and supports the original Coasian position that the key difference is that markets do not rely on resource allocation by means of authority whereas firms do (Coase 1937). 'Authority' is a problematic word, because it is often invested with too narrow a meaning; for example, detailed direction and supervision (Foss and Foss 2002). Ultimately, the meaning of having authority is that one can restrict the decisions of one's subordinate, overrule him, and perhaps fire him. This means that although decision rights may be delegated, we can still trace the chain of authority in a firm, and we will always realize that ultimate decision-making power resides at the top. As this chapter has illustrated, all subordinates' decision rights 'are loaned, not owned' (Baker, Gibbons, and Murphy 1999: 56). Fundamentally, it can never be otherwise. This is because ultimate decision-making rights can only be transferred from bosses to subordinates in one way; namely, by transferring ownership (Hart 1995). However, transferring ownership amounts to spinning off the person to whom ownership is given. It means creating a new firm. It is this fundamental difference in how ownership is allocated that underlies the problem of selective intervention. The analysis in this chapter thus makes direct contact with important modern theories of economic organization (Hart 1995; Williamson 1996a; Baker, Gibbons, and Murphy 2002) that stress the importance of ownership for the understanding of the nature of firms and firm boundaries.

Conclusion

To many firms the adoption of new, hybrid organizational forms is increasingly seen as imperative. However, rather little theoretical and empirical research has treated, particularly, internal hybrids. This chapter has examined a specific experiment with adopting and later strongly modifying a radical internal hybrid, in an attempt to identify some possible liabilities of the adoption of such organizational forms. In particular, the focus has been on motivational problems that may be caused by problems of committing to refraining from harmful selective intervention. A main argument was that problems of selective intervention are particularly prevalent in organizations that adopt radical internal hybrids. In contrast, firms with more traditional hierarchical structures better shield themselves from these problems. Managers may commit to non-intervention by means of rationally choosing to be ignorant or by making it harmful to themselves selectively to intervene. Finally, the problem of selective intervention is a prime candidate for understanding the incentive liabilities of hierarchies and internal hybrids vis-à-vis markets or external hybrids.

Although this chapter has thus exemplified the interpretative power of organizational economics, it must be admitted that organizational economics only tells part of the story. From an organizational economics perspective the spaghetti organization represented a matrix of rights and incentives that are helpful for understanding its liabilities, and how these liabilities gave rise to certain organizational dynamics (i.e. the partial abandonment of the spaghetti organization). However, it may indeed also be understood in terms of an attempt to, for example, foster dynamic capabilities (Ravasi and Verona 2000), a perspective that lies outside organizational economics. Thus, the full story of the Oticon spaghetti experiment requires that more than one perspective be considered. Relatedly, the chapter has suggested that organizational economics should consider to a fuller extent psychological insights into motivation and cognition. While it is possible to tell stories of managerial commitment, selective intervention, and stifled incentives based only on organizational economics, there is little reason to be so narrow. A vast literature on procedural justice in organization, psychological contracts, and (biased) cognition exists, the insights of which may be combined with organizational-economics insights in order to further the understanding of problems of managerial commitment, including problems of selective intervention (cf. also Miller 1992; Lindenberg 2000).

Notes

1. See Teece (2003) for a study that is complementary to this chapter. Teece studies an internal hybrid (the organization of the Law and Economics Consulting Group) that is organized on very different principles from those of the Oticon spaghetti organization.
2. However, a main purpose of conducting analysis of single cases is often to be able to pose competing explanations for the same set of events (and perhaps to indicate how these explanations may be applied to other situations) (Yin 1989). Moreover, basic considerations of internal validity dictate that alternative explanations be considered. However, while I shall indeed make reference to and discuss other possible explanations of some of the relevant events (e.g. ideas from motivation theory and information processing theory), the main emphasis is on developing one specific interpretation. While an eclectic, multiple-perspective approach may be superior in the abstract, more insight may arguably be provided in the concrete by pursuing, in a relatively narrow fashion, one specific interpretation and exploring the limits of this interpretation.
3. The possibility that external hybrids or market contracting may be alternatives to internal hybrids never seems to have been considered in Oticon. Thus, that incentives may be strengthened by relying on the *real* market (rather than the simulated internal one) by spinning off functions and departments (Aron 1991) does not appear to have been seen as a serious alternative to internal disaggregation.
4. Exceptions may occur when giving subordinates more extensive rights (e.g. a package of initiation, ratification, and implementation rights) strengthens employee incentives (see Aghion and Tirole 1997; Baker, Gibbons, and Murphy 1999; and Foss and Foss 2002 for analyses of this).
5. For example, it could reflect attempts to curb moral hazard in project teams. However, the increased use of high-powered incentives and more widespread employee ownership were designed to remedy problems of moral hazard.
6. In addition, a motivation theory perspective would suggest that while employees' lower-level needs were not sufficiently satisfied (low income, uncertainty because of the reorganization and lay-offs), management already tried to address their higher-level needs (more comprehensive tasks, more responsibility). Thanks to an anonymous reviewer for this point.
7. Eskerod (1997, 1998) in particular documents this. My later interview with the chief HRM officer strongly confirmed Eskerod's finding that the multi-job concept had severe costs in terms of problems of coordination and frustrating employees.
8. Nor would this have been possible, as nobody in Oticon, not even the Products and Projects Committee, kept track of the total number of development projects. Records were only kept of the ten-to-twenty major projects. An estimate is that under the spaghetti organization an average of seventy projects were continously running (Eskerod 1998: 80).

9. In fact, the more structured project organization gradually implemented from 1996 has established controls that ensure that the coordination and time-allocation problems that beset the original spaghetti organization are kept at bay.

10. Interview with HRM manager Henrik Holck.

11. Somewhat later the literature on internal-transfer prices revealed the existence of various incentive problems that may beset this organizational practice (e.g. Holmström and Tirole 1991).

12. This should be understood in a broad sense. A 'project' may refer to many different types of decisions or clusters of decisions.

13. See Simons (2002) for a highly pertinent discussion of employees' perception of the fit between managers' words and actions, and the motivational consequences of this perception.

14. Since behavior was apparently difficult to measure, a more output-based system could have been tried (Prendergast 1999); for example, contracts that specified rewards for specific accomplishments (e.g. a system that rewarded according to milestones in a development project). However, it is doubtful whether such a contract could actually be made court-enforceable. A managerial-commitment problem would again result.

8

Performance and Organization in the Knowledge Economy: Innovation and New Human Resource Management Practices

Introduction

The ongoing restructuring of management and organization practices designed to cope with an increasingly complex and rapidly changing knowledge-based economy has received increasing attention from scholars from a diversity of disciplines and fields (Bowman and Singh 1993; Huselid 1995; Guest 1997; Zenger and Hesterly 1997). In particular, much attention has been given to the restructuring of the employment relation in the form of changed human resource management (henceforth 'HRM') practices that has accompanied the emergence of firms specialized to compete in dynamic, information-rich environments (Ichniowski et al. 1996). These practices encompass various types of team-based organization, continuous (often internal and team-based) learning, decentralization of decision rights and incentives, systems for mobilizing employee proposals for improvements, quality circles, emphasis on internal knowledge dissemination, etc. (Lado and Wilson 1994; Zenger and Hesterly 1997; Mendelson and Pillai 1999).

While many of these new practices may not, strictly speaking, be entirely novel, some of the broad generalizations about new HRM practices refer to trends that appear to be truly recent (Osterman 2000). Thus, new HRM practices appear to follow a steep diffusion curve (ibid.), and they tend to be adopted in a system-like manner rather than as individual components (Ichniowski, Shaw, and Prennushi 1997; Laursen and Mahnke 2001). Moreover, there are some indications that they tend to be associated with high innovation performance (Mendelson and Pillai 1999; Michie and Sheehan 1999). It is these emerging 'stylized facts', and particularly the latter two, that we try theoretically and empirically to address and substantiate in this chapter.

The increased attention paid to new HRM practice has been particularly prevalent in the fields of strategic management, human resource management, and, increasingly, the economics of organization. For example, strategy scholars have argued that human resources are particularly likely to be sources of

This chapter is co-authored with Keld Laursen.

sustained competitive advantage and that HRM practices should therefore be central to strategy (Barney 1991; Lado and Wilson 1994; Barney 1995). One reason for this is the system-like—or, in the terminology that we shall make use of, '(Edgeworth) complementary'—way in which HRM practices may connect: complex interaction between many complementary practices is arguably harder for would-be imitators to copy than stand-alone practices (Barney 1991; Porter and Rivkin 1997). The complementary nature of many of the elements of (formal and informal) organizational structure has been examined in an emerging important literature in organizational economics (notably Milgrom and Roberts 1990*a*; Aoki and Dore 1994; Milgrom and Roberts 1995; Holmström and Roberts 1998). Insights from this literature have made some impact in the human resource management field (Baron and Kreps 1999*ab*).

The connection between firms' internal organization and their innovativeness has certainly never been neglected in the innovation and evolutionary-economics literature. After all, the increasing bureaucratization of the R&D function was a key theme in Schumpeter's later work. However, it is also fair to say that these literatures are characterized by relatively scant attention being paid to new (complementary) HRM practices and how they influence innovation performance.[1] Something similar may be said of the HRM literature; here, too, is a lack of theoretical and empirical treatment of how new HRM practices impact on innovation performance.[2] In sum, there is clearly in a number of fields and disciplines an emerging theoretical and empirical understanding of how HRM practices and complementarities between these impact on productivity and, in turn, on financial performance, but that understanding needs to be extended to also encompass innovation performance. Accordingly, the purpose of this chapter is to add to the theoretical and empirical understanding of how HRM practices and complementarities assist in explaining innovation performance. Thus, we shall argue and empirically demonstrate that new HRM practices, and complementarities between these, impact on innovation performance; that is, on future competitive advantages.

This chapter is one of the first major empirical examinations of the link between innovation performance and complementary new HRM practices. Only a few other chapters are available on this topic, including Michie and Sheehan (1999). Thus, for example, while Gjerding (1997) and Mendelson and Pillai (1999) do examine the HRM/performance link, they do not incorporate considerations of complementarity. Lorenz (1998) presents an analysis of complementarities between the use of new HRM practices and so-called new pay policies, but he does not include a measure of performance in the analysis. And Ichniowski, Shaw, and Prennushi (1997) discuss the complementarity/ performance (productive efficiency) link, but they do not deal with innovation performance. In contrast, we link together complementarity and innovation performance. Furthermore, in our analysis the HRM 'systems' (i.e. particular combinations of HRM practices) *emerge* out of the empirical analysis (namely, from our principal-component analysis), while Ichniowski, Shaw, and Prennushi (1997) and Michie and Sheehan (1999) *assume* their different systems from the outset. Arguably, Ichniowski, Shaw, and Prennushi (1997) are able to define fine-grained controls, since they focus on HRM complementarities found in steel-finishing lines only. However, the drawback is that the conclusions drawn do not concern the entire economy as such. In contrast, we test hypotheses that articulate the HRM/innovation link on a large Danish data set—the DISKO database—which contains cross-sectional information on the HRM practices and innovation performances of 1,900 privately owned Danish firms in both manufacturing and non-manufacturing industries.

We contribute to several literatures. For instance, our finding that complementarity obtains in HRM practices provides further empirical support for theoretical work on complementarity in organizational economics and elsewhere. Our investigation of the links between complementary HRM practices and innovation performance contributes to the firm-strategy literature as well as to the innovation literature. However, we see this chapter as most directly linking up with work in evolutionary economics and innovation studies. Much of this work has had an aggregate focus in which the internal organization of the firm has been given less attention, and where the main interest has centered on issues such as appropriability, firm size, market structure, complementary assets, etc. as determinants of innovation performance. The findings in this chapter may be taken as an indication of the importance of internal factors for the understanding of innovation (while not denying the importance of other factors).

The design of the chapter is as follows. In the section, 'Complementarity, New HRM Practices, and Innovation Performance: Theoretical Considerations' we begin by reviewing recent work on complementarities in organizational economics. The notion of complementarities allows us better to understand the 'systemic' quality which may characterize not only technologies but also the organizational elements that constitute the internal organization of firms. Thus, we argue that complementarities allow us better to understand the clustering of HRM practices in firms. Moreover, the notion of complementarity is helpful for understanding how performance is influenced by such systemicness. Thus, complementarities between HRM practices influence not only the firm's profits but also, as we argue, its innovation performance. In the section, 'Empirical Analysis' we specify an empirical model that allows us to test these ideas on the data set represented by the DISKO database. We apply an ordered probit model as the relevant means of estimation. Using principal-component analysis, we identify two HRM systems which are both conducive to innovation. The first is one in which seven of nine HRM variables matter (almost) equally for the ability to innovate. The second system is dominated by firm-internal and -external training. Hence, we conclude that application of HRM practices does matter for the likelihood of a firm being an innovator. Furthermore, since the two HRM systems are strongly significant in explaining innovation performance, while only two individual practices (out of the total of nine) are found to be strongly significant, we find support for the hypothesis stating the importance of complementarities between certain HRM practices (within each of the two HRM systems) for explaining innovation performance.

Complementarity, New HRM Practices, and Innovation Performance: Theoretical Considerations

The HRM–Innovativeness Link: A Black Box?

Contributions that not only mention but actually theoretically and empirically address the link between HRM practices and innovation performance are surprisingly few in number. To be sure, there is a large, somewhat heterogeneous, literature on the management of innovation and technology. However, much of this literature is largely taken up with strategy issues connected to the exogenous dynamics of technology (e.g. technology life cycles), large-scale organizational issues, and questions relating to appropriability (e.g. Tushman and Moore 1988). Of course, beginning with Burns and Stalker (1961), the organizational-behavior field has stressed the link between 'organic' organizational structures and innovation performance. A recent stream of pertinent organizational-behavior research has been prompted by March's distinction (1991) between 'exploration' and 'exploitation'.

However, it is not too unfair to say that more precise theoretical identifications of the mechanisms underlying the hypothesized links between HRM practices and innovativeness are virtually non-existent. This is true of both the technology-management and the organizational-behavior literatures. To offer further illustrative examples, Baron and Kreps's economics-inspired treatise on human-resource management (1999) does not treat innovativeness as a relevant performance variable. Michie and Sheehan (1999), while empirically finding a link between HRM practices and innovation performance, do not offer a theory of this link. Virtually all of the economics literature on the firm-level determinants of innovation has dealt with issues such as the famous debates on the relation between firm size and innovation performance (Acs and Audretsch 1988; Cohen and Klepper 1996). The organizational factors which may mediate any such relations have largely been black-boxed. Finally, while the emerging evolutionary economics literature on the firm (e.g. Kogut and Zander 1992; Dosi and Marengo 1994; Henderson 1994; Granstrand, Patel, and Pavitt 1997; Pavitt 1998; Laamanen and Autio 2000) has stressed complementarities between diverse technologies, and the learning that such complementarities may give rise to, the organizational requirements for coordinating and reaping benefits from these complementarities have not been investigated in any detail.

In sum, therefore, while a number of contributors have noted a link between new HRM practices and innovation performance, and while some contributions have stressed the link between complementary-knowledge stocks and innovation performance, no contributions appear (as far as we know) to have put forward theoretical arguments asserting a link between complementary new HRM practices and innovation performance. However, as indicated, various literatures do contain ideas that are pertinent to the understanding of the link between HRM practices, complementarities between these, and innovation performance. We briefly discuss such ideas below.

Complementarities

One of the most important strides forward in the economics of organization during the last decade is the increasing use that has been made of the notion of Edgeworth complementarities (Milgrom and Roberts 1990a; Milgrom, Qian, and Roberts 1991; Aoki and Dore 1994; Holmström and Milgrom 1994; Milgrom and Roberts 1995; Ichniowski, Shaw, and Prennushi 1997; Holmström and Roberts 1998; Baron and Kreps 1999). Without doubt, the pioneers in this application have been Paul Milgrom and John Roberts. As they define it, complementarity between activities obtains if 'doing more of one thing increases the returns to doing (more of) the others' (Milgrom and Roberts 1995: 181). Formally, this will be seen closely to correspond to mixed partial derivatives of a pay-off function with standard assumptions about smoothness of this function. However, as Milgrom and Roberts argue, drawing on the mathematical field of lattice theory, the notion of complementarity is not wedded to the conventional differentiable framework.[3] Mathematically, complementarity between a set of variables obtains when a function containing the relevant variables as arguments is super-modular.[4]

There are a number of reasons why scholars in a diverse set of fields, including evolutionary economics, technology studies, and organizational behavior, should take an interest in the notion of complementarities (and the associated formalisms). At the most fundamental level, it provides an understanding of those systemic features of technologies that have traditionally interested such scholars (e.g. national systems of innovation, technology systems).[5] The other side of the coin is that complementarity is an important source of path-dependence: successful change has to involve many, perhaps all, relevant variables of a system and involve them in specific ways.[6] This also helps to explain why complementarities are an important source of self-propelled change (cf. Milgrom, Qian, and Roberts 1991); that is, 'cumulative change'.[7] Thus, the notion of complementarity is helpful for understanding, for example, technological paradigms and national systems of innovation. At the level of the firm, the notion of complementarity may assist in the understanding of diversification patterns (Granstrand, Patel, and Pavitt 1997)—for example, it implies that firms will find most profitable new activities (or technologies) in areas that are complementary to newly increased activities (technologies). As we shall argue further, the notion of complementarity is also helpful for understanding the links between organizational variables—specifically, what is here called 'new human resource management practices'—and innovation performance.

Innovation, Complementarities, and New HRM Practices

To repeat, 'new HRM practices' is the overall label put on a host of contemporary changes in the organization of the employment relation, referring to team-based organization, continuous (often team-based) learning, decentralization of decision rights and incentives, emphasis on internal-knowledge dissemination, etc. While there may be strong financial-performance effects, productivity effects, and flexibility advantages of such new HRM practices—as documented by Huselid (1995), Ichniowski, Shaw, and Prennushi (1997), and Mendelsson and Pillai (1999) respectively—our main emphasis is on the impact on innovation performance; in particular, on product innovation.

New HRM practices can be conducive to innovative activity for a number of reasons. With respect to process innovations/improvements, one notable feature of many new HRM practices is that they increase decentralization, in the sense that problem-solving rights are delegated to the shop floor. Accomplished in the right way, this amounts to delegating rights in such a way that they are co-located with relevant knowledge, much of which may be inherently tacit (and thus require decentralization for its efficient use). In other words, increased delegation may better allow for the discovery and utilization of local knowledge in the organization, particularly when there are incentives in place that foster such discovery (Hayek 1948; Jensen and Meckling 1992). Indeed, much of the ability of Japanese firms to engage in ongoing, incremental process innovation turns on a successful co-location of problem-solving rights and localized knowledge combined with appropriate pecuniary and non-pecuniary incentives (Aoki and Dore 1994).

Relatedly, the increased use of teams that is an important component in the package of new HRM practices also means that better use can be made of local knowledge, leading to improvements in processes and perhaps also to minor product improvements. However, teams can do something more, since they are often composed of different human-resource inputs. This may imply that teams bring together knowledge that hitherto existed separately, potentially resulting in non-trivial process improvements (when teams are on the shop floor) or 'new combinations' that lead to novel products (Schumpeter 1912/34)(when teams are in product-development departments). Training of the workforce may be expected to be a force pulling in the direction of a higher rate of process improvements and may possibly also lead to product innovations, depending on the type, amount, and quality of the relevant training. Generally, increased knowledge diffusion, for example through job rotation, and increased information dissemination, for example through IT, may also be expected to provide a positive contribution to the firm's innovation performance, for rather obvious reasons.

Thus, there are grounds for expecting that among the benefits from adopting new HRM practices will be increased innovation performance. Arguably, the adoption of a single such practice may sometimes provide a contribution to innovative performance. For example, the increasingly widespread practice of rewarding shop-floor employees for putting forward suggestions for process improvements (e.g. by giving them a share of the cost savings) is likely to increase such incremental innovation activity (Bohnet and Oberholzer-Gee 2001) more or less regardless of the specific firm in which the reward system is implemented. However, other practices may not be expected to have a significant impact on innovation performance if merely implemented in isolation. At least to the extent that implementing new HRM practices is associated with extra effort or with disutility of changing to new routines, etc., employees will have somehow to be compensated. Thus, we would expect many new HRM practices to work well (in terms of both profits and innovation performance) only if accompanied by new, typically more incentive-based, remuneration schemes. Evidence appears to support this (Ichniowski, Shaw, and Prennushi 1997).

In general, we should on a priori grounds expect new HRM practices to be most conducive to innovation performance when adopted not in isolation but as a system of mutually reinforcing practices. The arguments in favor of this are relatively straightforward. For example, the benefits from giving shop floor employees more problem-solving rights will probably depend positively on the level of training of such employees. The converse is also likely to hold: employees may invest more in upgrading their skills if they are also given extensive problem-solving rights (i.e. actually utilize those skills), particularly if they are given the right (intrinsic or extrinsic) motivation. Relatedly, rotation and job-related training may be complements in terms of their impact on innovative activity. All such practices are likely to be complements to various incentive-based remuneration schemes (whether based on individual, team, or firm performance), profit-sharing arrangements, and promotion schemes (Zenger and Hesterly 1997).

In sum, while individual new HRM practices may be expected have some positive impact on innovation performance, theory would lead us to expect that because of complementarities between these practices systems of HRM practices will be significantly more conducive to innovation than individual practices. Below we examine these ideas empirically.

Empirical Analysis

The Empirical Model

Based on the discussion above, the probability of introducing an innovation may be specified as follows:

$$a = f(\beta_1 z, \beta_2 x). \tag{1}$$

Here, a is the probability of introducing an innovation associated with a certain degree of novelty, β_1 and β_2 are parameter vectors, and z is a set of (exogenous) determinants of innovation, related to the application of human-resource-management practices, while x is a set of other variables explaining innovative performance across business firms. The variables included in the vector x are arguably standard variables in the literature aiming at explaining innovation performance (Geroski 1990; Kleinknecht 1996). The model may be made operational in the following way:

$$\text{Prob}(A_i = 0 .. j) = \alpha SIZE_i + \chi SECT_i + \delta LINK_i + \phi EXREL_i$$
$$+ \varphi SUBSID_i + \eta_j HRMP_i^j + .. + \eta_n HRMP_i^n + \varepsilon_i, \tag{2}$$

where $\text{Prob}(A_i = 0 .. j)$ expresses the firm's probability of introducing an innovation associated with a certain degree of novelty on the market. If the firm in question is a non-innovator, the variable takes the value of 0; if the firm has introduced (in the period 1993–5) a product or service new to the firm the value is 1; if the firm has introduced a product that is new in a Danish context over the period the value is 2; while the value for this variable is 3 if the firm has introduced a product (or service) that is new to the world.[8] Our sample includes 928 non-innovators, 728 firms that produced products/services which were new only to the firm itself and 125 firms that produced products/services that were new to the national market, while 103 firms introduced products/services that were new to the world. Since our dependent variable is a discrete variable we apply an ordered-probit model as the means of estimation.[9]

As is common in studies aimed at explaining innovative performance (e.g. Geroski 1990; Michie and Sheehan 1999), we control for firm size (*SIZE*) and for sectoral affiliation (*SECT*). We include nine sector categories. For what concerns the sectoral classification, we apply the taxonomy developed by Pavitt (1984) and the four corresponding sectors for manufacturing firms. For the service firms in our sample we construct five additional sectors. Explanations of the sectoral classification that we apply may be found in Appendices 1 and 2 to this chapter (on pp. 207–9 below). As argued by Geroski (1990), such sectoral controls can be interpreted as capturing the differences in technological opportunities which face firms located in different sectors.

Other control variables include whether or not the firm in question has increased its vertical interaction with other firms, whether upstream or downstream (*LINK*). This variable is supposed to pick up the effect of interactions with suppliers and users for innovation performance as stressed by, for example, Lundvall (1988) and Hippel (1988).

EXREL expresses whether the firm has increased its interaction with knowledge institutions, including technical-support institutions, consultancies, or universities. In this context it may be noted that Brouwer and Kleinknecht (1996) found that firms which had consulted an innovation center were more likely to innovate than other firms. Although both *LINK* and *EXREL* concern whether firms have increased their external linkages, we interpret these variables more broadly as measuring the strength of the respective linkages. Thus, we argue that respondents who have strong linkages with external partners are very likely to answer that they have *increased* interaction with partners. Finally, we control for whether or not the firm is a subsidiary of a larger firm. The effect of this variable is, however, ambiguous. On the one hand, firms with centralized R&D departments might not wish their subsidiaries to be innovative, as this might hamper economies of scale in R&D. On the other hand, as argued by Harris and Trainor (1995), subsidiary firms might benefit from the larger resource base and experience of the parent firm. Some early empirical studies (e.g. Howells 1984) found a negative effect of this variable on innovation performance, while more recent studies have detected a positive effect (Harris and Trainor 1995; Love, Ashcroft, and Dunlop 1996).

The variables $HRMP^j_i \ldots HRMP^n_i$ are our new HRM variables; that is, those variables that are key to the analysis. We include nine discrete variables pertaining to new HRM practices. They express the degree to which firms apply (i) interdisciplinary work groups, (ii) quality circles, (iii) systems for collection of employee proposals, (iv) planned job rotation, (v) delegation of responsibility (i.e. decision rights), (vi) integration of functions, (vii) performance-related pay, (viii) firm-internal training, and finally (ix) firm-external training. For the first seven variables the possible values are 0, 1, 2, and 3, which corresponds to the fact that $0 < 25$ per cent, 25–50 per cent and >50 percent of the employees are involved in a given practice respectively. For the last two variables the possible values are 0, 1, and 2, which corresponds to the fact that $0 < 50$ per cent and >50 per cent of the employees are involved in a given practice, respectively.

However, as argued earlier, the literature on complementarities suggests that HRM practices are more effective when they are applied in systems than on a stand-alone basis. Hence, we will estimate models where HRM practices enter the equation to be estimated in specific configurations or systems:

$$\text{Prob}(A_i = 0 \ldots j) = \alpha SIZE_i + \chi SECT_i + \delta LINK_i + \phi EXREL_i$$
$$+ \; \varphi SUBSID_i + \varpi_j HRMS^j_i + \ldots + \varpi_n HRMS^n_i + \varepsilon_i, \quad (3)$$

where the notation is the same as in Equation (3). $HRMS_i^j \dots HRMS_i^n$ denote HRM systems, made up by configurations of our nine HRM practices.[10] Subsequently, we shall estimate both Equations (2) and (3) separately and compare the significance of the estimations made when applying the HRMPs individually and when they appear in an HRM system.[11]

Concerning the signs of the parameters for each variable, we expect all signs to be positive, except for the $SECT$ variable. In this case the interpretation has to be made relative to the other sector categories. For what concerns $SIZE$, we expect larger firms to be more likely to innovate, while we expect the likelihood of innovation at the level of the sector to correspond to what is normally thought of as a high-tech/low-tech typology.

The Data

The main source of data for this chapter is the $DISKO$ database. The database is compiled from a questionnaire which aims at tracing the relationship between technical and organizational innovation in a way that permits an analysis of new principles for work organization and their implications for the use and development of the employee's qualifications in firms in the Danish private-business sector. The survey was carried out by the DISKO project at Aalborg University in 1996. The questionnaire was submitted to a national sample of 4,000 firms selected among manufacturing firms with at least twenty full-time employees and non-manufacturing firms with at least ten full-time employees.[12] Furthermore, all Danish firms with at least a hundred employees were included in the sample; that is, a total of 913 firms. The resulting numbers of respondents was 684 manufacturing and 1,216 non-manufacturing firms, corresponding to response rates of, respectively, 52 per cent and 45 per cent.[13] The first descriptive analysis of the survey can be found in Gjerding (1997). The database is held by Statistics Denmark, and the data on the firms in the database can be linked to regular register data (which are also held by Statistics Denmark). For the purposes of this chapter we have obtained data on the size of the firms in the sample from regular register data.

Table 8.1*a–c* displays descriptive statistics for our explanatory variables.[14] It can be seen from the table that the most widely dispersed HRM practice is 'delegation of responsibility', since only 15.9 per cent of the firms do not apply this practice at all. A percentage of 39.1 of the firms use this practice while involving more than 50 per cent of their employees. The least diffused practice is 'planned job rotation', where 64.3 per cent of the firms do not use this practice at all. A percentage of 94.5 of the firms apply at least one of the HRMPs, while 66.7 per cent apply at least three such practices. For what concerns the distribution on sectors and across size categories, it may be seen that none of the groups is either extremely large, or extremely small. Since the analysis contains many different variables, each reflecting different aspects of HRMPs, we use

TABLE 8.1. Descriptive statistics for a set of DISKO variables (n = 1,884)

| Variable | Percentage of firms using an HRMP | | | |
	0	<25	25–50	>50
	Percentage of employees involved for each firm			
Interdisciplinary work groups	51.0	27.0	12.9	9.1
Quality circles	62.5	18.7	9.0	9.8
Systems for collection of employee proposals	56.1	18.0	7.2	18.7
Planned job rotation	64.3	22.0	7.1	6.6
Delegation of responsibility	15.9	22.0	23.0	39.1
Integration of functions	43.7	28.9	14.3	13.1
Performance-related pay	61.0	16.6	6.9	15.5

| Variable | Percentage of firms using an HRMP | | |
	0	<50	>50
	Percentage of employees involved for each firm		
Firm-internal training	48.2	23.0	28.8
Firm-external training	30.7	38.7	30.6

Variable	Percentage of total sample
Applies at least two HRMPs (HRMPONE)	94.5
Applies at least three HRMPs (HRMPTHREE)	66.7
Scale-intensive	13.5
Supplier-dominated	11.9
Science-based	3.6
Specialized suppliers	7.3
Crafts	14.5
Wholesale trade	17.7
Specialized traditional services	19.6
Scale-intensive services	5.0
ICT-intensive services	6.9
1–10 employees	11.7
11–50 employees	52.0
51–100 employees	10.9
101 + employees	25.4

principal-component analysis in order to reduce the amount of variables in the regression analysis to be carried out subsequently. The principal-component technique—which is a form of factor analysis—estimates linear combinations of the underlying variables; in this case, the indices of various work practices that 'explain' the highest possible fraction of the remaining variance in the data set. Thus, the first principal component is estimated to explain the highest possible fraction of the total variance, the second principal component the highest possible fraction of the variance which is not explained by the first principal component, etc. By maximizing the 'explained residual variance' in each round, the first m ($< n$) principal component will explain a relatively large proportion of the total variance. Since our variables are discrete, we have followed the normal procedure by transforming (or 'smoothing') the variables using the method of alternating least squares, before conducting the principal-component analysis.

An economic interpretation of the sets of factor loadings[15] ('factors') from the factor analysis is that the 'typical' pattern is one in which some of the above-mentioned work practices play a major role. Accordingly, we interpret each of the factors as 'HRM systems'. The sets of factor loadings for each factor are reported in Table 8.2. It can be seen from this table that we include two factors in the analysis. The reason for retaining two factors is that Factor 2 is the last factor (of the potential nine factors), where the Eigenvalue exceeds 1. In other words, Factor 2 explains more of the total variance than each of the nine individual HRMP variables does, whereas Factor 3 explains less than one of the nine original variables. The factors have been rotated using orthogonal Varimax rotation. This operation 'amplifies' the initial (non-rotated) factors, so that the factors become more distinct.[16]

Factor 1 in Table 8.2 is the first of our HRM systems. In this case the factor loadings are all positive and all have approximately the same size (factor loadings of about 0.5–0.7), except for firm-internal and firm-external training, cases in which the values of the factor loadings are rather low. Nevertheless, Factor 1 expresses an HRM system in which seven of our nine HRMPs are equally important. Note that each individual firm which scores high on Factor 1 is not necessarily applying all seven HRMPs simultaneously.[17] However, it does imply that a firm which scores high on Factor 1 applies several of the seven HRMPs.

TABLE 8.2. Factor loadings for nine organizational variables (Varimax rotation, n = 1,884)

Variable	Factor 1	Factor 2
HRMP1: Interdisciplinary work groups	0.71	0.14
HRMP2: Quality circles	0.66	0.15
HRMP3: Systems for collection of employee proposals	0.65	0.04
HRMP4: Planned job rotation	0.62	0.08
HRMP5: Delegation of responsibility	0.57	0.03
HRMP6: Integration of functions	0.65	−0.05
HRMP7: Performance-related pay	0.55	0.05
HRMP8: Firm-internal training	0.14	0.90
HRMP9: Firm-external training	0.02	0.92
Cumulative %	0.33	0.50

Hence this system (Factor 1) is one in which all seven practices are applied in just about equal proportions. In the same manner Factor 2 is dominated by firm-internal and firm-external training (factor loadings of 0.9).

Estimation

The estimations of our models can be found in Table 8.3. First, it may be noted that the null hypothesis that the slopes of the explanatory variables are zero is strongly rejected by the likelihood ratio test for all of our three specifications. Furthermore, it may be seen from the table that large firms are more likely to innovate than small firms (e.g., in model i), although the effect is not particularly strong. Given that our dependent variable is not a measure of the frequency of innovation this finding is not surprising, but should be controlled for.[18]

It can be seen from Table 8.3 that the likelihood of firms being innovators, given their sectoral affiliation, can be ranked as follows: (1) specialized suppliers, (2) ICT-intensive services, (3) science-based, (4) wholesale trade, (5) scale-intensive, (6) supplier-dominated, (7) scale-intensive services, (8) specialized traditional services, and (9) crafts. Such a ranking may be said to be in agreement with what one would expect on more intuitive grounds, since it is so clearly related to whether sectors are 'high-tech' or 'low-tech' (OECD 1996).

The results also confirm that the external linkages of firms are important to innovation, since the parameters for both vertical linkages (*LINK*) and for other knowledge linkages (*EXREL*) are significantly different from zero. It may be noted, however, that upstream or downstream linkages are particularly important, given the high parameter for this variable. The latter finding is in line with the predictions of Lundvall (1988) and Hippel (1988), and with the empirical findings of Rothwell et al. (1974) and Malerba (1992). The variable for being a subsidiary has a positive sign, and is significant in models (i) and (iii).

By inserting the two retained factors from the principal-component analysis described above into the regression, we find that both HRM systems are conducive to innovation.[19] The first is Factor 1 from Table 8.2, in which seven of our nine HRM variables (namely, 'interdisciplinary workgroups', 'quality circles', 'systems for collection of employee proposals', 'planned job rotation', 'delegation of responsibility', 'integration of functions', and 'performance-related pay') matter (almost) equally for firm's ability to innovate. The second system which is found to be conducive to innovation (Factor 2 from Table 8.2) is dominated by 'firm-internal' and 'firm-external training'. Nevertheless, based on the principal-component regression we can—as a first step—conclude that HRMPs matter for the ability of firms to innovate. It should be noted that while the significant estimates for the HRMP variables are consistent with the view that the application of 'new' HRM practices is conducive to innovation performance, it is equally clear that—given the cross-sectional nature of the present data—strong

TABLE 8.3. Ordered-probit regressions, explaining innovative performance across 1,884 Danish firms

	Model (i)		Model (ii)		Model (iii)	
Variable	Estimate	p-value	Estimate	p-value	Estimate	p-value
Sector controls						
Scale-intensive	−0.242	0.061	−0.182	0.172	−0.247	0.063
Supplier-dominated	−0.275	0.037	−0.190	0.162	−0.301	0.026
Science-based	−0.143	0.418	−0.111	0.536	−0.132	0.469
Specialized suppliers	0.082	0.567	0.181	0.215	0.079	0.590
Crafts	−0.948	0.000	−0.877	0.000	−0.964	0.000
Wholesale trade	−0.203	0.098	−0.176	0.161	−0.210	0.098
Specialized traditional services	−0.722	0.000	−0.654	0.000	−0.725	0.000
Scale-intensive services	−0.694	0.000	−0.631	0.000	−0.748	0.000
ICT-intensive services	Benchmark		Benchmark		Benchmark	
SIZE	0.016	0.043	0.015	0.064	0.018	0.029
LINK	0.614	0.000	0.598	0.000	0.595	0.000
EXREL	0.267	0.000	0.247	0.000	0.270	0.000
SUBSID	0.127	0.042	0.098	0.123	0.130	0.043
Factor 1	0.192	0.000	–	–	–	
Factor 2	0.063	0.027	–	–	–	
HRMP1	–	–	0.025	0.466	–	
HRMP2			–	0.010	0.744	–
HRMP3	–	–	0.042	0.114	–	–
HRMP4	–	–	0.041	0.246	–	–
HRMP5	–	–	0.055	0.066		
HRMP6			0.067	0.024		
HRMP7			0.051	0.059		
HRMP8			0.154	0.000		
HRMP9			−0.004	0.924		
HRMPONE	–	–	–		0.423	0.027
HRMPTHREE	–	–	–		0.378	0.000
Log-likelihood	–		–		–	
		1757.5		1742.0		1755.8
Restricted log-likelihood	–		–		–	
		1987.8		1987.8		1987.8
Log-likelihood test		460.4		491.6		464.0

inferences about causality cannot be made. In fact, Capelli and Neumark (2001) use panel data and find only weak evidence for the effect of 'high-performance' work practices on labour productivity.

Concerning our hypothesis on the complementarity of HRMP, it may be seen from Table 8.3 (model (ii)) that only four of the HRMPs are individually significant, and moreover, that only 'integration of functions' (*HRMP6*) and 'firm-internal training' (*HRMP8*) are significant at the 5-per-cent level. However, when seven HRMPs (all but firm-external and -internal training) of the HRMPs are combined into a single variable (a 'system'), this 'synthetic' variable (Factor 1) is strongly significant. Seven out of the nine HRMPs appear to be complementary, since they jointly (as expressed by Factor 1) give rise to better innovation performance. This pattern applies to one group of firms, while for another group of firms complementarity between firm-internal training and firm-external training (as expressed by Factor 2) appears to be the important factor with respect to explaining firms' ability to innovate. Factor 2 is significant at the 5-per-cent level. We take the two positive and significant results for the system variables as evidence of the existence of Edgeworth complementarities between the HRMPs in our analysis.

However, it is not evident why the HRMPs cluster in exactly these ways, and we can only speculate on the reasons for the above pattern, since the data set does not allow us to resolve the issue. In this context one can argue that it is surprising that as many as seven of the total of nine practices turn out to be complementary (as expressed by Factor 1). However, it should be noted that we have not selected at random the work practices examined. Rather, we have chosen some of the practices already identified in the literature as being relevant candidates for obtaining complementarities (with other practices). The majority of the variables underlying Factor 1 are intuitively complementary. For instance—and as argued in the theoretical section of this chapter—'performance-related pay' appears to go hand in hand with team-based practices such as 'interdisciplinary work groups' and 'quality circles'. Moreover, it appears that the team practices can successfully be used jointly with 'delegation of responsibility', since the use of such team-based practices does not make much sense without at the same time allocating the appropriate decision rights down to the team level. However, some of the work practices underlying Factor 1 could be seen to be substitutes, rather than complements. For instance, 'planned job rotation' and 'integration of functions' could, at a first glance, be seen to be substitutes. However, on closer inspection—and as pointed out by Aoki (1990) in the context of product development—the use of teamwork involving job rotation increases the interaction between the different key actors in various successive stages (basic conceptualization, successive phases of detailed design, prototype fabrication, testing, redesign, mass production, and marketing) of product development. Since processes of product development are characterized by various feedback loops between the 'phases' (Kline and Rosenberg 1986), job rotation among different engineering offices, as well as between engineering jobs and supervisory jobs at the factory, facilitates the knowledge sharing needed for horizontal coordination among the different phases of development.

With respect to the two training variables, captured by Factor 2, it is surprising that these practices were found not to be complementary to other HRM practices. However, note that while these may conceivably be expected on a priori grounds to be complementary to other HRM practices (e.g. 'performance-related pay' or 'delegation of responsibility') captured by Factor 1, one may also point out that these practices are arguably the most traditional of the nine HRMPs that we consider; for example, even very traditional, hierarchical industrial firms are likely to make use of some internal training. Thus, one can expect firms that otherwise will not apply HRMPs to make use of some training. Moreover, there may be a significant size bias here, since small firms that (because of their smallness) need not make use of HRMPs to any great degree may still make considerable use of external training. Taken together these effects may help explain the pattern in the application of HRMPs.

Another way of gauging HRMP complementarities is to look at whether it is sufficient to apply at least one HRMP, rather than it being necessary to apply several practices together. In Table 8.3, model (iii) we test the hypothesis of the positive effect of having at least one HRMP against the alternative hypothesis stating the positive effect of applying three or more HRMPs at the same time. Both variables, *HRMPONE* and *HRMPTHREE*, are binary variables, taking into account only whether or not a certain practice is used, and not the degree to which the practice is used within each firm (in contrast to the previous analysis). Although having at least one practice (*HRMPONE*) is positive and significant when entered in the regression alone (not shown for reasons of space), *HRMPONE* is significant only at the 5-per-cent level when taken together with the variable expressing whether or not each firm applies three or more HRM practices (*HRMPTHREE*). In contrast *HRMPTHREE* is highly significant ($p < 0.0001$). We take this as further evidence of the importance of complementarities between new HRM practices with respect to determining innovation performance.[20]

The final part of our analysis is devoted to the assessment of whether sectoral regularities in the application of the two (successful) HRM systems can be detected. Despite the fact that the correlation coefficients are not very high in Table 8.4, we find that of our total of nine sectors the four manufacturing sectors correlate positively with the first system. Firms belonging to wholesale trade and to the ICT-intensive service sectors tend to be associated with the second system (firms in the scale-intensive sector tend to be associated with the second system as well, although the association is rather weak). Hence, it seems fair to conclude that, generally speaking, sectoral regularities in the effect of HRMP complementarities on innovation performance exist.

Conclusion

We began by noting a number of stylized facts that relate to the ongoing changes in the nature of the employment relation—often conceptualized by the term

TABLE 8.4. Correlations among HRM systems and the firm's sectoral affiliation

	Factor 1	p-value	Factor 2	p-value
Scale-intensive	0.16	0.000	0.05	0.031
Supplier-dominated	0.08	0.001	−0.09	0.000
Science-based	0.12	0.000	0.02	0.490
Specialized suppliers	0.15	0.000	−0.07	0.002
Crafts	−0.20	0.000	−0.11	0.000
Wholesale trade	0.00	0.936	0.08	0.001
Specialized traditional services	−0.17	0.000	0.06	0.006
Scale-intensive services	−0.05	0.041	−0.09	0.000
ICT-intensive services	0.03	0.178	0.12	0.000

'new HRM practices'—to the apparently systemic nature of these practices, and to their adoption by innovative firms. We argued that the notion of complementarities (and the associated theorizing and formalisms) is helpful for allowing us to construct explanations of these stylized facts. In particular, we argued that while the adoption of individual HRM practices may be expected positively to influence innovation performance, adopting a package of complementary HRM practices could be expected to impact much more strongly on innovation performance. However, we have not offered a finely honed theory about why this should be so. In general, there is very clearly a theoretical deficit in this area. Future work will be devoted to more comprehensively theorizing the links between complementary HRM practices and innovation performance. However, the main emphasis of this chapter is empirical.

In our empirical analysis of these overall ideas and hypotheses we began by finding that strong linkes to users or suppliers are conducive to innovation (while controlling for size and sectoral affiliation). Moreover, strong links to knowledge institutions, including technical-support institutions, consultancies, or universities, were similarly found to be conducive to innovation. With respect to the application of new HRM practices, we applied principal-component analysis in order to compress the information from the survey and in order to identify possible patterns of HRM practices. Hence, in our analysis the HRM 'systems' emerged out of the principal-component analysis, while previous contributions in the field have assumed different systems from the outset. Using the principal-component tool we identified two HRM systems that are conducive to innovation. The first is one in which seven of our nine HRM variables matter (almost) equally for the ability to innovate. The second system which was found to be conducive to innovation is dominated by firm-internal training in addition to firm-external training. Hence, we conclude that the application of HRM practices does matter for the likelihood of a firm being an innovator. Furthermore, since the two HRM systems were strongly significant in explaining innovation performance, while only two individual practices (out of nine) were found to be strongly significant, we found support for the hypothesis of the importance of Edgeworth complementarities between certain HRM practices within each of the two HRM systems.

The final part of our analysis was devoted to assessing whether sectoral regularities in the application of the two (successful) HRM systems could be detected. Of our total of nine sectors we found that the four manufacturing sectors correlate with the first system. Firms belonging to the wholesale-trade sector and to the ICT-intensive service sector tend to be associated with the second system. Theoretical analysis has focused almost exclusively on identifying organizational practices and complementarities between such practices, disregarding the type of activity in question (e.g. Milgrom and Roberts 1995). Hence, in order to inform future theoretical research in the field, further empirical research should be devoted to the more detailed unfolding of sectoral regularities in the effect of HRM-practice complementarities on innovation performance.[21]

Notes

1. The clear exception is some scholars' interest in Japanese economic organization and how this connects to innovativeness. Thus, Freeman (1988: 335) explicitly notes how in 'Japanese management, engineers and workers grew accustomed to thinking of the entire production process as a system and of thinking in an integrated way about product design and process design', and he makes systematic reference to quality management, horizontal information flows, and other features of new HRM practices. One could also construct an argument that already the concern with horizontal information flows in the late 1960s Project SAPPHO demonstrates a long-standing awareness of the relation between HRM practices and innovation performance. However, exceptions can always be found, and we think it is a fair judgment that other determinants of innovation performance, such as appropriability, market structure, control of complementary assets, etc. have played bigger roles in the literatures.

2. For example, Guest's programmatic discussion (1997) does not mention innovation as a relevant performance variable.

3. In terms of the intuition of the notion of complementarity, the notion represents a strong possible conceptualization of such concepts as 'synergy', '(organizational) fit', and 'consistency' (Porter 1996; Baron and Kreps 1999ab).

4. Given a real-valued function f on a lattice X, f is supermodular and its arguments are complements if for any x and y in X, $f(x) - f(x \wedge y) \leq f(x \vee y) - f(y)$ (Milgrom and Roberts 1995: 183). A lattice $(X, \geq)$ is a set (X) with a partial order $(\geq)$ with the property that for any x and y in X there is a smallest element $(x \vee y)$ that is larger than x and y and largest element $(x \wedge y)$ that is smaller than both.

5. At the method level it is attractive that complementarities (and the underlying mathematical lattice theory) do not involve the drastic divisibility and concavity assumptions that have often been criticized by evolutionary economists (e.g. Nelson 1980).

6. Not surprisingly, the notion has been extensively used in recent research in comparative systems (e.g. Dewatripont and Roland 1997).

7. As Milgrom and Roberts (1995: 187) point out, a 'movement of a whole system of complementary variables, once begun, tends to continue', thus providing an aspect of the understanding of co-evolution.

8. Hence, only the final category qualifies for being an innovation in the strict(est) sense of the word.

9. Hence, the method is maximum-likelihood estimation (MLE), which provides a means of choosing an asymptotically efficient estimator for a set of parameters. (For an exposition of the properties of ML estimators see Greene 1997: 129.) Although MLE has been criticized for having less than optimal small-sample properties (may be biased, since the MLE of the variance in sampling from a normal distribution is biased downwards), this is unlikely to be a major problem, given the fact that our sample contains about 1,900 firms.

10. The way in which the HRM practices are transformed into 'systems' will be explained in the section below.

11. If the effect of individual practices as well as the systems of practices were estimated in the same model this would result in perfect collinearity.

12. In the stratification of the sample, firms with less than ten employees were excluded from the analysis. However, in our analysis we have a size category containing firms with less than ten employees. The reason for this is that when the sample was stratified, size was measured at a given point in time. However, in this chapter we measure size as the number of full-time employees over a full year.

13. The full questionnaire is available in English as appendix 1 to Lund and Gjerding (1996).

14. Of the total of 1,900 responding firms, data are not available for size or for sectoral affiliation for 16 of those firms. Hence, we conduct our analysis using information on 1,884 firms.

15. The factor loadings are the parameters relating the original variables to the principal components.

16. We have experimented with oblique rotation methods as well, but the choice of oblique rather than orthogonal methods does not change the results in any important way.

17. Admittedly, it is a weakness of the principal-component methodology that the size of each factor loading chosen, for one to conclude that an underlying variable is 'important', is somewhat arbitrary.

18. The marginal effects from the probit analysis (corresponding to the coefficients shown in Table 8.3), are reported in the Appendix Table 8.5. They show that the probability of introducing an innovation increases with firm size, since the marginal effect for the size variable is negative only in the case of no innovation ($A = 0$), while the marginal effect is positive in the case of innovation at all levels of novelty ($A = 1$, 2, 3). Indeed, this is the interpretation which can be put on all of the significant coefficients (including the parameters for the HRM variables), since the marginal effects are negative only in the case of no innovation ($A = 0$) for all significant coefficients. However, it can also be noted that the marginal effects are larger for

A = 1 (than for A = 2 and A = 3); that is, the explanatory variables have the strongest effect on introducing a product 'new to the firm'.

19. Other examples of principal-component regression include Arvanitis and Hollenstein (1996), in which the effects on innovation performance of various sources of innovation are examined. In the field of international economics Dalum, Laursen, and Verspagen (1999) analyzed the effect of international patterns of specialization on economic growth, while applying the methodology.

20. It can be noted that we have tested our models not only by using an ordered-probit model, as documented in Table 8.3, but also by making standard binary probit estimations (collapsing our discrete dependent variable into a binary variable which takes the value of 0 if the firm does not innovate and takes the value of 1 if the firm innovates). This change of estimation method does not change our results in any important way.

21. For a preliminary empirical analysis in this direction see Laursen (2002).

Appendix 1: The Sectoral Classification Applied in this Chapter

Pavitt (1984) identifies differences in the importance of different sources of innovation according to which broad sector the individual firm belongs to. The Pavitt taxonomy—which is based on grouping firms according to their principal activity—emerged out of a statistical analysis of more than 2,000 post-war innovations in Britain. The underlying explanatory variables are the sources of technology; the nature of users' needs; and firms' means of appropriation. Based on this, four overall types of firms were identified; namely, supplier-dominated firms, scale-intensive firms, specialized suppliers, and science-based firms. *Supplier-dominated* firms are typically small. Most technology comes from suppliers of equipment and material. *Scale-intensive* firms are found in bulk materials and assembly. Their internal sources of technology are production engineering and R&D departments. External sources of technology include mainly interactive learning with specialized suppliers, but inputs from science-based firms are also of some importance. *Specialized suppliers* are small firms which are producers of production equipment and control instrumentation. Their internal sources of technology are design and development. External sources are users (science-based and scale-intensive firms). *Science-based firms* are found in the chemical and electronic sectors. Their main internal sources of technology are internal R&D and production engineering. Important external sources of technology include universities, but also specialized suppliers.

Because the Pavitt taxonomy was created mainly with the manufacturing sector in mind (although our *crafts* sector (see below) could be included in the *supplier-dominated* sector, if one were to follow the original Pavitt taxonomy), and since we are conducting an analysis of firms in both manufacturing as well as in services, we have added five additional service sectors. *ICT-intensive services* are firms providing business services and financial services. *Wholesale trade* consists of firms selling bulk materials or machines. *Scale-intensive services* consist typically of large firms in the transport industries, cleaning services, as well as of supermarkets and warehouses. *Specialized services* is made up of smaller firms, including miscellaneous shops, hotels and restaurants, taxi companies etc. *Crafts* consists of firms in construction industries, as well as of automobile repair shops.

For a detailed assignment of all industries into our nine sectors see Appendix 2 to this chapter.

Appendix 2: The Assignment of Industries into Nine Sectoral Categories

No.	Industry	Sector	No.	Industry	Sector
1	Production etc. of meat and meat products	SCAI	43	Sale of motor vehicles, motorcycles, etc.	SSER
2	Manufacture of dairy products	SCAI	44	Maintenance and repair of motor vehicles	CRAF
3	Manufacture of other food products	SCAI	45	Service stations	SSER
4	Manufacture of beverages	SCAI	46	Wholesale of agricultural raw materials, live animals	WTRA
5	Manufacture of tobacco products	SCAI	47	Wholesale of food, beverages, and tobacco	WTRA
6	Manufacture of textiles and textile products	SDOM	48	Wholesale of household goods	WTRA
7	Manufacture of clothes; dressing etc. of fur	SDOM	49	Wholesale of wood and construction materials	WTRA
8	Manufacture of leather and leather products	SDOM	50	Wholesale of other raw materials and semi-manufactures	WTRA
9	Manufacture of wood and wood products	SDOM	51	Wholesale of machinery, equipment, and supplies	WTRA
10	Manufacture of pulp, paper, and paper products	SDOM	52	Commission trade and other wholesale trade	WTRA
11	Publishing of newspapers	SDOM	53	Retail sale of food in non-specialized stores	SCIS
12	Publishing activities, excluding newspapers	SDOM	54	Retail sale of food in specialized stores	SSER
13	Printing activities, etc.	SDOM	55	Department stores	SCIS
14	Manufacture of refined petroleum products, etc.	SCAI	56	Retail sale of pharmaceutical goods, cosmetic art. etc.	SSER
15	Manufacture of chemical raw materials	SCIB	57	Retail sale of clothing, footwear, etc.	SSER
16	Manufacture of paints, soap, cosmetics, etc.	SCAI	58	Retail sale of furniture, household appliances	SSER
17	Manufacture of pharmaceuticals, etc.	SCIB	59	Retail sale in other specialized stores	SSER
18	Manufacture of plastics and synthetic rubber	SCAI	60	Repair of personal and household goods	SSER

No.	Industry	Sector	No.	Industry	Sector
19	Manufacture of glass and ceramic goods, etc.	SDOM	61	Hotels, etc.	SSER
20	Manufacture of cement, bricks, concrete industry etc.	SCAI	62	Restaurants, etc.	SSER
21	Manufacture of basic metals	SCAI	63	Transport via railways and buses	SCIS
22	Manufacture of metal construction materials, etc.	SCAI	64	Taxi operation and coach services	SSER
23	Manufacture of hand tools, metal packaging, etc.	SDOM	65	Freight transport by road and via pipelines	SSER
24	Manufacture of marine engines, compressors, etc.	SPEC	66	Water transport	SCIS
25	Manufacture of other general-purpose machinery	SPEC	67	Air transport	SCIS
26	Manufacture of agricultural and forestry machinery	SPEC	68	Cargo handling, harbours, etc., travel agencies	SCIS
27	Manufacture of machinery for industries, etc.	SPEC	69	Monetary intermediation	ITIS
28	Manufacture of domestic appliances n.e.c.	SCAI	70	Other financial intermediation	ITIS
29	Manufacture of office machinery and computers	SCIB	71	Insurance and pension funding	ITIS
30	Manufacture of radio and communication equipment, etc.	SCIB	72	Activities auxiliary to financial intermediates	ITIS
31	Manufacture of medical and optical instruments, etc.	SPEC	73	Letting of own property	SSER
32	Building and repairing of ships and boats	SCAI	74	Real-estate agents, etc.	SSER
33	Manufacture of transport equipment excluding ships, etc.	SCAI	75	Renting of machinery and equipment, etc.	SSER
34	Manufacture of furniture	SDOM	76	Computer and related activity	ITIS
35	Manufacture of toys, gold and silver articles, etc.	SDOM	77	Research and development	ITIS
36	General contractors	CRAF	78	Legal activities	ITIS
37	Bricklaying	CRAF	79	Accounting, bookkeeping, and auditing activities	ITIS
38	Installation of electrical wiring and fittings	CRAF	80	Consulting engineers, architects, etc.	ITIS
39	Plumbing	CRAF	81	Advertising	ITIS
40	Joinery installation	CRAF	82	Building-cleaning activities	SCIS
41	Painting and glazing	CRAF	83	Other business services	ITIS
42	Other construction work	CRAF			

Note: CRAF = Crafts; ITIS = ICT-intensive services; SCAI = Scale-intensive firms; SDOM = Supplier-dominated firms; SCIB = Science-based firms; SCIS = Scale-intensive services; SPEC = Specialized suppliers; SSER = Specialized services; WTRA = Wholesale trade

Appendix 3

TABLE 8.5. Marginal effects from the ordered-probit analysis (Table 8.3)

Variable	$A = 0$	$A = 1$	$A = 2$	$A = 3$
Model (i)				
SIZE	−0.0059	0.0037	0.0012	0.0010
LINK	−0.2387	0.1493	0.0483	0.0412
EXREL	−0.0986	0.0617	0.0199	0.0170
SUBSID	−0.0390	0.0244	0.0079	0.0067
HRMP1: *Interdisciplinary workgroups*	−0.0099	0.0062	0.0020	0.0017
HRMP2: *Quality circles*	−0.0042	0.0026	0.0008	0.0007
HRMP3: *Systems for collection of employee proposals*	−0.0167	0.0104	0.0034	0.0029
HRMP4: *Planned job rotation*	−0.0162	0.0101	0.0033	0.0028
HRMP5: *Delegation of responsibility*	−0.0219	0.0137	0.0044	0.0038
HRMP6: *Integration of functions*	−0.0268	0.0168	0.0054	0.0046
HRMP7: *Performance-related pay*	−0.0202	0.0126	0.0041	0.0035
HRMP8: *Firm-internal training*	−0.0615	0.0385	0.0124	0.0106
HRMP9: *Firm-external training*	0.0015	−0.0010	−0.0003	−0.0003
Model (ii)				
SIZE	−0.0063	0.0039	0.0013	0.0011
LINK	−0.2451	0.1510	0.0503	0.0438
EXREL	−0.1066	0.0657	0.0219	0.0191
SUBSID	−0.0507	0.0312	0.0104	0.0091
Factor 1	−0.0766	0.0472	0.0157	0.0137
Factor 2	−0.0253	0.0156	0.0052	0.0045
Model (iii)				
SIZE	−0.0070	0.0043	0.0014	0.0012
LINK	−0.2372	0.1469	0.0482	0.0421
EXREL	−0.1076	0.0666	0.0219	0.0191
SUBSID	−0.0520	0.0322	0.0106	0.0092
NWPONE	−0.1689	0.1046	0.0343	0.0300
NWPTHREE	−0.1509	0.0934	0.0307	0.0268

9

Cognitive Leadership and Coordination in the Knowledge Economy

Introduction

Why are major organizational restructurings often communicated through large-scale gatherings where top management addresses employees through face-to-face contact instead of relying on, for example, electronic mail? Why do many corporations spend substantial amounts of money on flying in managers from foreign subsidiaries to tell them things in personal meetings with top management that they could easily be told over the telephone, by fax or by e-mail? More generally, why are executives so fond of face-to-face, verbal communication, when in many situations written communication or other means of communication would appear to be appropriate substitutes?

The phenomena described may seem to be ritualistic and ceremonial, perhaps only susceptible of explanation in terms of group psychology or the desire to achieve legitimacy through conforming to institutional requirements, etc. For such reasons, it may be argued that they lie outside the orbit of 'rational' social science. However, it will be argued in this chapter that simple ideas from (mostly) game theory suggest a rational explanation. More specifically, the hypothesis here is that the above phenomena are manifestations of the exercise of *cognitive leadership* designed to coordinate the complementary actions of many people through the creation of belief conditions that (at least) approximate common knowledge. Indeed, the overall argument is that leadership, coordination, and common beliefs/knowledge are closely related phenomena, and that cognitive leadership is a prominent member of the set of 'alternative institutions for resolving coordination problems' (Cooper, DeJong, Forsythe, and Ross 1994). The argument is developed using simple ideas from non-cooperative game theory on coordination games, and on exploring these ideas from a decision-theoretic point of view in a non-formal manner; hence the emphasis on the epistemic states of players.

To get an intuitive idea of the argument, consider the following story as told by Kevin Kelly, the Executive Editor of *Wired*. Kelly (1999: 17) recounts participating in 1995 in a computer-graphics conference organized by Loren Carpenter where one of the events consisted in having all 5,000 attendees simultaneously operate a submarine simulator. Thus, the challenge for the 5,000 co-pilots, each one equipped with their own joystick

was to steer a submarine through a 3D undersea world to capture some sea monster eggs. [...] The sub could go up/down, open claws, close claws, and so on [...] when the audience first took command of the submarine, nothing happened. Audience members wiggled this control and that, shouted and counter-shouted instructions to one another, but nothing moved. Each person's instructions were being canceled by another person's orders. There was no cohesion. The sub didn't budge.

Finally Loren Carpenter's voice boomed from a loudspeaker at the back of the room. 'Why don't you guys go to the right?', he hollered. Click! Instantly the sub zipped off to the right. With emergent coordination the audience adjusted the steering details and smoothly set off in search of sea-monster eggs. In the terms of the argument of this chapter, Mr Carpenter was exercising cognitive leadership aimed at coordinating the complementary actions of many people through the creation of common knowledge. An underlying theme in the chapter is that this kind of leadership will become increasingly important in the knowledge economy to the extent that this economy is characterized by the need to coordinate distributed knowledge in networked systems.

As an academic subject leadership is characterized by huge differences with respect to the basic conceptualization of the phenomenon. No doubt this is because many disciplines have contributed to the study of leadership and because leadership behavior is manifest in many diverse social settings. It is therefore advisable to be explicit about what is meant by leadership. And the literature on leadership has in general heeded such advice. Even a casual reading of the literature reveals that it is very rich indeed with respect to providing conceptualizations. In fact, it is much richer in this respect than with respect to providing explanations of the phenomenon.

In this chapter I define cognitive leadership as the ability to resolve coordination problems by influencing beliefs. This is both a conceptualization and a stab at an explanation. For some reason, the leader is able to spot and resolve coordination problems by influencing beliefs more effectively than other people. For example, the leader may have privileged information about some state of nature that perturbs the underlying game. Because, as will often be the case in practice, the leader's own pay-offs are somehow tied to the pay-offs of his followers (and they know this), they are actually prepared to believe and follow him. The leader's announcement of what strategy should be followed is effective in resolving the underlying coordination problem because it creates a belief structure that at least approximates common knowledge. It is well known from the literatures on conventions, focal points, the robustness of game-theoretical equilibria, etc. that whether common knowledge obtains or not, the extent to which it is approximated by beliefs, etc. may make crucial differences for outcomes (e.g. Monderer and Samet 1989; Rubinstein 1989; Crawford and Haller 1990).

This overall explanation arguably grasps much—if certainly not all—of what is meant by leadership, both in common parlance and in the scholarly literature. Because the emphasis is on the coordination of beliefs (e.g. of people in an organization), it is appropriate to make use of a particular class of games, namely coordination games. Indeed, this chapter may be read as a contribution to a small but growing literature that tries to cast organizational phenomena in terms of resolving interaction problems that can be represented by various types of coordination games (notably Camerer and Knez 1994, 1996, 1997; Greenan and Guellec 1994; Weber 1998). However, this literature has not dealt with leadership. Another important source of inspiration is political-science contributions on leadership (notably Frohlich, Oppenheimer, and Young 1971; Hardin 1982; Calvert 1992, 1995) that clearly identify a link between leadership and coordination problems (particularly Calvert 1992), but without using the epistemic arguments presented in this chapter.

The design of the chapter is as follows. First comes a rather selective literature review. Instead of reviewing the enormous and diverse literature on leadership, I concentrate briefly on the few economics approaches to leadership. I then argue that a different approach to leadership may be developed—one that both retains a rational-choice orientation and links up with those contributions to the leadership literature that have stressed the cognitive aspects of leadership; that is, how leaders influence what people believe. I then go on to present some basic game-theory ideas. Even at an elementary level we can make the basic point that coordination games aren't trivial, somewhat contrary to common perception, and that they are likely to capture the essence of a large number of real-world situations. Notably, they are likely to help us gain an improved understanding of important aspects of leadership. What is offered in the following pages is not a finely honed theory about leadership behavior (as in Hermalin 1998). Rather, it is an explorative discussion (somewhat in the style of Kreps 1990a and Langlois 1998), aimed at convincing organizational scholars of the value of basic game-theoretic ideas, and economists of organization of the possibility of alternative routes of research.

Leadership: A Highly Partial Literature Review

Leadership has been defined as 'leading others along a way, guiding'. There are clearly two distinct aspects involved in the exercise of leadership; namely, first, selecting a goal, and, second, making others follow that goal (Gardner 1990: 11). From the perspective of the economics of organization, 'the problem of motivating employees to follow a vision is the standard agency problem' (Brickley, Smith, and Zimmerman 1996: 309). Below, I shall briefly discuss a few contributions that work from a similar logic, and then suggest the possibility of an alternative view that, while it is consistent with a rational choice approach, puts more stress on cognition and belief formation than on motivation per se.

Some Recent Economics Contributions

That social-interaction problems and leadership are somehow connected is not a new recognition in social-science research. At least, political scientists have often made the link explicit (Frohlich, Oppenheimer, and Young 1971; Hardin 1982; Calvert 1992, 1995). In contrast, economists have had relatively little to say about leadership, and when they have addressed the issue it is fair to say that one specific modeling heuristic has been dominant. To see this, consider three important economics contributions to the leadership literature; namely Kreps (1990), Rotemberg and Saloner (1993), and Hermalin (1998). All three work out of contract-economics approaches. Thus, Kreps and Rotemberg and Saloner begin from an incomplete-contract setting, whereas Hermalin takes his starting point in the Holmström (1982) (complete contracts) team-model. Consider each of these in turn.

Strictly speaking, Kreps's paper is not about leadership per se, but rather about corporate culture, and how the reputation that a corporate culture may help build provides an important part of the explanation of firm organization. Nevertheless, it certainly makes provision for leadership. Beginning from the property rights/incomplete-contracts theory (Grossman and Hart 1986; Hart 1995), Kreps argues that incompleteness of contracts may produce a need for implicit contracts. However, in the face of unforeseen contingencies it is not clear how implicit contracts should be administered; in particular, it is not clear how well standard reputation arguments work with unforeseen contingencies. The possible role of leadership in this setting is to provide general principles (i.e. focal points) that instruct employees and suppliers about how unforeseen contingencies will be handled in the future by management (see also Shleifer and Summers 1990).

Rotemberg and Saloner are more taken up with how leadership styles are influenced by environmental contingencies. However, the same basic insight as in Kreps—namely, that the provision of incentives is not straightforward under incomplete contracting—plays a key role in their paper. Specifically, they consider the problem of compensating middle managers who develop project ideas, when compensation cannot be based on the manager's unobservable effort but has to be based on whether the project is implemented, and where the CEO may have difficulties committing to implementation; hence, contracting is incomplete and commitment is imperfect. Leadership style affects employees' beliefs about how they will be compensated in various circumstances. Assuming that shareholders will select the firm's leadership style to maximize profits, they will appoint 'empathic' leaders (whose utility functions include the utility of their manager) if the firm operates in an opportunity-rich environment, whereas 'selfish' leaders (whose utility functions do not include the utility of their managers) will be appointed in stable environments.

Finally, Hermalin studies incentive problems in the context of the team model of Holmström (1982). The problem here is that the leader for some reason has privileged information about what the team should do, but—because she shares in team output—has an incentive to exaggerate the value of effort devoted to the common activity. In Hermalin's main case the problem may be solved if the leader acts as a Stackelberg leader and expends effort earlier than the other team members. Based on their observation of effort, the other team members form beliefs about the leader's information. Interestingly, this produces the conclusion that the leader works harder than she would do under symmetric information. The leader indeed 'leads by example'.

To be sure, these modeling efforts are neat, logical, and produce interesting, sometimes counter-intuitive, conclusions. However, they are limited in various ways that are typical of recent contract economics. The basic thrust of this literature is to conceptualize virtually any issue related to economic organization in terms of solving incentive conflicts. The motivation for this presumably is an underlying argument that in the absence of such conflicts the first-best can be reached without major obstacles (e.g. Hart 1995). Thus, the essence of the above contributions is that (business) leaders exist because they resolve incentive conflicts, albeit sophisticated and non-standard ones. However, other perspectives on leadership are certainly possible, and insights from related disciplines are likely to enrich economic approaches to leadership.

Towards a Different View

The view that all, or most, organizational phenomena are reducible to problems of aligning incentives is one that is implicitly (and sometimes explicitly) contradicted by contributions to organization studies (Thompson 1967), the executive and leadership literature (Barnard 1948; Carlsson 1951; Selznick 1957; Kotter 1996), political science (Calvert 1992, 1995), (rational-choice) sociology (Coleman 1990), and in some quarters of the economics of organization (Milgrom and Roberts 1992: ch. 4; Camerer and Knez 1994, 1996, 1997; Langlois 1998; Weber 1998; Langlois and Foss 1999). Many of these contributions are directly relevant to the issue of leadership.

For example, Coleman (1990) observes that charismatic authority may be a response to coordination problems that don't necessarily turn on misaligned incentives (see also Langlois 1998). In fact, Coleman's discussion suggests that he has an assurance game in mind. Calvert (1992, 1995) and Camerer and Knez (1994, 1996, 1997) argue that attention should be shifted to coordination games (rather than cooperation games) in seeking a foundation for the understanding of organizational phenomena. Although he has placed primary emphasis on problems of *ex post* opportunism, Williamson (1991: 278) has not been blind to the possibility of coordination problems, noting that failures of coordination 'may arise because autonomous parties read and react to signals differently, even though their purpose is to achieve a timely and compatible combined response'. While making much room for the role of incentives in organization, Chester Barnard also emphasized the importance of 'the inculcation of belief in the real existence of a common purpose', which he considered to be 'an essential executive function' (Barnard 1948: 87). Indeed, he very clearly argued that 'an organization can secure the efforts necessary to its existence . . . either by the objective inducements it provides or by changing states of mind' (ibid. 141).

The aim of the following pages is to develop some of these suggestions. Thus, in line with Calvert (1992, 1995), Camerer and Knez (1994, 1996, 1997) and Weber (1998), the focus is on coordination games rather than on cooperation games. And in line with Barnard, and others who have stressed the cognitive aspects of leadership (e.g. Selznick 1957), the emphasis will be on 'the inculcation of belief' and on 'changing states of mind'; for example, through (credible) communication. In contrast, all incentive problems will be suppressed. Basic game-theory ideas will be used to explicate the reasoning.

Coordination Problems and Coordination Games

Cooperation and Coordination Games

Criticism of the predominant incentive-alignment heuristic in the economics of organization has often been cast in terms of basic game theory (e.g. Camerer and Knez 1994, 1996, 1997; Foss 1996). Thus, the critics have argued that all the emphasis has been on cooperation games; that is, games where the pay-off space of the game is such that the efficient outcomes are not supportable as equilibria (at least in one-shot play). The key problem that such a game leads one to ponder is how to avoid the Pareto-inferior outcome. Indeed, the basic hold-up situation has a prisoners' dilemma structure (Milgrom and Roberts 1992: 128), and this is also the case with the team-production problem and other problems with information externalities and moral hazard (Holmström 1982, 1999). Accordingly, the literature is taken up with how reallocating incentives and property rights may improve on outcomes. In contrast, the economics-of-organization literature is characterized by a corresponding lack of interest in the interaction problems that may be represented by coordination games—a somewhat surprising neglect given the the increasing emphasis on such problems in other areas of economics, such as standards (Farrell and Saloner 1985; Witt 1997), conventions

(Young 1996), learning behavior (Crawford and Haller 1990), and macro-economics (Cooper 1999) (Friedman 1994).

There is a distinction between shared-interest (or 'pure') coordination games and coordination games with mixed interests. In the former category players' preferences over equilibria coincide. In symmetric, shared-interest coordination games all equilibria are efficient and pay-off equivalent, so that players are indifferent about which equilibrium is chosen, so long as one is in fact chosen. The coordination problem in question concerns actually choosing an equilibrium (Bicchieri 1993). In contrast, non-symmetric, shared-interest coordination games exhibit multiple Pareto-ranked equilibria. This (sub-)category encompasses assurance games where the coordination problem is caused by the riskiness of coordination on the Pareto optimal equilibrium (Cooper 1999). While coordination games with mixed interests will also exhibit multiple equilibria, these equilibria are ranked differently by the players (cf. the battle of the sexes or the chicken games), so that the problem again is choosing one of the equilibria. In this chapter reference will mostly be to shared-interest coordination games.

Coordination Problems and Approaches to Organizational Phenomena

Much recent work in game theory has consisted in refining a number of equilibrium concepts, most of them variations on the basic notion of Nash equilibrium. In general, the refinement literature analyzes alternative equilibrium concepts in terms of the epistemic states of players; that is, what they know or believe about other players's beliefs, knowledge, rationality, etc., and about the game (Aumann and Brandenburger 1995). Thus, the literature has a strong decision-theoretic, even 'subjectivist', orientation. Complicated interactive epistemics is involved, and impressive reasoning skills are imputed to players. Critics may easily gain the impression that classical game theory solves the coordination problem by defining it away; that is to say, by assuming that agents by means of pure ratiocination can reason their way to equilibrium. And such critics may argue that the literature begins from what is basically an existence claim; namely, that if rational players have commonly known and identical beliefs about all other players' strategies, then those beliefs are consistent with some equilibrium in the game. A problem with this is that nothing is said about the origin and formation of beliefs, and it is in principle possible that although there is an equilibrium in players' strategies, they may never be able to realize that equilibrium.

Along the lines of classical game theory, most of today's formal economics of organization proceeds on the assumption that players can choose the efficient game form for regulating their trade and can also choose any desired equilibrium thereof. It is a story of unproblematic coordination, given the constraints. Although information asymmetries and conflicting incentives may hinder reaching the first-best outcome, there is no problem picking the equilibrium that is induced by these constraints (and the rationality of the players, etc.). In this literature, one does not encounter, say, two pay-off-equivalent second-best outcomes, with players confronting the coordination problem of choosing between the two. Such problems are defined away. Of course, this is a short cut to conceptualizing various contractual arrangements as equilibria of some properly specified underlying games, involving conflicting incentives, and it may be argued that suppressing coordination problems is justified because it allows one to concentrate on the essentials (but see Foss and Foss 2000*a*). Moreover, it may be claimed that coordination problems are in fact not suppressed in the formal economics of organization, since the whole point of these exercises is to show how agents may coordinate to avoid inefficiency, or at least reach the second best. However, something different is involved here. More specifically, the argument is that organizations, and leaders, do more than make agents avoid inefficiencies in prisoners' dilemma-like interaction situations. For example, a proponent of institutional organization theory may argue that a function of organization is to define what strategies are available, in the sense of being 'legitimate' relative to some environment (Powell and DiMaggio 1991). An entrepreneurship scholar may point out that the function of leadership is to alert to new business opportunities. Although placing primary emphasis on the hold-up problem, Williamson (1985, 1996*a*, 1998) has long argued—following a time-honoured tradition in organization theory (March and Simon 1958)— that an organization also serves the purpose of alleviating bounds on rationality.

To be sure, it is hard to make game-theoretic sense of such functions of organization and leadership. For example, if the leader's function lies in his 'defining new strategies', this amounts to introducing a new game, and it is not at all clear what is gained by comparing a string of different games. However, more unconventional ideas (relative to economics) on 'symbolic leadership', the leader's 'inculcation of belief' among those being led, etc. can in fact be treated in relatively simple game-theoretic terms. Camerer and Knez (1994, 1996, 1997) and Weber (1998) have already demonstrated the usefulness of a coordination-game perspective for understanding a host of organizational phenomena. The following may be taken as an extension of the basic thrust of their arguments to the phenomenon of leadership in organizations. To understand the argument it is, however, necessary to spend some time arguing that, somewhat contrary to common perception, coordination games are non-trivial and quite fundamental.

Coordination Games are Non-trivial and Fundamental

The dominant implicit attitude among social scientists appears, at least until recently, to have been that coordination games, particularly of the shared-interests type, are basically trivial. The sources of this attitude are hard to trace, but the verdict issued in R. Duncan Luce and Howard Raiffa's very influential book *Games and Decisions* (1957: 59), that at least in pure coordination games 'everything is trivial', seems to be a possible—and likely—source. In contrast to what may be called 'the Luce and Raiffa legacy', a growing literature asserts that coordination games, even pure ones, are not so trivial as they may appear at first glance. Moreover, they are fundamental in the sense that they help identify fundamental interaction problems (e.g. interactive belief formation) and how such problems are resolved (e.g. through conventions). Finally, coordination games are fundamental not only in the sense that a host of everyday situations conform to their structure(s) (Schelling 1960, 1978) but also in the sense that from a theoretical perspective problems of equilibrium selection, which may often be seen as coordination problems, are very common.

Fundamentally, coordination games are (very often) non-trivial because their multiplicity of equilibria serves to highlight the importance for outcomes of agents' beliefs about each others' beliefs. And such interactive epistemology can be quite a complicated business, as both the philosophical (Lewis 1969; Dupuy 1989; Gilbert 1992; Bicchieri 1993), theoretical (Rubinstein 1989; Bacharach 1993; Aumann and Brandenburger 1995; Sugden 1995; Colman 1997; Colman and Bacharach 1997), and experimental (Cooper et al. 1992, 1994; Bacharach and Bernasconi 1997; Colman and Stirk 1998) literatures confirm. Thus, equilibrium-selection theories have been devised for rationalizing certain outcomes rather than others in asymmetric coordination games (Harsanyi and Selten 1988); there is a body of work on how repeated play may lead to convergence to an equilibrium (Crawford and Haller 1990); work has been done on how players' labeling of their strategies influences their beliefs (Sugden 1995); and there is a literature on communication in coordination games (Farrell 1987; Rabin 1990)—all of which is far from trivial.

Moreover, coordination games are fundamental in a number of ways—first of all, in the basic phenomenological sense of being pervasive in social life (Schelling 1960, 1978). Second, they provide a useful conceptualization of one class of interaction situations that may lead to the emergence of social institutions (Calvert 1995; Young 1996) or organizational phenomena (Camerer and Knez 1994, 1996, 1997). Moreover, they are fundamental in a theoretical sense, too, since recent work in game theory has revealed that coordination problems (that may be represented in terms of coordination games) emerge in a multiplicity of game situations. In particular, this is the case as dynamics is introduced, the number of players is increased, and less knowledge is ascribed to players.

Types of Coordination Problem

A possible categorization of coordination problems that may be illustrated by means of coordination games lies in the following distinction between three broad classes of coordination problems:

(1) the problem of coordinating on an equilibrium when agents are initially outside equilibrium (i.e. have inconsistent beliefs, lack of common knowledge), and don't know, for example, how strategies are labeled;

(2) the problem of coordinating on one equilibrium out of a multitude, when strategies, pay-offs, and rationality are common knowledge (e.g. the battle-of-the-sexes game); and

(3) the problem of moving from an inferior equilibrium to the efficient equilibrium, when strategies, pay-offs, and rationality are common knowledge (e.g. the assurance game).

What is common to all three problems is that belief dynamics is essential to them. They are briefly considered seriatim.

Coordinating on an equilibrium.   This is the problem of rationalizing the formation of those beliefs that will make it possible for agents to realize some equilibrium. To be sure, there has been an increasing interest in defining equilibria in terms of the beliefs and conjectures of agents, for example in connection with interpreting the notion of mixed strategies (where the relevant probabilities are interpreted as subjectively held probabilities) (Aumann and Brandenburger 1995). However, the problem of actually rationalizing the emergence of equilibrium beliefs—rather than 'simply' providing conditions for these—has attracted less general interest, at least until recently.

Thus, in a much cited paper, Crawford and Haller (1990) study how fully strategic agents may learn to coordinate in the context of a repeated coordination game where they initially have no shared information about how the strategies are labeled or how the game is presented (e.g. the normal form of the game), where strategies are symmetric (i.e. yield the same pay-offs), and where the players are also symmetric in the sense that they are in identical strategic positions in the game. Although they are playing the same game, they may (and probably will) perceive it differently. This effectively excludes any focal points based on the description of the game. However, after some play the players will develop distinctions between strategies and players, and when these distinctions become common knowledge, coordination may take place very quickly. The assumption that sets in motion, as it were, the right belief dynamics that establishes common knowledge is that players follow the meta-strategy of repeating successful strategies.

Of course, one should be extremely cautious in drawing inferences from the very simplified setting of Crawford and Haller (ibid.) to more complicated (and realistic) settings, where the problem of reaching an equilibrium may be complicated by, for example, the imperfection as guides to future behavior of precedents generated in earlier play when players play against different players (Knez 1998). However, one important feature of the Crawford and Haller analysis lies in their demonstration that in the situations they analyze 'it is sometimes optimal to forsake an efficient strategy forever in favor of an ineffi-cient one that is less costly to locate' (1990: 584). In other words, although coordination sometimes takes place quickly, there is no guarantee that agents coordinate in an efficient manner.

Selecting among multiple equilibria. It is well known that prisoners'-dilemma games with many players or hidden information imply many different ways of motivating cooperation, and that a key problem is making players choose beliefs that will pick out one of these solutions (Calvert 1995: 242). However, somewhat in contrast to the situation analyzed in Crawford and Haller (1990), there may be a coordination problem even in the presence of common knowledge. The conventional illustration of this is the symmetric pure coordination game, such as game (*a*) in Figure 9.1.

The problem is that classical game theory is not terribly helpful with respect to telling us how players will avoid coordination failure in such situations. Of course, when a (one-shot) game has multiple Nash equilibria in pure strategies it often has a unique mixed-strategy equilibrium (Nash 1951). But the basic problem of rationalizing the beliefs that lead players to play mixed strategies, and choose certain probabilities (and believe that others choose certain probabilities) rather than other ones, is not really addressed. There is still a fundamental problem of rationalizing the formation of equilibrating beliefs. In one interpret-ation of Nash equilibrium—namely, that it is the outcome of non-binding pre-play communication leading to the selection of a self-enforcing agreement (Farrell 1987)—the problem can, of course, be handled. It is arguably outside the conventional interpretation of games in normal form, such as the one in matrix 9.1(*a*), where the players make their choices simultaneously and there is no explicitly modeled stage in which they can communicate. However, in an exploratory chapter such as the present one, we wish to allow for this possibility, too.

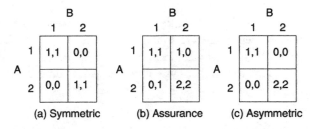

Figure 9.1. Coordination games.

Moving away from an inferior equilibrium.   The simultaneous-move-assurance game (matrix 9.1(*b*)) has become a popular pedagogical device for illustrating coordination failures, and it is one of the work horses of the experimental game theorist (e.g. Cooper et al. 1988, 1992; Van Huyck et al. 1990). Of course, this is motivated by the game's ability to portray risky coordination and strategic complementarity. Relatedly, the game connects to the theoretical issue of equilibrium selection in situations in which the existing refinement procedures do not work. For example, Harsanyi and Selten (1988) forcefully argue that the pay-off-dominant outcome ((2, 2) in matrix 9.1(*b*)) is a natural focal point. However, there is experimental evidence that coordination failure 'almost always' occurs (in the absence of pre-play communication) (Van Huyck et al. 1990; Cooper et al. 1992).

Perhaps less obviously, rationalizing the pay-off-dominant outcome as the focal point in the apparently less risky asymmetric pure coordination game (matrix 9.1(*c*)) is far from trivial (Farrell 1988; Colman 1997; Colman and Bacharach 1997). The basic problem is that A appears to have no rational grounds for choosing strategy 2 unless he has grounds for believing that B will choose strategy 2, because if A went to choose the strategy 1, B would do better also to choose strategy 1. Of course, B is in the same epistemic situation, and the reasoning process winds up in infinite regress. Pre-play communication does not necessarily help, for how can one player be sure that the other player has understood him? There still seems to be a problem of justifying beliefs. So how can we justify everybody's strong intuition—that the pay-off-dominant outcome will in fact be chosen?

Colman and Bacharach (ibid.) suggest that players may solve the problem by using something they call the 'Stackelberg heuristic'. Essentially, this heuristic works by letting agents mentally transform a normal-form game to an extensive-form game. Thus, they know that they will choose simultaneously but think as if they will choose sequentially. Specifically, player A will simulate the game by thinking of himself as moving first. Then B has to move with knowledge of A's choice, choosing a best-reply meta-strategy; namely strategy 1 if A also chooses 1 and strategy 2 if A also chooses 2. Of course, the latter choice is best for A. Having performed this simulation, A, returning to the real game, chooses what is (in the mental simulation) the utility-maximizing strategy provided that B responds with a best reply (namely strategy 2). Player B, performing the same simulation, makes the same choice. However, the requirement for the Stackelberg heuristic to do its work is that these simulations are common knowledge; in other words, that the heuristic itself is common knowledge.

Summing Up and Looking Ahead

The preceding pages have established that coordination games are non-trivial and fundamental. They are extremely helpful mental laboratories that assist in exploring the boundaries of game theory (e.g. Harsanyi and Selten 1988; Young 1996; Colman and Bacharach 1997), and in providing indirect rationales for phenomena, such as conventions (Lewis 1969; Young 1996) and other social phenomena that somehow turn on the issue of belief dynamics. The suggestion that will be developed in the following pages is that coordination games are also helpful for understanding the cognitive aspects of leadership; that is, what Barnard (1938) referred to as 'the inculcation of belief in the real existence of a common purpose'. The argument is not different in kind from other arguments pertaining to how coordination problems are solved in reality; namely, through the effect on the beliefs that players hold of communication, the formation of conventions, etc. Thus, leadership is an important member of the set of 'alternative institutions for resolving coordination problems' (Cooper, DeJong, Forsythe, and Ross 1994). However, the argument is, if one likes, 'comparative-institutional', in the sense that it is claimed that leadership may, in certain situations, be a low-cost alternative to these other methods of coordination.

Leadership

Conceptualizing Leadership

In much of the organization-theory literature it is held that the essence of organization is coordinated response to volatility; for example, in technologies or preferences (Thompson 1967; Galbraith 1973). Obviously, management and leadership have key roles here, for some volatility cannot be handled by organizational routine but requires judgment and decision. As we have seen, the economics of organization, to the extent that it relates to leadership and management issues, is not taken up with managers' and leaders' concrete actions and the judgments that inform such actions. However, it surely is informative with respect to leaders' and managers' roles in the design of explicit and implicit contracts (Kreps 1990a; Miller 1992; Rotemberg and Saloner 1993; Hermalin 1998), and much of the nature of leadership and managerial work may be conceptualized in this way. Thus, a classic contribution on the nature of managerial work (Mintzberg 1973: 5) lists six basic reasons why organizations need managers:

1. The prime purpose of the manager is to ensure that his organization serves its basic purpose [...] 2. The manager must design and maintain the stability of his organization's operations [...] 3. The manager must take charge of his organization's strategy-making system, and therein adapt his organization in a controlled way to its changing environment [...] 4. The manager must ensure that his organization serves the ends of those persons who control it [...] 5. The manager must serve as the key informational link between his organization and its environment [...] 6. As formal authority, the manager is responsible for the operating of his organization's status system.

On the face of it, much of this sounds largely consistent with the basic thrust of the economics of organization. It is indeed possible to cast virtually all of the above six points in terms of monitoring and the design of implicit and explicit contracts.

However, if one reads Mintzberg's own further detailing of what the six points actually mean and imply, it turns out that an economics-of-organization conceptualization does not do full justice to them. For Mintzberg is clear that the production of 'values' and 'atmosphere' through 'directing', disseminating information, and acting as 'spokesman', 'negotiator', and 'figurehead' is what lies behind the above managerial roles. Such roles and functions have so far not been treated from the perspective of the mainstream economics of organization.

The symbolic and cognitive aspects that Mintzberg associates with management become even more pronounced if one turns to the large and diverse literature on leadership in organizations (e.g. Vecchio 1997; Conger and Canungo 1998). Here, the leader is seen as engaging in numerous activities, such as planning strategy, changing standard practice, creating vision and meaning for the organization, and inducing changes in values, attitudes, and behavior. The reason why the economics literature on leadership may look somewhat meager (if considerably more precise) relative to the richness in the leadership literature overall arguably turns on the difficulty of providing economic interpretations of the cognitive and entrepreneurial aspects of leadership in particular. Of course, the aim should not be to present the phenomenon in all its complexity, but it is hard to escape the conclusion that economic approaches to leadership miss some essential aspects of the phenomenon, particularly those relating to the cognitive dimensions.

Below, I shall suggest that the basic ideas on coordination games that have been discussed so far are helpful for understanding precisely those aspects of leadership. More specifically, I shall develop a notion of leadership as the taking of actions that coordinate the complementary actions of many people through the creation of knowledge (or belief) conditions that at least approximate common knowledge, and where these actions characteristically consist of some act of communication directed at those being led.

Beliefs and Coordination Problems

An example of the type of belief dynamics that I am taken up with here involves the crucial epistemic construction in H. C. Andersen's well-known fairy tale 'The Emperor's New Clothes' that knowledge may be held identically (i.e. everybody knows that x is the case), but not in common. The child's loud announcement that the emperor really isn't wearing any clothes creates the belief dynamics that transforms the situation from one in which everybody knows that the emperor is not wearing any clothes to one in which everybody knows this and knows that everybody else knows it. The transformation essentially works because something else is common knowledge; namely, that everybody knows that everybody knows what the child has exclaimed.

One, possibly far-fetched, interpretation of the situation described in the tale is that a sort of assurance game is involved. Everybody would prefer that the truth be told, but because pay-offs (and possibly also rationality) are not common knowledge, telling the truth is risky. (Scorn may be heaped upon you!) Only the 'mediation' of the non-calculative child allows for beliefs to be coordinated on the superior equilibrium. In his classic contribution Schelling (1960) explicitly linked what he called 'mediators' to coordination problems:

a mediator can do more than simply constrain communications—putting limits on the order of offers, counter-offers, and so forth—since he can invent contextual material of his own and make potent suggestions. That is, he can influence [. . .] expectations on his own initiative [. . .] When there is no apparent point for agreement, he can create one by his power to make a dramatic suggestion.

In other words, when 'Schelling competence'—that is, players' capacity to coordinate by means of focal points (Bacharach and Bernasconi 1997: 2)—is low, coordination by means of a 'dramatic suggestion' may be required. Although Schelling doesn't spell this out, we may suggest that the creation of common-knowledge conditions is what is involved in his notion of mediation. A first hint, then, derived from Andersen and Schelling, is that part of the leader's function may be the break-up of an epistemic stalemate through acts of communication that influence 'in the right way' the beliefs held by players.

Coordination and Communication

The formalization (Crawford and Sobel 1982; Farrell 1988; Rabin 1990) and empirical investigation (Cooper et al. 1989, 1992, 1994) of communication is a relatively recent undertaking in game theoy. Thus, Cooper et al. (1992) experimentally evaluated the effect of 'cheap talk' under one-way communication and under two-way communication in the context of an assurance game. They found that with no communication, coordination failure was universal (the efficient equilibrium was never reached), with one-way communication, coordination substantially improved (the efficient equilibrium was reached about 50 per cent of the time), and two-way communication almost completely eliminated any coordination failures.

Intuitively, things are even simpler in pure, symmetric coordination games (Rabin 1990), where one would expect one-way communication to be more successful than in the context of assurance games. Thus, one person's communicative act may create a focal point that becomes common knowledge, such as the child's announcement in the H. C. Andersen fairy tale. But there is an apparent difficulty here (Monderer and Samet 1989). For whereas it was implicitly assumed in the discussion above that a public announcement automatically becomes common knowledge, it is not at all obvious that such an assumption is always warranted, particularly as the group to which a message is directed grows in size. For example, there may be a probability, however small, that somebody in the group was inattentive at the time of the announcement, which effectively means that the announced message will not be common knowledge.

In a famous note Rubinstein (1989) pointed out that whether or not common knowledge obtains may matter dramatically for outcomes. In his 'electronic-mail-game' example, nature chooses one of two two-person, risky coordination games with equal probabilities. If the state of nature is common knowledge, coordinating on the desired equilibrium is taken by Rubinstein to be straight-forward. Not so if what Rubinstein calls 'almost common knowledge' obtains; that is, if only a finite (but possibly very large) number of propositions of the sort '1 knows that 2 knows that A knows . . . that the state x (a or b) obtains' are true. Effectively, this situation implies that the game becomes one of incomplete information, although the players are allowed to communicate.

In the example the first player knows which one of the two games will be played and he sends a message to the second player informing him about this. The second player acknowledges receipt of the message, player 1 acknowledges receipt of the acknowledgment, and so on. However, there is a small probability that a message gets lost in the process, in which case the process of communication is brought to a halt. The problem now is that neither of the players knows whether it is his message or the other player's acknowledgment that was lost. Rubinstein proves that the uncertainty caused by incomplete information implies that under almost common knowledge there is actually only one Nash equilibrium in the game. Thus, there is no 'convergence' to the common-knowledge situation, where the players will play a certain strategy if state 'a' obtains and the other strategy if state 'b' obtains. Clearly, the agents would be better off if some mechanism could somehow throw a condition of common knowledge into their game.

It is of course easy to construct an argument that because we, strictly speaking, can never be absolutely certain that something is common knowledge many potential Pareto improvements are never realized. Some may even argue that common knowledge is a useless fiction. However, in a stimulating paper Monderer and Samet (1989) argued that common knowledge can be approximated (in a way they make precise) by the notion of common belief. Using Aumann's (1976) model, in which knowledge is partitions and beliefs are posterior probabilities, belief may be defined as being 'common' in the conventional way; namely, when an infinite hierarchy obtains. The difference is that beliefs are held with a probability, such that a common r-belief may be defined for each r in [0,1]. Monderer and Samet then show that when 'r' approaches 1, common r-belief approximates common knowledge. This line of reasoning further suggests, if only loosely, that not only are agents' successes at coordinating their strategies dependent on the beliefs they hold about each others' beliefs, but that the more well-founded these beliefs are the better they are able to coordinate strategies. This brings us directly to leadership; for one role of leadership is to influence how well founded agents think certain beliefs are.

Leadership and Coordination

For the purposes of this chapter leadership has been defined as the taking of actions that coordinate the complementary actions of many people through the creation of belief conditions that (at least) substitute for common knowledge, and where these actions characteristically consist of some act of communication directed at those being led. It is time to make something more out of this tentative definition.

Why may coordination problems cause a need for leadership in the above sense? In order to get a take on this issue, it is convenient to create a distinction between coordination problems (represented by means of coordination games) in which common knowledge (or, at least a common r-belief where r is close to 1) about pay-offs and strategies obtains initially and those in which it does not. Moreover, it is convenient to make a distinction between games where agents can communicate by exchanging cheap talk (at no or low cost) and those in which they can't (or communication is very costly). However, the leader will be privileged by being the only player who can always communicate if he so chooses. These distinctions produce four cases in which leadership plays different roles (Table 9.1). They are considered seriatim.

Case 1 represents the case where leadership is least likely to play a role, since knowledge is common and agents can communicate at low or no cost. If communication costs are strictly 0, coordination will be instantaneous. However, with positive (if small) communication costs, delay is a possibility. For example, the relevant game may be a pure symmetric coordination game without any focal points (e.g. matrix 9.1(a)). In this situation agents want to delay decisions because they first want to communicate with other agents. The incentives for delay are caused by the complementarity of actions that implies gains from coordination. These incentives may, however, cause an inefficiency, since there is no social gain from delay (Gale 1995). In this situation the exercise of leadership, that is the picking of some strategy, may economize on delay and communication costs.

Case 2 differs from case 1 by not allowing agents to engage in communication. However, the common-knowledge assumption is maintained. As we have seen, there is substantial empirical evidence that agents may not choose the efficient equilibrium when they cannot communicate, for example in

TABLE 9.1. The role of leadership under alternative assumptions about common knowledge and communication

			The role of leadership
Coordination games	With common knowledge	With communication	**Case 1:** Leadership may economize on delay and communication costs, particularly in many-players situations.
		Without communication	**Case 2:** Leadership may be required when 'Schelling competence' is low and/or there is coordination failure because agents avoid the risky, but efficient, equilibrium, and/or agents have to go through complex and costly reasoning processes in order to reach their preferred equilibrium (e.g. leaders may 'build assurance' in assurance-game situations).
	Without common knowledge	With communication	**Case 3:** Leadership economizes on the communication costs of establishing common-knowledge conditions (e.g. leaders may help convince players that there are gains from coordination).
		Without communication	**Case 4:** Leadership helps establish common-knowledge conditions by influencing beliefs, or chooses one equilibrium out of a multiplicity.

assurance-game situations (e.g. matrix 9.1(*b*)), although they have full common knowledge about pay-offs, strategies, and rationality. In this situation the leader may, by playing the efficient equilibrium and making this common knowledge, induce the other player to play the efficient equilibrium.

Moreover, agents may have difficulties coordinating on an equilibrium, when their 'Schelling competence' is low (i.e. there are no obvious focal points), or they have to go through complex and costly reasoning processes à la Stackelberg heuristic of Colman and Bacharach (1997), or they have to invest in flexibility (i.e. choose several actions at the same time by incurring some costs—see Galesloot and Goyal 1997) in order to reach their preferred equilibrium. Through the signal provided by the leader picking some strategy these coordination problems may be resolved.

Case 3 refers to the situation where knowledge is not held in common, but where agents may communicate at no or low cost. If communication costs are strictly 0, one would expect common-knowledge conditions to be established instantaneously, and coordination follows in the same split second. However, if communication costs are positive, but small, there may still be a role for leadership, particularly with respect to convincing players that there are gains to be had from coordination.

Case 4 refers to the situation where knowledge is not held in common, and where agents cannot communicate (at reasonable cost). Although theoretically extreme, this is also the most realistic of the four cases. The real world of managers and leaders is not a world of simple two-strategies, two-players coordination games with costless cheap talk and common knowledge, but of rather large-scale games with imperfect recall, state-contingent uncertainty, etc. In this situation players are likely to have incomplete information (or none at all) about other players, available strategies, previous plays, etc., and games will have to be redefined and played anew (Calvert 1995). In a large-scale game, individual belief formation may at most proceed from extrapolating the current aggregate behavior of the population. There is not likely to be an exact (if any) correspondence between players, strategies, and outcomes in various 'repetitions' of 'the game'. There will probably be multiple equilibria. In such a situation, leadership may be conceptualized as picking one equilibrium out of a multiplicity (Calvert 1992); for example, by establishing belief conditions that approximate common knowledge.

To be more specific about how leadership works by influencing beliefs in the absence of common knowledge, consider Colman and Bacharach's work on the 'Stackelberg heuristic' (1997) mentioned earlier. In their work no player is, strictly speaking, a leader; the Stackelberg element is introduced by thinking of oneself as a Stackelberg leader. However, we may find room for more genuine leadership if we provide a realistic interpretation of the fundamental assumption in the model that any conclusion about which strategy to play reached by player A will be perfectly anticipated by player B, and vice versa (i.e. is common knowledge). This may make sense for small groups characterized by a long period of interaction (Camerer and Knez 1994). But in larger-scale settings with less of a history of interaction players may not have such an easy time performing the Stackelberg heuristic. In such situations it may make sense to condition one's strategy choices on the choices of one particular player—who will be, in a sense, a leader.

Another example relates to the electronic-mail game of Rubinstein (1989). Organizational phenomena that are akin to the electronic-mail game may be represented by problems of coordinating in an administrative hierarchy. If senior management's strategic plan calls for new initiatives if certain conditions obtain and these new initiatives require inter-departmental coordination, what should division managers do (Rumelt 1995)? Moving first may be costly, but communication regarding concerted action will not lead to common knowledge. Top management may circumvent these problems simply by ordering all division managers to show up at a particular place and date, communicating their new initiatives, and making sure that all division managers publicly and explicitly agree on coordinating their actions. This may help establish the required condition of common knowledge (or an approximation in terms of common beliefs).

To sum up on the above, leadership may be thought of in terms of remedying (1) problems of coordinating on an equilibrium when agents are initially outside equilibrium; (2) problems of coordinating on one equilibrium out of a multitude; and (3) problems of moving from an inferior equilibrium to the efficient equilibrium by influencing the beliefs that agents hold. The question then arises of how the leader accomplishes this and what motivates his followers to follow him.

Leadership, Knowledge, and Communication

The story that has been sketched in the preceding pages relies heavily on the notion of common knowledge (or at least common r-belief with a high r). However, it has already been noted that common knowledge may be an unrealistic assumption because we, strictly speaking, can never be absolutely certain that something is common knowledge. One may conclude that in interaction we will always suffer from the inefficiencies illustrated by Rubinstein's electronic-mail game (1989). However, such a conclusion is premature.

One interpretation of the notion of common knowledge is not actually to think of it as involving conscious, ever ascending processes of reasoning, but rather as something that players recognize heuristically, somewhat akin to Monderer and Samet's notion of common r-belief (1989). For example, if players have a long history of interaction this may be sufficient to allow them to short-cut the infinite processes of reasoning involved in the common-knowledge assumption. For example, from the observed body language of the other players or through eye contact, etc. they may conclude on the basis of their earlier history of interaction that common knowledge is being formed (or, r is approaching 1). They simply know.[1] Hence, the importance of face-to-face contact in the examples with which I began this chapter. Other social practices in firms—notably various kinds of social gatherings at which management typically insists that a substantial percentage of employees be present—may play a similar role. They are mechanisms for installing common knowledge among employees. For example, they may help to build up the 'precedents' (Knez 1998) that Kreps analyzes (1990) as an important part of corporate culture, and which means that all employees know that everybody knows that in situations of type x the thing to do is y.

Judgment, Motivation and Commitment

So far, I have tacitly assumed that the leader is a sort of benevolent deus ex machina, who spots and resolves coordination problems to the benefit of all concerned. This raises a number of problems that have been sidestepped so far.

The first problem relates to the informational advantage of leaders, the second relates to the leader's motivation for leading, and the third relates to how he ensures that those he wants to lead actually follow him.

With respect to the first issue Hermalin (1998) begins his analysis by assuming that the leader already has some informational advantage. The ability to glimpse or intuitively judge what is the 'true' structure of a situation (say, an ongoing battle) and take action on the basis of that judgment is a common interpretation (perhaps, rather, definition) of successful leadership. It is, however, not clear that traditional social science has much to contribute to the understanding of the cognitive and psychological issues of what makes the leader's judgment superior to other players' judgment or, conversely, why leaders sometimes fail in their judgment of a situation. However, it is certainly possible to address a number of issues that are connected to the exercise of judgment, such as the consequences of the exercise of judgment and the motivation of leaders and followers.

With respect to the motivation of the leader we may well make standard assumptions with respect to his behavior. As portrayed so far, the leader's activities create additional utility for the relevant players; by making players change their strategies, he moves them towards better equilibria. He can be paid out of this extra value, or, if he is one of the players in the game himself, he will automatically gain from his activities (supposing the relevant games are coordination games such as those in matrices 9.1(a)–(c)).

With respect to the issue of how to motivate followers to actually follow, things are slightly more complicated. As discussed so far, leadership consists in influencing beliefs so that better equilibria can be reached; for example through explicit (speech act) and more tacit (body language) communication and through 'leading by example' by being the first to pick a certain strategy. That the issues of communication and commitment are closed linked has often been pointed out. Thus, Kotter, an expert on leadership, argues that 'people will not make sacrifices [...] unless they think that the potential benefits of change are attractive and unless they really believe that transformation is possible. Without credible communication, and a lot of it, employees' minds and hearts are never captured' (Kotter 1996: 9). In the way that Kotter uses the concept here, 'credible communication' corresponds closely to the point that leaders may be instrumental in installing common knowledge conditions among players. Thus, if everybody believes that everybody else will move to a superior equilibrium when such a change has been communicated by the leader, and if it is common knowledge that players condition their behavior on the leader and that the leader himself gains by the change, then the leader's communication is very credible indeed. To put it in simpler terms, in pure coordination games we would clearly expect 'cheap talk' to be credible, since it is clearly in the interest of the announcing player to follow what he himself announces.

Evidence

Existing experimental evidence has a bearing, directly or indirectly, on the issues under consideration here. For example, it is a rather robust result that coordination on the efficient equilibrium in weakest-link games is virtually impossible for groups of ten people or more (Van Huyck, Battalio, and Beil 1990; Camerer and Knez 1994). Of course, this doesn't prove the need for leadership, but it does suggest that various institutions, and among them leadership, exist for the purpose of building assurance. One device that for a wide class of games improves coordination—both in theory and in experiments—is communication (Farrell 1987, 1988; Cooper, DeJong, Forsythe, and Ross 1989, 1992, 1994), and communication and leadership have indeed been connected in this chapter.

However, there is reason to be cautious here, for communication is not always helpful. Thus, Weber, Camerer, Rottenstreich, and Knez (1998) conducted experiments with weakest-link games and found that letting one member of a large group take the role of a speaker and engage in brief one-way, pre-play communication did not improve the success with which the group coordinated. It may of course be objected that weakest-link games are extreme games (they are very risky) in a broad class of coordination games and that the experimental subjects that were picked as speaker/leaders were inexperienced students, not real managers. However, the results of Weber et al. (1998) do indicate that communication is not necessarily effective across the board and that in some interaction situations communicative leadership will have to be backed up by other means that can further build assurance (cf. Kotter 1996).

Moreover, recent experimental work has begun to discern some basic mistakes that leaders may be prone to commit. Thus, Weber (1998) investigated the dependence of successful coordination in weakest-link games (generalized-assurance games) on the size of the group that played the game. His results indicate that starting with small groups and then 'growing' them at a slow rate (corresponding to 'controlled growth' in firms) led to successful coordination in large groups, whereas successful coordination was impossible if the size of the group was initially large. Weber then allowed for the possibility that one of the players may become a 'leader' in the sense that he is allowed to determine the growth path of group size. The experiments suggest that leaders tend to increase group size too quickly. In other words, they tend not to have the correct cognition of the situation. Again, the easy objection is the same as above—that is, weakest-link games are extreme games in the broad class of coordination games and the experimental subjects are inexperienced students— but the results certainly do indicate the potential importance of behavioral aspects for the understanding of leadership (cf. also Heath, Knez, and Camerer 1993).

Applications

The primary aim of this chapter has been to put forward a conceptualization of leadership that while based on simple game theoretical ideas can capture much of what is meant by leadership from a cognitive or symbolic perspective, and goes some way towards rationalizing such a notion. The ideas here should be judged relative to how well they make sense out of cognitive and symbolic understandings of leadership, and how they illuminate business practices in an increasingly networked knowledge economy. The emerging knowledge economy is very often characterized in terms of increasing information richness. However, the flip side of this information richness, increasing connectivity, is usually given less attention, although it is everywhere, from the linking of primitive cash registers into smart inventory-management systems to the amazing connectivity we can observe on the internet. Another word for 'connectivity' is 'network', although connectivity goes way beyond those industries that have traditionally been considered 'network industries', such as telecommunications, operating systems, and the like. Networks introduce critical mass through network externalities. Actions become increasingly interdependent, and coordination problems of the kind that have just been considered become increasingly important to cope with. Below I argue that establishing knowledge conditions approximating common knowledge will be an increasingly important capability in this economy.

Organization

The argument that there may be a connection between common knowledge and economic organization has occasionally been made. Thus, Camerer and Knez (1996) suggest that total-quality management may play a role akin to the role that this chapter has ascribed to leadership; namely, helping to establish focal points that ease coordination of actions. Kreps (1990a) puts forward a similar argument with respect to corporate culture. This perspective may be generalized, drawing on the ideas of this chapter. Thus, the currently highly fashionable emphasis on 'knowledge management' may be interpreted as an attempt to create knowledge conditions among employees that approximate common knowledge. In such an interpretation the practice of knowledge management—which may roughly be interpreted as a practice of disseminating and sharing knowledge that was hitherto more asymmetrically distributed—is useful, not because it disseminates valuable knowledge per se, but rather because the process of knowledge management is a vehicle for establishing knowledge conditions that more closely resemble those of common knowledge (Foss and Mahnke 2003). Thus, knowledge-intensive organizations engage in knowledge management projects not (just) because this allows for more efficient use of the knowledge that is available to the organization, but because these firms typically have a coordination need (e.g. because employees are hard-to-monitor professionals, organization structures are flat) that cannot easily be resolved by means of existing hierarchical mechanisms. Establishing common knowledge conditions helps here.

However, much depends on how knowledge management exercises are actually carried out. Notably, there is a tendency in the knowledge management movement to think that technology can replace face-to-face contact. This line of thinking has become influential, because it seemingly helps drastically to cut travel budgets, reduce the opportunity costs of meeting activity, etc. As Nancy Dixon (2000: 4) laconically observes, '[a]lthough this sounds reasonable, it unfortunately just doesn't always work out that way'. She finds that the knowledge-management systems she studied unavoidably gravitate towards a mix of technology and face-to-face meetings. In her story, one of the causes of this is that much knowledge is tacit, and hence not directly open to transfer through existing knowledge-management technologies. A common-knowledge perspective suggests a complementary explanation. Thus, if knowledge is placed in a central 'storehouse', employee A may know that a particular piece of information is located there; for example, because he himself supplied it. He also knows that all other employees may retrieve it. But he doesn't know whether they have retrieved it; that is, whether they, in fact, know. And even if he guesses that they know, how does he know that they know that he knows. Well, he doesn't. Only more direct contact, and preferably direct meetings, can guarantee this kind of common knowledge. The implication is that knowledge that it is crucial that all employees know and where coordination requirements necessitate that all know that all know should not be disseminated through conventional knowledge-management techniques.

The relevance of common knowledge/coordination also applies to corporate values and what such values can accomplish for firms. As previously discussed, in many industries traditional 'Taylorist' authority in the sense of detailed order-giving and control is waning in importance, as knowledge workers increasingly control strategically important assets, have attractive exit options, and are anyway increasingly difficult to monitor and control, because of their expert knowledge. Traditional hierarchy and supervision is giving way to empowerment, delegation, and autonomy and disintegration into molecular team-based units. However, firms still often need to take concerted action. They also need to share knowledge, for example, for the purpose of taking such concerted action. It is not immediately clear how firms can fulfil these aims at the same time as they are restructuring their organizations towards much more decentralized structures. Corporate cohesion would seem to be threatened in the face of the centrifugal forces of decentralization. As a consequence of this, more and more firms are working not only on installing shared value bases that are intended to compensate for (and more) those formal communication channels that decentralization may have swept away. However, they often fail to do it in the right way. Insights into coordination problems and common knowledge show us why.

Although corporate value bases are currently all the rage, very many firms communicate these value bases in a surprisingly naive manner. Often the initial training session is the only time during her career in which an employee is explicitly exposed to the corporate value base. Such an exercise is, at best, useless. For corporate value bases to help in internal coordination tasks they have to be in the nature of what Danish marketing executive turned guru Jesper Kunde (1997) strikingly calls 'corporate religion'. Though perhaps a bit tasteless (at least to the believer), the religion metaphor is nevertheless descriptively highly apposite. This is because a living religion is not the holy Scriptures per se, but is the lived practice and the feeling of community implied by and revolving around those Scriptures. Most religions thus consider active participation in the community, including participating in services, essential. Common knowledge helps us to understand why this is so. Thus, common knowledge is best established through being physically present at the same location and, if possible, through eye contact. Rituals perform much of this function (Chwe 2001). Corporate value bases are not something that should only be communicated from a human-resources manager to a prospective or new employee; they are something that is meant for large-scale, relatively frequent (perhaps yearly) gatherings, involving as many of the firm's employees as possible, allowing for eye contact and other aspects of bodily language. This is the way to maximize the chances that any employee knows that any other employee knows that any given action is or is not in conformity with corporate values, with 'the way we do it "round here" '; something which we have seen is a great assisting force in resolving coordination problems.

In this connection note that while Taylorist authority may indeed be waning in the information-rich, networked economy, this is not the case for what Max Weber called 'charismatic authority'. The successful charismatic leader is not only the one who makes each individual believe in the real existence of a common purpose; he also succeeds in making all those he leads believe that everybody believes in this common purpose. This kind of authority is certainly a source of cohesion also in those firms that adopt radical decentralizing exercises. Perhaps it is the only source left.

Strategy

Arguments on the role of common knowledge in resolving coordination problems may be applied to strategy, particularly strategy in a networked knowledge economy. It goes almost without saying that beliefs must be crucial to the enterprise of strategy. Thus, beliefs are central to the phenomenon of entrepreneurship (individual and corporate), clearly an important part of how competitive advantages are created and maintained. The ambitious notion of 'vision'—as propagated by Gary Hamel and C. K. Prahalad (1994)—refers to corporate beliefs and how these may help mold future competitive landscapes. Shorter-run aspects of strategizing, such as signaling tactics, are also ultimately rooted in what is believed about competitors, what they believe about you, what you believe that they believe about you, etc. (Tirole 1988). And the outcomes of bargaining with, for example, suppliers or employees also depend very much on the beliefs you and your suppliers or employees hold.

In fact, according to Barney's argument (1986) considered in Chapter 3, the very phenomenon of competitive advantage—arguably the fundamental subject of strategic management—is ultimately a matter of beliefs. The core of the argument is that buyers and sellers may hold different beliefs with respect to the value-creating potential of a resource, and that superior insight, or luck, may help to exploit those differences.[2] Because beliefs are so obviously central to strategy, and underlie its central phenomenon, one would expect the formal study of belief management to constitute the central core of strategy. This is not the case. Apart from a few contributions (Barney 1986; Phelan 2000), beliefs have been given surprisingly little attention in the strategy literature. To be sure game theorists, psychologists, marketing specialists, etc. are taken up with beliefs, how they are formed, how they interact, how they may be influenced. Strategic-management scholars are much less so. Rather, strategists are instructed to utilize the information that they, and no (or only a few) others, possess in order to be able to utilize possible divergences in the beliefs about the true values of resources on factor markets. This is taking the beliefs of others as given, and hence unchanging.

However, there are reasons to believe that to the extent that the emergence of the knowledge economy is also the emergence of an increasingly networked economy, as many argue (e.g. Kelly 1999; Tapscott 1999; Varian and Shapiro 1999; Teece 2000), the ability to influence beliefs will increasingly be a central strategic capability. It will be one that goes significantly beyond the marketing function (although it will bring marketing and strategy closer together); it will be central to managing supply networks, to influencing customers and users; and it will be the key to managing employees. Firms will increasingly be confronted with coordination problems that arise for various reasons, primary among which are network effects. Standards represent an example that is so familiar that it will not be discussed further here. Instead, implications that relate to consumption rather than production are discussed below.

Organizing Consumption through Cognitive Leadership

To be able to consume in an intelligent manner one has to be able to rank the relevant consumption, process available information, understand why and how various goods and services produce utility, and compute what is the optimal bundle of goods and services one can afford to buy. The conventional assumption—certainly in economics, but to some extent also in marketing—is that once given sufficient information in the form of advertising, the consumer can easily and autonomously choose his most-preferred, 'utility-maximizing' bundle of goods. In a competitive equilibrium the consumer needs to know the menu of available goods, the prices of these goods, his own preferences (which are of course 'given'), and his own wealth. Knowing all of the goods in the economy is already mind-boggling. But there is one thing this consumer does not have to do; namely, care at all about the consumption choices of other consumers, since all interaction effects that are not transmitted through the price system are squeezed out of this model. Moreover, she knows exactly how the various goods and services that she may purchase produce utility for her. Her 'consumption capabilities' (Langlois and Cosgel 1998) are perfect.

In more realistic settings, such as our increasingly networked economy, consumers are not likely to come equipped with such perfect consumption capabilities. Moreover, everything is not somehow mysteriously organized for the consumer (or user) so that all he must do is pick his preferred bundle. Think of how beer drinkers now organize to influence the traditional breweries to produce higher-quality beers; or the role of the hobbyists in the development of the emerging PC industry, and, in general, how much of innovation activity is really a matter of interaction between users and producers. Or think of how much of advertising is really educating you as a consumer not only about prices and where to get the goods, but also about how products fit with each other, how you will 'fit' with all other buyers once you have purchased the product, or how—ironically, and ultimately self-defeatingly—you will not fit with the other consumers if you buy a certain product. In all these cases you are being educated about how your consumption pattern may fit into the consumption patterns of other consumers. Sometimes this is done in less than subtle ways ('fifty million Americans can't be wrong', etc.), but often it is done in very subtle ways indeed.[3]

A particularly subtle example, discovered and ingeniously interpreted by Michael Chwe (2001), is Super Bowl advertising. The Super Bowl is the most popular program that occurs regularly on network television. It is likely to be seen by a majority of American households. In fact, any American household is likely to know that a majority of other households have seen it. The Super Bowl, in other words, is one giant common-knowledge generator. Chwe examined what kind of products are typically advertised on the Super Bowl transmission, and noticed that it is products such as the Macintosh, the Discover card, Chrysler's Neon automobile, and various Nike and Reebok trainers. Is there anything special about such goods? Yes, indeed: buying each one of them constitutes a coordination problem. In fact, Chwe talks about 'coordination goods' as a separate category of products.[4]

To illustrate, imagine that you are back in 1984. Why does buying a Macintosh constitute a coordination problem for you? Well, the answer is of course that when you consider buying a Macintosh you want as many others to buy a Mac as well, so as to be able to exchange programs, documents, games, etc. This is the network externality. Your problem is that you don't know whether a sufficient number of other buyers will in fact buy a Mac; you don't know whether there will be 'critical mass'. Enter the Super Bowl transmission. As a potential Mac buyer, at least this will make you know that other potential Mac buyers have seen the Mac ad. In fact, this goes for any potential Mac buyer who has seen the Super Bowl transmission. In other words, common knowledge is established.

Now, coordination goods may possess this quality for various reasons. Thus, in some cases the potential buyer is interested in connectivity and a large network for purely technical reasons. In other cases, such as those of Nike or Reebok trainers, technical complementarity has very little to do with purchasing decisions. Rather, consumers purchase such goods because they are interested in having others form certain beliefs about them; for example, that they, too, are members of a certain in-group. Thus, consumption may in itself carry information and reduce uncertainty. Or, consumers' preferences are influenced by the number and character of other purchasers, quite apart from considerations of expediency. Purchase may be purely a matter of snobbery. However, in all these cases consumers face a coordination problem. And in all of these cases establishing common knowledge may be key to consumers solving their coordination problems—and to firms succeeding. Some firms, if certainly not all, are acutely aware of this. A striking example was an increasingly squeezed WordPerfect filing a court complaint against Microsoft to make the court stop the Microsoft claim that Word was the globally most popular software for word-processing purposes. Another example is Netscape's Navigator campaign which revolved around the slogan, 'Netscape Everywhere'.

Conclusion

This chapter has had an exploratory, yet ambitious, agenda. At the overall level it has been suggested—following the lead of Camerer and Knez (1994, 1996, 1997)—that coordination games carry important lessons for the study of organizational phenomena, including leadership in organizations, and that they also help to illuminate aspects of strategy in a networked knowledge economy. The innovation of this chapter is to suggest and sketch a notion of leadership that links up with cognitive notions of leadership—in which the 'inculcation of beliefs' is central—but which is founded on a rational-choice methodology and draws upon simple ideas in game theory. Thus, the chapter suggests that leadership is an important member of the set of institutions for resolving coordination problems; it is closely connected to issues of communication; it may arise as a response to significant communication costs in large-scale groups; it functions partly through communication; and it partakes of its coordinative role by establishing common-knowledge conditions (or, belief conditions approximating these).

The aim of this chapter has primarily been to take the first step in conceptualizing the leadership phenomenon in a way that while linking up with important strands in the leadership literature is founded on rational-choice methodology, and to suggest some applications of this conceptualization that may be particularly pertinent to the knowledge economy. To the extent that the knowledge bases to which firms need access become increasingly distributed whilst economic activity becomes increasingly networked, the cognitive concept of leadership developed here may become increasingly relevant.

Notes

1. Chwe (2001) explicitly argues that in everyday interaction we often succeed in short-cutting the infinite regress involved in common knowledge. In particular, eye contact helps to establish such epistemic conditions that 'I don't have to think through anything; I can simply infer from past experience that usually when we make eye contact, common knowledge is formed' (ibid. 77). Focal-point coordination implies much the same. When there is a focal point, you don't have to think through anything; you can just play the focal-point strategy.
2. A fairly well-known example concerns the initial sources of Microsoft wealth creation, which was very much based on landing a lucrative contract with IBM for an operating system (which MS still had to develop) and then discovering a small OS developer whose product was acquired for the (comparatively) miniscule sum of $50,000 (US), keeping the IBM contract entirely secret.
3. One important means of trying to establish common knowledge is through emphasizing simplicity. A classic example that pertains to a coordination product is movies, specifically the very different ads for Steven Spielberg's *Jaws* and Robert Altman's *Nashville*, both from 1975 (Chwe 2001: 81). While the *Jaws* poster showed little more than a swimming (and naked) woman and a shark, the *Nashville* poster showed the whole twenty-four character cast emblazoned on the back of a blue denim jacket. The simpler poster is likely to be noticed and remembered by many more than the more complicated poster. It is therefore more likely to help create common knowledge. Karl Weick (1979: 164) argued that as a general matter, managers engage in processes of 'enactment', whereby they 'construct, rearrange, single out, and demolish many "objective" features of their surroundings. They unrandomize variables [and] insert vestiges of orderliness.' Enactment, in Weick's description, is essentially making order by means of simplification that helps agents to construct shared understandings with which they can interpret reality and act in a cohesive way. While Weick had organizational action in mind, my argument implies that firms

should try to enact their external environment not only for themselves, but just as much for their customers.

4. Many goods are actually coordination goods, even if this is seldom realized, such as car oil or photo copying machine. There isn't necessarily anything fancy about coordination goods.

References

Acs, Zoltan J., and Audretsch, David D. (1988), 'Innovation in Large and Small Firms: An Empirical Analysis', *American Economic Review*, 78: 678–90.

Adler, Paul S. (2001), 'Market, Hierarchy and Trust: The Knowledge Economy and the Future of Capitalism', *Organization Science*, 12: 215–34.

—— and Borys, B. (1996), 'Two Types of Bureaucracy: Enabling vs. Coercive', *Administrative Science Quarterly*, 4: 61–89.

Aghion, Philippe, and Tirole, Jean (1997), 'Formal and Real Authority in Organizations', *Journal of Political Economy*, 105: 1–29.

Aghion, Philippe, and Bolton, Patrick (1987), 'Contracts as Barriers to Entry', *American Economic Review*, 77: 388–401.

Aharoni, Yair (1993), 'In Search for the Unique: Can Firm-Specific Advantages Be Evaluated?', *Journal of Management Studies*, 30: 31–49.

Akerlof, George (1970), 'The Market for Lemons', in Akerlof (1984), *An Economic Theorist's Book of Tales* (Cambridge: Cambridge University Press).

Alchian, Armen A. (1965), 'Some Economics of Property Rights', in Alchian (1977), *Economic Forces at Work* (Indianapolis, Ind.: Liberty).

—— and Demsetz, Harold (1972), 'Production, Information Costs, and Economic Organization', *American Economic Review*, 62: 772–95.

Allan, D., and Lueck, D. (1992), 'Contract Choice in Modern Agriculture: Crop-Share versus Cash Rent', *Journal of Law and Economics*, 35: 397–426.

Amit, Raphael, and Schoemaker, Paul J. H. (1993), 'Strategic Assets and Organizational Rent', *Strategic Management Journal*, 14: 33–46.

Andrews, Kenneth (1971), *The Concept of Corporate Strategy* (Homewood, Ill.: Irwin).

Aoki, Masahiko (1984), *The Cooperative Game Theory of the Firm* (Cambridge: Cambridge University Press).

—— (1990), 'Toward an Economic Model of the Japanese Firm', *Journal of Economic Literature*, 28: 1–27.

—— and Dore, Ronald (1994) (eds.), *The Japanese Firm: The Sources of Competitive Strength* (Oxford: Oxford University Press).

Argyres, Nicolas S. (1996), 'Evidence on the Role of Firm Capabilities in Vertical Integration Decisions', *Strategic Management Journal*, 17: 129–50.

—— and Liebeskind, Julia Porter (1998), 'Privatizing the Intellectual Commons: Universities and the Commercialization of Biotechnology', *Journal of Economic Behavior and Organization*, 35: 427–54.

—— (1999), 'Contractual Commitments, Bargaining Power, and Governance Inseparability: Incorporating History into Transaction Cost Theory', *Academy of Management Review*, 24: 49–63.

Argyres, Nicolas S. and Mui, Vai-Lam (2000), 'Rules of Engagement, Informal Leaders, and the Political Economy of Organizational Dissent', paper presented to the

International Society of New Institutional Economics Conference, Tübingern, 22–4 September 2000.

Armour, Henry O., and Teece, David J. (1978), 'Organizational Structure and Economic Performance: A Test of the Multidivisional Hypothesis', *Bell Journal of Economics*, 9: 106–22.

Aron, Debra J. (1991), 'Using the Capital Market as a Monitor: Corporate Spin-offs in an Agency Framework', *RAND Journal of Economics*, 22: 505–18.

Arora, Ashish, and Gambardella, Alfredo (1994), 'The Changing Technology of Technical Change: General and Abstract Knowledge and the Division of Innovative Labour', *Research Policy*, 23: 523–32.

Arrow, Kenneth J. (1962), 'Economic Welfare and the Allocation of Resources for Invention', in R. R. Nelson (ed.), *The Rate and Direction of Inventive Activity: Economic and Social Factors* (Princeton, NJ: Princeton University Press).

Arvanitis, S., and Hollenstein, H. (1996), 'Industrial Innovation in Switzerland: A Model-based Analysis with Survey Data', in Alfred Kleinknecht (ed.), *Determinants of Innovation: The Message from New Indicators* (London: Macmillan).

Athey, Susan, Gans, Joshna, Schacfer, Scott, and Stern, Scott (1994), *The Allocation of Decisions in Organizations* (Standford, Calif.: Mimeo).

Athey, Susan, and Stern, Scott (1998), 'An Empirical Framework for Testing Theories About Complementarity in Organizational Design', NBER working paper no. 6600.

Aumann, Robert, (1976), 'Agreeing to Disagree', *The Annals of Statistics*, 4: 1236–9.

—— and Brandenburger, Adam (1995), 'Epistemic Conditions for Nash Equilibrium', *Econometrica*, 63: 1161–80.

Bacharach, Michael (1993), 'Variable Universe Games', in Ken Binmore, Alan Kirman, and P. Tani (eds.), *Frontiers of Game Theory* (Cambridge, Mass.: MIT Press).

—— and Bernasconi, Michele (1997), 'The Variable Frame Theory of Focal Points: An Experimental Study', *Games and Economic Behavior*, 19: 1–45.

Badaracco, Joseph L. (1991), 'The Boundaries of Firms', in Amitai Etzioni and Paul R. Lawrence, *Socio-Economics: Toward a New Synthesis* (Armonk: Sharpe).

Bain, Joe S. (1959), *Industrial Organisation* (New York: Wiley).

Baker, George, Gibbons, Robert, and Murphy, Kevin J. (1999), 'Informal Authority in Organizations', *Journal of Law, Economics and Organization*, 15: 56–73.

—— (2002), 'Relational Contracts and the Theory of the Firm', *Quarterly Journal of Economics*, 117: 39–83.

Bandura, Albert (1977), *Social Learning Theory* (Englewood Cliffs, NJ: Prentice Hall).

Barnard, Chester I. (1948), *The Functions of the Executive* (Cambridge, Mass.: Harvard University Press).

Barney, Jay B. (1986), 'Strategic Factor Markets', *Management Science*, 32: 1231–41.

—— (1991), 'Firm Resources and Sustained Competitive Advantage', *Journal of Management*, 17: 99–120.

—— (1995), 'Looking Inside for Competitive Advantage', *Academy of Management Executive*, 9: 49–61.

—— (1997), *Gaining and Sustaining Competitive Advantage* (Reading, Mass.: Addison-Wesley).

—— (2001), 'Is the Resource-Based "View" a Useful Perspective for Strategic Management Research? Yes', *Academy of Management Review*, 26: 41–56.

—— and Onchi, William G. (1986), *Organizational Economics: Toward in New Paradigm for Studying and Understanding Organizations* (San Francisco, Calif.: Jossey-Bass).

Baron, James N., and Kreps, David M. (1999*a*), *Strategic Human Resources: Frameworks for General Managers*, (New York: Wiley).

—— (1999*b*), 'Consistent Human Resource Practices', *California Management Review*, 41: 29–53.

Barr, Jason, and Saraceno, Francesco (2002), 'A Computational Theory of the Firm', *Journal of Economic Behavior and Organization*, 49: 345–61.

Barzel, Yoram (1982), 'Measurement Costs and the Organization of Markets', *Journal of Law and Economics* 25: 27–48.

—— (1989), *Economic Analysis of Property Rights* (Cambridge: Cambridge University Press).

—— (1994), 'The Capture of Wealth by Monopolists and the Protection of Property Rights', *International Review of Law and Economics*, 14: 393–409.

—— (1997), *Economic Analysis of Property Rights*, 2nd edn. (Cambridge: Cambridge University Press).

Baumol, William S., Panzar, John, and Willig, Robert D. (1982), *Contestable Markets and the Theory of Industry Structure* (New York: Harcourt Brace Jovanovich).

Bazerman, Max (1994), *Judgment in Managerial Decision Making* (New York: Wiley).

Berman, Eli, Bound, John, and Griliches, Zvi (1994), 'Changes in the Demand for Skilled Labor Within U.S. Manufacturing: Evidence from the Annual Survey of Manufacturing', *Quarterly Journal of Economics*, 109: 367–98.

Best, Michael (1990). *The New Competition* (Oxford: Polity).

Bettenhausen, Kenneth and Murnighan, J. Keith (1985), 'The Emergence of Norms in Competitive Decision-Making Groups', *Administrative Science Quarterly*, 30: 350–72.

Bettis, Richard, Bradley, Steven, and Hamel, Gary (1992), 'Outsourcing and Industrial Decline', *Academy of Management Executive*, 6/1: 7–22.

Bicchieri, Christina (1993), *Rationality and Coordination* (Cambridge: Cambridge University Press).

Bikhchandani, Sushil, Hirshleifer, David, and Welch, Ivo (1992), 'A Theory of Fads, Fashions, Custom, and Cultural Change as Informational Cascades', *Journal of Political Economy*, 100: 992–1026.

Binmore, Ken, and Dasgupta, Patha (1986) (eds.), *Economic Organizations as Games* (Oxford: Oxford University Press).

Birkinshaw, Julian (1996), 'How Multinational Subsidiary Mandates are Gained and Lost', *Journal of International Business Studies*, 27: 467–95.

Blackler, Frank (1995), 'Knowledge, Knowledge Work, and Organizations: An Overview and Interpretation', *Organization Studies*, 16: 1021–46.

Blaug, Mark (1985), *Economic Theory in Retrospect*, 4th edn. (Cambridge: Cambridge University Press).

Boddy, David, and Paton, Robert (1998), *Management: An Introduction* (London: Prentice Hall).

Bohnet, Iris, and Oberholzer-Gee, Felix (2001), 'Pay for Performance: Motivation and Selection Effects', mimeo (Cambridge, Mass.: Harvard Business School).

Boisot, Max H. (1998), *Knowledge Assets: Securing Competitive Advantage in the Information Economy* (Oxford: Oxford University Press).

Bolton, Patrick, and Farrell, Joseph (1990), 'Decentralization, Duplication, and Delay', *Journal of Political Economy*, 98 (1998): 803–26.

Bolton, Patrick, and Dewatripont, Mathias (1994), 'The Firm as a Communication Network', *Quarterly Journal of Economics*, 115: 809–39.

Børsens Nyhedsmagasin (1991), 'For Gud, Schrøder og Oticon', 1 March, p. 42.

—— (1999), 'Opgør med Kolinds kaos', 8 November, 14–22.

Bowman, Cliff, and Ambrosini, Veronique (2000), 'Value Creation versus Value Capture: Towards a Coherent Definition of Value in Strategy', *British Journal of Management*, 11: 1–16.

Bowman, Edward H., and Singh, Harbir (1993), 'Corporate Restructuring: Reconfiguring the Firm', *Strategic Management Journal*, 14: 5–14.

Brandenburger, Adam M., and Stuart, Harborne W. Jr. (1996), 'Value-Based Business Strategy', *Journal of Economics and Management Strategy*, 5: 5–24.

Brass, D. J. (1984), 'Being in the Right Place: A Structural Analysis of Individual Influence in an Organization', *Administrative Science Quarterly*, 29: 518–39.

Brennan, Geoffrey, and Buchanan, James M. (1985), *The Reason of Rules* (Cambridge: Cambridge University Press).

Bresnahan, Timothy, Brynjolfsson, Erik, and Hitt, Lorin M. (2002), 'Information Technology, Workplace Organization, and the Demand for Skilled Labor: Firm-level Evidence', *Quarterly Journal of Economics*, 117: 339–76.

Brickley, Jim, Smith, Cliff, and Zimmerman, Jerry (1996), *Organizational Architecture* (Toronto: Irwin).

Brockner, J., Tyler, T. R., Cooper, L. L., and Shneider, R. (1992), 'The Influence of Prior Commitment to an Institution on Reactions to Perceived Unfairness: The Higher They Are, the Harder They Fall', *Administrative Science Quarterly*, 37: 241–61.

Bromiley, Philip, and Fleming, L. (2002), 'The Resource-based View of Strategy: A Behaviorist Critique', in Mie Augier and James G. March (eds.), *The Economics of Choice, Change and Organization: Essays in Memory of Richard M. Cyert* (Cheltenham: Elgar).

Brouwer, E., and Kleinknecht, A. (1996), 'Determinants of Innovation: A Microeconometric Analysis of Three Alternative Innovation Output Indicators', in Alfred Kleinknecht (ed.) *Determinants of Innovation: The Message from New Indicators* (London: Macmillan).

Brown, John Seely, and Duguid, Paul (2002), 'Organizing Knowledge', in Stephen E. Little, *Managing Knowledge: An Essential Reader* (London: Sage).

Brown, Shona L., and Eisenhardt, Kathleen M. (1998), *Competing on the Edge: Strategy as Structured Chaos* (Boston, Mass.: Harvard Business School Press).

Brozen, Yale (1971), 'The Persistence of "High Rates of Return" in High-Stable Concentration Industries', *Journal of Law and Economics*, 14: 501–12.

Brusoni, Stefano, Prencipe, Andrea, and Pavitt, Keith (2001), 'Knowledge Specialization, Organizational Coupling, and the Boundaries of the Firm: Why Do Firms Know More Than They Make?', *Administrative Science Quarterly*, 46: 597–621.

Brynjolfsson, Erik (1994), 'Information Assets, Technology, and Organization', *Management Science*, 40: 1645–62.

—— Hitt, Lorin M., and Yang, Shinkyu (2002), 'Intangible Assets: Computers and Organizational Capital', Center for e-Business at MIT, working paper no. 138.

—— Malone, Thomas W., Gurbaxani, Vijay, and Kambil, Ajit (1994), 'Does Information Technology Lead to Smaller Firms?', *Management Science*, 40: 1628–44.

Bulow, Jeremy, Geanakoplos, John D., and Klemperer, Paul D. (1985), 'Multimarket Oligopoly: Strategic Substitutes and Complements', *Journal of Political Economy*, 93: 488–511.

Burns, Tom, and Stalker, G. M. (1961), *The Management of Innovation* (London: Tavistock).

Business Intelligence (1993), 'A Non-Traditional Performance and Process Measurement System', in Mette Morsing and Kristian Eiberg (1998) (eds.), *Managing the Unmanageable for a Decade* (Hellerup: Oticon).

Calvert, Randall L. (1992), 'Leadership and its Basis in Problems of Social Coordination', *International Political Science Review*, 13: 7–24.

—— (1995), 'The Rational Choice Theory of Social Institutions: Cooperation, Coordination, and Communication', in Jeffrey S. Banks and Eric A. Hanushek (eds.), *Modern Political Economy: Old Topics, New Directions* (Cambridge: Cambridge University Press).

Camerer, Colin, and Knez, Marc (1994), 'Creating Expectational Assets in the Laboratory: Coordination in "Weakest-Link" Games', *Strategic Management Journal*, 15: 101–19.

—— (1996), 'Coordination, Organizational Boundaries and Fads in Business Practice', *Industrial and Corporate Change*, 5: 89–112.

—— (1997), 'Coordination in Organizations: A Game-Theoretic Perspective', in Zur Shapira (ed.), *Organizational Decision Making* (Cambridge: Cambridge University Press).

Camuffo, Arnaldo (2002), 'The Changing Nature of Internal Labor Markets', *Journal of Management and Governance*, 6: 281–94.

Capelli, Peter, and Neumark, David (2001), 'Do "High-Performance" Work Practices Improve Establishment-Level Outcomes?', *Industrial and Labor Relations Review*, 54: 737–75.

Carlsson, Sune (1951), *Executive Behavior*, 1991 edn. (Uppsala: Acta Universitatis Upsaliensis).

Casson, Mark (1994), 'Why are Firms Hierarchical?', *International Journal of the Economics of Business*, 1: 47–76.

—— (1997), *Information and Organisation* (Oxford: Oxford University Press).

—— and Wadeson, Nigel (1997), 'Bounded Rationality, Meta-Rationality, and the Theory of International Business', working paper no. 242 (discussion papers in international investment and management), Dept. of Economics, University of Reading.

Castells, Manuel (1996), *The Rise of the Network Society: The Information Age: Economy, Society and Culture* (Oxford: Blackwell).

Caves, Richard E. (1980), 'Industrial Organization, Corporate Structure, and Strategy', *Journal of Economic Literature*, 18: 64–92.

Chandler, Alfred D. (1962), *Strategy and Structure*, new edn. 1990 (Cambridge, Mass.: MIT Press).

—— (1977), *The Visible Hand* (Cambridge, Mass.: Belknap).

Chandler, Alfred D., Jr. (1992), 'Organizational Capabilities and the Theory of the Firm', *Journal of Economic Perspectives*, 6: 79–100.

Cheung, Stephen S. N. (1969), 'The Structure of a Contract and the Theory of a Non-Exclusive Resource', *Journal of Law and Economics*, 10: 49–70.

—— (1983), 'The Contractual Nature of the Firm', *Journal of Law and Economics*, 26: 1–22.

Chi, Tailan (1994), 'Trading in Strategic Resources: Necessary Conditions, Transaction Cost Problems, and Choice of Exchange Structure', *Strategic Management Journal*, 15: 271–90.

Child, John, and McGrath, Rita (2001), 'Organizations Unfettered: Organizational Form in an Information Intensive Economy', *Academy of Management Journal*, 44: 1135–48.

Chwe, Michael Suk-Young (2001), *Rational Ritual: Culture, Coordination, and Common Knowledge* (Princeton, NJ: Princeton University Press).

Coase, Ronald H. (1937), 'The Nature of the Firm', *Economica* (NS), 4: 386–405.

—— (1960), 'The Problem of Social Cost', in Coase (1988), *The Firm, the Market and the Law* (Chicago, Ill: University of Chicago Press).

—— (1972), 'Internal Organization: A Proposal for Research', in Victor E. Fuchs (ed.), *Policy Issues and Research Opportunities in Industrial Organization* (New York: NBER).

—— (1988), 'The Nature of the Firm: Origin, Meaning, Influence', *Journal of Law, Economics and Organization*, 4: 3–47.

—— (1992), 'The Institutional Structure of Production', *American Economic Review*, 82: 713–19.

Cockburn, Iain, and Henderson, Rebecca (1999), 'Measuring Competence: Exploring Firm Effects in Pharmaceutical Research', *Strategic Management Journal*, 15: 63–84.

Coddington, Alan (1983), *Keynesian Economics: The Search for First Principles* (London: George Allen and Unwin).

Coff, Russell W. (1997), 'Human Assets and Management Dilemmas: Coping with Hazards on the Road to Resource-Based Theory', *Academy of Management Review*, 22(2): 374–402.

—— (1999), 'When Competitive Advantage Doesn't Lead to Performance: The Resource-based View and Stakeholder Bargaining Power', *Organization Science*, 10: 119–35.

—— (2002), 'Human Capital, Shared Expertise, and the Likelihood of Impasse in Corporate Acquisitions', *Journal of Management*, 28: 115–37.

—— (2003), 'The Emergent Knowledge-based Theory of Competitive Advantage: An Evolutionary Approach to Integrating Economics and Management', *Managerial and Decision Economics*, 24: 245–51.

Cohen, Michael, and Bacdayan, Paul (1994), 'Organizational Routines are Stored as Procedural Memory', *Organization Science*, 5: 554–68.

Cohen, Michael D., Burkhart, Roger, Dosi, Giovanni, Egidi, Massimo, Marengo, Luigi, Warglien, Massimo, and Winter, Sidney (1996), 'Routines and Other Recurrent

Action Patterns of Organizations: Contemporary Research Issues', *Industrial and Corporate Change*, 5: 653–98.

Cohen, Moshe, and Regan, Robert A. (1996), 'Managing Internal Consistency in Technology Intensive Design Projects', *Competitiveness Review*, 6: 42–59.

Cohen, Wesley M., and Klepper, Steven (1996), 'A Reprise of Size and R&D', *Economic Journal*, 106: 925–51.

Cohen, Wesley, and Levinthal, Daniel (1990), 'Absorptive Capacity: A New Perspective on Learning and Innovation', *Administrative Science Quarterly*, 35: 128–52.

Coleman, James S. (1990), 'Rational Organization', *Rationality and Society*, 2: 94–105.

Colman, Andrew M. (1997), 'Salience and Focusing in Pure Coordination Games', *Journal of Economic Methodology*, 4: 61–81.

—— and Stirk, Jonathan A. (1998), 'Stackelberg Reasoning in Mixed-Motive Games: An Experimental Investigation', *Journal of Economic Psychology*, 19: 279–93.

—— and Bacharach, Michael (1997), 'Pay-Off Dominance and the Stackelberg Heuristic', *Theory and Decision*, 43: 1–19.

Conger, J., and Kanungo, R. (1988), 'The Empowerment Process: Integrating Theory and Practice', *Academy of Management Review*, 13: 471–82.

—— (1998), *Charismatic Leadership in Organizations* (London: Sage).

Conlisk, John (1996), 'Why Bounded Rationality?', *Journal of Economic Literature*, 34: 669–700.

Conner, Kathleen R. (1991), 'A Historical Comparison of Resource-Based Theory and Five Schools of Thought within Industrial Organization Theory: Do We Have a New Theory of the Firm', *Journal of Management*, 17: 121–55.

—— and Prahalad, C. K. (1996), 'A Resource-based Theory of the Firm: Knowledge vs. Opportunism,' *Organization Science*, 7: 477–501.

Coombs, Rod, and Metcalfe, Stanley (2000), 'Organizing for Innovation: Co-ordinating Distributed Innovation Capabilities,' in Nicolai J. Foss and Volker Mahnke (eds.), *Competence, Governance, and Entrepreneurship* (Oxford: Oxford University Press).

Cooper, Russell W. (1999), *Coordination Games: Complementarities and Macroeconomics* (Cambridge: Cambridge University Press).

—— and John, Andrew (1988), 'Coordinating Coordination Failures in Keynesian Models', *Quarterly Journal of Economics*, 103: 441–63.

—— DeJong, Douglass V., Forsythe, Robert, and Ross, Thomas (1989), 'Communication in the Battle of the Sexes Game: Some Experimental Results,' *RAND Journal of Economics*, 20: 568–87.

—— (1992), 'Communication in Coordination Games', *Quarterly Journal of Economics*, 107: 739–71.

—— (1994), 'Alternative Institutions for Resolving Coordination Problems: Experimental Evidence on Forward Induction and Preplay Communication', in J. Friedman (ed.), *Problems of Coordination in Economic Activity* (Norwell: Kluwer).

Cosgel, Metin (1994), 'Audience Effects in Consumption,' *Economics and Philosophy*, 10: 19–30.

Coughlan, A. T., and Narasimhan, C. (1992) 'An Empirical Analysis of Sales-Force Compensation Plans', *Journal of Business*, 65: 93–121.

Drucker, Peter (1999), *Management Challenges for the Twenty-first Century* (Oxford: Butterworth-Heinemann).

Dundas, K. N. M., and Richardson, P. R. (1980), 'Corporate Strategy and the Concept of Market Failure', *Strategic Management Journal*, 1: 177–88.

Dupuy, Jean-Pierre (1989), 'Common Knowledge, Common Sense', *Theory and Decision*, 27: 37–62.

Dyer, Jeffrey H., and Nobeoka, Kentaro (2000), 'Creating and Managing a High-Performance Knowledge-Sharing Network: The Toyota Case', *Strategic Management Journal*, 21: 345–67.

Eggertson, Thrainn (1990), *Economic Behavior and Institutions* (Cambridge: Cambridge University Press).

Egidi, Massimo (1992), 'Organizational Learning, Problem-Solving, and the Division of Labor', in Herbert A. Simon (ed.), *Economics, Bounded Rationality, and the Cognitive Revolution* (Aldershot: Elgar).

—— (2001), 'Biases in Organizational Behavior', unpublished paper.

Eisenhardt, Kathleen M., and Martin, Joanna A. (2000), 'Dynamic Capabilities: What Are They', *Strategic Management Journal*, 21: 1105–21.

Elzinga, Kenneth, and Mills, David (2001), 'Independent Service Organizations and Economic Efficiency', *Economic Inquiry*, 39: 549–60.

Eskerod, Pernille (1997), *Nye perspektiver på fordeling af menneskelige ressourcer i et projektorganiseret multiprojekt-miljø*, Ph.D. thesis (Sønderborg: Handelshøjskole Syd).

—— (1998), 'Organising by Projects: Experiences From Oticon's Product Development Function', in Mette Morsing and Kristian Eiberg (eds.), *Managing the Unmanageable for a Decade* (Hellerup: Oticon).

Ewing, Michael T. (2002), 'Employment Branding in the Knowledge Economy', *International Journal of Advertising*, 21: 3–22.

Fama, Eugene, and Jensen Michael C. (1983), 'Separation of Ownership and Control', *Journal of Law and Economics*, 26: 301–25.

Farrell, Joseph (1987), 'Cheap Talk, Coordination, and Entry', *RAND Journal of Economics*, 18: 34–9.

—— (1988), 'Communication, Coordination, and Nash Equilibrium', *Economics Letters*, 27: 209–14.

—— and Saloner, Garth (1985), 'Standardization, Compatibility, and Innovation', *RAND Journal of Economics*, 16: 70–83.

—— Monroe, Hunter K., and Saloner, Garth (1998), 'The Vertical Organization of Industry: Systems Competition Versus Component Competition', *Journal of Economics and Management Strategy*, 7: 143–82.

Feenstra, R. C. (1998), 'Integration of Trade and Disintegration of Production in the Global Economy', *Journal of Economic Perspectives*, 12: 31–50.

Felin, Teppo, and Foss, Nicolai J. (2004), 'Methodological Individualism and the Organizational Capabilities Approach', working paper no. 5 <http://cbs.dk/ckg/working.php>

Felin, Teppo, and Hesterly, William (2004), 'The Knowledge-based View and the Individual: Philosophical Considerations on the Locus of Knowledge', working paper, David Eccles School of Business, University of Utah.

Field, Alexander (1984), 'Microeconomics, Norms, and Rationality', *Economic Development and Cultural Change*, 32: 683–711.

Ford, D. (1990), *Understanding Business Markets: Interaction, Relationships, Networks* (London: Academic).

Foss, Kirsten (1996), 'Transaction Costs and Technological Development', *Research Policy*, 25: 531–47.

—— (2001), 'Organizing Technological Interdependencies: A Coordination Perspective on the Firm', *Industrial and Corporate Change*, 10: 151–78.

—— (2002), 'Lead Time and the Modularisation of Products and Organization', working paper.

—— and Foss, Nicolai (2000*a*), 'Competence and Governance Perspectives: How Do They Differ? And How Does It Matter?', in Nicolai J. Foss and Volker Mahnke (eds.), *Competence, Governance, and Entrepreneurship* (Oxford: Oxford University Press).

—— (2000*b*), 'Theoretical Isolation in Contract Economics', *Journal of Economic Methodology*, 7: 313–39.

—— (2001), 'Assets, Attributes and Ownership', *International Journal of the Economics of Business*, 8: 19–37.

—— (2002*a*), 'Authority and Discretion: Tensions, Credible Delegation, and Implications for New Organizational Forms', <http://www.cbs.dk/link/papers>

—— (2002*b*) 'Economic Organization and the Trade-off Between Destructive and Productive Entrepeneurship', in Nicolai J. Foss and Peter G. Klein (eds.), *Entrepreneurship and the Firm: Austrian Perspectives and Economic Organization* (Aldershot: Edward Elgar).

—— (2004), 'Value Creation and Appropriation, Resources, and Transaction Costs', unpublished MS.

—— and Vazquez, Xosé (2004), 'Credible Commitments and Opportunistic Managerial Intervention: Some Evidence', unpublished MS.

Foss, Kirsten, Nicolai, J. Foss, Klein, Peter G., and Klein, Sandra (2002), 'Heterogeneous Capital, Entrepreneurship, and Economic Organization', *Journal des Economistes et des Etudes Humaine*, 12: 79–96.

Foss, Nicolai J. (1993), 'Theories of the Firm: Contractual and Competence Perspectives', *Journal of Evolutionary Economics*, 3: 127–44.

—— (1994), *The Austrian School and Modern Economics: Essays in Reassessment* (Copenhagen: Munksgaard).

—— (1996*a*), 'Strategy, Economics, and Michael Porter', *Journal of Management Studies*, 33: 1–24.

—— (1996*b*), 'Whither the Competence Perspective?', in Nicolai J. Foss and Christian Knudsen, *Towards a Competence Theory of the Firm* (London: Routledge).

—— (1997*a*), *Resources, Firms, and Strategies* (Oxford: Oxford University Press).

—— (1997*b*), 'On the Rationales of Corporate Headquarters', *Industrial and Corporate Change*, 6: 313–39.

—— (1998*a*), 'The Competence-Based Approach: Veblenian Ideas in the Modern Theory of the Firm', *Cambridge Journal of Economics*, 22: 479–96.

—— (1998*b*), 'The New Growth Theory: Some Intellectual Growth Accounting', *Journal of Economic Methodology*, 5: 223–46.

—— (2000), *Organization and Economic Behavior* (London: Routledge).

—— (2001), 'Neither Hierarchy nor Identity: Knowledge Governance Mechanisms and the Theory of the Firm', *Journal of Management and Governance*, 5: 381–99.

—— (2002), ' "Cognitive Failures" and "Combinative Failure" ', *Journal of Management and Governance*, 6: 252–60.

Grandori, Anna, and Kogut, Bruce (2002), 'Dialogue on Organization and Knowledge', *Organization Science*, 13: 224–32.

Granstrand, Ove, Patel, Pari, and Pavitt, Keith L. R. (1997), 'Multi-Technology Corporations: Why They Have "Distributed" Rather than "Distinctive Core" Competencies', *California Management Review*, 39: 8–25.

Grant, Robert M. (1991), 'The Resource-based Theory of Competitive Advantage', *California Management Review*, 33: 114–35.

—— (1996), 'Toward a Knowledge-Based Theory of the Firm', *Strategic Management Journal*, 17: 109–22.

—— (2002), 'Knowledge Management and the Knowledge-based Economy: Taking Stock', *General Management Review*, 3 (Jan.–Mar. 2002).

Greenan, Nathalie, and Guellec, Dominique (1994), 'Coordination Within the Firm and Endogenous Growth', *Industrial and Corporate Change*, 3: 173–96.

Greene, W. H. (1997), *Econometric Analysis* (Upper Saddle River, NJ: Prentice Hall).

Grossman, Sanford, and Hart, Oliver (1986), 'The Costs and Benefits of Ownership: A Theory of Vertical Integration', *Journal of Political Economy*, 94: 691–719.

Guest, D. E. (1997), 'Human Resource Management and Performance: a Review and Research Agenda', *International Journal of Human Resource Management*, 8: 263–76.

Halal, William E., and Taylor, K. B. (1998), *Twenty-First Century Economics: Perspectives of Socioeconomics for a Changing World* (New York: St Martin's).

Halal, William E., Geranmayeh, Ali, and Pourdehnad, John (1993), *Internal Markets: Bringing the Power of Free Enterprise Inside Your Organization* (New York: Wiley).

Halberstam, David (1986), *The Reckoning* (New York: Avon).

Halpern, Joseph Y., and Moses, Yoram (1990), 'Knowledge and Common Knowledge in a Distributed Environment', *Journal of the Association for Computing Machinery*, 37: 549–87.

Hamel, Gary (1991), 'Competition for Competence and Inter-Partner Learning within International Strategic Alliances', *Strategic Management Journal*, 12 (summer special issue): 83–103.

—— and Prahalad, C. K. (1991), 'Expeditionary Marketing', *Harvard Business Review*, 69(4): 81–93.

—— (1994), *Competing for the Future* (New York: Wiley).

Hammond, Thomas H., and Miller Gary J. (1985), 'A Social Choice Perspective on Expertise and Authority in Bureaucracy', *American Journal of Political Science*, 29: 611–38.

Hansen, Morten T. (1999), 'The Search-Transfer Problem: The Role of Weak Ties in Sharing Knowledge Across Organizational Subunits', *Administrative Science Quarterly*, 44: 82–111.

Hardin, Russell (1982), *Collective Action* (Baltimore, Md.: Johns Hopkins University Press).

Harris, R. I. D., and Trainor, M. (1995), 'Innovations and R&D in Northern Ireland Manufacturing: A Schumpeterian Approach', *Regional Studies*, 29: 593–604.

Harryson, S. J. (2000), *Managing Know-Who Based Companies* (Cheltenham: Elgar).

Harsanyi, John, and Selten, Reinhard (1988), *A General Theory of Equilibrium Selection in Games* (Cambridge: MIT Press).

Hart, Oliver (1990), 'Is "Bounded Rationality" an Important Element of a Theory of Institution?', *Journal of Institutional and Theoretical Economics*, 146: 696–702.

—— (1995), *Firms, Contracts and Financial Structure* (Oxford: Oxford University Press).

—— (1996), 'An Economist's View of Authority', *Rationality and Society*, 8: 371–86.

—— and Moore, John (1990), 'Property Rights and the Nature of the Firm', *Journal of Political Economy*, 98: 1119–58.

Hart, Sergiu (1989), 'Shapley Value', in John Eatwell, Murray Milgate, and Peter Newman (eds.), *The New Palgrave: Game Theory* (New York: Norton).

Hayek, Friedrich A. von (1935), 'Socialist Calculation: the State of the Debate', in Hayek (1948), *Individualism and Economic Order* (Chicago, Ill.: University of Chicago Press).

—— (1937), 'Economics and Knowledge', in Hayek (1948), *Individualism and Economic Order* (Chicago, Ill.: University of Chicago Press).

—— (1945), 'The Use of Knowledge in Society', in Hayek (1948), *Individualism and Economic Order* (Chicago, Ill.: University of Chicago Press).

—— (1948), *Individualism and Economic Order* (Chicago, Ill.: University of Chicago Press).

—— (1952), *The Counter Revolution of Science* (Chicago, Ill.: University of Chicago Press).

—— (1964), 'The Theory of Complex Phenomena', in Hayek (1978), *Studies in Philosophy, Economics, and Politics* (London: Routledge & Kegan Paul).

—— (1973), *Law, Legislation and Liberty*, i. *Rules and Order* (Chicago, Ill.: University of Chicago Press).

—— (1988), *The Fatal Conceit: The Errors of Constructivism* (London: Routledge).

Heath, C., Knez, Mark, and Camerer, Colin (1993), 'The Strategic Management of the Entitlement Process in the Employment Relationship', *Strategic Management Journal*, 14: 75–93.

Heiman, Bruce, and Nickerson, Jack A. (2002), 'Towards Reconciling Transaction Cost Economics and the Knowledge-based View of the Firm: The Context of Interfirm Collaborations', *International Journal of the Economics of Business*, 9: 97–116.

Helfat, Constance E., and Peteraf, Margaret A. (2003), 'The Dynamic Resource-based View: Capability Lifecycles', *Strategic Management Journal*, 24: 997–1010.

Helper, Susan, MacDuffie, J.P., and Sabel, Charles (2000), 'Pragmatic Collaborations: Advancing Knowledge While Controlling Opportunism', *Industrial and Corporate Change*, 9: 443–87.

Hemmer, Thomas (1995), 'On the Interrelation Between Production Technology, Job Design, and Incentives', *Journal of Accounting and Economics*, 19: 209–45.

Henderson, Rebecca (1994), 'The Evolution of Integrative Capabilities: Innovation in Cardiovascular Drug Discovery', *Industrial and Corporate Change*, 3: 607–30.

—— and Cockburn, Ian (1996), 'Scale, Scope, and Spillovers: The Determinants of Research Productivity in Drug Discovery', *RAND Journal of Economics*, 27/1: 32–59.

Henderson, Richard I. (2000), *Compensation Management in a Knowledge-based World* (London: Prentice Hall).

Hendry, John (2002), 'The Principal's Other Problem: Honest Incompetence and the Specification of Objectives', *Academy of Management Review*, 27: 98–113.

Hennart, Jean-Francois (1993), 'Explaining the Swollen Middle: Why Most Transactions Are a Mix of "Market" and "Hierarchy" ', *Organization Science*, 4: 529–47.

Hermalin, Benjamin (1998), 'Toward an Economic Theory of Leadership: Leading by Example', *American Economic Review*, 88: 1188–206.

—— (1999), 'The Firm as a Non-Economy: Some Comments on Holmström', *Journal of Law, Economics and Organization*, 15 (1999) 103–5.

Hicks, John (1979), *Causality in Economics* (New York: Basic).

Hintikka, J. (1962), *Knowledge and Belief* (Ithaca, NY: Cornell University Press).

Hippel, Eric von (1988), *The Sources of Innovation* (New York/Oxford: Oxford University Press).

—— (1994), ' "Sticky Information" and the Locus of Problem Solving: Implications for Innovation', *Management Science*, 40: 429–39.

Hodgson, Geoff. (1988), *Economics and Institutions: A Manifesto for a Modern Institutional Economics* (Cambridge: Polity).

—— (1998), *Economics and Utopia* (London: Routledge).

—— (2002), 'The Legal Nature of the Firm and the Myth of the Firm–Market Dichotomy', *International Journal of the Economics of Business*, 9: 37–60.

Hofer, Charles, and Schendel, Dan (1978), *Strategy Formulation: Analytical Concepts* (Minneapolis, Minn.: St Paul).

Holland, C. P., and Lockett, A. G. (1997), 'Mixed Network Structures: The Strategic Use of Electronic Communication by Organizations', *Organization Science*, 8: 475–88.

Holmström, Bengt (1979), 'Moral Hazard and Observability', *Bell Journal of Economics*, 10: 74–91.

—— (1982), 'Moral Hazard in Teams', *Bell Journal of Economics*, 13: 324–40.

—— (1989), 'Agency Costs and Innovation', *Journal of Economic Behavior and Organization*, 12: 305–27.

—— (1999), 'The Firm as a Subeconomy', *Journal of Law, Economics, and Organization*, 15: 74–102.

—— and Milgrom, Paul (1987), 'Aggregation and Linearity in the Provision of Intertemporal Incentives', *Econometrica*, 55: 303–28.

—— (1990), 'Regulating Trade Among Agents', *Journal of Institutional and Theoretical Economics*, 146: 85–105.

—— (1991), 'Multitask Principal–Agent Analysis: Incentive Contracts, Asset Ownership and Job Design', *Journal of Law, Economics and Organization*, 7: 24–54.

—— (1994), 'The Firm as an Incentive System', *American Economic Review*, 84: 972–91.

Holmström, Bengt, and Ricart i Costa, Joan (1986), 'Managerial Incentives and Capital Management', *Quarterly Journal of Economics*, 101: 835–60.

Holmström, Bengt, and Roberts, John (1998), 'The Boundaries of the Firm Revisited', *Journal of Economic Perspectives*, 12: 73–94.

Holmström, Bengt, and Tirole, Jean (1991), 'Transfer Pricing and Organizational Form', *Journal of Law, Economics and Organization*, 7: 201–28.

Holmström, Bengt, and Tirole, Jean (1989), 'The Theory of the Firm', in Richard Schmalensee and Robert D. Willig (eds.), *Handbook of Industrial Organization*, i (Amsterdam: North-Holland).

House, Robert J., and Baetz, Mary L. (1979), 'Leadership: Some Empirical Generalizations and New Research Directions', *Research in Organizational Behavior*, 1: 341–423.

Howells, Jeremy (1984), 'The Localisation of Research and Development: Some Observations and Evidence from Britain', *Regional Studies*, 18: 13–29.

Hubbard, Thomas N. (2000), 'The Demand for Monitoring Technologies: The Case of Trucking', *Quarterly Journal of Economics*, 115: 533–60.

Hunt, Shelby (2000), *A General Theory of Competition* (London: Sage).

Huselid, Mark A. (1995), 'The Impact of Human Resource Management Practices on Turnover, Productivity, and Corporate Financial Performance', *Academy of Management Journal*, 38: 635–72.

Hutchins, Edwin (1995), *Cognition in the Wild* (Cambridge, Mass.: MIT Press).

Ichniowski, C., Kochan, T.A., Levine, D., Olson, C., and Strauss, G. (1996), 'What Works at Work: Overview and Assessment', *Industrial Relations*, 35: 299–333.

Ichniowski, C., Shaw, K., and Prennushi, G. (1997), 'The Effects of Human Resource Management Practices on Productivity: A Study of Steel Finishing Lines', *American Economic Review*, 87: 291–313.

Jacobides, Michael (2002), 'Where Do Intermediate Markets Come From?', working paper, London Business School.

—— and Winter, Sidney G. (2003), 'Capabilities, Transaction Costs and Evolution: Understanding the Institutional Structure of Production', working paper, Centre for the Network Economy, London Business School.

Jacobson, Robert (1992), 'The Austrian School of Strategy', *Academy of Management Review*, 17: 782–807.

Jensen, Frank Dybdal (1998), *Værdibaseret Ledelse—styring mellem regler og visioner* (Copenhagen: Jurist-og Økonomforbundets Forlag).

Jensen, Michael C., and Meckling, William H. (1976), 'The Theory of the Firm: Managerial Behavior, Agency Costs, and Ownership Structure', *Journal of Financial Economics*, 3: 305–60.

—— (1992), 'Specific and General Knowledge and Organizational Structure', in L. Werin and H. Wijkander (eds.), *Contract Economics* (Oxford: Blackwell).

Jensen, Michael C., and Wruck, Karen (1994), 'Science, Specific Knowledge and Total Quality Management', in Michael C. Jensen (1998) (ed.), *Foundations of Organizational Strategy* (Cambridge Mass.: Harvard University Press).

Jeppesen, Lars Bo (forthcoming), 'The Implications of "User Toolkits for Innovation" ', *Journal of Product Innovation Management*.

Jones, Gareth R. (1983), 'Transaction Costs, Property Rights, and Organizational Culture: An Exchange Perspective', *Administrative Science Quarterly*, 28: 454–67.

Jorgenson, Dale W., and Fraumeni, Barbara M. (1995), 'Investment in Education and U.S. Economic Growth', in Dale W. Jorgenson (1995) (ed.), *Productivity, i. Postwar Economic Growth* (Cambridge, Mass.: MIT Press).

Kaplan, Sarah, Schenkel, A., Krogh, Georg von, and Weber, C. (2001), 'Knowledge-based Theories of the Firm in Strategic Management: A Review and Extension', working paper no. 4216-01, MIT.

Kelly, Kevin (1999), *New Rules for the New Economy* (London: Fourth Estate).

Kenney, Roy W., and Klein, Benjamin (1983), 'The Economics of Block Booking', *Journal of Law and Economics*, 26: 497–540.

Keynes, John Maynard (1936), *Collected Writings, vii. The General Theory of Employment, Interest, and Money* (London: Macmillan/Cambridge University Press).

Kim, Jongwook, and Mahoney, Joseph T. (2002), 'Resource-based and Property Rights Perspectives on Value Creation: The Case of Oil Field Unitization', *Managerial and Decision Economics*, 23: 225–45.

Kirzner, Israel M. (1973), *Competition and Entrepreneurship* (Chicago, Ill.: University of Chicago Press).

—— (1997), 'Entrepreneurial Discovery and the Competitive Market Process: An Austrian Approach', *Journal of Economic Literature*, 35: 60–85.

Klein, Benjamin (1988), 'Vertical Integration as Organizational Ownership: The Fisher Body–General Motors Relationship Revisited', *Journal of Law, Economics, and Organization*, 4: 199–213.

Klein, Benjamin. (1991), 'Organizational Capital and the Theory of the Firm', in Oliver E. Williamson and Sidney G. Winter (eds.), *The Nature of the Firm* (Oxford: Blackwell).

—— and Leffler, Keith (1981), 'The Role of Market Forces in Assuring Contractual Performance', *Journal of Political Economy*, 89: 615–41.

Klein, Peter G. (2001), 'Government, Technology and the New Economy', slides for a presentation at the Danish Ministry of Economics.

—— and Shelanski, Howard A. (1995), 'Empirical Research in Transaction Cost Economics: A Review and Assessment', *Journal of Law, Economics and Organization*, 11: 335–61.

Kleinknecht, Alfred (1996) (ed.), *Determinants of Innovation: The Message from New Indicators* (London: Macmillan).

Kline, S., and Rosenberg, N. (1986), 'An Overview of Innovation', in R. Landau and N. Rosenberg (eds.), *The Positive Sum Strategy: Harnessing Technology for Economic Growth* (Washington, DC: National Academy Press).

Knez, Mark (1998), 'Precedent Transfer in Experimental Conflict-of-Interest Games', *Journal of Economic Behavior and Organization*, 34: 239–49.

Knight, Frank H. (1921), *Risk, Uncertainty and Profit*, repr. 1965 (Chicago, Ill.: Kelley).

Knott, Anne Marie (1998), 'The Organizational Routines Factor Market Paradox', working paper, The Wharton School, University of Pennsylvania.

—— (2003), 'Persistent Heterogeneity and Sustainable Innovation', *Strategic Management Journal*, 24: 687–705.

—— and McKelvey, Bill (1999), 'Nirvana Efficiency: A Comparative Test of Residual Claims and Routines', *Journal of Economic Behavior and Organization*, 38: 365–83.

Knott, Anne Marie, Bryce David J., and Posen, Hart (2002), 'On the Strategic Accumulation of Intangible Assets', working paper, The Wharton School, University of Pennsylvania.

Kogut, Bruce, (2000), 'The Network as Knowledge: Generative Rules and the Emergence of Structure', *Strategic Management Journal*, 21: 405–25.

—— and Zander, U. (1992), 'Knowledge of the Firm, Combinative Capabilities, and the Replication of Technology', *Organization Science*, 3: 383–97.

—— (1993), 'Knowledge of the Firm and the Evolutionary Theory of the Multinational Corporation', *Journal of International Business Studies*, 24: 625–46.

—— (1996), 'What Firms Do? Coordination, Identity and Learning', *Organization Science*, 7: 502–18.

Kolind, Lars (1990), 'Think the Unthinkable', in Mette Morsing and Kristian Eiberg (1998) (eds.), *Managing the Unmanageable For a Decade* (Hellerup: Oticon).

—— (1994), 'The Knowledge-Based Enterprise', in Mette Morsing and Kristian Eiberg (1998) (eds.), *Managing the Unmanageable for a Decade* (Hellerup: Oticon).

Kor, Yasemin Y., and Mahoney, Joseph T. (2000), 'Penrose's Resource-based Approach: The Process and Product of Research Creativity', *Journal of Management Studies*, 37/1: 109–39.

Kotter, John (1996), *Leading Change* (Boston, Mass.: Harvard Business School Press).

Krajewski, Wladyslaw (1977), *Correspondence Principle and Growth of Science* (Dordrecht: Reidel).

Kramarz, F. (1996), 'Dynamic Focal Points in N-Person Coordination Games', *Theory and Decision*, 40: 277–313.

Kreps, David M. (1990a), 'Corporate Culture and Economic Theory', in James G. Alt and Kenneth Shepsle (eds.), *Perspectives on Positive Political Economy* (Cambridge: Cambridge University Press).

—— (1990b), *Game Theory and Economic Modelling* (Oxford: Oxford University Press).

—— (1996), 'Markets and Hierarchies and (Mathematical) Economic Theory', *Industrial and Corporate Change*, 5: 561–95.

Kuhn, Thomas S. (1970), *The Structure of Scientific Revolutions*, 2nd edn. (Chicago, Ill.: University of Chicago Press).

Kunde, Jesper (1997), *Corporate Religion* (København: Børsens).

Laamanen, Tomi, and Autio, Erkko (2000), 'Dynamic Complementarities and Technology Acquisition', in Nicolai J. Foss and Paul L. Robertson (eds.), *Resources, Technology, and Strategy* (London: Routledge).

LaBarre, Polly (1996), 'This Organization is Dis-Organization', <Wysiwyg//93/http://fastcompany.com/online/03/oticon.html>, accessed July 2004.

Lado, A., and Wilson, M. C. (1994), 'Human Resource Systems and Sustained Competitive Advantage: A Competency-Based Perspective', *Academy of Management Review*, 19: 699–727.

Lafontaine, F. (1992), 'Agency Theory and Franchising', *RAND Journal of Economics*, 23: 263–83.

Lambert, R., and Larker, D. (1987), 'An analysis of the use of accounting and market measures of performance in executive compensation contracts', *Journal of Accounting Research*, 25: 85–125.

Langlois, Richard N. (1992), 'Transaction Cost Economics in Real Time', *Industrial and Corporate Change*, 1: 99–127.

—— (1998), 'Personal Capitalism as Charismatic Authority: The Organizational Economics of a Weberian Concept', *Industrial and Corporate Change*, 7: 195–214.

—— (1999), 'Rule-Following, Expertise, and Rationality: A New Behavioral Economics?', in Kenneth Dennis (ed.), *Rationality in Economics: Alternative Perspectives* (Dordrecht: Kluwer).

Langlois, Richard N. (2002), 'Modularity and Organizations', in Nicolai J. Foss and Peter G. Klein (eds.), *Entrepreneurship and the Firm: Austrian Perspectives on Economic Organization* (Aldershot: Elgar).

—— (2003), 'The Vanishing Hand: The Changing Dynamics of Industrial Capitalism', *Industrial and Corporate Change*, 12: 351–85.

—— and Cosgel, Metin M. (1998), 'The Organization of Consumption', in Marina Bianchi (ed.), *The Rational Consumer* (London: Routledge).

Langlois, Richard N., and Foss, Nicolai J. (1999), 'Capabilities and Governance: The Rebirth of Production in the Theory of Economic Organization', *KYKLOS*, 52: 201–18.

Langlois, Richard N., and Robertson, Paul L. (1995), *Firms, Markets, and Economic Change* (London: Routledge).

Laroche, Mireille, Mérette, Marcel, and Ruggeri, G. C. (1999), 'On the Concept and Dimensions of Human Capital in a Knowledge-based Economy Context', *Canadian Public Policy—Analyse de Politique*, 25: 87–100.

Larsen, Jakob Norvig (2001), 'Knowledge, Human Resources and Social Practice: The Knowledge-intensive Business Service Firm as a Distributed Knowledge System', *Service Industries Journal*, 21: 81–103.

Laursen, K. (2002), 'The Importance of Sectoral Differences in the Application of Complementary HRM Practices for Innovation Performance', *International Journal of the Economics of Business*, 9(1): 139–56.

—— and Mahnke, V. (2001), 'Knowledge Strategies, Firm Types, and Complementarity in Human-Resource Practices', *Journal of Management and Governance*, 5: 1–27.

Lavoie, Don (1985), *Rivalry and Central Planning* (Cambridge: Cambridge University Press).

Lawler, Edward, Mohrman, Susan A. and Ledford, Gerald E. (1998), *Strategies for High Performance Organizations: The CEO Report—Employee Involvement, TQM, and Reengineering Programs in Fortune 1000 Corporations* (San Francisco, Calif.: Jossey-Bass).

Lazear, Edward (1995), *Personnel Economics* (Cambridge, Mass.: MIT Press).

Lazonick, W. (1991), *Business Organization and the Myth of the Market Economy* (Cambridge: Cambridge University Press).

Leadbetter, Charles (1999), *Living on Thin Air: The New Economy* (London: Viking).

Leibold, Marius, Probst, Gilbert, and Gibbert, Michael (2002), *Strategic Management in the Knowledge Economy: New Approaches and Business Applications* (Winheim: Wiley).

Lessard, Donald R., and Zaheer, Srilata (1996), 'Breaking the Silos: Distributed Knowledge and Strategic Responses to Volatile Exchange Rates', *Strategic Management Journal*, 17: 513–34.

Lewin, Peter, and Phelan, Steven A. (1999), 'Firms, Strategies, and Resources', *Quarterly Journal of Austrian Economics*, 2: 3–18.

—— (2000), 'An Austrian Theory of the Firm', *Review of Austrian Economics*, 13: 59–79.

Lewis, David (1969), *Convention: A Philosophical Study* (Cambridge, Mass.: Harvard University Press).

Lewis, Tracy, and Sappington, David (1991), 'Technological Change and the Boundaries of the Firm', *American Economic Review*, 81: 887–900.

Liebeskind, Julia P. (1996), 'Knowledge, Strategy, and the Theory of the Firm', *Strategic Management Journal*, 17: 93–107.

—— 'Keeping Organizational Secrets: Protective Institutional Mechanisms and their Costs', *Industrial and Corporate Change*, 6: 623–63.

—— Oliver, A. L., Zucker, L. G., and Brewer, M. B. (1995), 'Social Networks, Learning, and Flexibility: Sourcing Scientific Knowledge in New Biotechnology Firms', Cambridge: NBER working paper No. W5320, Cambridge.

Lindenberg, Siegwart (2003*a*), 'It Takes both Trust and Lack of Mistrust: The Workings of Cooperation and Relational Signaling in Contractual Relationships', *Journal of Management and Governance*, 4: 11–33.

—— (2003*b*), 'The Cognitive Side of Governance', *Research in the Sociology of Organizations*, 20: 47–76.

Lippman, Steven A., and Rumelt, Richard P. (1982), 'Uncertain Imitability: An Analysis of Interfirm Differences Under Competition', *Bell Journal of Economics*, 13: 418–38.

—— (2003*a*), 'A Bargaining Perspective on Resource Advantage', *Strategic Management Journal*, 24: 1069–86.

—— (2003*b*), 'The Payments Perspective', *Strategic Management Journal*, 24: 903–27.

Lipsey, Richard, G., and Steiner, Peter O. (1981), *Economics*, 6th edn. (New York: Harper & Row).

Lippman, Steven, McCardle, Kevin F., and Rumelt, Richard P. (1991), 'Heterogeneity Under Competition', *Economic Inquiry*, 24: 774–82.

Loasby, Brian (1976), *Choice, Complexity and Ignorance* (Cambridge: Cambridge University Press).

—— (1995), 'Running a Business: An Appraisal of *Economics, Organization and Management* by Paul Milgrom and John Roberts', *Industrial and Corporate Change*, 4: 471–89.

—— (1991), *Equilibrium and Evolution* (Manchester: Manchester University Press).

Lorentz, E. (1998), 'Organisational Innovation, Governance Structure and Innovative Capacity in British and French Industry', mimeo (Compiégne: University of Compiégne).

Lotz, Peter (1998), 'The Paradox of High R&D and Industry Stability: Technology and Structural Dynamics in the Global Hearing Instruments Industry', *Industry and Innovation*, 5: 113–37.

Lovas, Bjorn, and Ghoshal, Sumantra (2000), 'Strategy as Guided Evolution', *Strategic Management Journal*, 21: 875–96.

Love, J. H., Ashcroft, B., and Dunlop, S. (1996), 'Corporate Structure, Ownership and the Likelihood of Innovation', *Applied Economics*, 28: 737–46.

Lucas, Robert E. (1978), 'On the Size Distribution of Firms', *Bell Journal of Economics*, 9: 508–23.

Luce, R. Duncan, and Raiffa, Howard (1957), *Games and Decisions* (New York: J. Wiley).

Lund, R., and Gjerding, A. N. (1996), 'The Flexible Company: Innovation, Work Organisation and Human Resource Management', DRUID working paper no. 17, Aalborg, IKE Group/DRUID, Department of Business Studies.

Lundvall, Bengt-Åke (1988), 'Innovation as an Interactive Process—From User–Producer Interaction to National Systems of Innovation', in G. Dosi, C. Freeman, R. Nelson, G. Silverberg, and L. L. G. Soete (eds.), *Technical Change and Economic Theory* (London: Pinter).

Lundvall, Bengt-Åke (2003), 'Why the New Economy is a Learning Economy', *Economia e Politica Industriale*, 117: 173–85.

—— and Johnson, Björn (1994), 'The Learning Economy', *Industry and Innovation*, 1: 23–42.

Lyles, Marjorie A., and Schwenk, Charles, R. (1992), 'Top Management, Strategy, and Organizational Knowledge Structures', *Journal of Management Studies*, 29: 155–74.

Lyregaard, Poul-Erik (1993), 'Oticon: Erfaringer og faldgruber', in Steen Hildebrandt and Leif H. Alken (eds.), *På vej mod helhedssyn i ledelse* (Kolding: Ankerhus).

MacEvily, Susan K., and Chakravarthy, Bala (2002), 'The Persistence of Knowledge-based Advantage: An Empirical Test for Product Performance and Technological Knowledge', *Strategic Management Journal*, 23: 285–305.

Machin, Stephen, and Van Reenen, John (1998), 'Technology and Changes in Skill Structure: Evidence from Seven OECD Countries', *Quarterly Journal of Economics*, 113: 1215–44.

Machlup, Fritz (1946), 'Marginal Analysis and Empirical Research', *American Economic Review*, 36: 519–54.

—— (1955), 'The Problem of Verification in Economics', in Machlup, *The Methodology of Economics and Other Social Sciences* (New York: Wiley).

Machovec, Frank M. (1995), *Perfect Competition and the Transformation of Economics* (London: Routledge).

MacNamara, Gerry, Vaaler, Paul M., and Devers, Cynthia (2003), 'Same as It Ever Was: The Search for Evidence of Increasing Hypercompetition', *Strategic Management Journal*, 24: 261–78.

Madhok, Anoop (1996), 'The Organization of Economic Activity: Transaction Costs, Firm Capabilities, and the Nature of Governance', *Organization Science*, 7: 577–90.

—— (2002), 'Reassessing the Fundamentals and Beyond: Ronald Coase, the Transaction Cost and Resource-based Theories of the Firm and the Institutional Structure of Production', *Strategic Management Journal*, 23: 535–50.

Mahoney, Joseph T. (1992), 'Organizational Economics within the Conversation of Strategic Management', in P. Shrivastava, A. Huff, and J. Sutton (eds.), *Advances in Strategic Management*, 8: 103–55.

—— (1995), 'The Management of Resources and the Resource of Management', *Journal of Business Research*, 33: 91–101.

—— (2001), 'A Resource-Based Theory of Sustainable Rents', *Journal of Management*, 27: 651–60.

—— and Kor, Yasemin (2000), 'Penrose's Resource-based Approach: The Process and Product of Research Creativity', *Journal of Management Studies*, 37: 109–39.

Mailath, George J. (1998), 'Do People Play Nash Equilibrium? Lessons From Evolutionary Game Theory', *Journal of Economic Literature*, 36: 1347–74.

Makadok, Richard (2003), 'Doing the Right Thing and Knowing the Right Thing to Do: Why the Whole is Greater Than the Sum of the Parts', *Strategic Management Journal*, 24: 1043–55.

—— and Barney, Jay B. (2001), 'Strategic Factor Market Intelligence: An Application of Information Economics to Strategy Formulation and Competitor Intelligence', *Management Science*, 47: 1621–38.

Makadok, Richard, and Coff, Russell (2002), 'The Theory of Value and the Value of Theory', *Academy of Management Review*, 27: 10–13.

Makowski, Louis, and Ostroy, Joseph M. (2001), 'Perfect Competition and the Creativity of Markets', *Journal of Economic Literature*, 39: 479–535.

Malerba, F. (1992), 'Learning by Firms and Incremental Technical Change', *Economic Journal*, 102: 845–59.

Malone, Thomas W., and Crowston, Kevin (1994), 'The Interdisciplinary Study of Coordination', *ACM Computing Surveys*, 26: 87–119.

Mandag Morgen (1991), 'Oticon satser dristigt, men resultaterne mangler', 15 Feb., 15–18.

March, James G. (1991a), 'Exploration and Exploitation in Organizational Learning', in Michael D. Cohen and Lee Sproull (1996) (eds.), *Organizational Learning* (London: Sage).

March, James G. (1991b), 'Exploration and Exploitation in Organizational Learning', *Organization Science*, 2: 71–87.

—— and Simon, Herbert A. (1958), *Organizations* (New York: Wiley).

Marengo, Luigi (1995), 'Structure, Competence, and Learning in Organizations', *Wirtschaftspolitische Blätter*, 6: 454–64.

—— Dosi, Giovanni, Legrenzi, Paolo, and Pasquali, Corrado (2000), 'The Structure of Problem-Solving Knowledge and the Structure of Organizations', *Industrial and Corporate Change*, 9: 757–88.

Marglin, Stephen A. (1974), ' "What Do Bosses Do?" The Origins and Functions of Hierarchy in Capitalist Production', *Review of Radical Political Economy*, 6: 33–60.

Marschak, Jacob, and Radner, Roy (1972), *The Theory of Teams* (New Heaven, Conn.: Yale University Press).

Marshall, Alfred (1920), *Principles of Economics* (London: Macmillan).

Maskell, Peter, Eskelinen, Heikki, Hannibalsson, Ingjaldur, Malmberg, Anders, and Vatne, Eirik (1998), *Competitiveness, Localised Learning and Regional Development: Specialisation and Prosperity in Small Open Economies* (London: Routledge).

Maskin, Eric, and Tirole, Jean (1999), 'Unforeseen Contingencies and Incomplete Contracts', *Review of Economic Studies*, 66: 83–114.

Masten, Scott (1991), 'A Legal Basis for the Firm', in O. E. Williamson and S. G. Winter (eds.), *The Nature of the Firm: Origins, Evolution, and Development* (Oxford: Oxford University Press).

Matusik, Sharon F., and Hill, Charles W. L. (1998), 'The Utilization of Contingent Work, Knowledge Creation, and Competitive Advantage', *Academy of Management Review*, 23: 680–97.

Ménard, Claude (1994), 'Organizations as Coordinating Devices', *Metroeconomica*, 45: 224–47.

Mendelson, H., and Pillai, R. R. (1999), 'Information Age Organizations, Dynamics, and Performance', *Journal of Economic Behavior and Organization*, 38: 253–81.

Meyer, Alan D., Tsui, Anne S., and Hinings, C. R. (1993), 'Configurational Approaches to Organizational Analysis', *Academy of Management Journal*, 36: 1175–95.

Meyer, C., 'How the Right Measures Help Teams Excel', *Harvard Business Review* (May–June 1994), 95–103.

Meyer, Martin (2001), 'Nelson and Winter's *Evolutionary Theory—A Citation Analysis*', unpublished paper.

Michie, J., and Sheehan, M. (1999), 'HRM Practices, R&D Expenditure and Innovative Investment: Evidence from the UK's 1990 Workplace Industrial Relations Survey', *Industrial and Corporate Change*, 8: 211–34.

Miles, Raymond E., and Snow, Charles C. (1992), 'Causes of Failure in Network Organizations', *California Management Review*, 32: 53–72.

Miles, Raymond E., Miles, G., and Snow, Charles C. (1998), 'Good for Practice: An Integrated Theory of the Value of Alternative Organizational Forms', in G. Hamel, C. K. Prahalad, H. Thomas, and D. O'Neal (eds.), *Strategic Flexibility: Managing in a Turbulent Environment* (New York: Wiley).

Miles, Raymond E., Snow, Charles C., Mathews, John A., Miles, Grant, and Coleman, Henry, J., Jr. (1997), 'Organizing in the Knowledge Age: Anticipating the Cellular Form', *Academy of Management Executive*, 11: 7–20.

Milgrom, Paul (1988), 'Employment Contracts, Influence Activities and Efficient Organization Design', *Journal of Political Economy*, 96: 42–60.

—— and John D. Roberts (1988), 'Economic Theories of the Firm: Past, Present, and Future', *Canadian Journal of Economics*, 21: 444–58.

—— (1990a), 'Bargaining Costs, Influence Costs, and the Organization of Economic Activity', in James E. Alt and Kenneth A. Shepsle (eds.), *Perspectives on Positive Political Economy* (Cambridge: Cambridge University Press).

—— (1990b), 'The Economics of Modern Manufacturing: Technology, Strategy, and Organization', *American Economic Review*, 80: 511–28.

—— (1992), *Economics, Organization, and Management* (Englewood Cliffs, NJ: Prentice Hall).

—— (1995), 'Complementarities and Fit: Strategy, Structure, and Organizational Change in Manufacturing', *Journal of Accounting and Economics*, 19: 179–208.

Milgrom, Paul, Qian, Y., and Roberts, John (1991), 'Complementarities, Momentum, and the Evolution of Modern Manufacturing', *American Economic Review (PaP)*, 81: 85–9.

Miller, Danny, and Shamsie, Jamal (1996), 'The Resource-based View of the Firm in Two Environments: the Hollywood Film Studios from 1936 to 1965', *Academy of Management Journal* 39: 519–43.

Miller, Gary (1992), *Managerial Dilemmas* (Cambridge: Cambridge University Press).

Mills, David E., and Smith, William (1996), 'It Pays to Be Different: Endogeneous Heterogeneity of Firms in an Oligopoly', *International Journal of Industrial Organization*, 14: 317–29.

Minkler, Alanson P. (1993), 'Knowledge and Internal Organization', *Journal of Economic Behavior and Organization*, 21: 17–30.

Mintzberg, Henry (1973), *The Nature of Managerial Work* (Englewood Cliffs, NJ: Prentice Hall).

Mises, Ludwig von (1949), *Human Action* (San Francisco, Calif.: Fox and Wilkes).

Moe, Timothy (1997), 'A Positive Theory of Public Bureacracy', in Dennis Mueller (ed.), *Perspectives in Public Choice: A Handbook* (New York: Cambridge University Press).

Monderer, Dov, and Samet, Dov (1989), 'Approximating Common Knowledge With Common Beliefs', *Games and Economic Behavior*, 1: 170–90.

Monteverde, Kirk (1995), 'Technical Dialog as an Incentive for Vertical Integration in the Semiconductor Industry', *Management Science*, 41: 1624–38.

Montgomery, Cynthia A., and Wernerfelt, Birger (1988), 'Diversification, Ricardian Rents, and Tobin's q', *RAND Journal of Economics*, 19: 623–32.

Moore, K., and Birkinshaw, Julian (1998), 'Managing Knowledge in Global Service Firms: Centers of Excellence', *Academy of Management Executive*, 12: 81–92.

Morck, Randall, and Yeung, Bernard (2001), 'The Economic Underpinnings of a Knowledge-based Economy', in Louis Lefebvre, Elisabeth Lefebvre, and Pierre Mohnen (2001), *Doing Business in the Knowledge-based Economy: Facts and Policy Challenges* (Boston, Mass.: Kluwer).

Morsing, Mette (1995), *Omstigning til Paradis? Oticon i processen fra hierarki til spaghetti* (Copenhagen: Copenhagen Business School Press).

—— and Eiberg, Kristian (1998) (eds.), *Managing the Unmanageable for a Decade* (Hellerup: Oticon).

Mosakowski, Elaine (1998a), 'Entrepreneurial Resources, Organizational Choices, and Competitive Outcomes', *Organization Science*, 9: 625–43.

—— (1998b), 'Managerial Prescriptions under the Resource-based View: The Example of Motivational Techniques', *Strategic Management Journal*, 19: 1169–82.

Mothe, John de la, and Link, Albert N. (2002) (eds.), *Networks, Alliances and Partnerships in the Innovation Process* (Dordrecht: Kluwer).

Munro, Don (2000), 'The Knowledge Economy', *Journal of Australian Political Economy*, 45: 5–17.

Murmann, J. P., Aldrich, H., Levinthal, D., and Winter, S. G. (2003), 'Evolutionery Thought in Management and Organization Theory at the Beginning of the New Millennium', *Journal of Management Inquiry*, 12: 1–9.

Murnighan, J. Keith (1994), 'Game Theory and Organizational Behavior', *Research in Organizational Behavior*, 16: 83–123.

Muthoo, Abhinay (1999), *Bargaining Theory With Applications* (Cambridge: Cambridge University Press).

Myers, Paul S. (1996) (ed.), *Knowledge Management and Organizational Design* (Boston Mass.: Butterworth-Heinemann).

Nahapiet, Janine, and Ghoshal, Sumantra (1999), 'Social Capital, Intellectual Capital, and the Organizational Advantage', *Academy of Management Review*, 23: 242–66.

Nakamura, Leonard I. (2000), 'Economics and the New Economy: The Invisible Hand Meets Creative Destruction', *Business Review of the Federal Reserve Bank of Philadelphia* (July/August), 15–30.

Nalebuff, Barry J., and Brandenburger, Adam M. (1996), *Co-operation* (London: Harper-Collins).

Nanda, Ashish (1996*a*), 'Implementing Organizational Change', working paper, Harvard Business School.

—— (1996*b*), 'Resources, Capabilities, and Competencies', in B. Moingeon and A. Edmondson, *Organizational Learning and Competitive Advantage* (London: Sage).

Nash, John (1951), 'Non-Cooperative Games', *Annals of Mathematics*, 54: 286–95.

Neef, D. (1998) (ed.), *The Knowledge Economy* (Boston, Mass.: Butterworth-Heinemann).

Nelson, Richard R. (1959), 'The Simple Economics of Basic Scientific Research', *Journal of Political Economy*, 27.

—— (1980) 'Production Sets, Technological Knowledge and R. and D.: Fragile and Overworked Constructs for Analysis of Productivity Growth', *American Economic Review*, 70: 62–7.

—— (1994), 'Why Are Firms Different? And How Does it Matter?' in Russett, Schendel, and Teece (eds.) *Fundamental Issues in Strategy* (Boston: Harvard Business School press).

—— and Winter, Sidney G. (1982), *An Evolutionary Theory of Economic Change* (Cambridge, Mass.: Belknap).

—— (2002), 'Evolutionary Theorizing in Economics', *Journal of Economic Perspectives*, 16: 23–46.

Neumann, John von, and Morgenstern, Oskar (1944), *Theory of Games and Economic Behavior* (Princeton NJ: Princeton University Press).

Newell, Allan, and Simon, Herbert A. (1972), *Human Problem Solving* (Englewood Cliffs, NJ: Prentice Hall).

Newell, Sue, Robertson, Maxine, Scarbrough, Harry, and Swan, Jacky (2003), *Managing Knowledge Work* (Basingstoke: Palgrave Macmillan).

Nickerson, Jackson (2000), 'Towards an Economizing Theory of Strategy', unpublished MS.

—— and Silverman, Brian (forthcoming), 'Why Firms Want to Organize Efficiently, and What Keeps Them From Doing So: Evidence From the For-hire Trucking Industry', *Administrative Science Quarterly*.

Nickerson, Jackson, and Van den Bergh, Roger (1999), 'Economizing in a Context of Strategizing: Governance Mode Choice in Cournot Competition', *Journal of Economic Behavior and Organization*, 40: 1–15.

Nickerson, Jackson, and Zenger, Todd (2002), 'A Knowledge-based Theory of Governance Choice—A Problem-solving Approach', *Organization Science* (forthcoming).

—— (2002), 'Being Efficiently Fickle: A Dynamic Theory of Organizational Choice', *Organization Science*, 13:547–66.

Nickerson, Jackson, Hamilton, Barton, and Wada, Tetsuo (2001), 'Market Position, Resource Profile, and Governance: Linking Porter and Williamson in the Context of International Courier and Small Package Services in Japan', *Strategic Management Journal*, 22: 251–73.

Nightingale, Paul (2003), 'If Nelson and Winter are Only Half Right About Tacit Knowledge, Which Half? A Searlean Critique of "Codification" ', *Industrial and Corporate Change*, 12: 149–83.

Nonaka, I., and Takeuchi, H. (1995), *The Knowledge-creating Company* (Oxford: Oxford University Press).

North, Douglass C. (1990), *Institutions, Institutional Change, and Economic Performance* (Cambridge: Cambridge University Press).

OECD (1996), *Technology and Industrial Performance: Technology Diffusion, Productivity, Employment and Skills, International Competitiveness* (Paris: OECD).

OECD (2001*a*), *The New Economy: Beyond the Hype* (Paris: OECD).

OECD (2001*b*), *Science, Technology and Industry Scoreboard: Towards a Knowledge-based Economy* (Paris: OECD).

Ojha, Abhoy K., Brown, John L., and Philips, Nelson (1997), 'Change and Revolutionary Change: Formalizing and Extending the Punctuated Equilibrium Paradigm', *Computational and Mathematical Organization Theory*, 3: 91–111.

Osterloh, Margit, and Frey, Bruno (2000), 'Motivation, Knowledge Transfer and Organizational Form', *Organization Science*, 11: 538–50.

Osterloh, Margit, and Frost, Jetta (2000), 'Motivation in a Knowledge-based Theory of the Firm', paper prepared for the LINK workshop on 'Learning, Incentives, and Corporate Disaggregation', Copenhagen, 26–7 October 2000.

Osterloh, Margit, Frost, Jetta, and Frey, Bruno (2002), 'The Dynamics of Motivation in New Organizational Forms', *International Journal of the Economics of Business*, 9: 61–77.

Osterman, Paul (2000), 'Work Reorganization in an Era of Restructuring: Trends in Diffusion and Effects on Employee Welfare', *Industrial and Labor Relations Review*, 53: 179–96.

Ouchi, William (1980), 'Markets, Bureaucracies and Clans', *Administrative Science Quarterly*, 25: 129–41.

Oxley, Joanne E. (1999), 'Institutional Environment and the Mechanism of Governance: The Impact of Intellectual Property Protection on the Structure of Inter-Firm Alliances', *Journal of Economic Behavior and Organization*, 38: 283–309.

Paganetto, Luigi (2004) (ed.), *Knowledge Economy, Information Technologies and Growth* (Aldershot: Ashgate).

Parnas, David L. (1972), 'On the Criteria for Decomposing Systems in to Modules', *Communications of the ACM*, 15: 1053–8.

Pavitt, K. L. R. (1984), 'Sectoral Patterns of Technical Change: Towards a Taxonomy and a Theory', *Research Policy*, 13: 343–73.

—— (1991), 'What Makes Basic Research Economically Useful?', *Research Policy*, 20: 109–19.

—— (1998), 'Technologies, Products and Organization in the Innovating Firm: What Adam Smith Tells us and Joseph Schumpeter Doesn't', *Industrial and Corporate Change*, 7: 433–52.

Peltzman, Sam (1977), 'The Gains and Losses from Industrial Concentration', *Journal of Law and Economics*, 20: 229–63.

Penrose, Edith T. (1959), *The Theory of the Growth of the Firm* (Oxford: Oxford University Press).

Richardson, Hettie A., Vandenberg, Robert J., Blum, Terry C., and Roman, Paul M. (2002), 'Does Decentralization Make a Difference for the Organization?', *Journal of Management*, 8: 217–44.

Robinson, S. L., and Morrison, E. W. (1995), 'Organizational Citizenship Behaviour: A Psychological Contract Perspective', *Journal of Organizational Behaviour*, 16: 289–98.

Robinson, Sandra L., and Rousseau, Denise M. (1994), 'Violating the Psychological Contract: Not the Exception but the Norm', *Journal of Organizational Behavior*, 15: 245–59.

Robinson, Sandra L., and Morrison, Elizabeth Wolfe (1995), 'Psychological Contracts and OCB: The Effects of Unfulfilled Obligations on Civic Virtue Behavior', *Journal of Organizational Behavior*, 16: 289–98.

Romer, Paul M. (1986), 'Increasing Returns and Long Run Growth', *Journal of Political Economy*, 94: 1002–37.

—— (1990), 'Endogenous Technological Change', *Journal of Political Economy*, 98: S71–102.

—— (1998), 'Bank of America Roundtable on the Soft Revolution', *Journal of Applied Corporate Finance*, 10: 9–14.

Rooney, David, Hearn, Greg, and Mandeville, Thomas (2003), *Public Policy in Knowledge-based Economies* (Cheltenham: Elgar).

Rosen, Sherwin (1991), 'Transaction Costs and Internal Labor Markets', in Oliver E. Williamson and Sidney G. Winter (eds.), *The Nature of the Firm: Origins, Evolution and Development* (Oxford: Blackwell).

Rost, John, (1991), *Leadership for the Twenty-First Century* (New York: Praeger).

Rotemberg, Julio J., and Saloner, Garth (1993), 'Leadership Style and Incentives', *Management Science*, 39: 1299–318.

Roth, K., and Morrison, A. J. (1992), 'Implementing Global Strategy: Characteristics of Global Subsidiary Mandates', *Journal of International Business Studies*, 23: 715–36.

Rothwell, R., Freeman, C., Jervis, P., Robertson, A., and Townsend, J. (1974), 'SAPPHO Updated—Project SAPPHO Phase 2', *Research Policy*, 3: 258–91.

Rousseau, Denise M. (1989), 'Psychological and Implied Contracts in Organizations', *Employee Responsibilities and Rights Journal*, 8: 121–39.

—— and Shperling, Zipi (2003), 'Pieces of the Action: Ownership and the Changing Employment Relationship', *Academy of Management Review*, 28: 553–70.

Rubin, Paul H. (1990), *Organizing Business Transactions* (New York: Free Press).

Rubinstein, Ariel (1982), 'Perfect Equilibrium in a Bargaining Model', *Econometrica*, 50: 97–109.

—— (1989), 'The Electronic Mail Game: Strategic Behavior under "Almost Common Knowledge" ', *American Economic Review*, 79: 385–91.

Rugman, Alan, and Verbeke, Alain (2002), 'Edith Penrose's Contribution to the Resource-based View of Strategic Management', *Strategic Management Journal*, 23: 769–80.

—— (2004), 'A Final Word on Edith Penrose', *Journal of Management Studies*, 41: 205–17.

Rumelt, Richard P. (1984), 'Towards a Strategic Theory of the Firm', in Richard B. Lamb (ed.), *Competitive Strategic Management* (Englewood Cliffs, NJ: Prentice Hall).

—— (1987), 'Theory, Strategy, and Entrepreneurship', in David J. Teece (ed.), *The Competitive Challenge* (New York: Harper & Row).

—— (1995), 'Inertia and Transformation', in Cynthia A. Montgomery (ed.), *Evolutionary and Resource-based Theories of the Firm* (Boston, Mass.: Kluwer).

—— Schendel, Dan, and Teece, David J. (1994), 'Fundamental Issues in Strategy', in Rumelt, Schendel, and Teece (eds.) *Fundamental Issues in Strategy: A Research Agenda* (Boston, Mass.: Harvard Business School Press).

Sah, Raaj, and Stiglitz, Joseph E. (1985), 'Human Fallibility and Economic Organization', *American Economic Review*, Papers and Proceedings, 75: 292–7.

Salanié, Bernard (1997), *The Economics of Contracts* (Cambridge, Mass.: MIT Press).

Salop, Stephen, and Scheffman, David (1983), 'Raising Rivals' Costs', *American Economic Review, Papers and Proceedings*, 73: 267–71.

Sanchez, Ron (1993), 'Strategic Flexibility, Firm Organization, and Managerial Work in Dynamic Markets: A Strategic Options Perspective', *Advances in Strategic Management*, 9: 251–91.

—— (2001), 'Resources, Dynamic Capabilities, and Competences: Building Blocks of Integrative Strategy Theory', in Tom Elfring and Henk Volberda (eds.), *Rethinking Strategy* (Thousand Oaks, Calif.: Sage).

Sanderson, Margaret, and Winter, Ralph A. (2002), ' "Profits" versus "Rents" in Antitrust Analysis: An Application to the Canadian Waste Services Merger', *Antitrust Law Journal*, 70: 485–511.

Schelling, Thomas (1960), *The Strategy of Conflict* (Cambridge, Mass.: Harvard University Press).

—— (1978), *Micro-motives and Macro-behaviour* (New York: Free Press).

Scherer, Frederick, and Ross, David (1990), *Industrial Market Structure and Economic Performance* (Boston, Mass.: Houghton-Mifflin).

Schilling, Melissa A., and Steensma, H. Kevin (2002), 'Disentangling the Theories of Firm Boundaries: A Path Model and Empirical Test', *Organization Science*, 13: 387–401.

Schmalensee, Richard (1987), 'Competitive Advantage and Collusive Optima', *International Journal of Industrial Organization*, 5: 351–67.

Schotter, Andrew (1981), *The Economic Theory of Social Institutions* (Cambridge: Cambridge University Press).

Schumpeter, Joseph A. (1912/34), *The Theory of Economic Development: An Inquiry into Profits, Capital, Credit, Interest and the Business Cycle* (London: Oxford University Press).

Segal, Ilya (1996), 'Modeling the Managerial Task', working paper, Department of Economics, UCLA.

Selten, Reinhardt (1990), 'Bounded Rationality', *Journal of Institutional and Theoretical Economics*, 146: 649–58.

Selznick, Philip (1957), *Leadership in Administration* (New York: Harper & Row).

Semler, Ricardo (1989), 'Managing Without Managers', *Harvard Business Review* (Sept.–Oct.), 76–84.

Seth, Anju, and Thomas, Howard (1994), 'Theories of the Firm: Implications for Strategy Research', *Journal of Management Studies*, 31: 165–91.

Shackle, George L. S. (1972), *Epistemics and Economics* (Cambridge: Cambridge University Press).

Shapiro, Carl (1989), 'The Theory of Business Strategy', *RAND Journal of Economics*, 20: 125–37.

—— and Varian, Hal (1999), *Information Rules* (Boston, Mass.: Harvard Business School Press).

Shelanski, H., and Klein, P. G. (1995), 'Empirical Research in Transaction Cost Economics: A Review and Assessment', *Journal of Law, Economics and Organization*, 11: 335–61.

Shin, Hyun Song, and Williamson, Timothy (1996), 'How Much Belief is Necessary for a Convention?', *Games and Economic Behavior*, 13: 252–68.

Shleifer, Andrei, and Summers, Lawrence (1990), 'Breach of Trust in Corporate Takeovers', in Alan Auerbach (ed.), *Corporate Takeovers: Causes and Consequences* (Chicago, Ill.: University of Chicago Press).

Silverman, Brian (1999), 'Technological Resources and the Direction of Corporate Diversification: Toward an Integration of the Resource-based View and Transaction Cost Economics', *Management Science*, 45: 1109–24.

Simon, Herbert A. (1947), *Administrative Behavior* (New York: Macmillan).

—— (1951), 'A Formal Theory of the Employment Relationship', in Herbert (1982), *Models of Bounded Rationality* (Cambridge: MIT Press).

—— (1955), 'A Behavioral Model of Rational Choice', *Quarterly Journal of Economics*, 69: 99–118.

Simon, Herbert A. (1962), 'The Architecture of Complexity', *Proceedings of the American Philosophical Society*, 156: 467–82.

—— (1973), 'The Structure of Ill-Structured Problems', *Artificial Intelligence*, 4: 181–201.

—— (1982), *Models of Bounded Rationality* (Cambridge, Mass.: MIT Press).

—— (1985), 'Human Nature in Politics', *American Political Science Review*, 79: 293–304.

—— (1991), 'Organizations and Markets', *Journal of Economic Perspectives*, 5: 25–44.

Simons, Tony (2002), 'Behavioral Integrity: The Perceived Alignment Between Managers' Words and Deeds as a Research Focus', *Organization Science*, 13: 18–35.

Sjöström, Thomas, and Weitzman, Martin (1996), 'Competition and the Evolution of Efficiency', *Journal of Economic Behavior and Organization*, 30: 25–43.

Skaperdas, Stergios (1994), 'Contest Success Functions', *Journal of Economic Theory*, 7: 283–90.

Sloan, R. G. (1992), 'Accounting Earnings and Top Executive Compensation', *Journal of Accounting and Economics*, 16: 55–100.

Smith, Keith (2000), 'What is the "Knowledge Economy"? Knowledge-Intensive Industries and Distributed Knowledge Bases', working paper, STEP group, Oslo.

Spangler, William E., and James M. Peters, (2001), 'A Model of Distributed Knowledge and Action in Complex Systems', *Decision Support Systems*, 31: 103.

Spender, J. C. (1996), 'Making Knowledge The Basis of a Dynamic Theory of the Firms', *Strategic Management Journal*, 17: 45–62.

—— (1998), 'The Geographies of Strategic Competence', in Alfred Chandler et al. (eds.), *The Dynamic Firm* (Oxford: Oxford University Press).

Starbuck, William H. (1992), 'Learning by Knowledge Intensive Firms', *Journal of Management Studies*, 29: 147–75.

Sugden, Robert (1995), 'A Theory of Focal Points', *Economic Journal*, 105: 533–50.

Sutton, John (1986), 'Non-Cooperative Bargaining Theory: An Introduction', *Review of Economic Studies*, 53: 709–24.

—— (1991), *Sunk Costs and Market Structure: Price, Competition, Advertising, and the Evolution of Concentration* (Cambridge, Mass.: MIT Press).

Szulanski, Gabriel (1996), 'Exploring Internal Stickiness: Impediments to the Transfer of Best Practice Within the Firm', *Strategic Management Journal*, 17 (special winter issue): 27–43.

Tallman, Steven (2003), 'The Significance of Bruce Kogut's and Udo Zander's Article, "Knowledge of the Firm and the Evolutionary Theory of the Multinational Corporation" ', *Journal of International Business Studies*, 34: 495–7.

Tapscott, D. (1999) (ed.), *Creating Value in the Network Economy* (Boston, Mass.: Harvard Business School Press).

Teece, David J. (1982), 'Towards an Economic Theory of the Multiproduct Firm', *Journal of Economic Behavior and Organization*, 3: 39–63.

—— (1986), 'Transaction Cost Economics and the Multinational Enterprise: An Assessment', *Journal of Economic Behavior and Organization*, 7: 21–45.

—— (1987), 'Profiting from Technological Innovation: Implications for Integration, Collaboration, Licensing and Public Policy', in Teece, *The Competitive Challenge* (Cambridge: Ballinger).

—— (1993), 'The Dynamics of Industrial Capitalism: Perspectives on Alfred Chandler's Scale and Scope', *Journal of Economic Literature*, 31: 199–225.

—— (2000), *Managing Intellectual Capital: Organizational, Strategic and Policy Dimensions* (Oxford: Oxford University Press).

—— (2001), 'Strategies for Managing Knowledge Assets: the Role of Firm Structure and Industrial Context', in Ikujiro Nonaka and David J. Teece (2001) (eds.), *Managing Industrial Knowledge: Creation, Transfer and Utilization* (London: Sage).

—— (2003), 'Explicating Dynamic Capabilities: Asset Selection, Coordination, and Entrepreneurship in Strategic Management Theory', working paper.

—— and Pisano, Gary (1994), 'The Dynamic Capabilities of Firms: An Introduction', *Industrial and Corporate Change*, 3: 537–56.

—— and Shuen, Amy (1997), 'Dynamic Capabilities and Strategic Management', *Strategic Management Journal*, 18: 509–33.

Teece, David J., Dosi, Giovanni, Rumelt, Richard P., and Winter, Sidney G. (1994), 'Understanding Corporate Coherence: Theory and Evidence', *Journal of Economic Behavior and Organization*, 23: 1–30.

Thomas, K., and Velthouse, B. (1990), 'Cognitive Elements of Empowerment: An Interpretive Model and Intrinsic Task Motivation', *Academy of Management Review*, 15: 666–81.

Thompson, Paul (2004), *Skating on Thin Ice: The Knowledge Economy Myth* (Glasgow: Big Thinking).

Thompson, James D. (1956), 'Authority and Power in "Identical" Organizations', *American Journal of Sociology*, 62: 290–301.

—— (1967), *Organizations in Action* (New York: McGraw-Hill).

Tirole, Jean (1988), *The Theory of Industrial Organization* (Cambridge, Mass.: MIT Press).

—— (1999), 'Incomplete Contracts: Where Do We Stand?', Walras-Bowley lecture, *Econometrica*, 67: 741.

Tomlinson, Mark (1999), 'The Learning Economy and Embodied Knowledge Flows in Great Britain', *Journal of Evolutionary Economics*, 9: 431–51.

Tsoukas, Haridimos (1996), 'The Firm as a Distributed Knowledge System: A Constructionist Approach', *Strategic Management Journal*, 17: 11–25.

Tushman, Michael L., and Moore, William L. (1988) (eds.), *Readings in the Management of Innovation* (Cambridge, Mass.: Ballinger).

Tyler, Tom R., and Blader, Steven (2000), *Cooperation in Groups: Procedural Justice, Social Identity, and Behavioral Engagement* (Hove: Psychology).

Ullmann-Margalit, Edna (1977), 'Invisible-hand Explanations', *Synthese*, 39: 263–91.

Vancil, Robert, and Buddrus, Lee E. (1979), *Decentralization: Managerial Ambiguity by Design* (Homewood, Ill.: Irwin).

Van Huyck, J. B., Battalio, R. C., and Beil, R. O. (1990), 'Tacit Coordination Games, Strategic Uncertainty, and Coordination Failure', *American Economic Review*, 80: 234–48.

—— (1991), 'Strategic Uncertainty, Equilibrium Selection, and Cooordination Failure in Average Opinion Games', *Quarterly Journal of Economics*, 106: 885–910.

Vandenberghe, A. S., and Siegers, J. (2000), 'Employees versus Independent Contractors for the Exchange of Labor Services: Authority as Distinguishing Characteristic?', paper delivered at the 17th Annual Conference on the European Association of Law and Economics, Gent, 14–16 Sept.

Varian, Hal, and Shapiro, Carl (1999), *Information Rules* (Boston, Mass.: Harvard Business School Press).

Vechhio, Robert P. (1997) (ed.), *Leadership: Understanding the Dynamics of Power and Influence in Organizations* (Notre Dame: University of Notre Dame).

Ven, A. H. V. de, Delbecq, A. L., and Koenig, R. Jr. (1976), 'Determinants of Coordination Modes within Organizations', *American Sociological Review*, 41: 322–38.

Verona, Gianmario, and Ravasi, Davide (1999), 'Organizational Capabilities for Continuous Innovation', unpublished MS.

Vining, Aidan (2003), 'Internal Market Failure: A Framework for Diagnosing Firm Inefficiency', *Journal of Management Studies*, 40: 431–57.

Vroom, V. H., and Jago, A. G. (1988), *The New Leadership: Managing Participation in Organizations* (Englewood Cliffs, NJ: Prentice Hall).

Wagner, John A. (1994), 'Participation's Effect on Performance and Satisfaction: A Reconsideration of Research Evidence', *Academy of Management Review*, 19: 312–30.

Wang, Q., and Tunzelman, G. N. von (2000), 'Complexity and the Functions of the Firm: Breadth and Depth', *Research Policy*, 29: 805–18.

Warglien, Massimo (1995), 'Hierarchical Selection and Organizational Adaptation', *Industrial and Corporate Change*, 4: 161–86.

Weber, Max (1947), *The Theory of Economic and Social Organization*, trans. A. M. Henderson and Talcott Parson, ed. Talcott Parson (New York: Oxford University Press).

Weber, Roberto (1998), 'Coordination Problems in Growing Firms: Insights From Experiments', unpublished MS.

—— Camerer, Colin, Rottenstreich, Y., and Knez, Mark (1998), 'The Illuson of Leadership: Misattribution of Cause in Coordination Games', unpublished MS.

Weick, Karl (1979), *The Social Psychology of Organizing* (New York: Random House).

Wernerfelt, Birger (1984), 'A Resource-based View of the Firm', *Strategic Management Journal*, 5: 171–80.

—— (1989), 'From Critical Resources to Corporate Strategy', *Journal of General Management*, 14: 4–12.

—— (1995), 'Resource-based Strategy in a Stochastic Model', in Cynthia A. Montgomery (1995) (ed.), *Resource-based and Evolutionary Theories of the Firm* (Boston, Mass.: Kluwer).

—— (1997), 'On the Nature and Scope of the Firm: An Adjustment Cost Theory', *Journal of Business*, 70: 489–514.

—— (2003), 'Resources, Adjustments, and Diversification: Evidence from Production Functions', Working paper, MIT.

Williams, Jeffrey A. (1992), 'How Sustainable is Your Competitive Advantage?', *California Management Review*, 34: 29–51.

Williamson, Oliver E. (1971), 'The Vertical Integration of Production: Market Failure Considerations', *American Economic Review*, 61: 112–23.

—— (1975), *Markets and Hierarchies* (New York: Free Press).

—— (1985), *The Economic Institutions of Capitalism* (New York: Free Press).

—— (1991), 'Strategizing, Economizing, and Economic Organization', in Richard P. Rumelt, Dan E. Schendel and David J. Teece (eds.), *Fundamental Issues in Strategy* (Boston, Mass.: Harvard Business School Press).

—— (1993), 'Transaction Cost Economics Meets Posnerian Law and Economics', *Journal of Institutional and Theoretical Economics*, 149: 99–118.

—— (1996a), *The Mechanisms of Governance* (Oxford: Oxford University Press).

—— (1996b), 'Economic Organization: The Case for Candor', *Academy of Management Review*, 21: 48–57.

—— (1998), 'Human Actors and Economic Organization', paper prepared for the 1998 Paris ISNIE conference.

—— (1999), 'Strategy Research: Governance and Competence Perspectives', *Strategic Management Journal*, 20: 1087–1108.

—— (2000), 'Strategy Research: Competence and Governance Perspectives', in Nicolai J. Foss and Volker Mahnke (eds.), *Competence, Governance, and Entreprenership* (Oxford: Oxford University Press).

Winter, Sidney G. (1964a), 'Economic "Natural" Selection and the Theory of the Firm', *Yale Economic Essays*, 4: 225–72.

—— (1964b), 'Review of Richard Cyert and James G. March, *A Behavioral Theory of the Firm*', *American Economic Review*, 54: 144–8.

—— (1986), 'The Research Program of the Behavioral Theory of the Firm: Orthodox Critique and Evolutionary Perspective', in Benjamin Gilad and Stanley Kaish (1986) (eds.), *Handbook of Behavioral Microeconomics, A* (Greenwich: JAI Press).

—— (1987), 'Knowledge and Competence as Strategic Assets', in David Teece (ed.), *The Competitive Challenge—Strategies for Industrial Innovation and Renewal* (Cambridge, Mass.: Ballinger).

—— (1991), 'On Coase, Competence, and the Corporation', in Oliver E. Williamson and Sidney G. Winter (1991) (eds.), *The Nature of the Firm: Origins, Evolution, and Development* (Oxford: Blackwell).

Winter, Sidney G. (2003), 'Understanding Dynamic Capabilities', *Strategic Management Journal*, 24: 991–95.

Witt, Ulrich (1997), ' "Lock-In" vs. "Critical Masses"—Industrial Change under Network Externalities', *International Journal of Industrial Organization*, 15: 753–73.

—— (1998), 'Imagination and Leadership: The Neglected Dimension of an Evolutionary Theory of the Firm', *Journal of Economic Behavior and Organization*, 35: 161–77.

—— (1999), 'Do Entrepreneurs Need Firms? A Contribution to a Missing Chapter in Austrian Economics', *Review of Austrian Economics*, 11: 99–109.

World Bank <http://www.worldbank.org.

Yin, Robert K. (1989), *Case Study Research: Design and Methods* (London: Sage).

Young, H. Peyton (1996), 'The Economics of Convention', *Journal of Economic Perspectives*, 10: 105–22.

Zajac, Edward J. (1992), 'Relating Economic and Behavioral Perspectives in Strategy Research', *Advances in Strategic Management*, 8: 69–96.

—— and Olsen, C. P. (1993), 'From Transaction Cost to Transactional Value Analysis: Implications for the Study of Interorganizational Strategies', *Journal of Management Studies*, 30: 131–45.

Zander, Udo, and Kogut, Bruce (1995), 'Knowledge and the Speed of the Transfer and Imitation of Organizational Capabilities', *Organization Science*, 6: 76–92.

Zandt, Timothy van (1998), 'Organizations with an Endogenous Number of Information Processing Agents', in M. Majumdar (ed.), *Organizations with Incomplete Information* (Cambridge: Cambridge University Press).

Zenger, Todd (2002), 'Crafting Internal Hybrids', *International Journal of the Economics of Business*, 9: 79–96.

Zenger, Todd, and Hesterly, William S. (1997), 'The Disaggregation of Corporations: Selective Intervention, High-Powered Incentives, and Molecular Units', *Organization Science*, 8: 209–22.

Zingales, Luigi (2000), 'In Search of New Foundations', *Journal of Finance*, 55: 1623–53.

Zollo, Maurizio, and Winter, Sidney G. (2002), 'Deliberate Learning and the Evolution of Dynamic Capabilities', *Organization Science*, 13: 339–52.

Zott, C. (2003), 'Dynamic Capabilities and the Emergence of Intra-industry Differential Firm Performance: Insights from a Simulation Study', *Strategic Management Journal*, 24: 97–125.

Zuboff, Shoshana (1988), *In the Age of the Smart Machine* (New York: Heinemann).

Zucker, Lynne (1991), 'Markets for Bureaucratic Authority and Control: Information Quality in Professions and Services', *Research in the Sociology of Organizations*, 8: 157–90.

Index